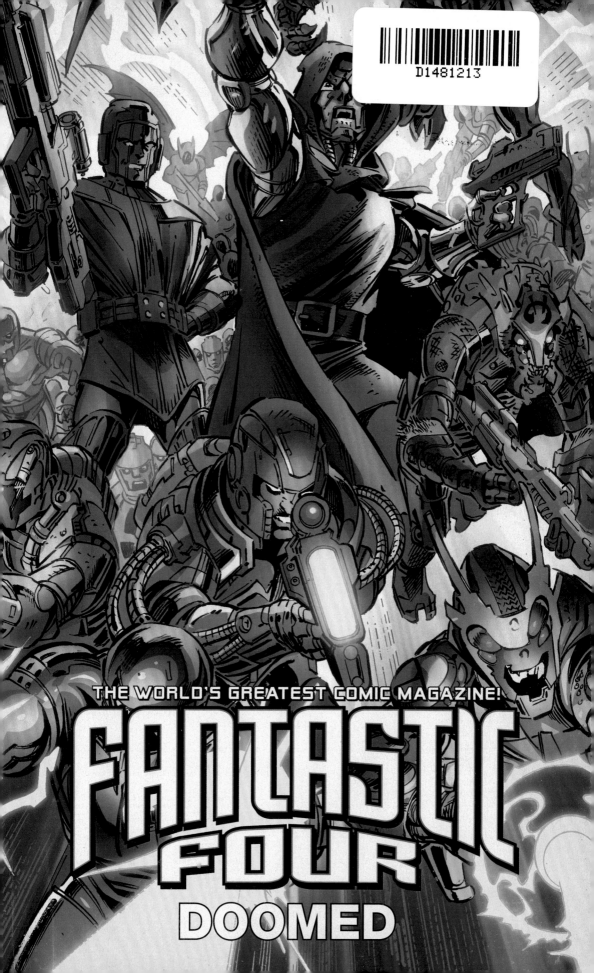

THE WORLD'S GREATEST COMIC MAGAZINE!

FANTASTIC FOUR

DOOMED

COLLECTION EDITOR **JENNIFER GRÜNWALD**
ASSOCIATE MANAGING EDITOR **ALEX STARBUCK**
EDITOR, SPECIAL PROJECTS **MARK D. BEAZLEY**
SENIOR EDITOR, SPECIAL PROJECTS **JEFF YOUNGQUIST**
SVP PRINT, SALES & MARKETING **DAVID GABRIEL**

EDITOR IN CHIEF **AXEL ALONSO**
CHIEF CREATIVE OFFICER **JOE QUESADA**
PUBLISHER **DAN BUCKLEY**
EXECUTIVE PRODUCER **ALAN FINE**

FANTASTIC FOUR VOL. 3: DOOMED. Contains material originally published in magazine form as FANTASTIC FOUR #9-16. First printing 2014. ISBN# 978-0-7851-8883-4. Published by MARVEL WORLDWIDE, INC., a subsidiary of MARVEL ENTERTAINMENT, LLC. OFFICE OF PUBLICATION: 135 West 50th Street, New York, NY 10020. Copyright © 2014 Marvel Characters, Inc. All rights reserved. All characters featured in this issue and the distinctive names and likenesses thereof, and all related indicia are trademarks of Marvel Characters, Inc. No similarity between any of the names, characters, persons, and/ or institutions in this magazine with those of any living or dead person or institution is intended, and any such similarity which may exist is purely coincidental. **Printed in Canada.** ALAN FINE, EVP - Office of the President, Marvel Worldwide, Inc. and EVP & CMO Marvel Characters B.V.; DAN BUCKLEY, Publisher & President - Print, Animation & Digital Divisions; JOE QUESADA, Chief Creative Officer; TOM BREVOORT, SVP of Publishing; DAVID BOGART, SVP of Operations & Procurement, Publishing; C.B. CEBULSKI, SVP of Creator & Content Development; DAVID GABRIEL, SVP Print, Sales & Marketing; JIM O'KEEFE, VP of Operations & Logistics; DAN CARR, Executive Director of Publishing Technology; SUSAN CRESPI, Editorial Operations Manager; ALEX MORALES, Publishing Operations Manager; STAN LEE, Chairman Emeritus. For information regarding advertising in Marvel Comics or on Marvel.com, please contact Niza Disla, Director of Marvel Partnerships, at ndisla@marvel.com. For Marvel subscription inquiries, please call 800-217-9158. **Manufactured between 1/17/2014 and 2/24/2014 by SOLISCO PRINTERS, SCOTT, QC, CANADA.**

10 9 8 7 6 5 4 3 2 1

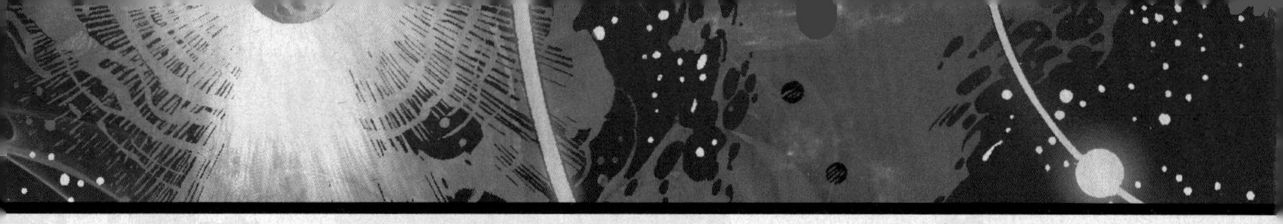

THE WORLD'S GREATEST COMIC MAGAZINE!

FANTASTIC FOUR

DOOMED

WRITER, #9-12
MATT FRACTION
WITH **CHRISTOPHER SEBELA** (#11-12)

STORY, #13-16
MATT FRACTION & **KARL KESEL**

SCRIPT, #13-16
KARL KESEL

PENCILERS
MARK BAGLEY (#9-13) & **RAFFAELE IENCO** (#14-16)

INKERS
MARK FARMER (#9-10), **JOE RUBINSTEIN** (#11-13)
& **RAFFAELE IENCO** (#14-16)

COLORISTS
PAUL MOUNTS
WITH **GURU-eFX** (#9)

EPILOGUE
STORY **KARL KESEL** & **LEE ALLRED**
SCRIPT **KARL KESEL**
PENCILER **JOE QUINONES**
INKER **MIKE ALLRED**
COLORIST **LAURA ALLRED**

LETTERER **VC'S CLAYTON COWLES**
COVER ARTISTS **MARK BAGLEY, MARK FARMER** & **PAUL MOUNTS**
ASSISTANT EDITOR **JAKE THOMAS**
EDITOR **TOM BREVOORT**

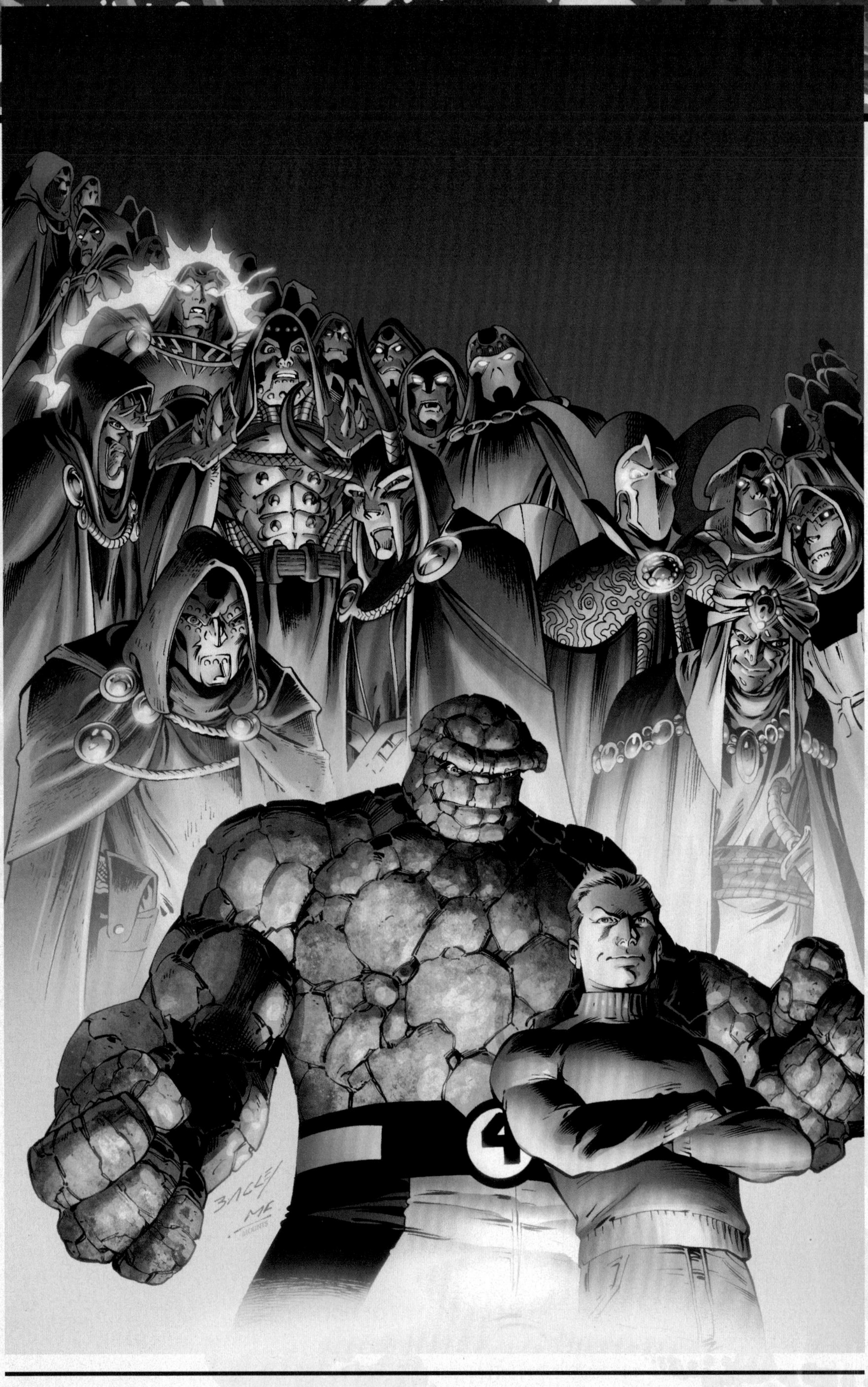

FANTASTIC FOUR #9 — “NATIVITY”

THE FANTASTIC FOUR

VALERIA RICHARDS
REED RICHARDS
MR. FANTASTIC
FRANKLIN RICHARDS
SUE STORM RICHARDS
INVISIBLE WOMAN
BEN GRIMM
THE THING
JOHNNY STORM
THE HUMAN TORCH

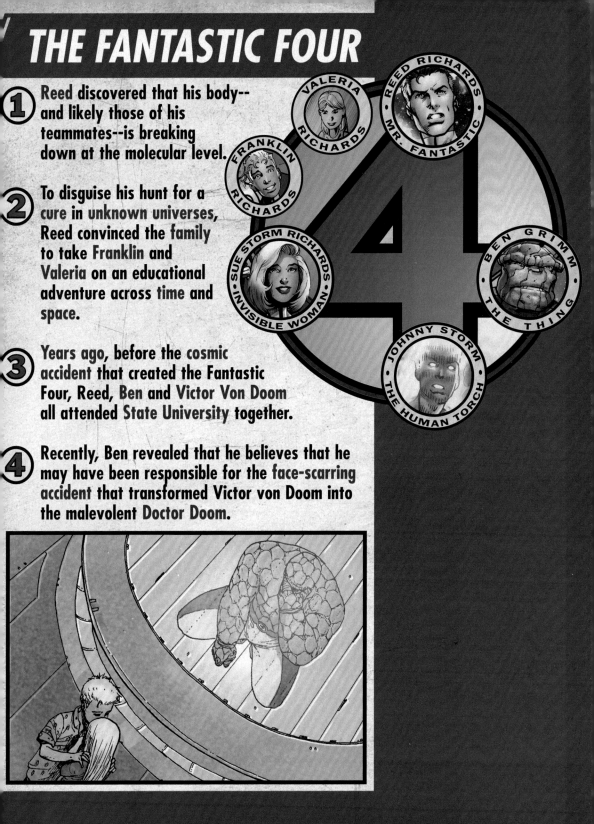

1. Reed discovered that his body--and likely those of his teammates--is breaking down at the molecular level.

2. To disguise his hunt for a cure in unknown universes, Reed convinced the family to take Franklin and Valeria on an educational adventure across time and space.

3. Years ago, before the cosmic accident that created the Fantastic Four, Reed, Ben and Victor Von Doom all attended State University together.

4. Recently, Ben revealed that he believes that he may have been responsible for the face-scarring accident that transformed Victor von Doom into the malevolent Doctor Doom.

I GOT IT!

HEY, PAL, SORRY ABOUT TH--

SIMPLETON!

MORON!

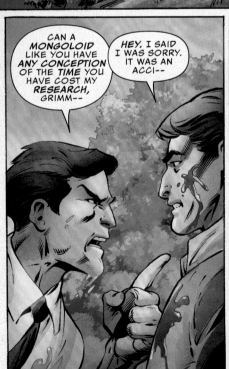

CAN A MONGOLOID LIKE YOU HAVE ANY CONCEPTION OF THE TIME YOU HAVE COST MY RESEARCH, GRIMM--

HEY. I SAID I WAS SORRY. IT WAS AN ACCI--

THERE ARE NO ACCIDENTS.

YOU CRETIN.

WHY THIS SO-CALLED UNIVERSITY ALLOWS SUBHUMAN THUGS TO ATTEND, I'LL NEVER KNOW.

HEY!

LET IT GO THERE, BENJY-BOY.

HE'S NOT WORTH IT.

BEN, C'MON, MAN! LET IT GO!

LIGHTEN UP--

--IT'S A PARTY!

AWW, MAN, LOOKIT *THAT*...

WELL, OF COURSE, THE REASON THEY DROP *OXYGEN MASKS* ON CRASHING AIRPLANES IS--

HEY, REED, LOOKIT WHAT THAT SPOILED BRAT PAL O' YOURS DID TO MY FAVORITE SWEATER.

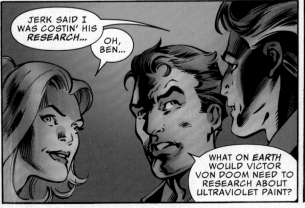

JERK SAID I WAS COSTIN' HIS *RESEARCH*...

OH, BEN...

WHAT ON *EARTH* WOULD VICTOR VON DOOM NEED TO RESEARCH ABOUT ULTRAVIOLET PAINT?

HOWZABOUT... *WHERE* WOULD HE BE NEEDIN' TO RESEARCH IT, PAL?

ANY CLUE?

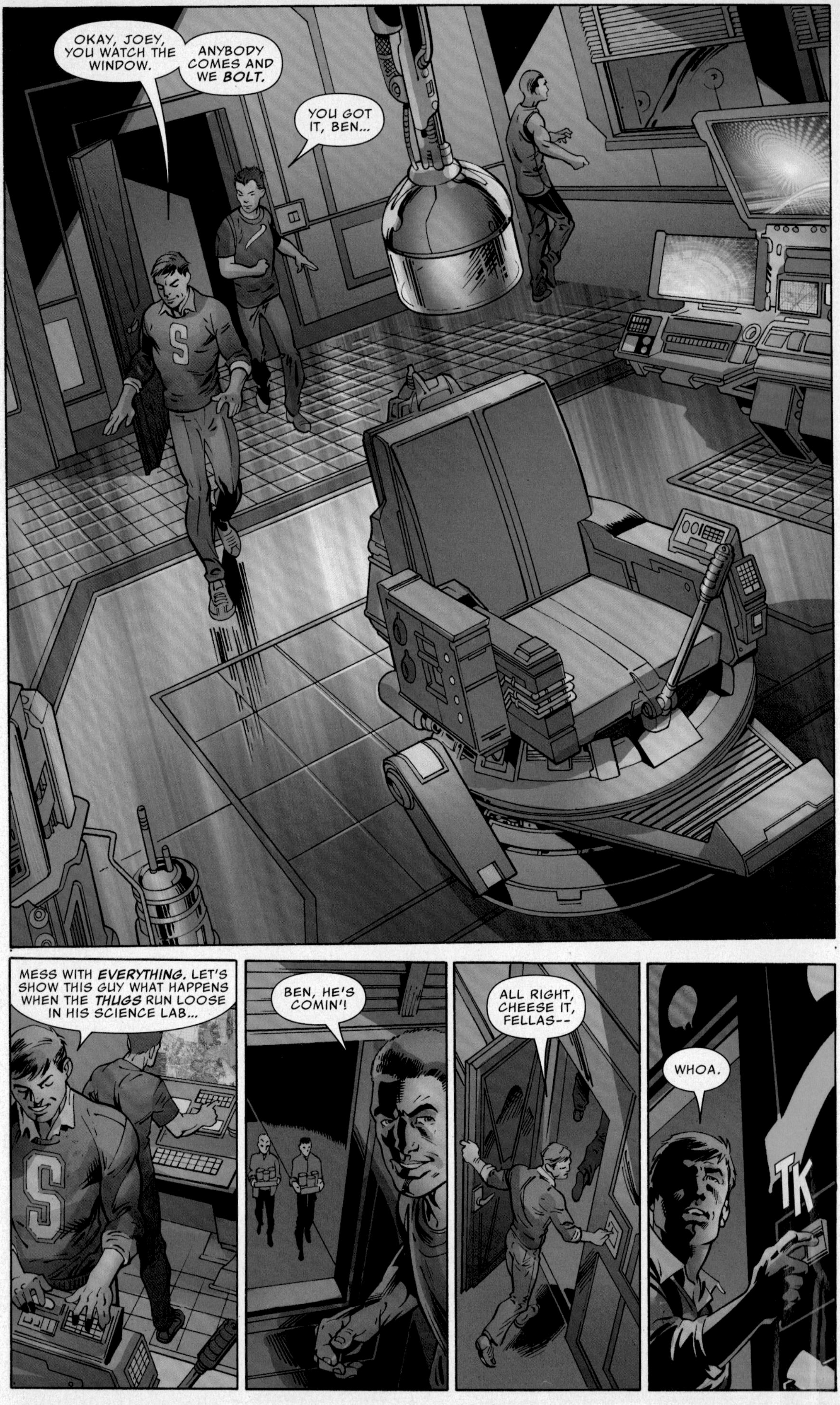
OKAY, JOEY, YOU WATCH THE WINDOW.
ANYBODY COMES AND WE *BOLT.*
YOU GOT IT, BEN...
MESS WITH *EVERYTHING.* LET'S SHOW THIS GUY WHAT HAPPENS WHEN THE *THUGS* RUN LOOSE IN HIS SCIENCE LAB...
BEN, HE'S COMIN'!
ALL RIGHT, CHEESE IT, FELLAS--
WHOA.
TK

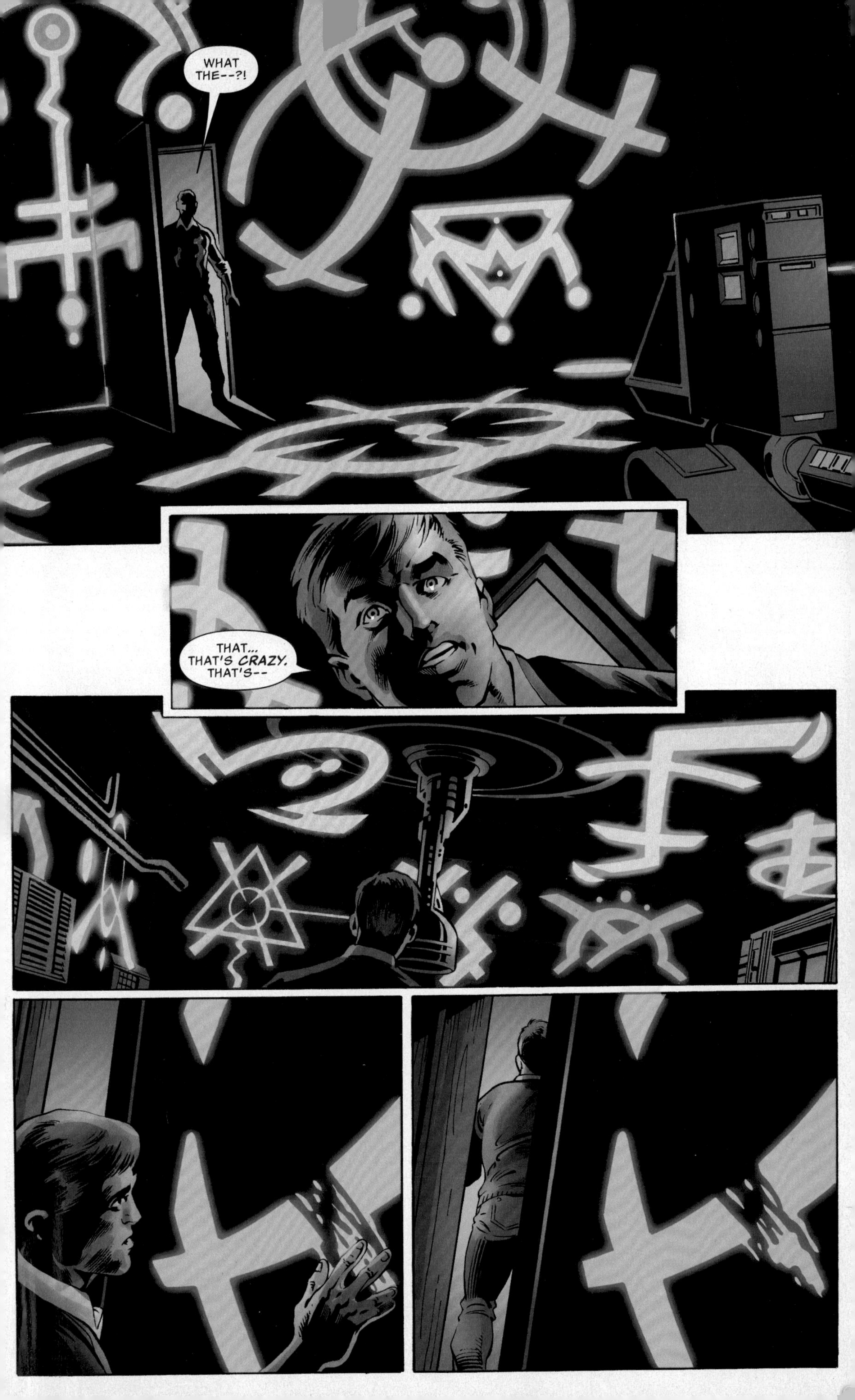
WHAT THE--?!
THAT... THAT'S *CRAZY*. THAT'S--

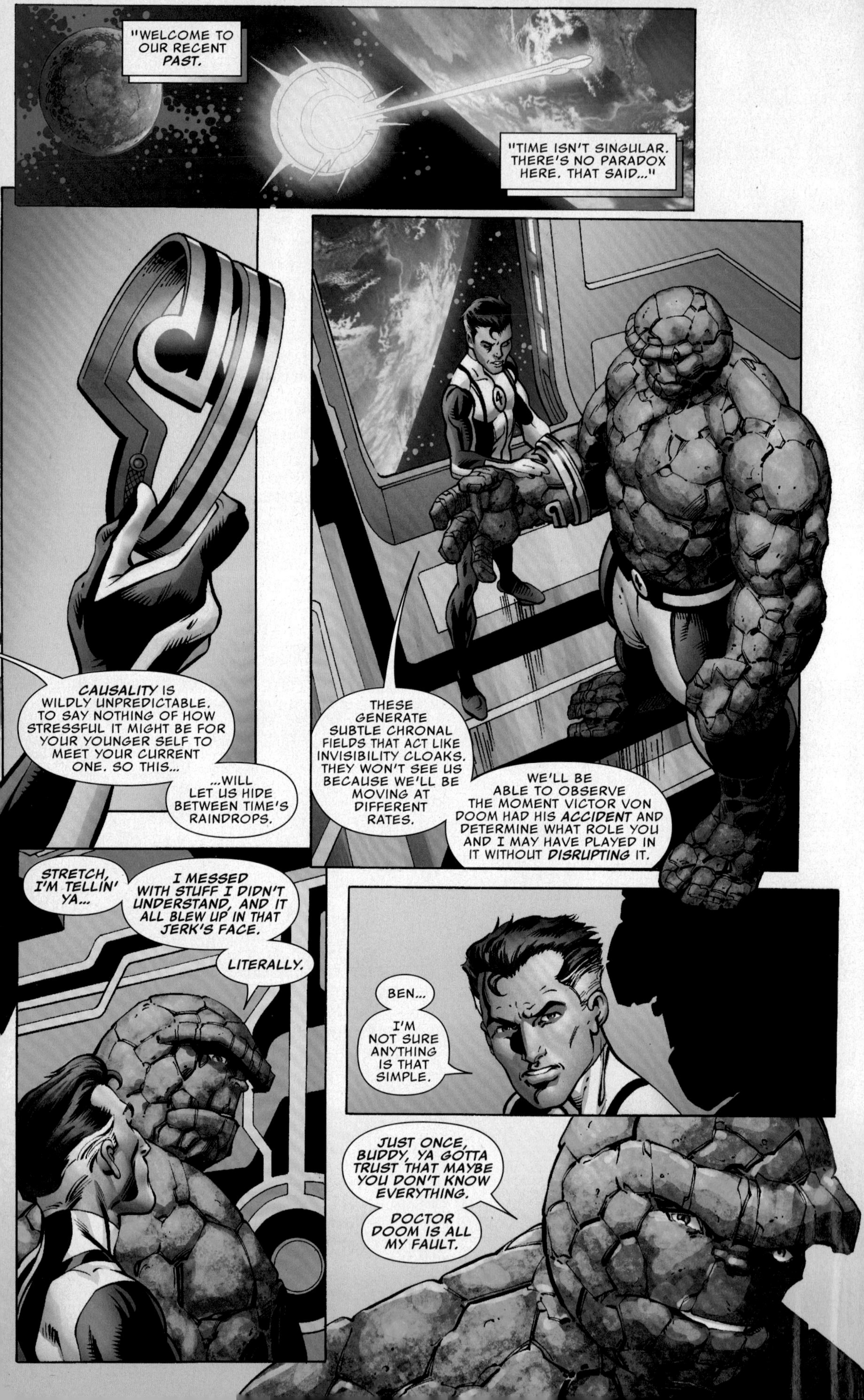
"WELCOME TO OUR RECENT PAST.
"TIME ISN'T SINGULAR. THERE'S NO PARADOX HERE. THAT SAID..."
CAUSALITY IS WILDLY UNPREDICTABLE. TO SAY NOTHING OF HOW STRESSFUL IT MIGHT BE FOR YOUR YOUNGER SELF TO MEET YOUR CURRENT ONE. SO THIS...
...WILL LET US HIDE BETWEEN TIME'S RAINDROPS.
THESE GENERATE SUBTLE CHRONAL FIELDS THAT ACT LIKE INVISIBILITY CLOAKS. THEY WON'T SEE US BECAUSE WE'LL BE MOVING AT DIFFERENT RATES.
WE'LL BE ABLE TO OBSERVE THE MOMENT VICTOR VON DOOM HAD HIS ACCIDENT AND DETERMINE WHAT ROLE YOU AND I MAY HAVE PLAYED IN IT WITHOUT DISRUPTING IT.
STRETCH, I'M TELLIN' YA...
I MESSED WITH STUFF I DIDN'T UNDERSTAND, AND IT ALL BLEW UP IN THAT JERK'S FACE.
LITERALLY.
BEN...
I'M NOT SURE ANYTHING IS THAT SIMPLE.
JUST ONCE, BUDDY, YA GOTTA TRUST THAT MAYBE YOU DON'T KNOW EVERYTHING.
DOCTOR DOOM IS ALL MY FAULT.

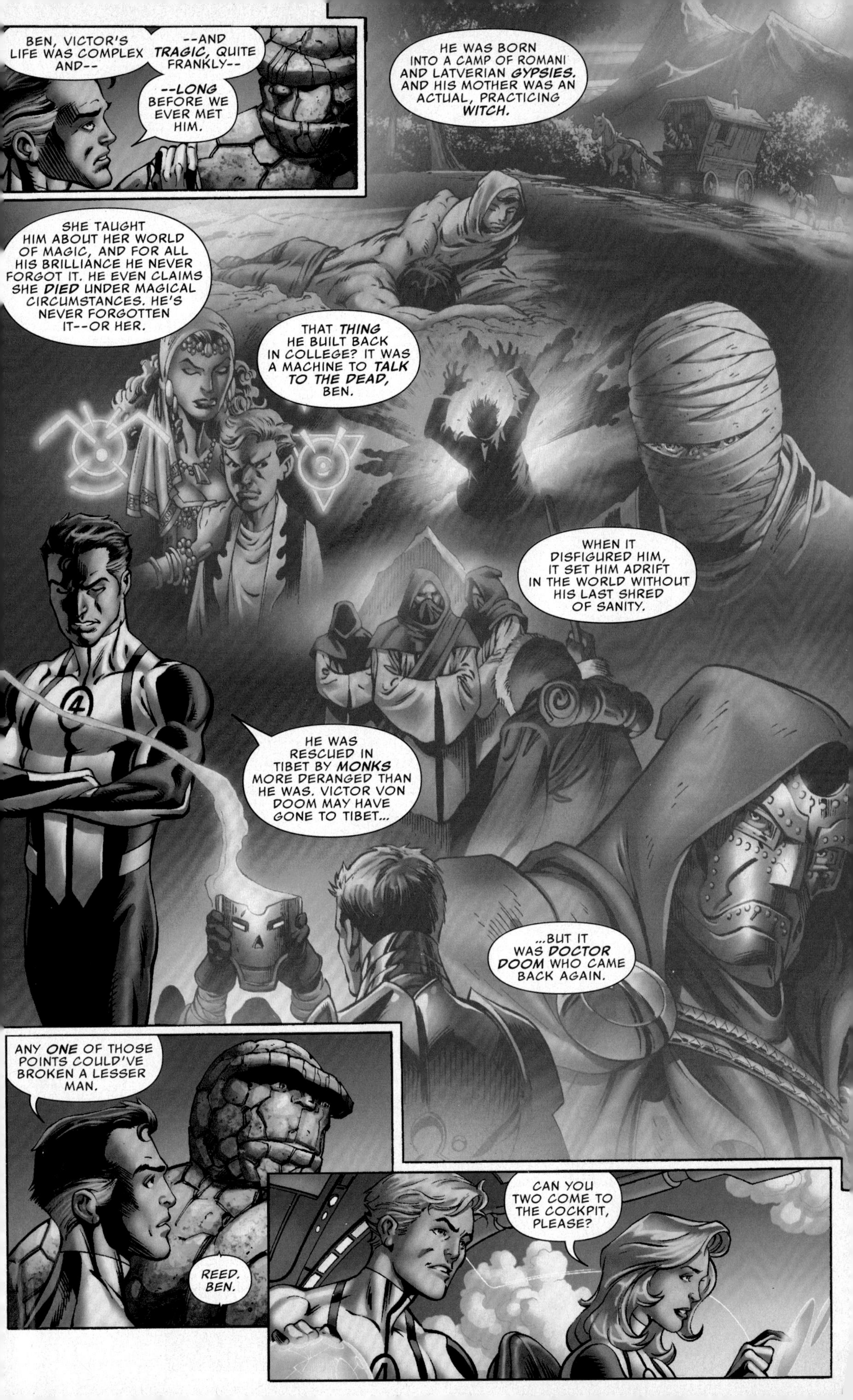
BEN, VICTOR'S LIFE WAS COMPLEX AND--
--AND TRAGIC, QUITE FRANKLY--
--LONG BEFORE WE EVER MET HIM.
HE WAS BORN INTO A CAMP OF ROMANI AND LATVERIAN GYPSIES. AND HIS MOTHER WAS AN ACTUAL, PRACTICING WITCH.
SHE TAUGHT HIM ABOUT HER WORLD OF MAGIC, AND FOR ALL HIS BRILLIANCE HE NEVER FORGOT IT. HE EVEN CLAIMS SHE DIED UNDER MAGICAL CIRCUMSTANCES. HE'S NEVER FORGOTTEN IT--OR HER.
THAT THING HE BUILT BACK IN COLLEGE? IT WAS A MACHINE TO TALK TO THE DEAD, BEN.
WHEN IT DISFIGURED HIM, IT SET HIM ADRIFT IN THE WORLD WITHOUT HIS LAST SHRED OF SANITY.
HE WAS RESCUED IN TIBET BY MONKS MORE DERANGED THAN HE WAS. VICTOR VON DOOM MAY HAVE GONE TO TIBET...
...BUT IT WAS DOCTOR DOOM WHO CAME BACK AGAIN.
ANY ONE OF THOSE POINTS COULD'VE BROKEN A LESSER MAN.
REED. BEN.
CAN YOU TWO COME TO THE COCKPIT, PLEASE?

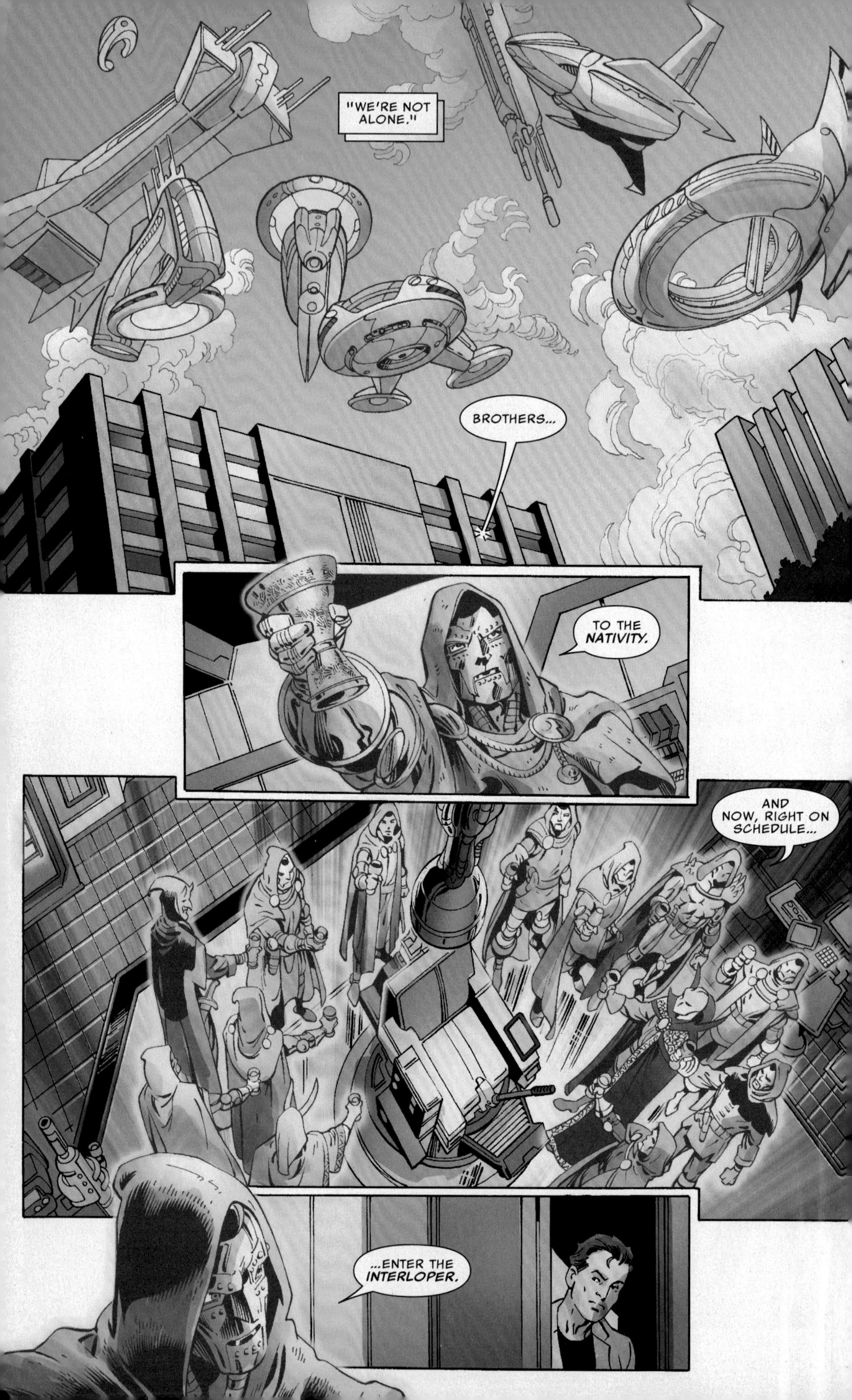
"WE'RE NOT ALONE."
BROTHERS...
TO THE NATIVITY.
AND NOW, RIGHT ON SCHEDULE...
...ENTER THE INTERLOPER.

LOOK AT HIM. MEDDLER. MORON.

RICHARDS THINKS HE CAN GRASP OUR GENIUS BY SIMPLY OBSERVING IT.

EASY NOW, DOOM...

IN HIS SIMPLE WAY HE'S TRYING TO HELP. HE KNOWS NO BETTER AND CAN ONLY PLAY HIS SMALL PART.

CONSIDER HIM LIKE A TOOL BEING USED IN OUR MANUFACTURE...

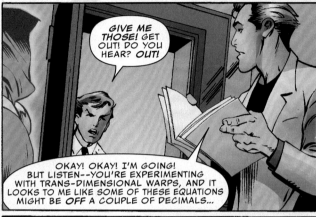

GIVE ME THOSE! GET OUT! DO YOU HEAR? OUT!

OKAY! OKAY! I'M GOING! BUT LISTEN--YOU'RE EXPERIMENTING WITH TRANS-DIMENSIONAL WARPS, AND IT LOOKS TO ME LIKE SOME OF THESE EQUATIONS MIGHT BE OFF A COUPLE OF DECIMALS...

HE IS BUT ONE THREAD OF MANY IN OUR INFERNAL TAPESTRY.

REMOVE ONE AND THE REST MAY UNRAVEL.

STILL. WE SHOULD HAVE KILLED HIM WHEN WE HAD THE CHANCE.

DOOM, NO--!

YOU CAN'T INTERFERE!

WHO ARE YOU TO DARE TOUCH DOOM?

THIS IS NUTTY, REED. YOU SURE THEY CAN'T SEE US?

IT'S LIKE WHEN ONE RADIO STATION BLEEDS THROUGH ANOTHER. WE'RE GETTING THE BLEED, BUT THEY AREN'T.

WELL, HAVE YOU EVER SEEN A BIGGER LINEUP OF CHUMPS IN YOUR LIFE?

THINK OF DOOM'S *MEGALOMANIA*, BEN-- IT MAKES SENSE HE'D WANT TO WITNESS THE MOMENT OF HIS OWN INCEPTION.

WELL, WHADDYA THINK? DID WE MESS ANYTHING UP?

I'VE GOT A LOT MORE TO LOOK AT, BEN, BUT AT THIS POINT EVERYTHING APPEARS TO BE IN WORKING ORDER.

DOOM'S FUNDAMENTAL *MATHEMATICS* WERE FLAWED. THERE WERE NO MECHANICAL *FAILURES* HERE...

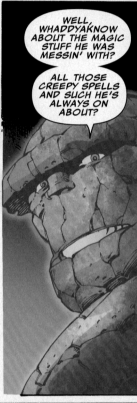

WELL, WHADDYAKNOW ABOUT THE MAGIC STUFF HE WAS MESSIN' WITH?

ALL THOSE CREEPY SPELLS AND SUCH HE'S ALWAYS ON ABOUT?

STOP BEING SO SUPERSTITIOUS, BEN. "MAGIC" ONLY MEANS THE RULES AND LAWS OF THE OBSERVABLE UNIVERSE WE'VE NOT UNCOVERED OR DEFINED PROPERLY YET. IT'S ALL *SCIENCE*.

OH, YEAH...?

WELL, WE'RE ABOUT TO SEE WHAT BEIN' SUPERSTITIOUS GETS YA, STRETCHO...

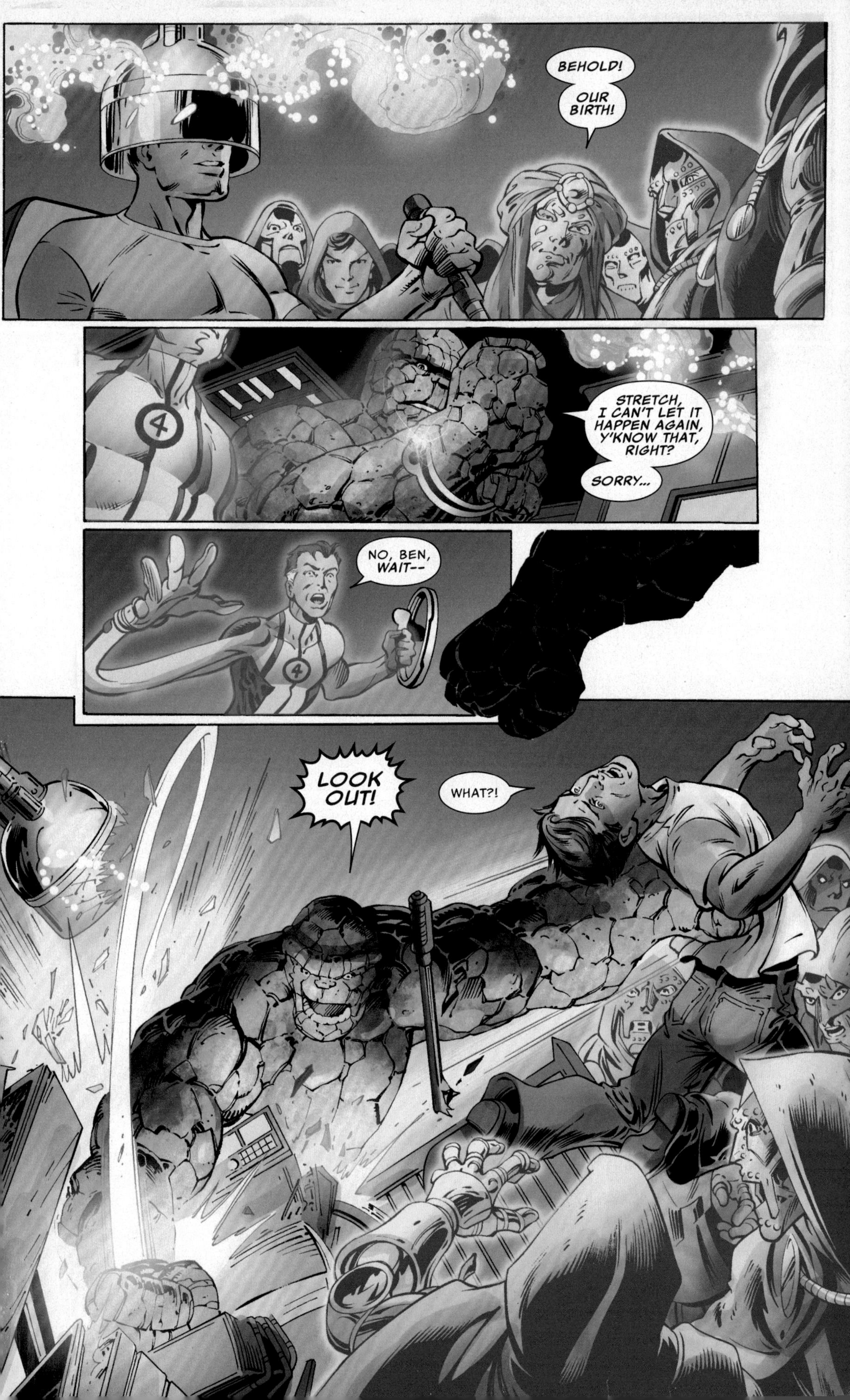
BEHOLD!
OUR BIRTH!
STRETCH, I CAN'T LET IT HAPPEN AGAIN, Y'KNOW THAT, RIGHT?
SORRY...
NO, BEN, WAIT--
LOOK OUT!
WHAT?!

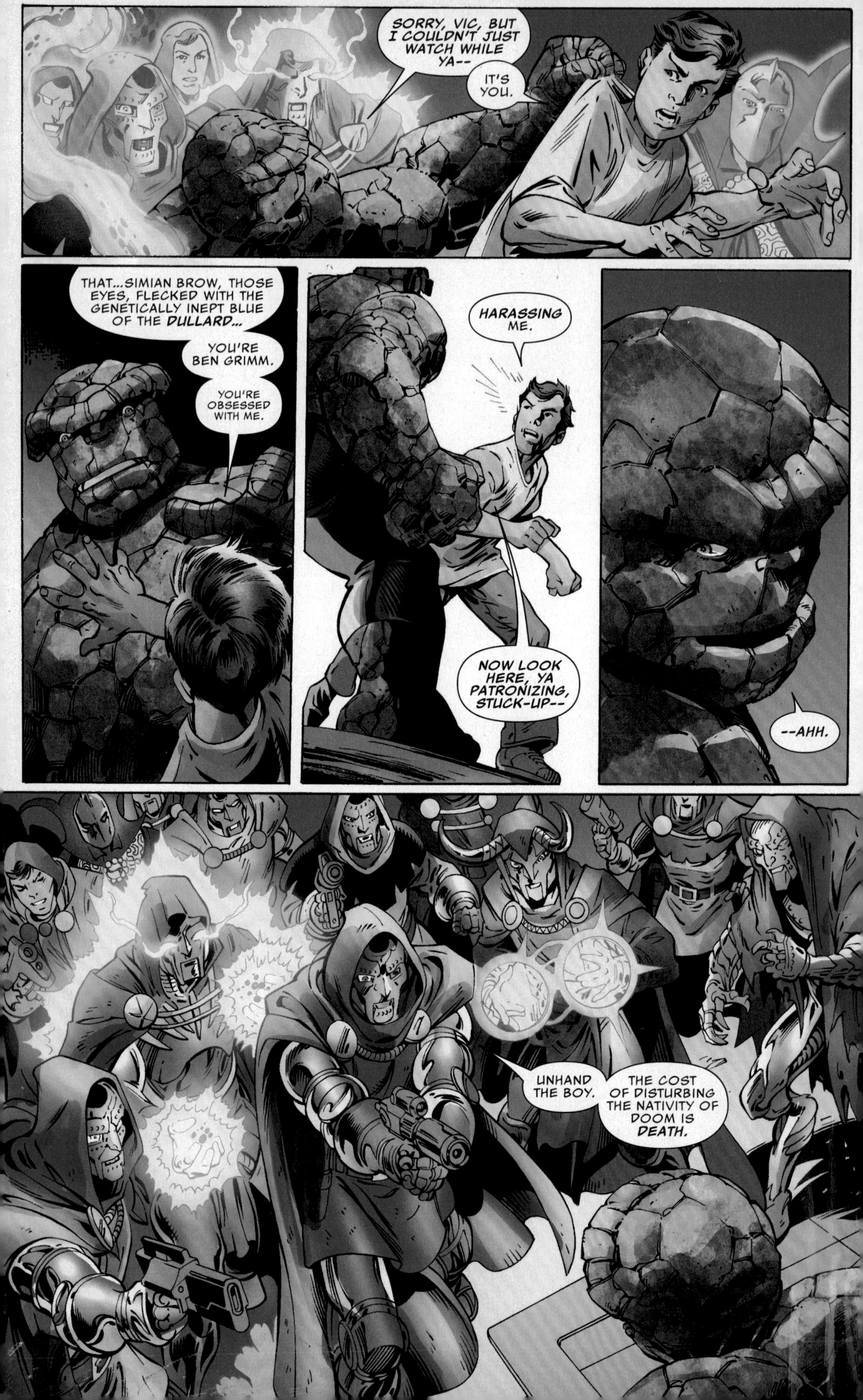

SORRY, VIC, BUT I COULDN'T JUST WATCH WHILE YA--
IT'S YOU.
THAT...SIMIAN BROW, THOSE EYES, FLECKED WITH THE GENETICALLY INEPT BLUE OF THE *DULLARD*...
YOU'RE BEN GRIMM.
YOU'RE OBSESSED WITH ME.
HARASSING ME.
NOW LOOK HERE, YA PATRONIZING, STUCK-UP--
--AHH.
UNHAND THE BOY.
THE COST OF DISTURBING THE NATIVITY OF DOOM IS *DEATH*.

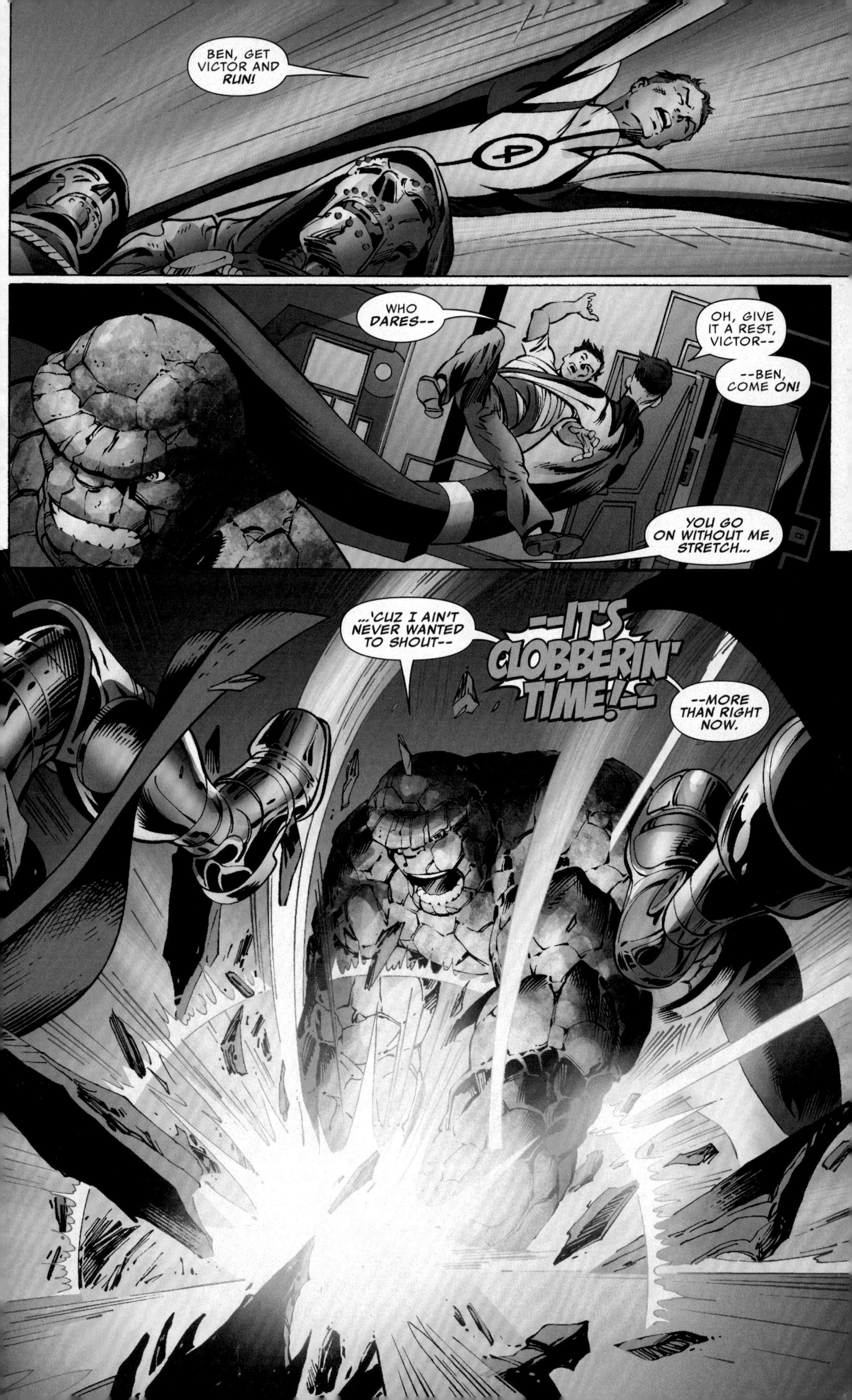
BEN, GET VICTOR AND RUN!
WHO DARES--
OH, GIVE IT A REST, VICTOR--
--BEN, COME ON!
YOU GO ON WITHOUT ME, STRETCH...
...'CUZ I AIN'T NEVER WANTED TO SHOUT--
--IT'S CLOBBERIN' TIME!--
--MORE THAN RIGHT NOW.

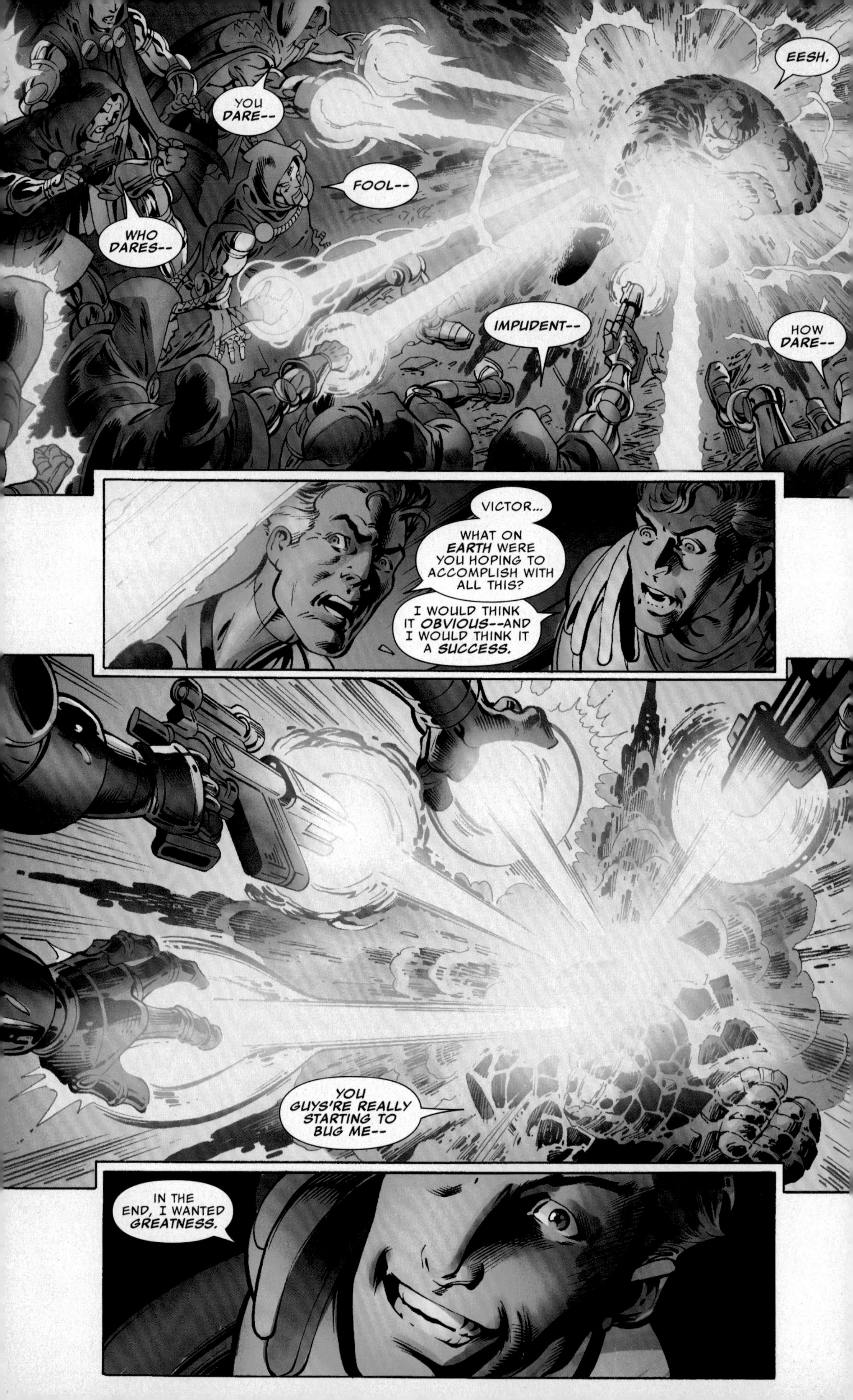
EESH.
YOU DARE--
FOOL--
WHO DARES--
IMPUDENT--
HOW DARE--
VICTOR...
WHAT ON EARTH WERE YOU HOPING TO ACCOMPLISH WITH ALL THIS?
I WOULD THINK IT OBVIOUS--AND I WOULD THINK IT A SUCCESS.
YOU GUYS'RE REALLY STARTING TO BUG ME--
IN THE END, I WANTED GREATNESS.

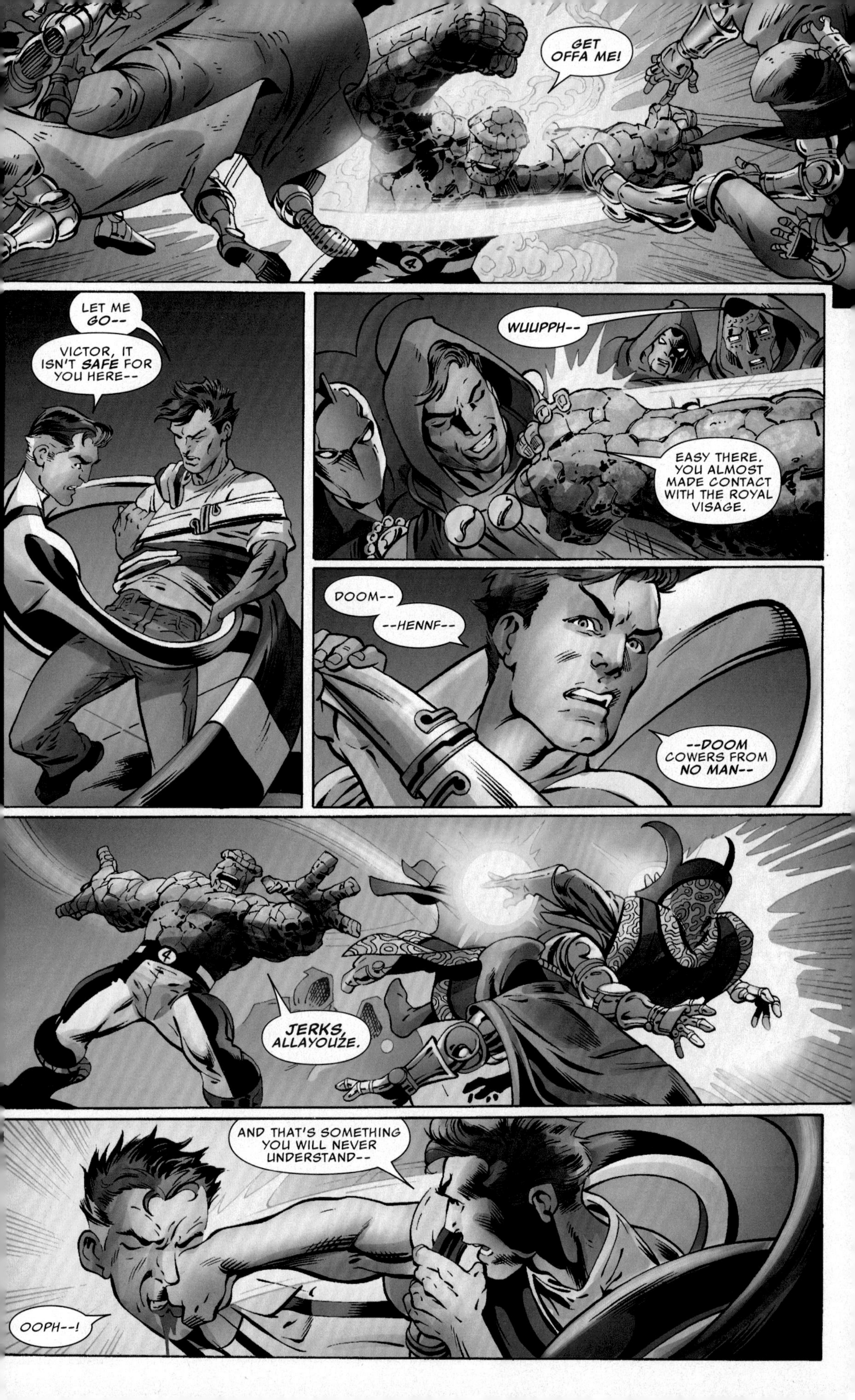
GET OFFA ME!
LET ME GO--
VICTOR, IT ISN'T SAFE FOR YOU HERE--
WUUPPH--
EASY THERE. YOU ALMOST MADE CONTACT WITH THE ROYAL VISAGE.
DOOM--
--HENNF--
--DOOM COWERS FROM NO MAN--
JERKS, ALLAYOUZE.
AND THAT'S SOMETHING YOU WILL NEVER UNDERSTAND--
OOPH--!

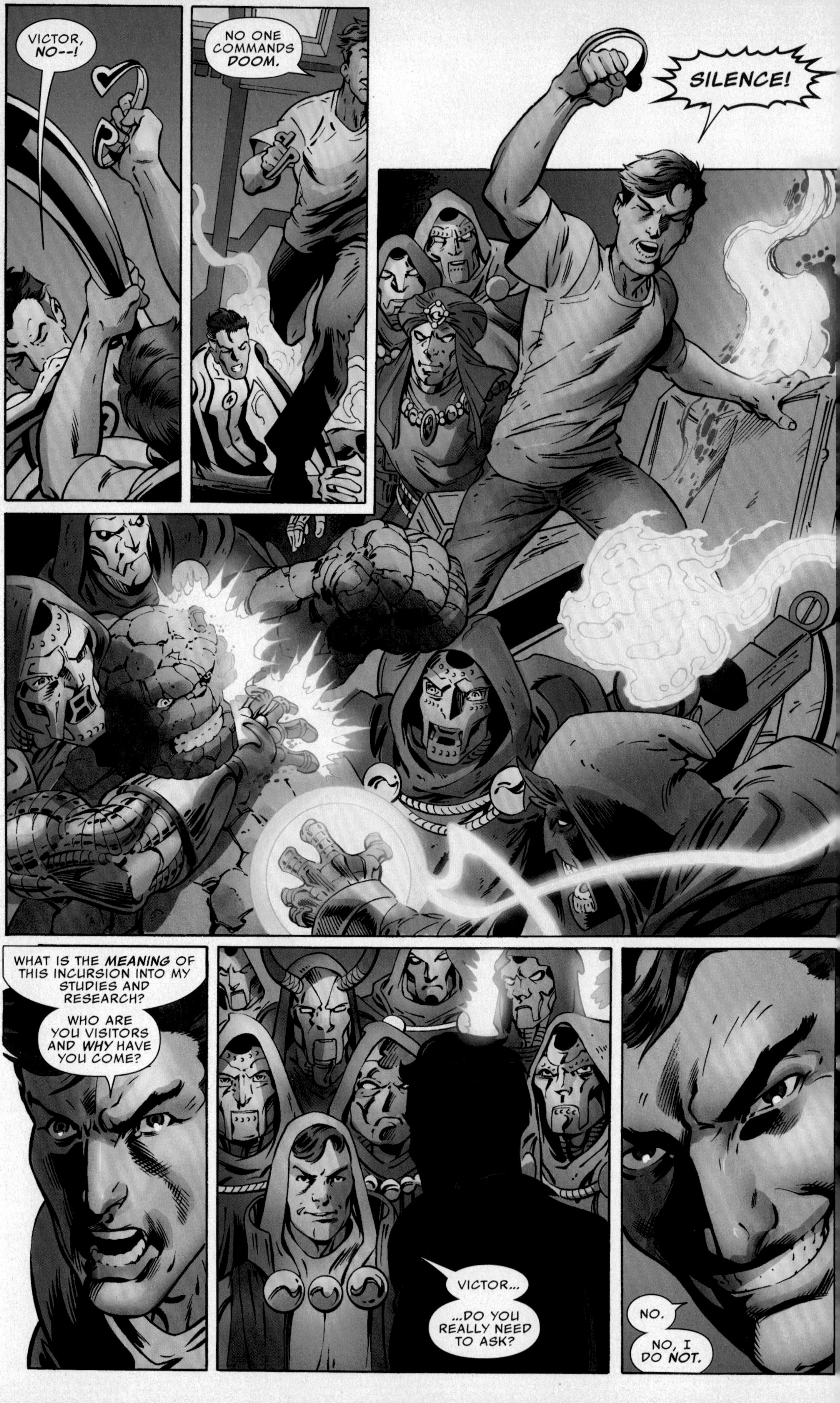
VICTOR, NO--!
NO ONE COMMANDS DOOM.
SILENCE!
WHAT IS THE MEANING OF THIS INCURSION INTO MY STUDIES AND RESEARCH?
WHO ARE YOU VISITORS AND WHY HAVE YOU COME?
VICTOR...
...DO YOU REALLY NEED TO ASK?
NO.
NO, I DO NOT.

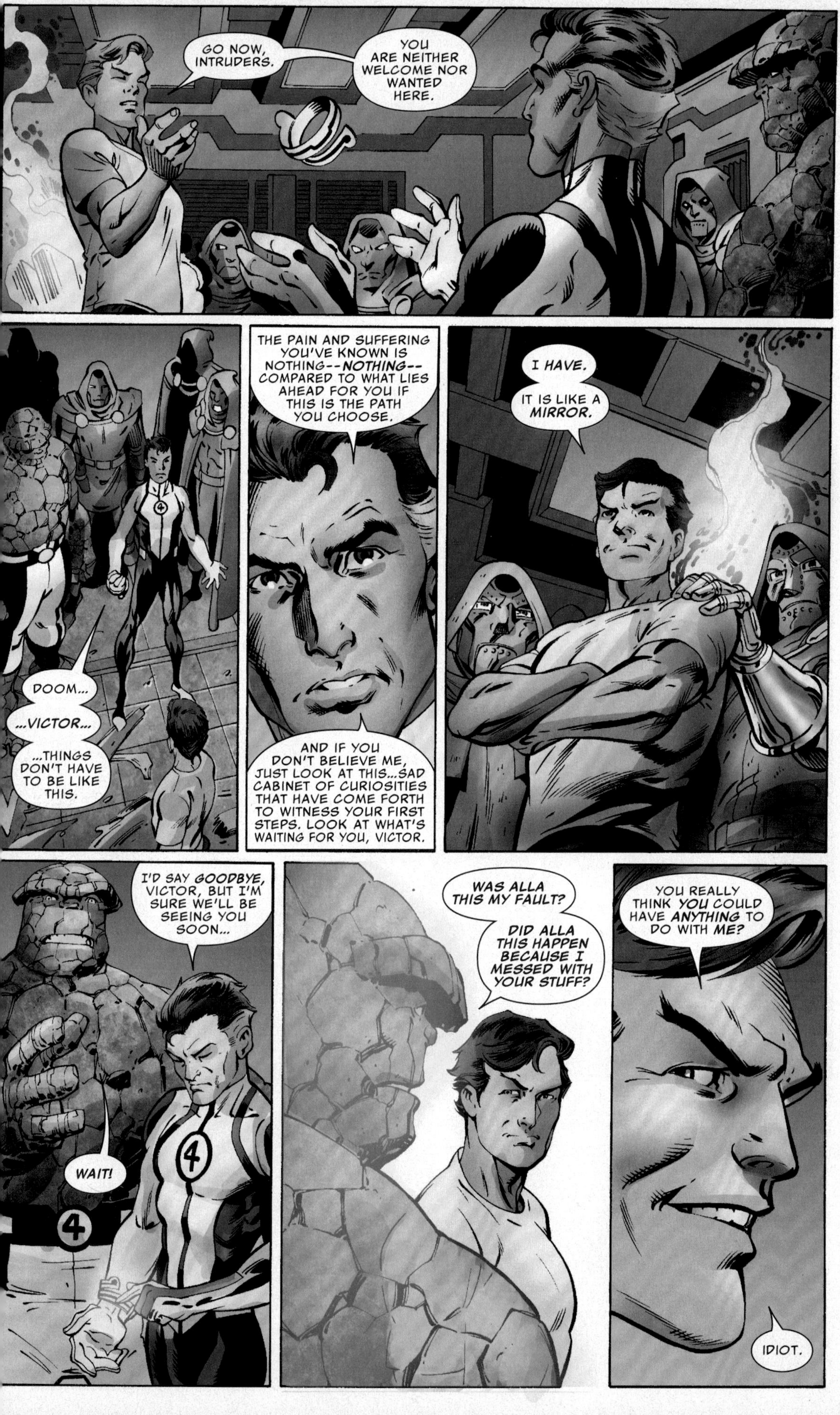
GO NOW, INTRUDERS.
YOU ARE NEITHER WELCOME NOR WANTED HERE.
DOOM...
...VICTOR...
...THINGS DON'T HAVE TO BE LIKE THIS.
THE PAIN AND SUFFERING YOU'VE KNOWN IS NOTHING--NOTHING--COMPARED TO WHAT LIES AHEAD FOR YOU IF THIS IS THE PATH YOU CHOOSE.
AND IF YOU DON'T BELIEVE ME, JUST LOOK AT THIS...SAD CABINET OF CURIOSITIES THAT HAVE COME FORTH TO WITNESS YOUR FIRST STEPS. LOOK AT WHAT'S WAITING FOR YOU, VICTOR.
I HAVE.
IT IS LIKE A MIRROR.
I'D SAY GOODBYE, VICTOR, BUT I'M SURE WE'LL BE SEEING YOU SOON...
WAIT!
WAS ALLA THIS MY FAULT?
DID ALLA THIS HAPPEN BECAUSE I MESSED WITH YOUR STUFF?
YOU REALLY THINK YOU COULD HAVE ANYTHING TO DO WITH ME?
IDIOT.

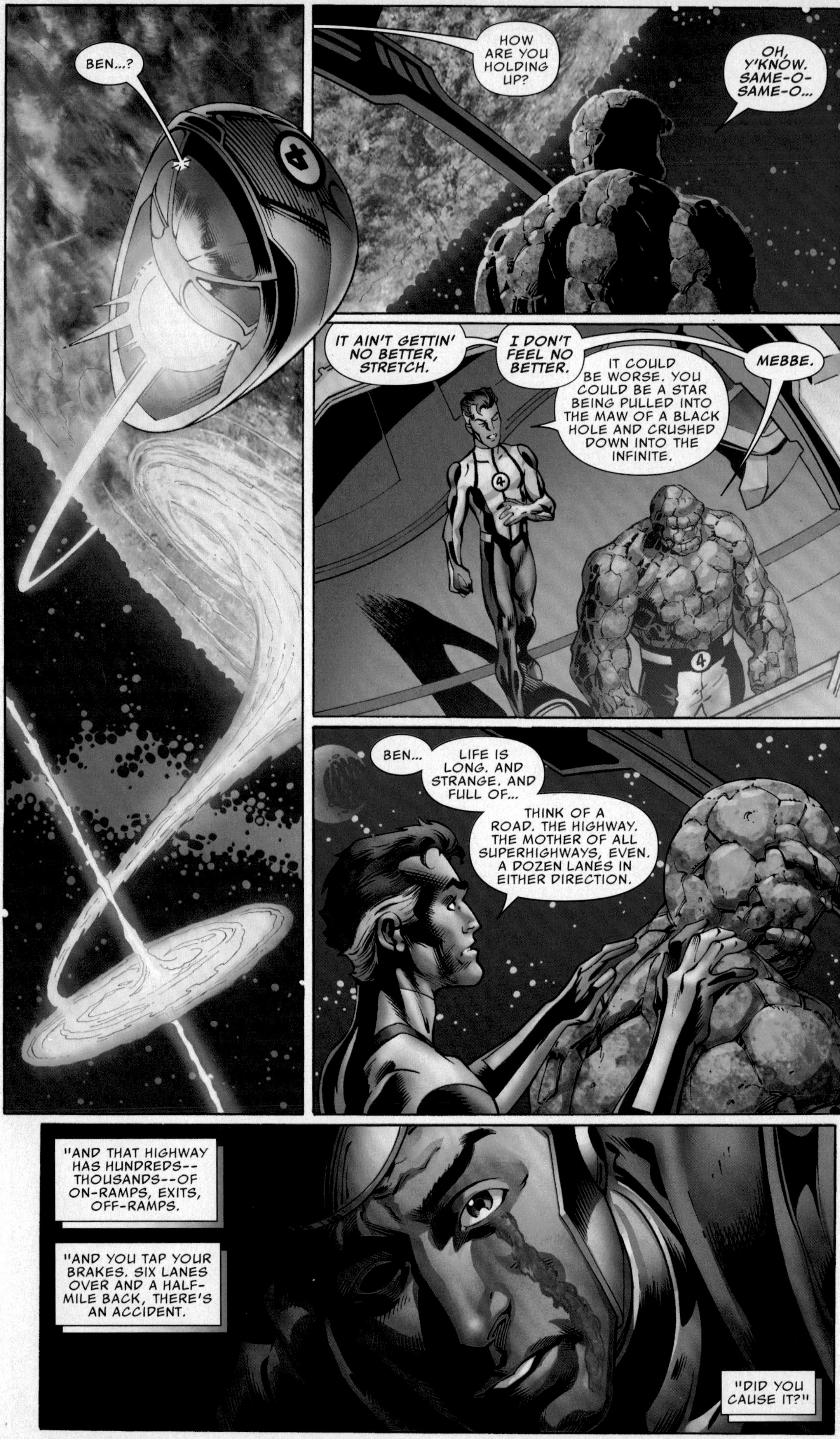
BEN...?
HOW ARE YOU HOLDING UP?
OH, Y'KNOW. SAME-O-SAME-O...
IT AIN'T GETTIN' NO BETTER, STRETCH.
I DON'T FEEL NO BETTER.
IT COULD BE WORSE. YOU COULD BE A STAR BEING PULLED INTO THE MAW OF A BLACK HOLE AND CRUSHED DOWN INTO THE INFINITE.
MEBBE.
BEN...
LIFE IS LONG. AND STRANGE. AND FULL OF...
THINK OF A ROAD. THE HIGHWAY. THE MOTHER OF ALL SUPERHIGHWAYS, EVEN. A DOZEN LANES IN EITHER DIRECTION.
"AND THAT HIGHWAY HAS HUNDREDS--THOUSANDS--OF ON-RAMPS, EXITS, OFF-RAMPS.
"AND YOU TAP YOUR BRAKES. SIX LANES OVER AND A HALF-MILE BACK, THERE'S AN ACCIDENT.
"DID YOU CAUSE IT?"

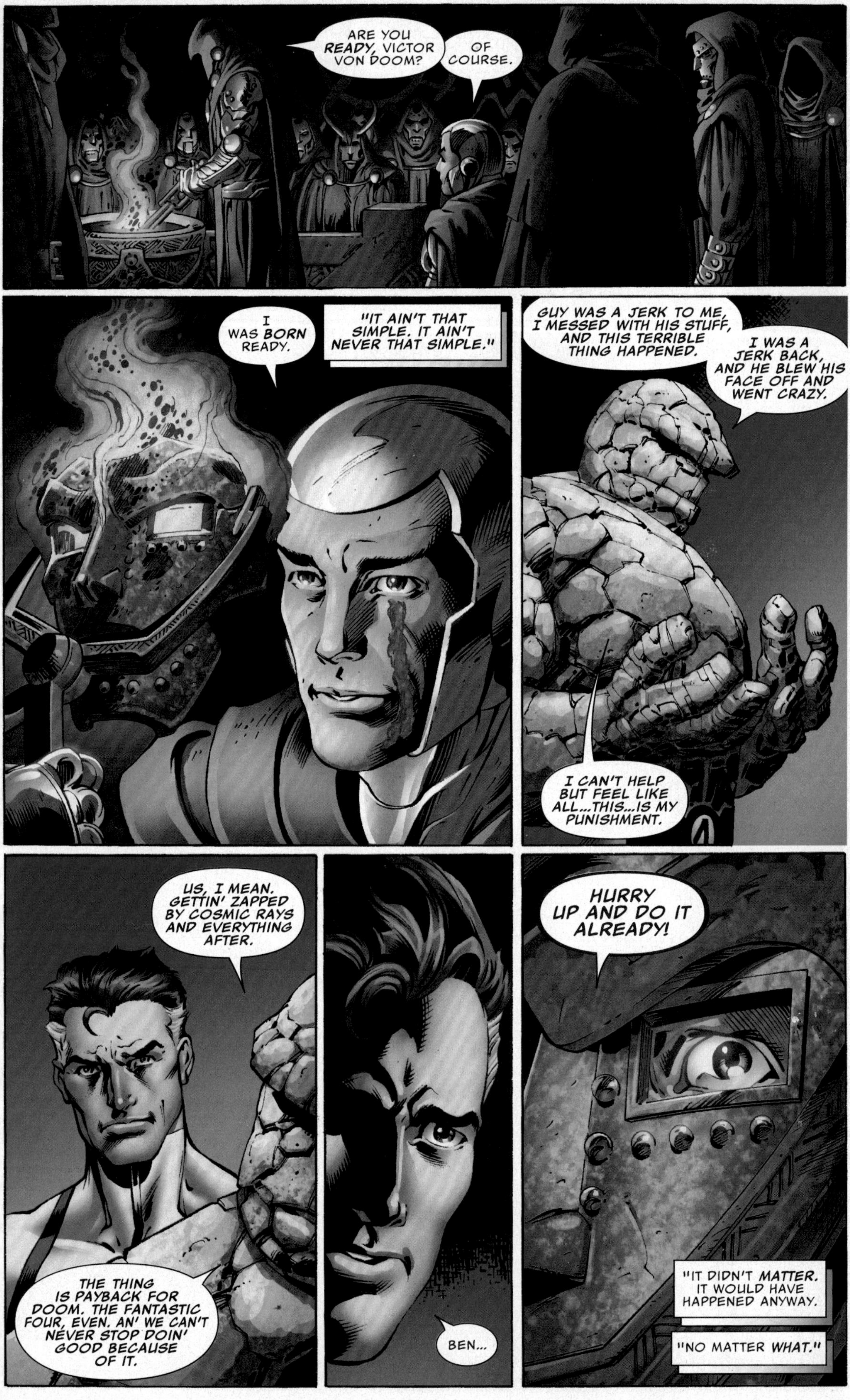
ARE YOU READY, VICTOR VON DOOM?
OF COURSE.
I WAS BORN READY.
"IT AIN'T THAT SIMPLE. IT AIN'T NEVER THAT SIMPLE."
GUY WAS A JERK TO ME, I MESSED WITH HIS STUFF, AND THIS TERRIBLE THING HAPPENED.
I WAS A JERK BACK, AND HE BLEW HIS FACE OFF AND WENT CRAZY.
I CAN'T HELP BUT FEEL LIKE ALL...THIS...IS MY PUNISHMENT.
US, I MEAN. GETTIN' ZAPPED BY COSMIC RAYS AND EVERYTHING AFTER.
THE THING IS PAYBACK FOR DOOM. THE FANTASTIC FOUR, EVEN. AN' WE CAN'T NEVER STOP DOIN' GOOD BECAUSE OF IT.
BEN...
HURRY UP AND DO IT ALREADY!
"IT DIDN'T MATTER. IT WOULD HAVE HAPPENED ANYWAY.
"NO MATTER WHAT."

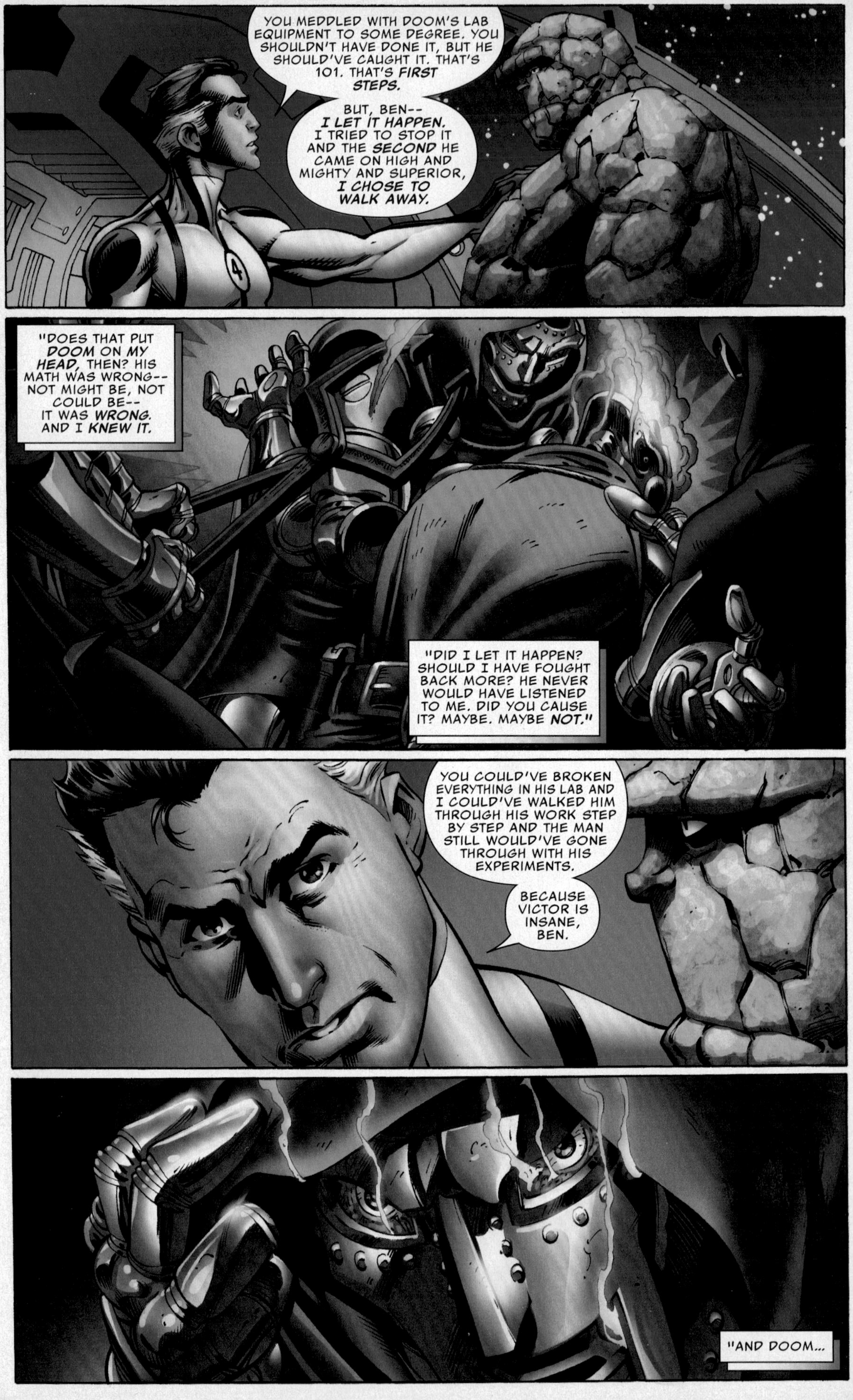
YOU MEDDLED WITH DOOM'S LAB EQUIPMENT TO SOME DEGREE. YOU SHOULDN'T HAVE DONE IT, BUT HE SHOULD'VE CAUGHT IT. THAT'S 101. THAT'S FIRST STEPS.
BUT, BEN-- I LET IT HAPPEN. I TRIED TO STOP IT AND THE SECOND HE CAME ON HIGH AND MIGHTY AND SUPERIOR, I CHOSE TO WALK AWAY.
"DOES THAT PUT DOOM ON MY HEAD, THEN? HIS MATH WAS WRONG-- NOT MIGHT BE, NOT COULD BE-- IT WAS WRONG. AND I KNEW IT.
"DID I LET IT HAPPEN? SHOULD I HAVE FOUGHT BACK MORE? HE NEVER WOULD HAVE LISTENED TO ME. DID YOU CAUSE IT? MAYBE. MAYBE NOT."
YOU COULD'VE BROKEN EVERYTHING IN HIS LAB AND I COULD'VE WALKED HIM THROUGH HIS WORK STEP BY STEP AND THE MAN STILL WOULD'VE GONE THROUGH WITH HIS EXPERIMENTS.
BECAUSE VICTOR IS INSANE, BEN.
"AND DOOM...

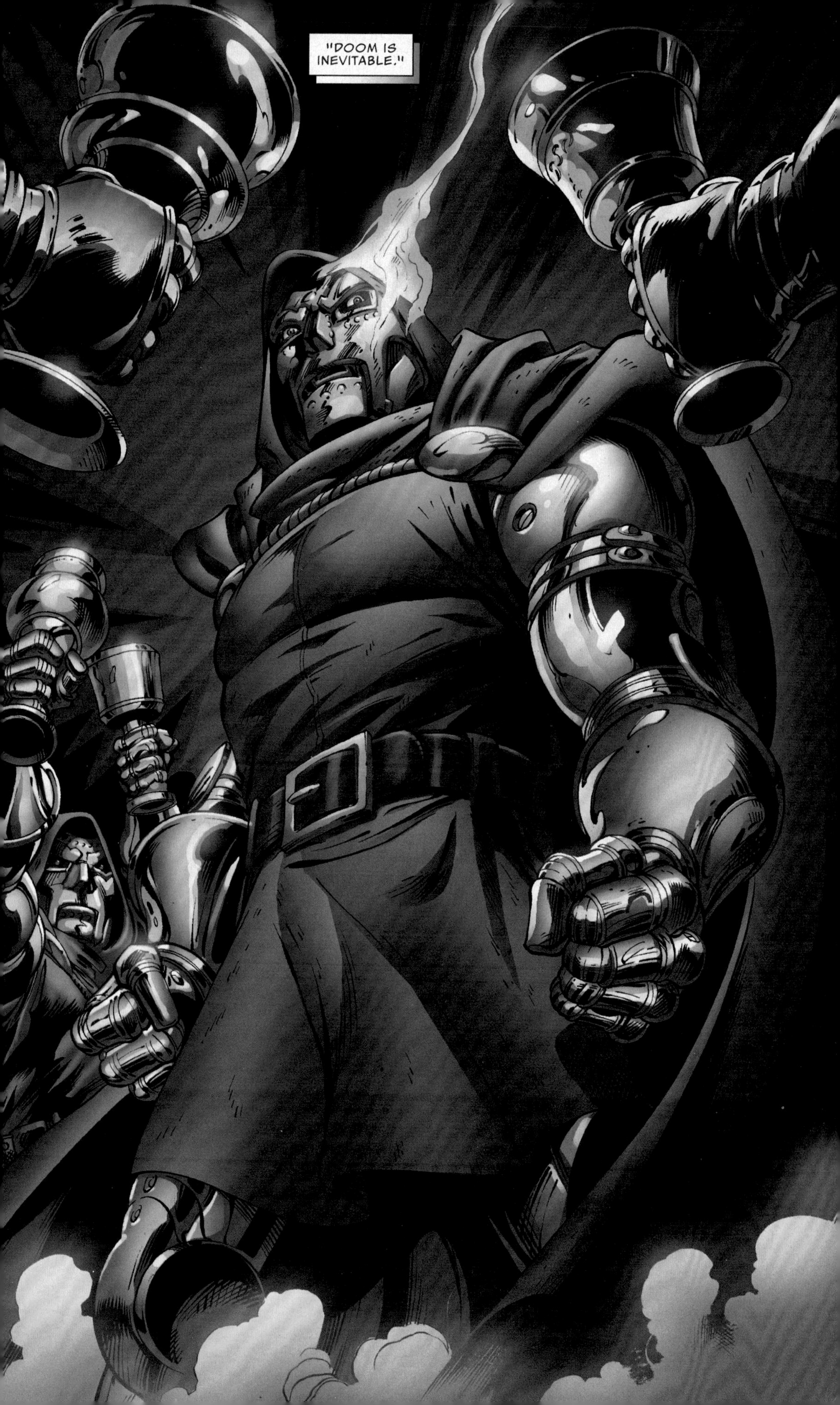
"DOOM IS INEVITABLE."

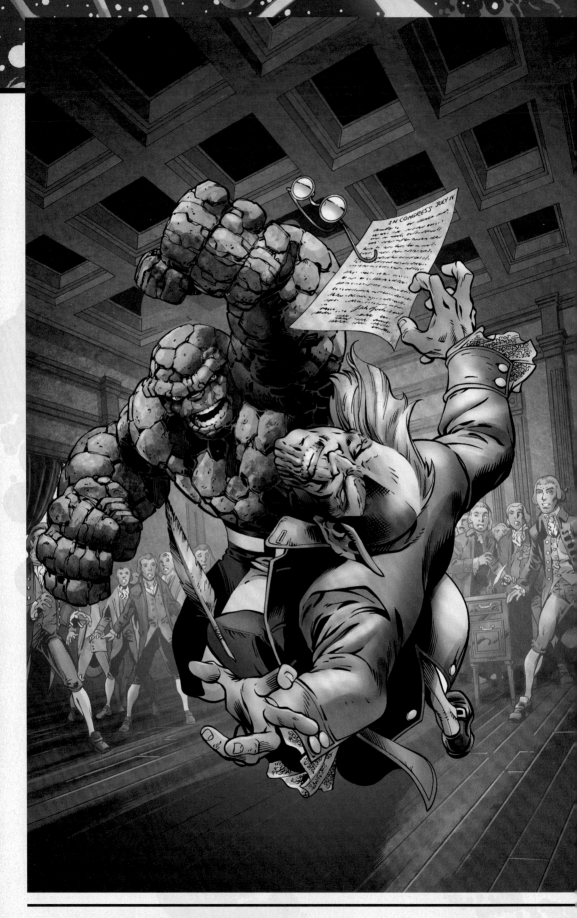

FANTASTIC FOUR #10 — "SELF-EVIDENT TRUTHS"

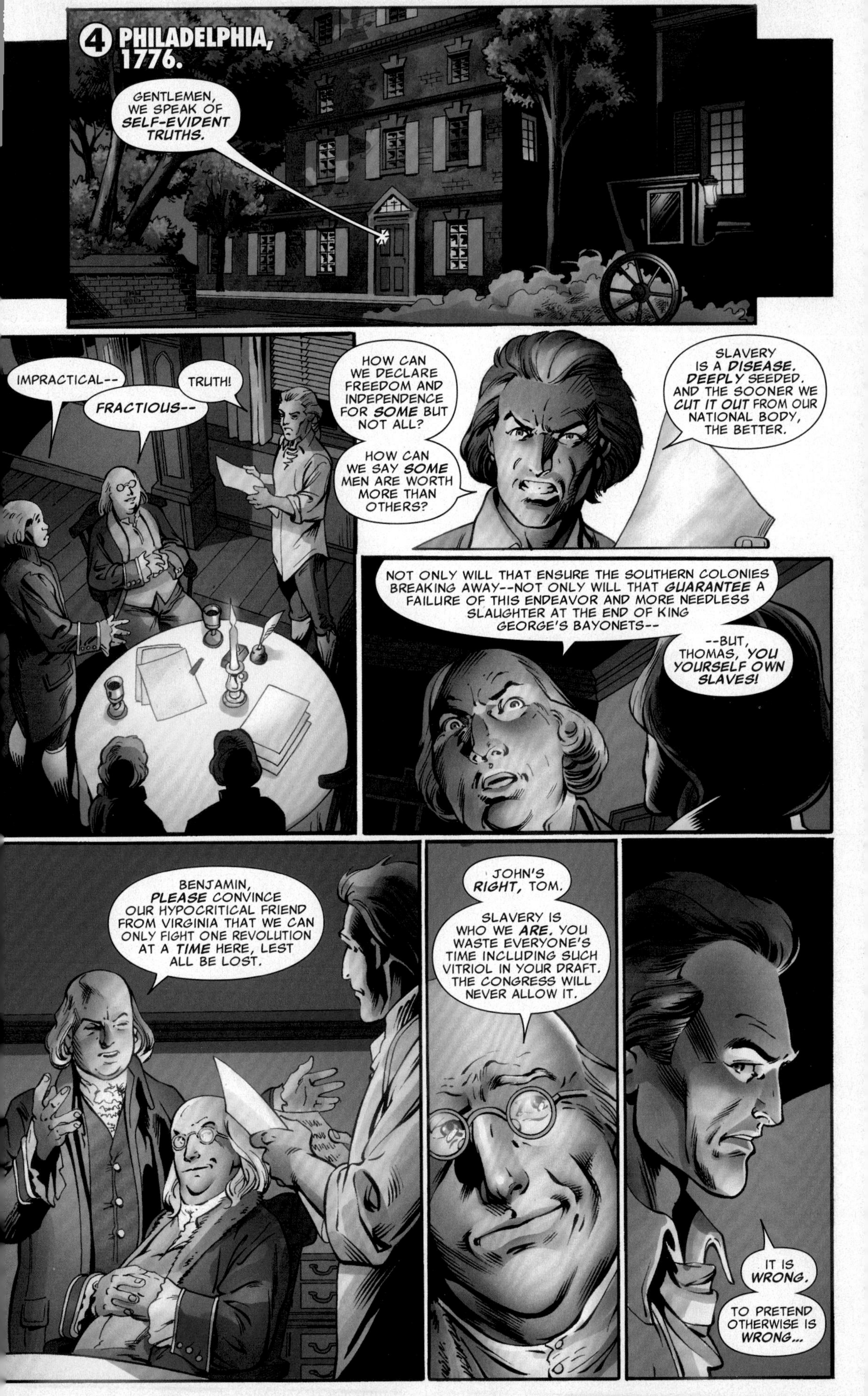
4 PHILADELPHIA, 1776.
GENTLEMEN, WE SPEAK OF SELF-EVIDENT TRUTHS.
IMPRACTICAL--
FRACTIOUS--
TRUTH!
HOW CAN WE DECLARE FREEDOM AND INDEPENDENCE FOR SOME BUT NOT ALL?
HOW CAN WE SAY SOME MEN ARE WORTH MORE THAN OTHERS?
SLAVERY IS A DISEASE. DEEPLY SEEDED. AND THE SOONER WE CUT IT OUT FROM OUR NATIONAL BODY, THE BETTER.
NOT ONLY WILL THAT ENSURE THE SOUTHERN COLONIES BREAKING AWAY--NOT ONLY WILL THAT GUARANTEE A FAILURE OF THIS ENDEAVOR AND MORE NEEDLESS SLAUGHTER AT THE END OF KING GEORGE'S BAYONETS--
--BUT, THOMAS, YOU YOURSELF OWN SLAVES!
BENJAMIN, PLEASE CONVINCE OUR HYPOCRITICAL FRIEND FROM VIRGINIA THAT WE CAN ONLY FIGHT ONE REVOLUTION AT A TIME HERE, LEST ALL BE LOST.
JOHN'S RIGHT, TOM.
SLAVERY IS WHO WE ARE. YOU WASTE EVERYONE'S TIME INCLUDING SUCH VITRIOL IN YOUR DRAFT. THE CONGRESS WILL NEVER ALLOW IT.
IT IS WRONG.
TO PRETEND OTHERWISE IS WRONG...

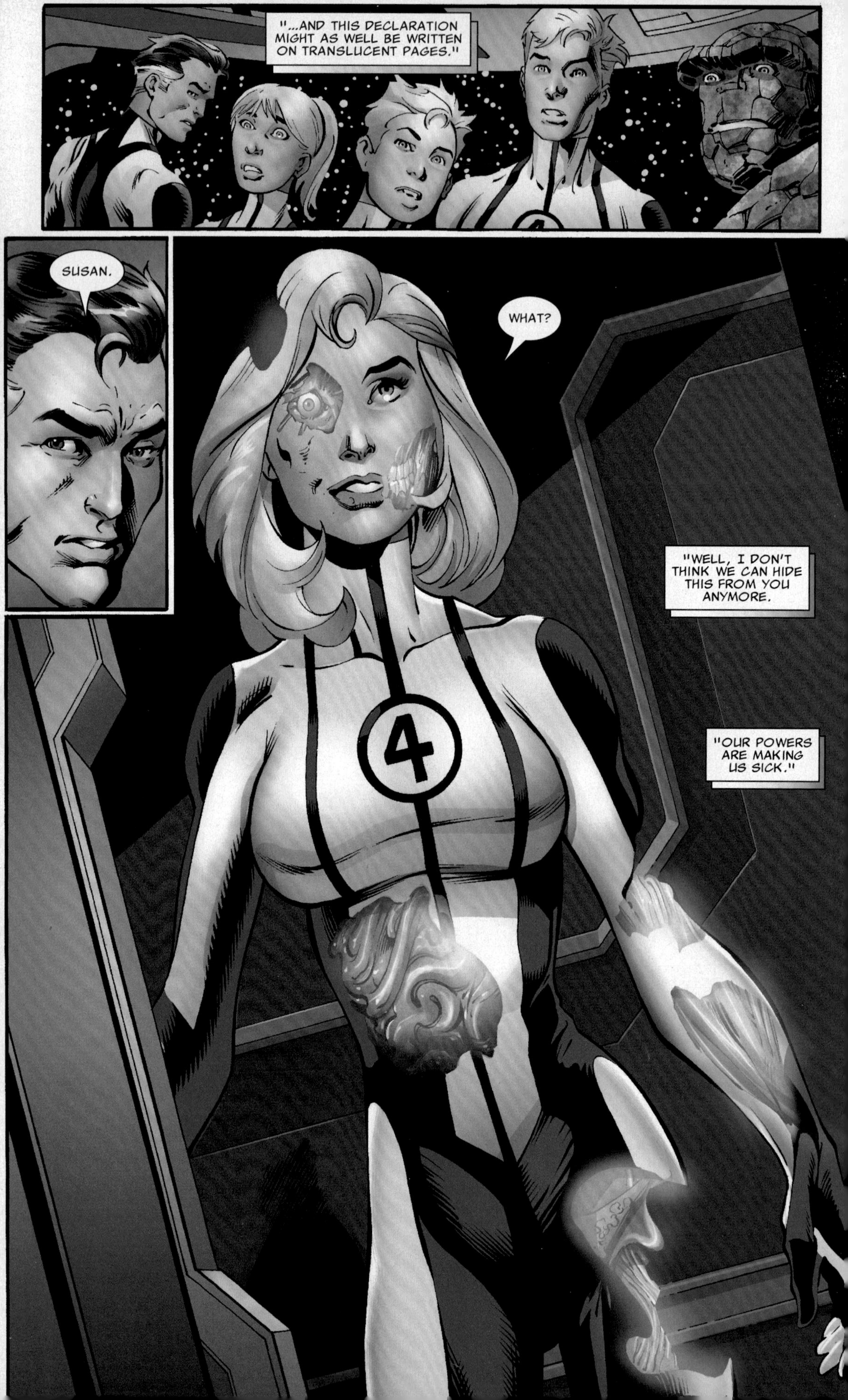
"...AND THIS DECLARATION MIGHT AS WELL BE WRITTEN ON TRANSLUCENT PAGES."
SUSAN.
WHAT?
"WELL, I DON'T THINK WE CAN HIDE THIS FROM YOU ANYMORE.
"OUR POWERS ARE MAKING US SICK."

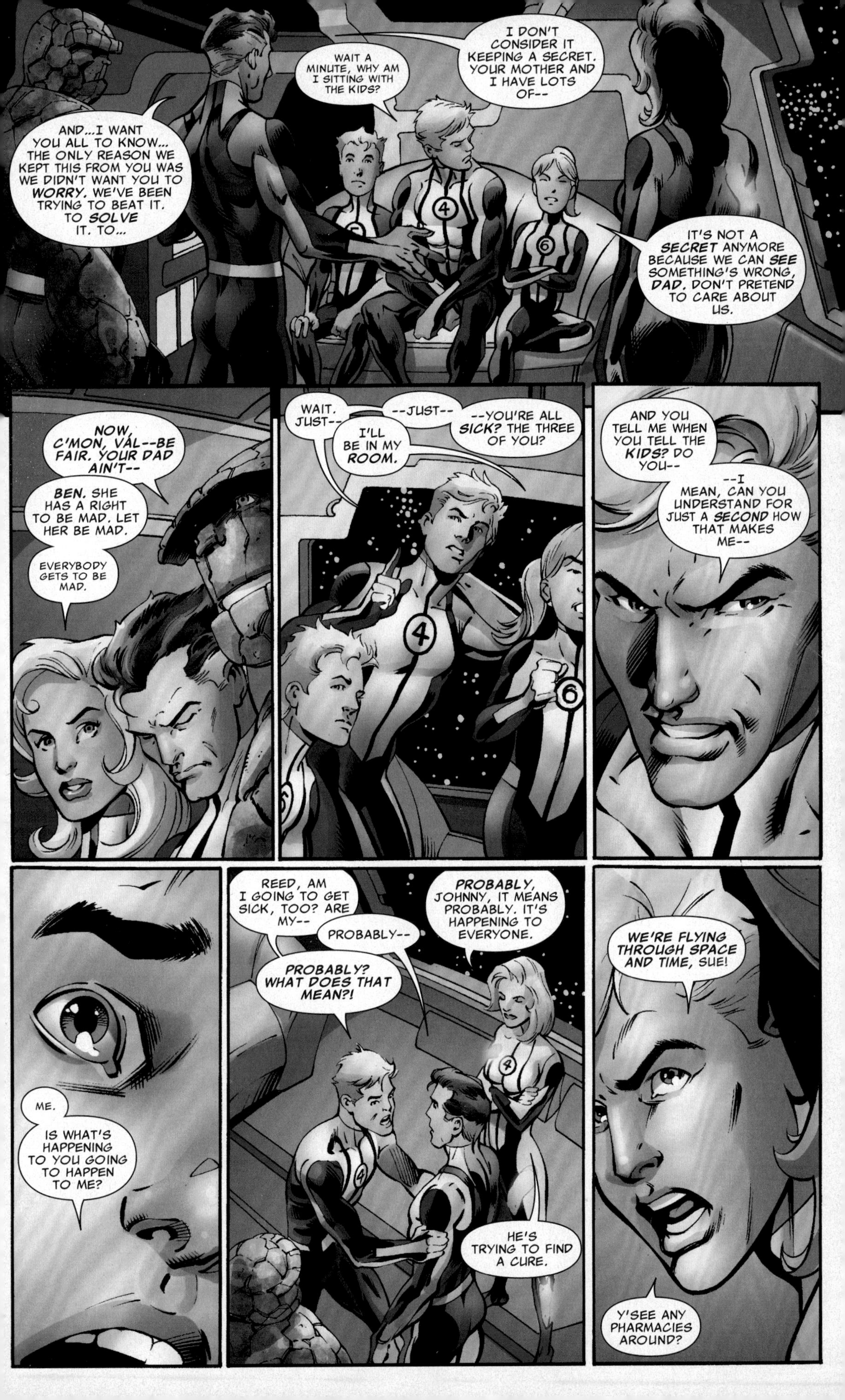

WAIT A MINUTE, WHY AM I SITTING WITH THE KIDS?
I DON'T CONSIDER IT KEEPING A SECRET. YOUR MOTHER AND I HAVE LOTS OF--
AND...I WANT YOU ALL TO KNOW... THE ONLY REASON WE KEPT THIS FROM YOU WAS WE DIDN'T WANT YOU TO WORRY. WE'VE BEEN TRYING TO BEAT IT. TO SOLVE IT. TO...
IT'S NOT A SECRET ANYMORE BECAUSE WE CAN SEE SOMETHING'S WRONG, DAD. DON'T PRETEND TO CARE ABOUT US.
NOW, C'MON, VAL--BE FAIR. YOUR DAD AIN'T--
BEN. SHE HAS A RIGHT TO BE MAD. LET HER BE MAD.
EVERYBODY GETS TO BE MAD.
WAIT. JUST--
--JUST--
--YOU'RE ALL SICK? THE THREE OF YOU?
I'LL BE IN MY ROOM.
AND YOU TELL ME WHEN YOU TELL THE KIDS? DO YOU--
--I MEAN, CAN YOU UNDERSTAND FOR JUST A SECOND HOW THAT MAKES ME--
ME.
IS WHAT'S HAPPENING TO YOU GOING TO HAPPEN TO ME?
REED, AM I GOING TO GET SICK, TOO? ARE MY--
PROBABLY--
PROBABLY? WHAT DOES THAT MEAN?!
PROBABLY, JOHNNY, IT MEANS PROBABLY. IT'S HAPPENING TO EVERYONE.
HE'S TRYING TO FIND A CURE.
WE'RE FLYING THROUGH SPACE AND TIME, SUE!
Y'SEE ANY PHARMACIES AROUND?

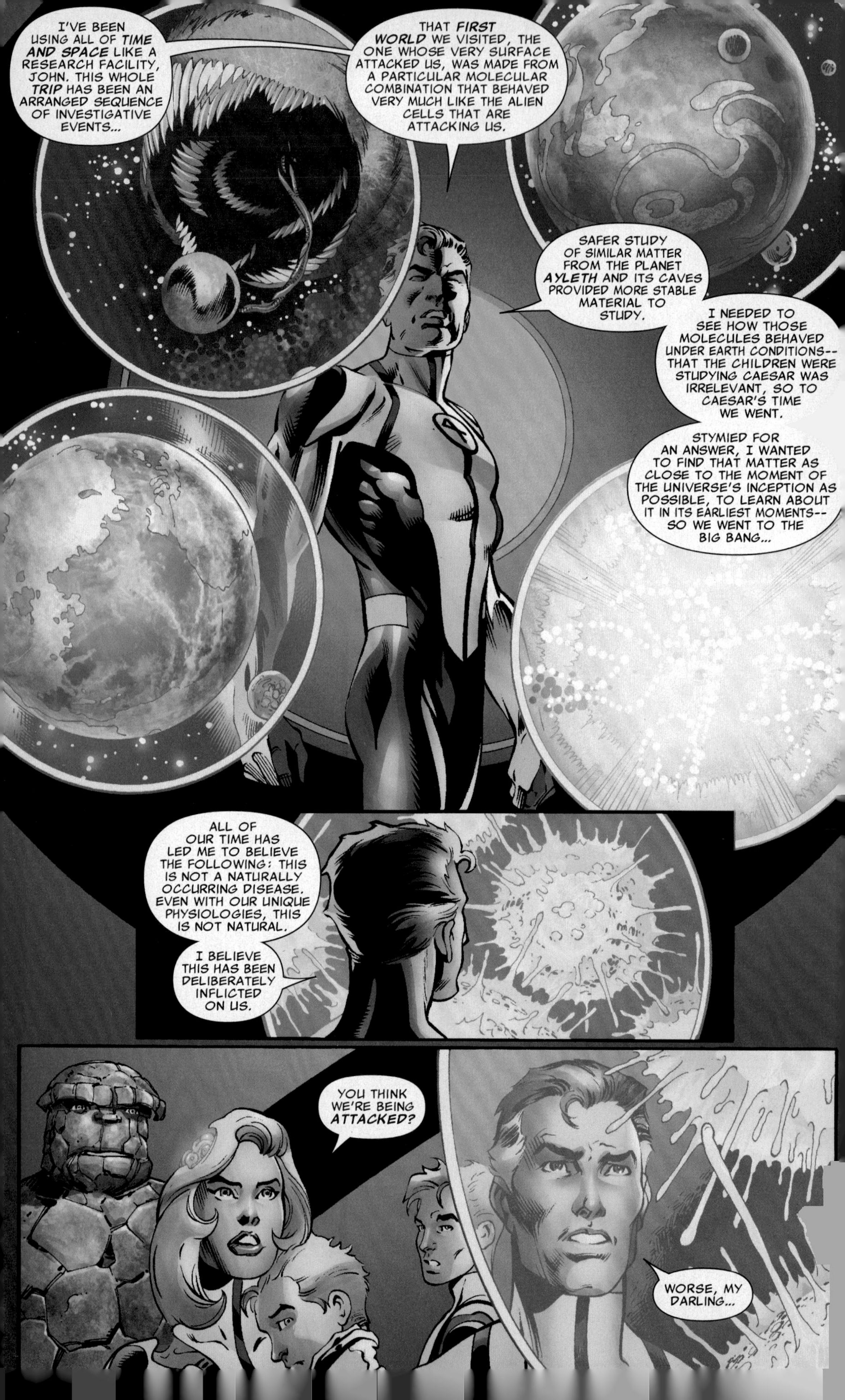
I'VE BEEN USING ALL OF TIME AND SPACE LIKE A RESEARCH FACILITY, JOHN. THIS WHOLE TRIP HAS BEEN AN ARRANGED SEQUENCE OF INVESTIGATIVE EVENTS...
THAT FIRST WORLD WE VISITED, THE ONE WHOSE VERY SURFACE ATTACKED US, WAS MADE FROM A PARTICULAR MOLECULAR COMBINATION THAT BEHAVED VERY MUCH LIKE THE ALIEN CELLS THAT ARE ATTACKING US.
SAFER STUDY OF SIMILAR MATTER FROM THE PLANET AYLETH AND ITS CAVES PROVIDED MORE STABLE MATERIAL TO STUDY.
I NEEDED TO SEE HOW THOSE MOLECULES BEHAVED UNDER EARTH CONDITIONS--THAT THE CHILDREN WERE STUDYING CAESAR WAS IRRELEVANT, SO TO CAESAR'S TIME WE WENT.
STYMIED FOR AN ANSWER, I WANTED TO FIND THAT MATTER AS CLOSE TO THE MOMENT OF THE UNIVERSE'S INCEPTION AS POSSIBLE, TO LEARN ABOUT IT IN ITS EARLIEST MOMENTS--SO WE WENT TO THE BIG BANG...
ALL OF OUR TIME HAS LED ME TO BELIEVE THE FOLLOWING: THIS IS NOT A NATURALLY OCCURRING DISEASE. EVEN WITH OUR UNIQUE PHYSIOLOGIES, THIS IS NOT NATURAL.
I BELIEVE THIS HAS BEEN DELIBERATELY INFLICTED ON US.
YOU THINK WE'RE BEING ATTACKED?
WORSE, MY DARLING...

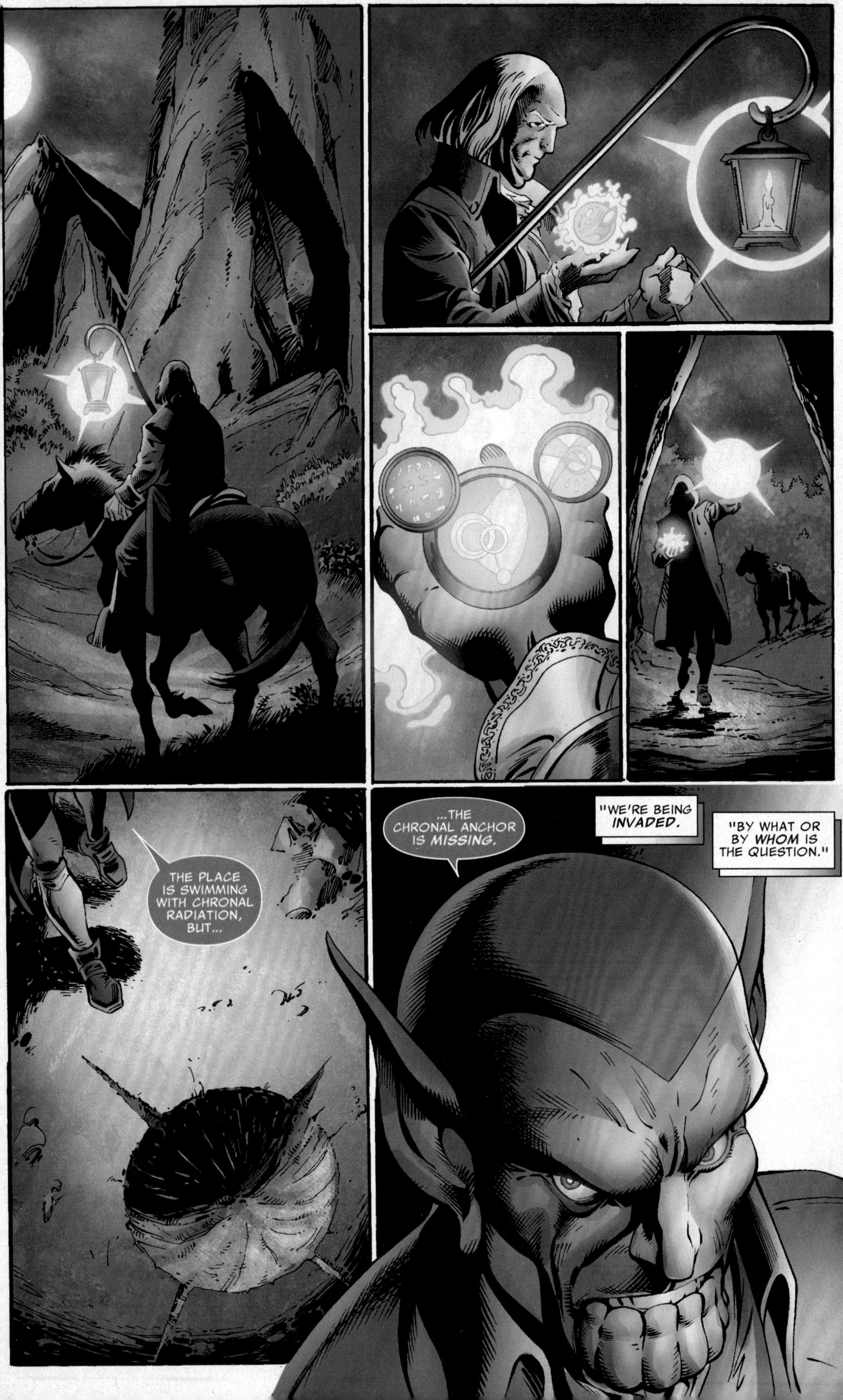
THE PLACE IS SWIMMING WITH CHRONAL RADIATION, BUT...
...THE CHRONAL ANCHOR IS MISSING.
"WE'RE BEING INVADED.
"BY WHAT OR BY WHOM IS THE QUESTION."

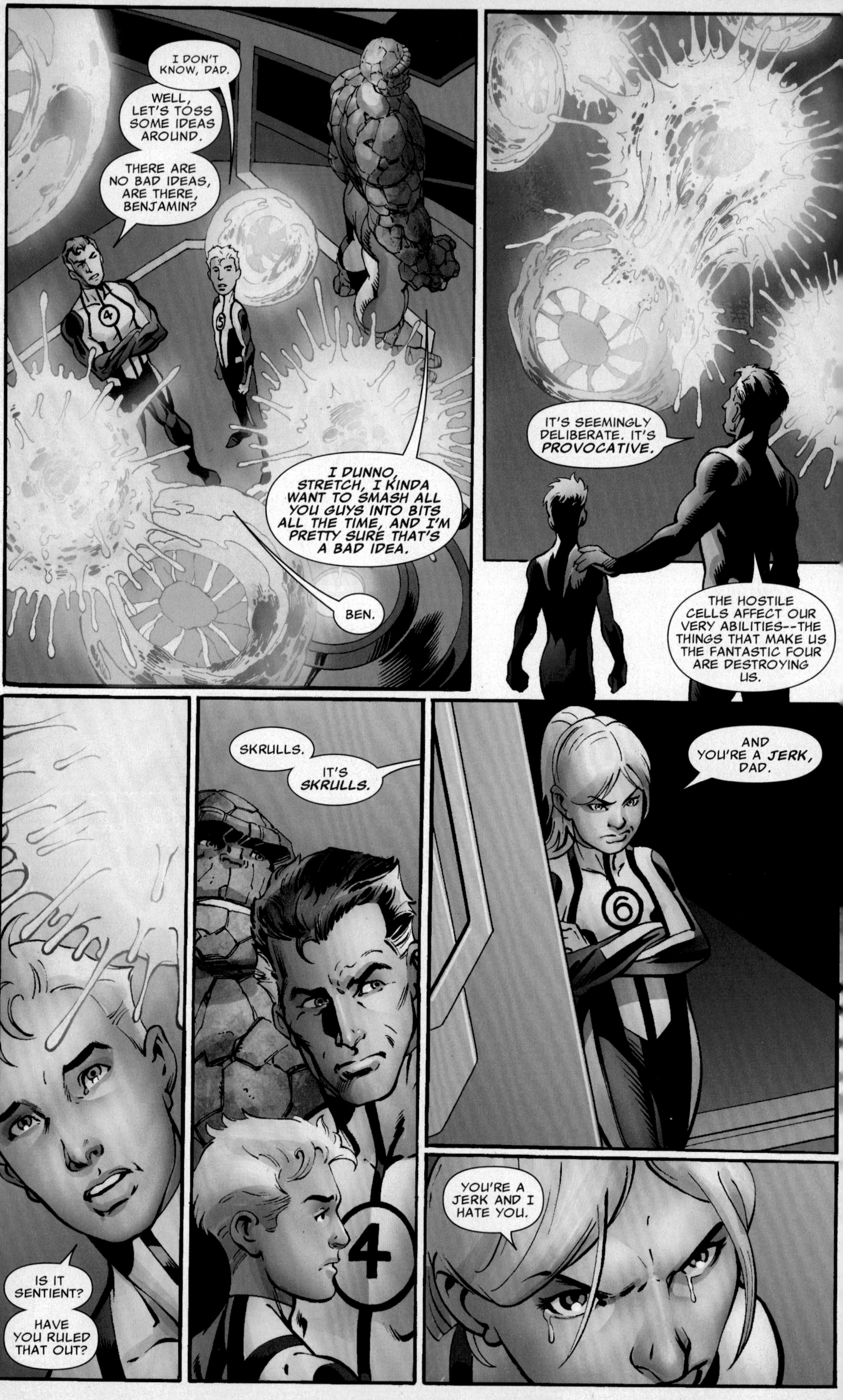
I DON'T KNOW, DAD.
WELL, LET'S TOSS SOME IDEAS AROUND.
THERE ARE NO BAD IDEAS, ARE THERE, BENJAMIN?
I DUNNO, STRETCH, I KINDA WANT TO SMASH ALL YOU GUYS INTO BITS ALL THE TIME, AND I'M PRETTY SURE THAT'S A BAD IDEA.
BEN.
IT'S SEEMINGLY DELIBERATE. IT'S PROVOCATIVE.
THE HOSTILE CELLS AFFECT OUR VERY ABILITIES--THE THINGS THAT MAKE US THE FANTASTIC FOUR ARE DESTROYING US.
IS IT SENTIENT?
HAVE YOU RULED THAT OUT?
SKRULLS.
IT'S SKRULLS.
AND YOU'RE A JERK, DAD.
YOU'RE A JERK AND I HATE YOU.

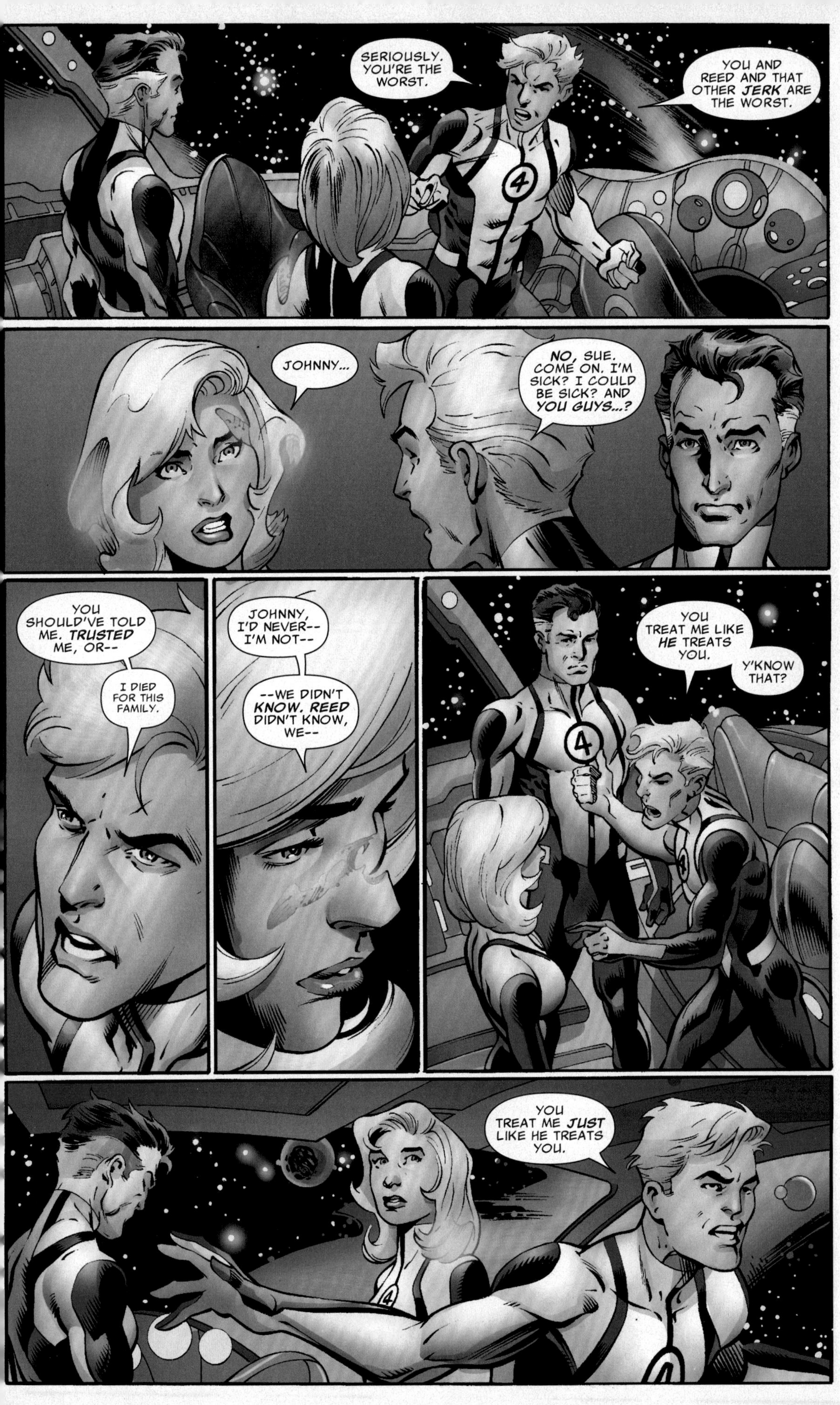
SERIOUSLY. YOU'RE THE WORST.
YOU AND REED AND THAT OTHER JERK ARE THE WORST.
JOHNNY...
NO, SUE. COME ON. I'M SICK? I COULD BE SICK? AND YOU GUYS...?
YOU SHOULD'VE TOLD ME. TRUSTED ME, OR--
I DIED FOR THIS FAMILY.
JOHNNY, I'D NEVER-- I'M NOT--
--WE DIDN'T KNOW. REED DIDN'T KNOW, WE--
YOU TREAT ME LIKE HE TREATS YOU.
Y'KNOW THAT?
YOU TREAT ME JUST LIKE HE TREATS YOU.

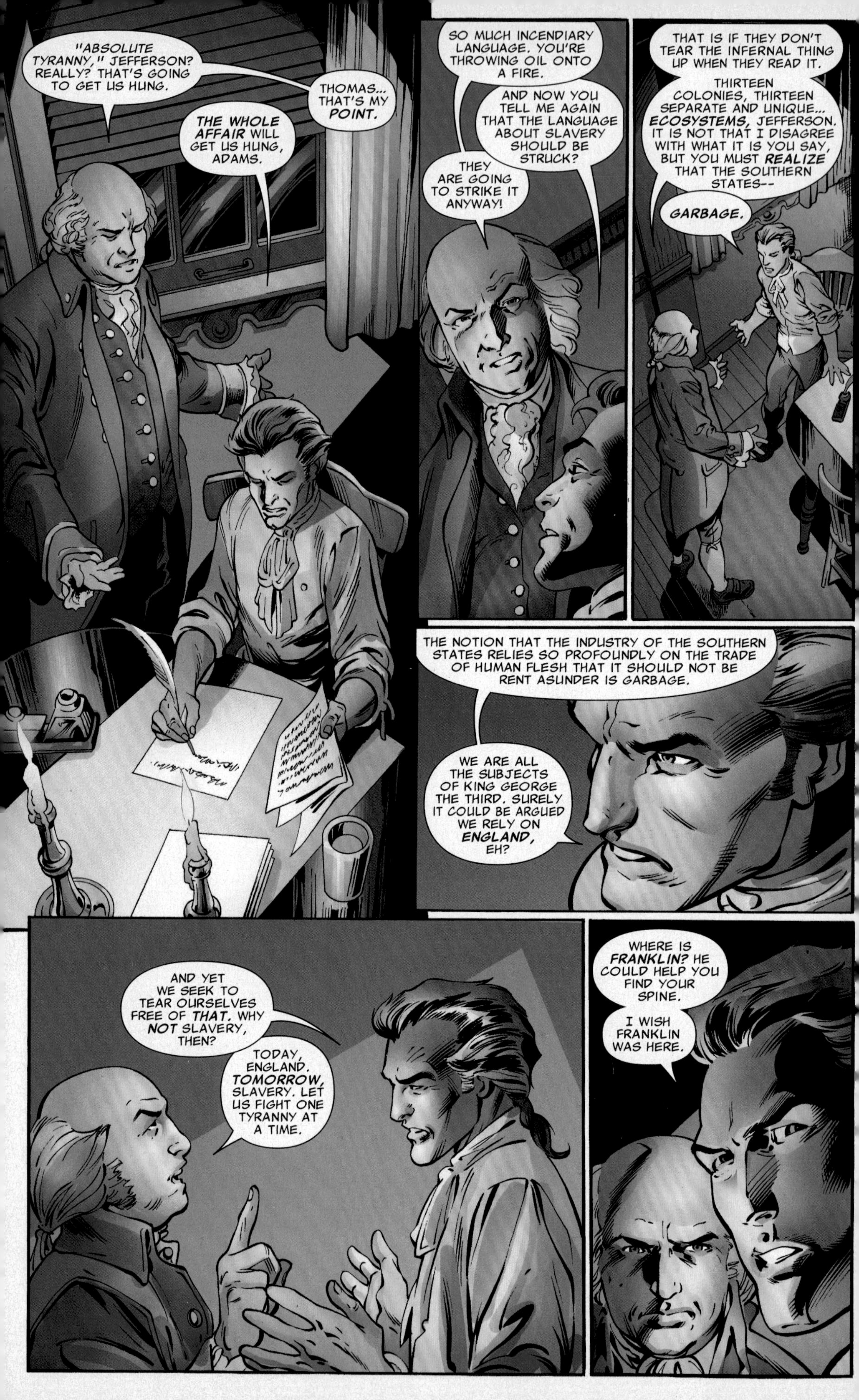
"ABSOLUTE TYRANNY," JEFFERSON? REALLY? THAT'S GOING TO GET US HUNG.
THOMAS... THAT'S MY POINT.
THE WHOLE AFFAIR WILL GET US HUNG, ADAMS.
SO MUCH INCENDIARY LANGUAGE. YOU'RE THROWING OIL ONTO A FIRE.
AND NOW YOU TELL ME AGAIN THAT THE LANGUAGE ABOUT SLAVERY SHOULD BE STRUCK?
THEY ARE GOING TO STRIKE IT ANYWAY!
THAT IS IF THEY DON'T TEAR THE INFERNAL THING UP WHEN THEY READ IT.
THIRTEEN COLONIES, THIRTEEN SEPARATE AND UNIQUE... ECOSYSTEMS, JEFFERSON. IT IS NOT THAT I DISAGREE WITH WHAT IT IS YOU SAY, BUT YOU MUST REALIZE THAT THE SOUTHERN STATES--
GARBAGE.
THE NOTION THAT THE INDUSTRY OF THE SOUTHERN STATES RELIES SO PROFOUNDLY ON THE TRADE OF HUMAN FLESH THAT IT SHOULD NOT BE RENT ASUNDER IS GARBAGE.
WE ARE ALL THE SUBJECTS OF KING GEORGE THE THIRD. SURELY IT COULD BE ARGUED WE RELY ON ENGLAND, EH?
AND YET WE SEEK TO TEAR OURSELVES FREE OF THAT. WHY NOT SLAVERY, THEN?
TODAY, ENGLAND. TOMORROW, SLAVERY. LET US FIGHT ONE TYRANNY AT A TIME.
WHERE IS FRANKLIN? HE COULD HELP YOU FIND YOUR SPINE.
I WISH FRANKLIN WAS HERE.

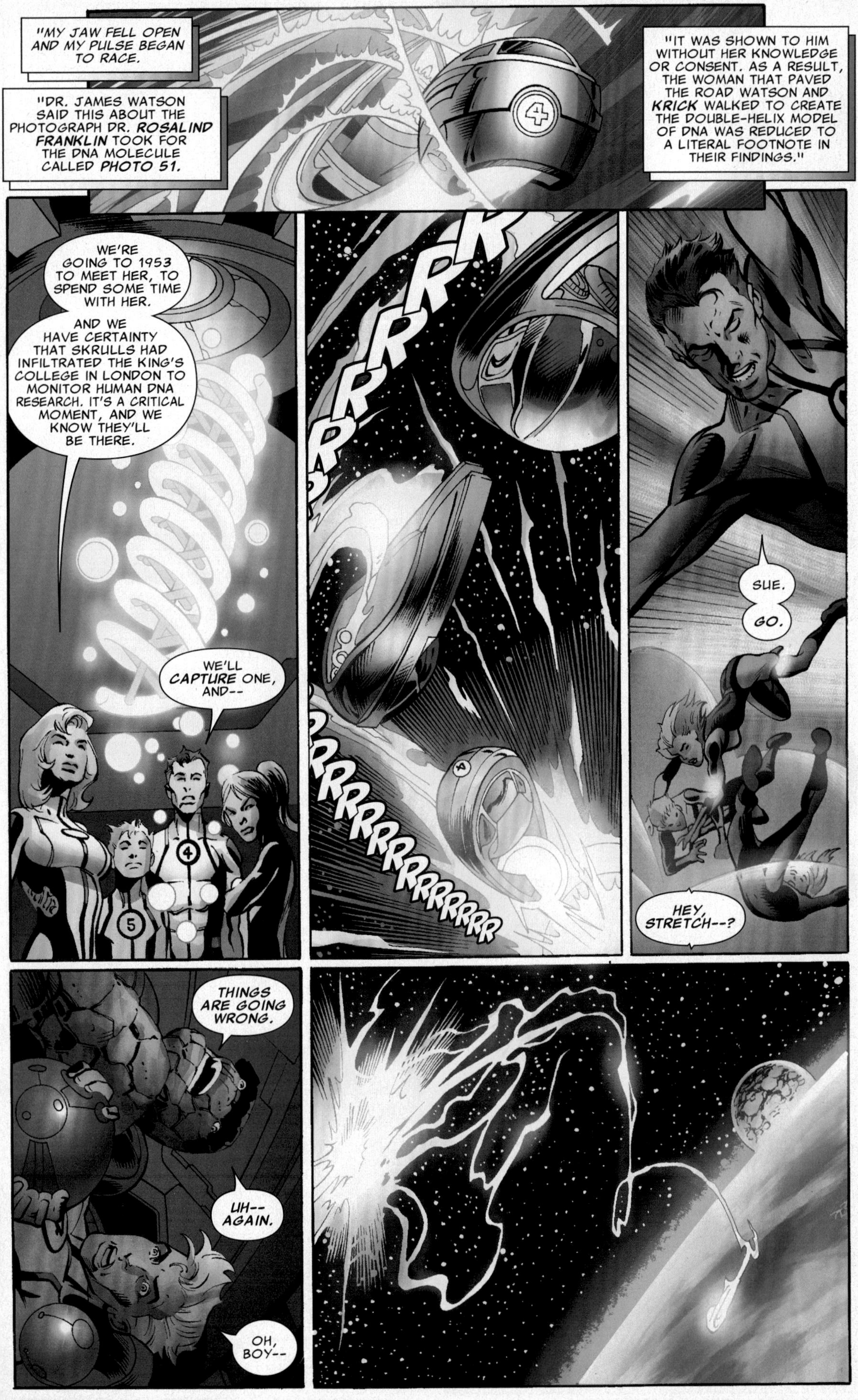
"MY JAW FELL OPEN AND MY PULSE BEGAN TO RACE.
"DR. JAMES WATSON SAID THIS ABOUT THE PHOTOGRAPH DR. ROSALIND FRANKLIN TOOK FOR THE DNA MOLECULE CALLED PHOTO 51.
"IT WAS SHOWN TO HIM WITHOUT HER KNOWLEDGE OR CONSENT. AS A RESULT, THE WOMAN THAT PAVED THE ROAD WATSON AND KRICK WALKED TO CREATE THE DOUBLE-HELIX MODEL OF DNA WAS REDUCED TO A LITERAL FOOTNOTE IN THEIR FINDINGS."
WE'RE GOING TO 1953 TO MEET HER, TO SPEND SOME TIME WITH HER.
AND WE HAVE CERTAINTY THAT SKRULLS HAD INFILTRATED THE KING'S COLLEGE IN LONDON TO MONITOR HUMAN DNA RESEARCH. IT'S A CRITICAL MOMENT, AND WE KNOW THEY'LL BE THERE.
WE'LL CAPTURE ONE, AND--
RRRRRRK
RRRRRRRRRRRRRRRR
SUE.
GO.
HEY, STRETCH--?
THINGS ARE GOING WRONG.
UH-- AGAIN.
OH, BOY--

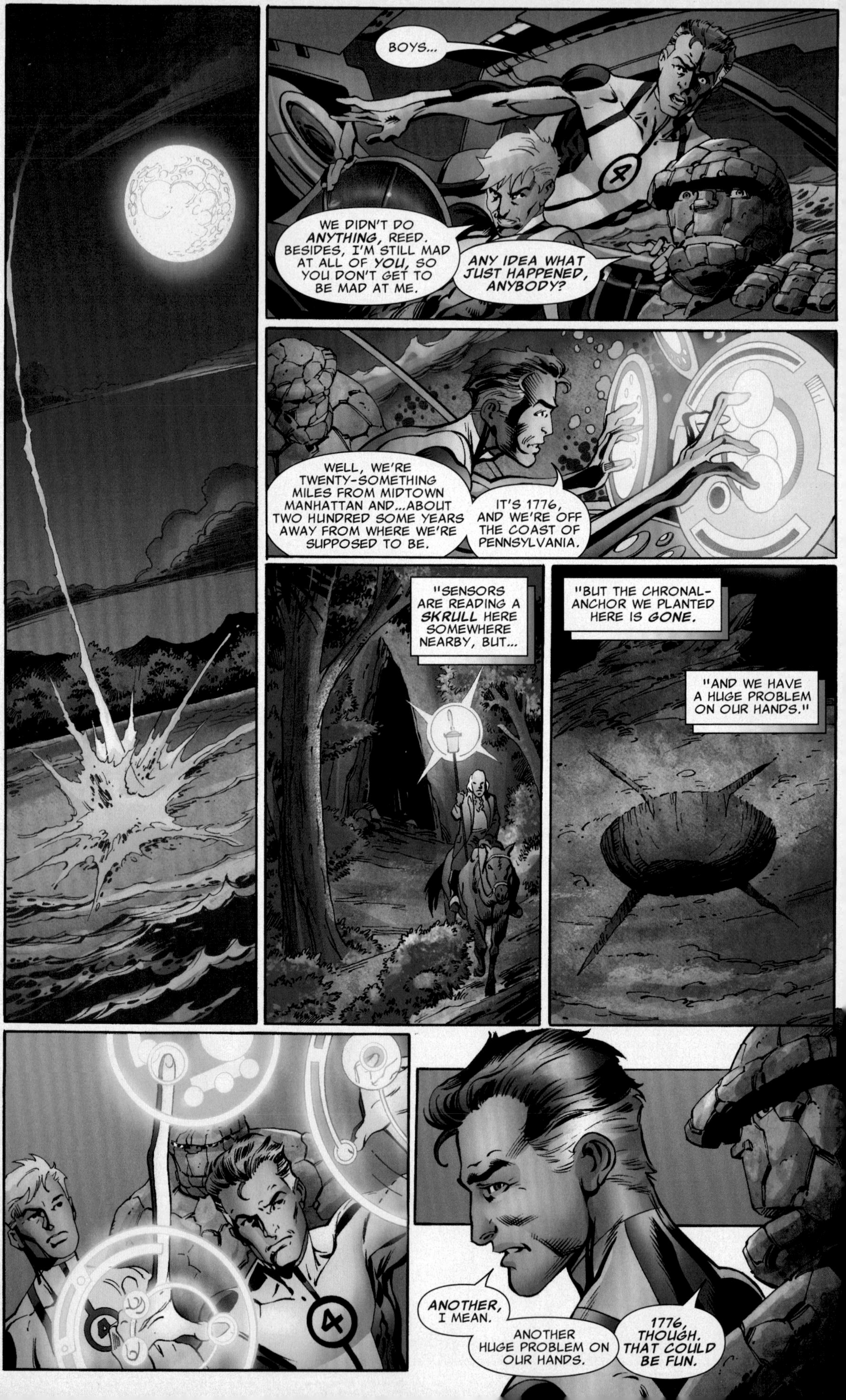
BOYS...
WE DIDN'T DO ANYTHING, REED. BESIDES, I'M STILL MAD AT ALL OF YOU, SO YOU DON'T GET TO BE MAD AT ME.
ANY IDEA WHAT JUST HAPPENED, ANYBODY?
WELL, WE'RE TWENTY-SOMETHING MILES FROM MIDTOWN MANHATTAN AND...ABOUT TWO HUNDRED SOME YEARS AWAY FROM WHERE WE'RE SUPPOSED TO BE.
IT'S 1776, AND WE'RE OFF THE COAST OF PENNSYLVANIA.
"SENSORS ARE READING A SKRULL HERE SOMEWHERE NEARBY, BUT...
"BUT THE CHRONAL-ANCHOR WE PLANTED HERE IS GONE.
"AND WE HAVE A HUGE PROBLEM ON OUR HANDS."
ANOTHER, I MEAN.
ANOTHER HUGE PROBLEM ON OUR HANDS.
1776, THOUGH. THAT COULD BE FUN.

GENTLEMEN, MY APOLOGIES.

I HAD THE MOST INCONVENIENCING EVENING...

FINALLY YOU ARRIVE.

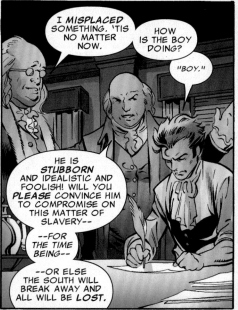

I MISPLACED SOMETHING. 'TIS NO MATTER NOW.

HOW IS THE BOY DOING?

"BOY."

HE IS STUBBORN AND IDEALISTIC AND FOOLISH! WILL YOU PLEASE CONVINCE HIM TO COMPROMISE ON THIS MATTER OF SLAVERY--

--FOR THE TIME BEING--

--OR ELSE THE SOUTH WILL BREAK AWAY AND ALL WILL BE LOST.

OUT WITH IT, THEN.

LET THEM.

THEN OUR GRAND EXPERIMENT SHALL FAIL AND FOR NAUGHT WILL GEORGE HAVE US IN CHAINS!

OR MAYBE EVEN SOMEONE WORSE.

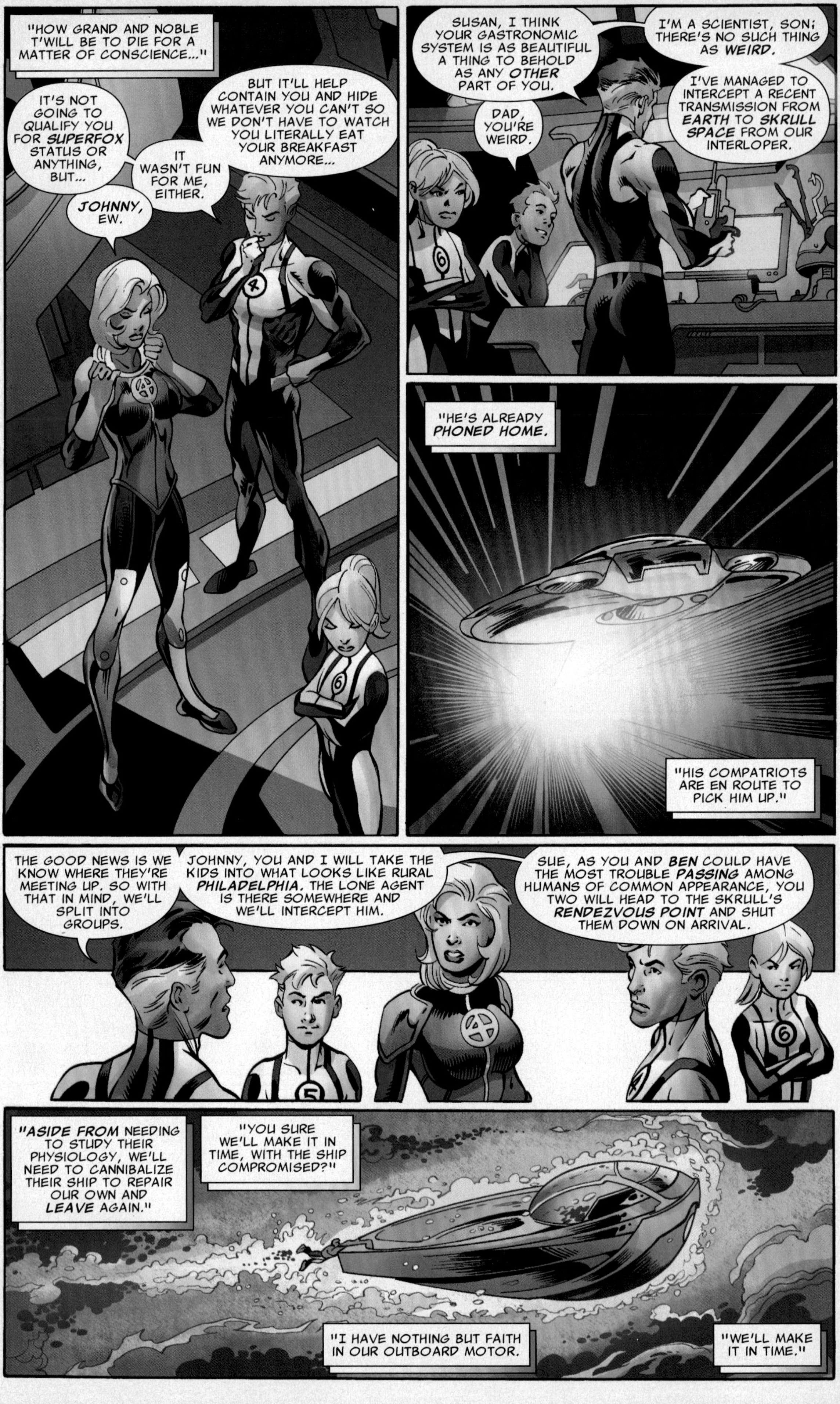
"HOW GRAND AND NOBLE T'WILL BE TO DIE FOR A MATTER OF CONSCIENCE..."
IT'S NOT GOING TO QUALIFY YOU FOR SUPERFOX STATUS OR ANYTHING, BUT...
BUT IT'LL HELP CONTAIN YOU AND HIDE WHATEVER YOU CAN'T SO WE DON'T HAVE TO WATCH YOU LITERALLY EAT YOUR BREAKFAST ANYMORE...
IT WASN'T FUN FOR ME, EITHER.
JOHNNY, EW.
SUSAN, I THINK YOUR GASTRONOMIC SYSTEM IS AS BEAUTIFUL A THING TO BEHOLD AS ANY OTHER PART OF YOU.
DAD, YOU'RE WEIRD.
I'M A SCIENTIST, SON; THERE'S NO SUCH THING AS WEIRD.
I'VE MANAGED TO INTERCEPT A RECENT TRANSMISSION FROM EARTH TO SKRULL SPACE FROM OUR INTERLOPER.
"HE'S ALREADY PHONED HOME.
"HIS COMPATRIOTS ARE EN ROUTE TO PICK HIM UP."
THE GOOD NEWS IS WE KNOW WHERE THEY'RE MEETING UP. SO WITH THAT IN MIND, WE'LL SPLIT INTO GROUPS.
JOHNNY, YOU AND I WILL TAKE THE KIDS INTO WHAT LOOKS LIKE RURAL PHILADELPHIA. THE LONE AGENT IS THERE SOMEWHERE AND WE'LL INTERCEPT HIM.
SUE, AS YOU AND BEN COULD HAVE THE MOST TROUBLE PASSING AMONG HUMANS OF COMMON APPEARANCE, YOU TWO WILL HEAD TO THE SKRULL'S RENDEZVOUS POINT AND SHUT THEM DOWN ON ARRIVAL.
"ASIDE FROM NEEDING TO STUDY THEIR PHYSIOLOGY, WE'LL NEED TO CANNIBALIZE THEIR SHIP TO REPAIR OUR OWN AND LEAVE AGAIN."
"YOU SURE WE'LL MAKE IT IN TIME, WITH THE SHIP COMPROMISED?"
"I HAVE NOTHING BUT FAITH IN OUR OUTBOARD MOTOR.
"WE'LL MAKE IT IN TIME."

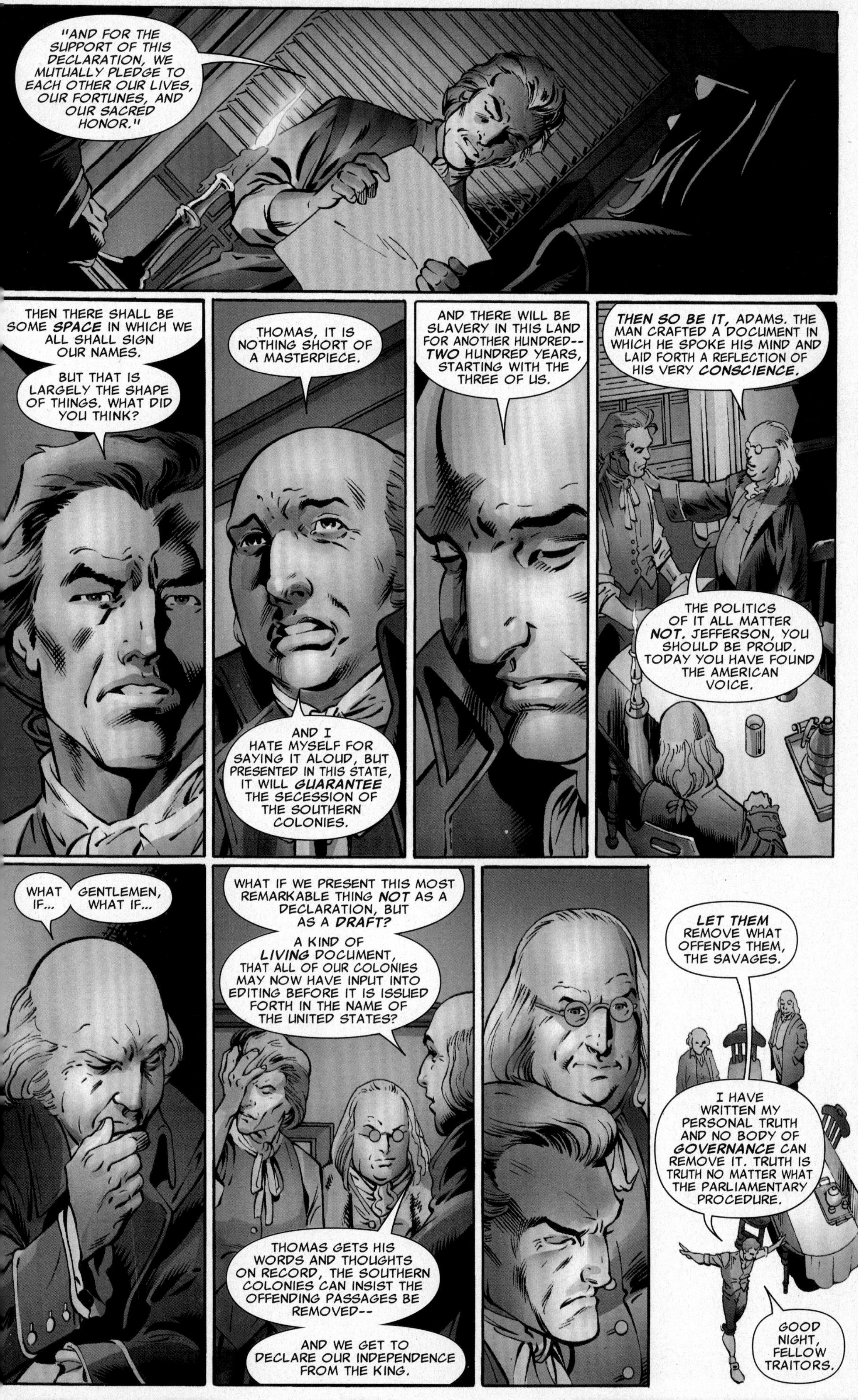
"AND FOR THE SUPPORT OF THIS DECLARATION, WE MUTUALLY PLEDGE TO EACH OTHER OUR LIVES, OUR FORTUNES, AND OUR SACRED HONOR."
THEN THERE SHALL BE SOME SPACE IN WHICH WE ALL SHALL SIGN OUR NAMES.
BUT THAT IS LARGELY THE SHAPE OF THINGS. WHAT DID YOU THINK?
THOMAS, IT IS NOTHING SHORT OF A MASTERPIECE.
AND I HATE MYSELF FOR SAYING IT ALOUD, BUT PRESENTED IN THIS STATE, IT WILL GUARANTEE THE SECESSION OF THE SOUTHERN COLONIES.
AND THERE WILL BE SLAVERY IN THIS LAND FOR ANOTHER HUNDRED--TWO HUNDRED YEARS, STARTING WITH THE THREE OF US.
THEN SO BE IT, ADAMS. THE MAN CRAFTED A DOCUMENT IN WHICH HE SPOKE HIS MIND AND LAID FORTH A REFLECTION OF HIS VERY CONSCIENCE.
THE POLITICS OF IT ALL MATTER NOT. JEFFERSON, YOU SHOULD BE PROUD. TODAY YOU HAVE FOUND THE AMERICAN VOICE.
WHAT IF...
GENTLEMEN, WHAT IF...
WHAT IF WE PRESENT THIS MOST REMARKABLE THING NOT AS A DECLARATION, BUT AS A DRAFT?
A KIND OF LIVING DOCUMENT, THAT ALL OF OUR COLONIES MAY NOW HAVE INPUT INTO EDITING BEFORE IT IS ISSUED FORTH IN THE NAME OF THE UNITED STATES?
THOMAS GETS HIS WORDS AND THOUGHTS ON RECORD, THE SOUTHERN COLONIES CAN INSIST THE OFFENDING PASSAGES BE REMOVED--
AND WE GET TO DECLARE OUR INDEPENDENCE FROM THE KING.
LET THEM REMOVE WHAT OFFENDS THEM, THE SAVAGES.
I HAVE WRITTEN MY PERSONAL TRUTH AND NO BODY OF GOVERNANCE CAN REMOVE IT. TRUTH IS TRUTH NO MATTER WHAT THE PARLIAMENTARY PROCEDURE.
GOOD NIGHT, FELLOW TRAITORS.

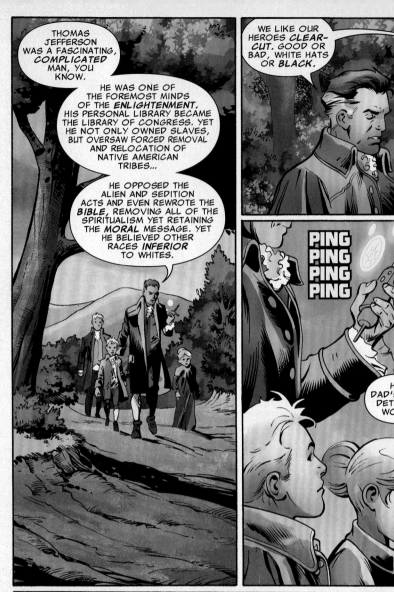

THOMAS JEFFERSON WAS A FASCINATING, *COMPLICATED* MAN, YOU KNOW.

HE WAS ONE OF THE FOREMOST MINDS OF THE *ENLIGHTENMENT*. HIS PERSONAL LIBRARY BECAME THE LIBRARY OF CONGRESS. YET HE NOT ONLY OWNED SLAVES, BUT OVERSAW FORCED REMOVAL AND RELOCATION OF NATIVE AMERICAN TRIBES...

HE OPPOSED THE ALIEN AND SEDITION ACTS AND EVEN REWROTE THE *BIBLE*, REMOVING ALL OF THE SPIRITUALISM YET RETAINING THE *MORAL* MESSAGE. YET HE BELIEVED OTHER RACES *INFERIOR* TO WHITES.

WE LIKE OUR HEROES *CLEAR-CUT*. GOOD OR BAD, WHITE HATS OR *BLACK*.

WE NEED OUR GOOD GUYS *ALL GOOD*. ANY SHADES OF COMPLEXITY OR CONTRADICTION DISRUPT OUR PREFERENCE FOR A *SIMPLE* HISTORICAL NARRATIVE.

YET IN MY EXPERIENCE, HISTORY, AND HEROES, ARE ANYTHING BUT.

PING PING PING PING

HEY, DAD'S IRONY DETECTOR WORKS.

CUTE, VAL.

HERE. HE'S IN HERE.

OH, KIDS, THIS JUST GOT VERY EXCITING FOR YOU, INDEED.

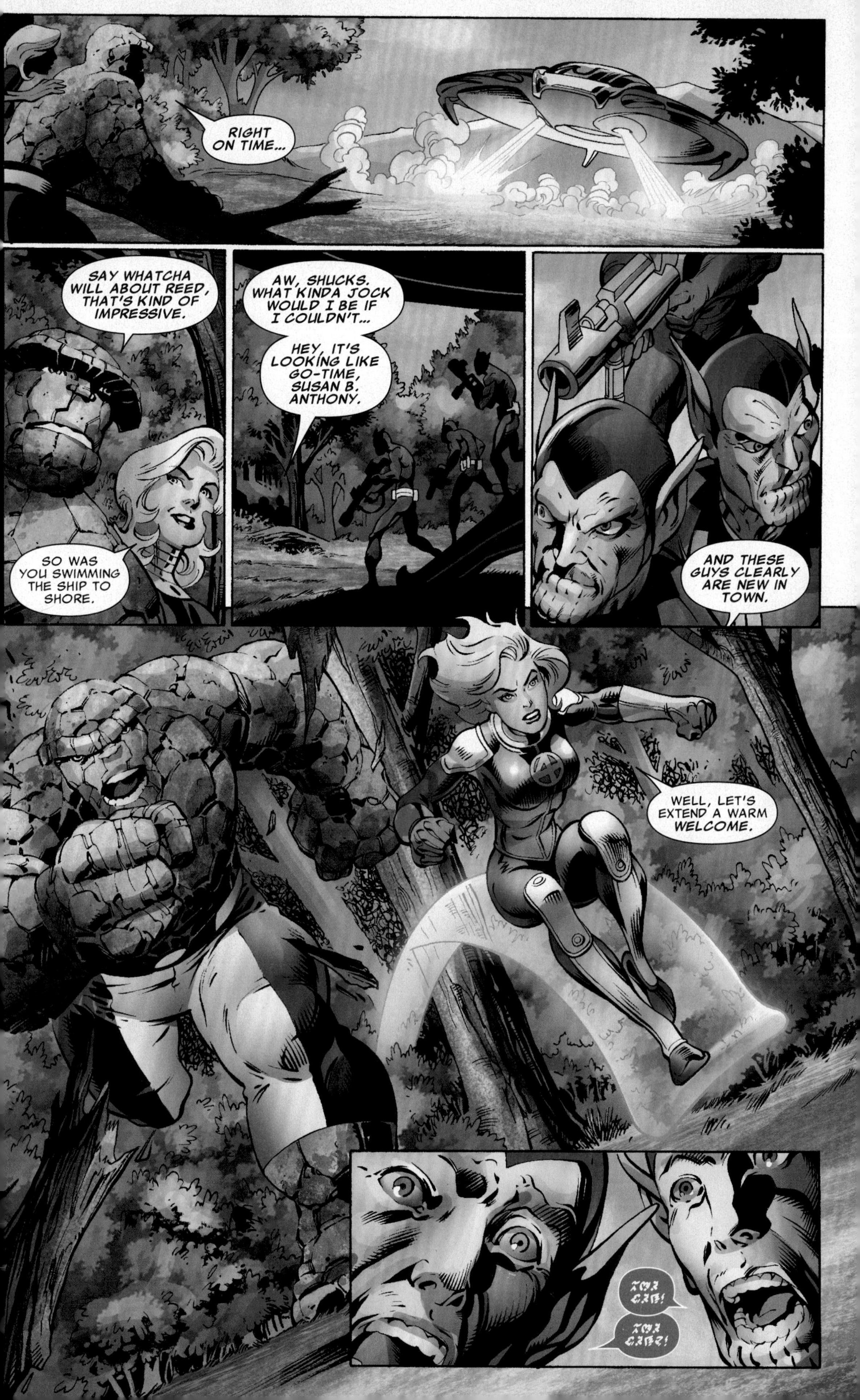
RIGHT ON TIME...
SAY WHATCHA WILL ABOUT REED, THAT'S KIND OF IMPRESSIVE.
SO WAS YOU SWIMMING THE SHIP TO SHORE.
AW, SHUCKS. WHAT KINDA JOCK WOULD I BE IF I COULDN'T...
HEY, IT'S LOOKING LIKE GO-TIME, SUSAN B. ANTHONY.
AND THESE GUYS CLEARLY ARE NEW IN TOWN.
WELL, LET'S EXTEND A WARM WELCOME.

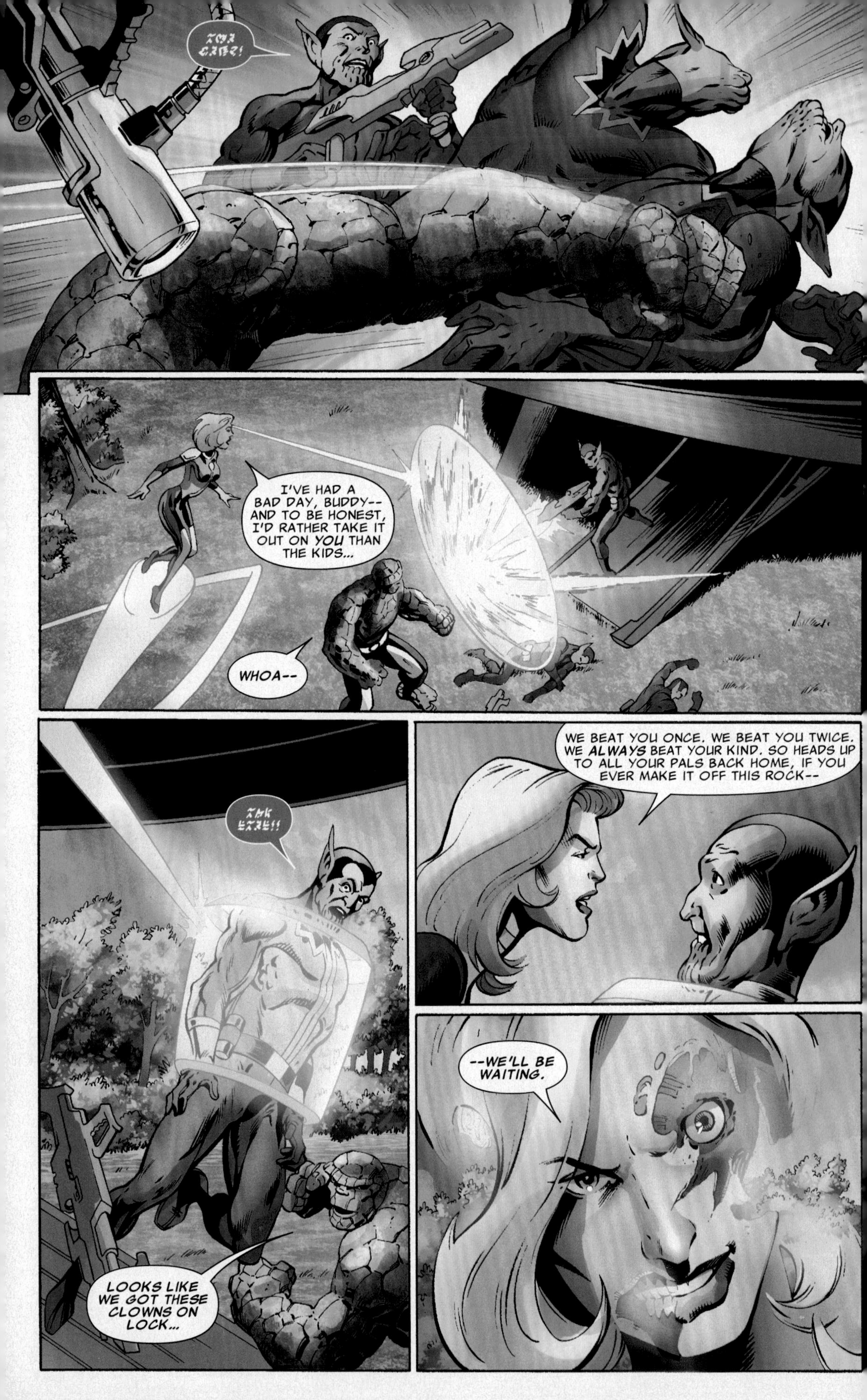
I'VE HAD A BAD DAY, BUDDY-- AND TO BE HONEST, I'D RATHER TAKE IT OUT ON *YOU* THAN THE KIDS...
WHOA--
LOOKS LIKE WE GOT THESE CLOWNS ON LOCK...
WE BEAT YOU ONCE. WE BEAT YOU TWICE. WE **ALWAYS** BEAT YOUR KIND. SO HEADS UP TO ALL YOUR PALS BACK HOME, IF YOU EVER MAKE IT OFF THIS ROCK--
--WE'LL BE WAITING.

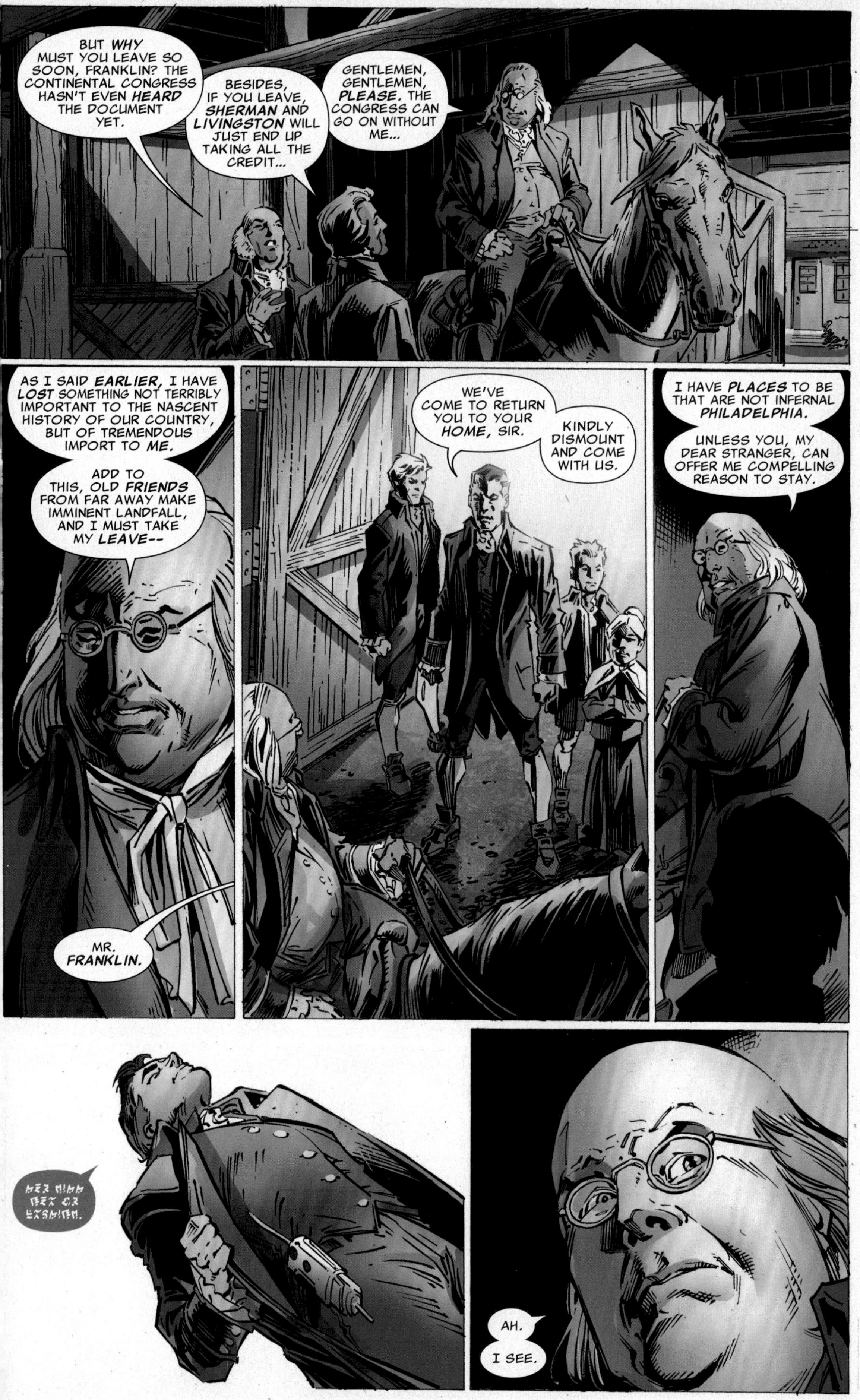
BUT WHY MUST YOU LEAVE SO SOON, FRANKLIN? THE CONTINENTAL CONGRESS HASN'T EVEN HEARD THE DOCUMENT YET.
BESIDES, IF YOU LEAVE, SHERMAN AND LIVINGSTON WILL JUST END UP TAKING ALL THE CREDIT...
GENTLEMEN, GENTLEMEN, PLEASE. THE CONGRESS CAN GO ON WITHOUT ME...
AS I SAID EARLIER, I HAVE LOST SOMETHING NOT TERRIBLY IMPORTANT TO THE NASCENT HISTORY OF OUR COUNTRY, BUT OF TREMENDOUS IMPORT TO ME.
ADD TO THIS, OLD FRIENDS FROM FAR AWAY MAKE IMMINENT LANDFALL, AND I MUST TAKE MY LEAVE--
MR. FRANKLIN.
WE'VE COME TO RETURN YOU TO YOUR HOME, SIR.
KINDLY DISMOUNT AND COME WITH US.
I HAVE PLACES TO BE THAT ARE NOT INFERNAL PHILADELPHIA.
UNLESS YOU, MY DEAR STRANGER, CAN OFFER ME COMPELLING REASON TO STAY.
AH.
I SEE.

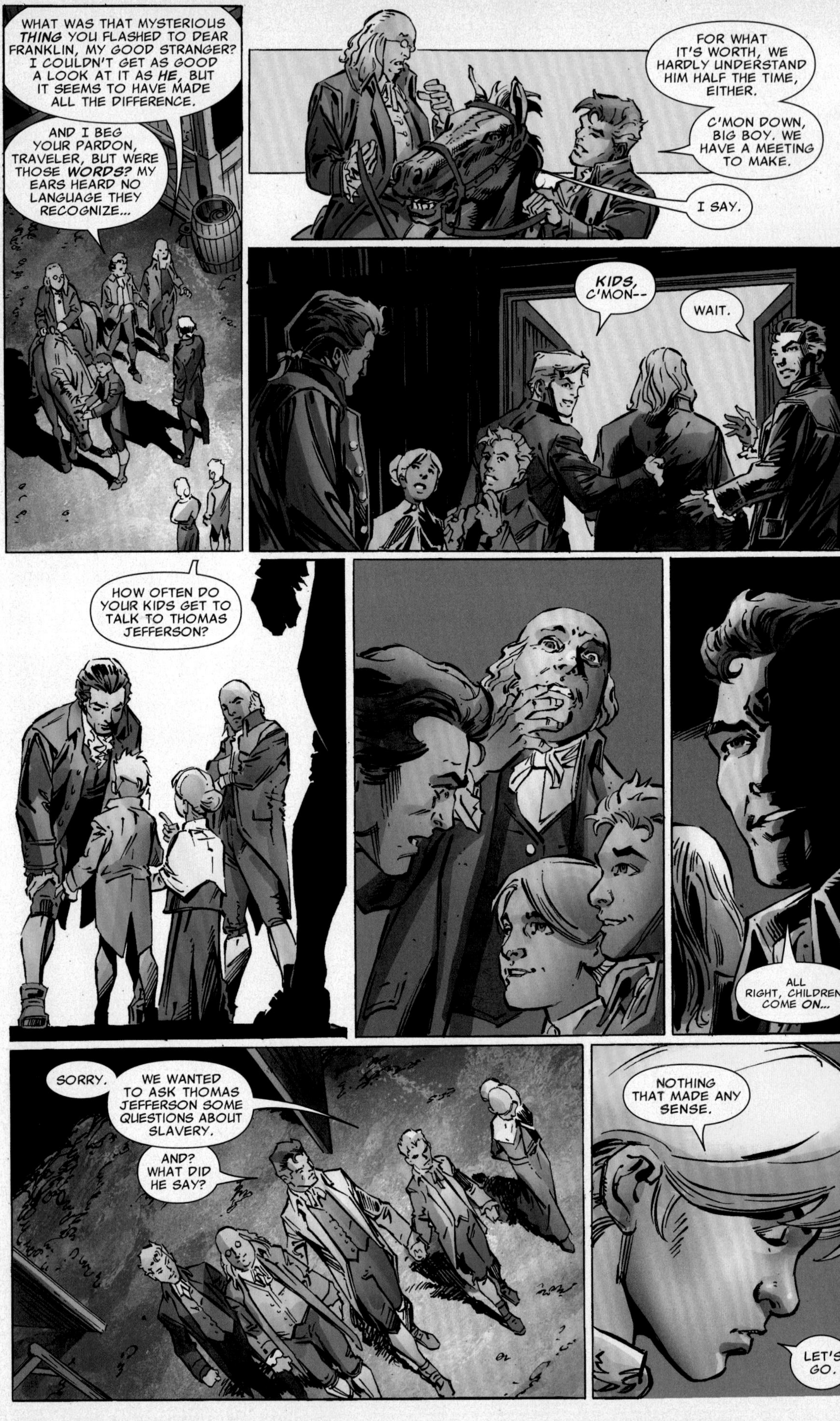
WHAT WAS THAT MYSTERIOUS THING YOU FLASHED TO DEAR FRANKLIN, MY GOOD STRANGER? I COULDN'T GET AS GOOD A LOOK AT IT AS HE, BUT IT SEEMS TO HAVE MADE ALL THE DIFFERENCE.
AND I BEG YOUR PARDON, TRAVELER, BUT WERE THOSE WORDS? MY EARS HEARD NO LANGUAGE THEY RECOGNIZE...
FOR WHAT IT'S WORTH, WE HARDLY UNDERSTAND HIM HALF THE TIME, EITHER.
C'MON DOWN, BIG BOY. WE HAVE A MEETING TO MAKE.
I SAY.
KIDS, C'MON--
WAIT.
HOW OFTEN DO YOUR KIDS GET TO TALK TO THOMAS JEFFERSON?
ALL RIGHT, CHILDREN, COME ON...
SORRY.
WE WANTED TO ASK THOMAS JEFFERSON SOME QUESTIONS ABOUT SLAVERY.
AND? WHAT DID HE SAY?
NOTHING THAT MADE ANY SENSE.
LET'S GO.

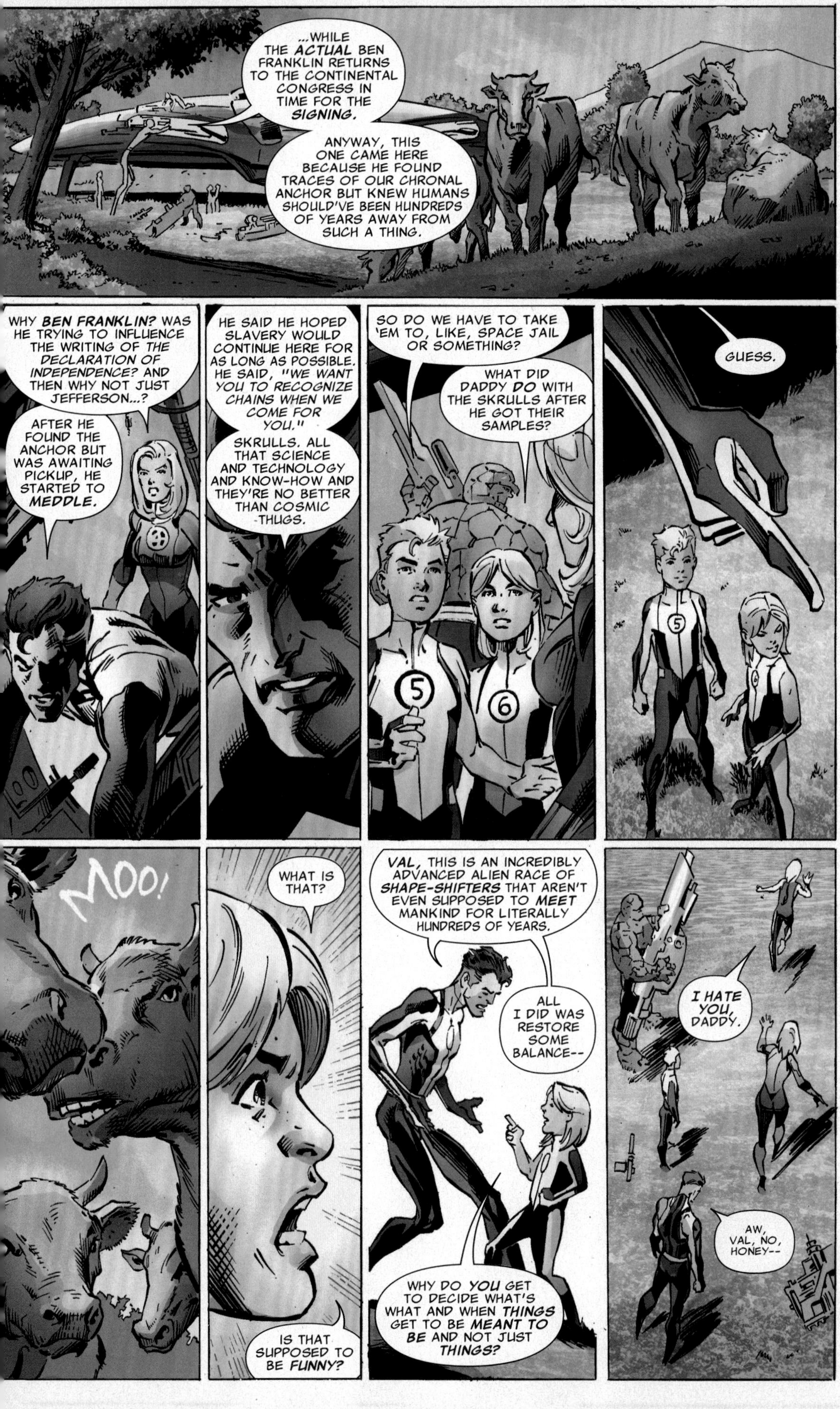
...WHILE THE ACTUAL BEN FRANKLIN RETURNS TO THE CONTINENTAL CONGRESS IN TIME FOR THE SIGNING.
ANYWAY, THIS ONE CAME HERE BECAUSE HE FOUND TRACES OF OUR CHRONAL ANCHOR BUT KNEW HUMANS SHOULD'VE BEEN HUNDREDS OF YEARS AWAY FROM SUCH A THING.
WHY BEN FRANKLIN? WAS HE TRYING TO INFLUENCE THE WRITING OF THE DECLARATION OF INDEPENDENCE? AND THEN WHY NOT JUST JEFFERSON...?
AFTER HE FOUND THE ANCHOR BUT WAS AWAITING PICKUP, HE STARTED TO MEDDLE.
HE SAID HE HOPED SLAVERY WOULD CONTINUE HERE FOR AS LONG AS POSSIBLE. HE SAID, "WE WANT YOU TO RECOGNIZE CHAINS WHEN WE COME FOR YOU."
SKRULLS. ALL THAT SCIENCE AND TECHNOLOGY AND KNOW-HOW AND THEY'RE NO BETTER THAN COSMIC -THUGS.
SO DO WE HAVE TO TAKE 'EM TO, LIKE, SPACE JAIL OR SOMETHING?
WHAT DID DADDY DO WITH THE SKRULLS AFTER HE GOT THEIR SAMPLES?
GUESS.
MOO!
WHAT IS THAT?
IS THAT SUPPOSED TO BE FUNNY?
VAL, THIS IS AN INCREDIBLY ADVANCED ALIEN RACE OF SHAPE-SHIFTERS THAT AREN'T EVEN SUPPOSED TO MEET MANKIND FOR LITERALLY HUNDREDS OF YEARS.
ALL I DID WAS RESTORE SOME BALANCE--
WHY DO YOU GET TO DECIDE WHAT'S WHAT AND WHEN THINGS GET TO BE MEANT TO BE AND NOT JUST THINGS?
I HATE YOU, DADDY.
AW, VAL, NO, HONEY--

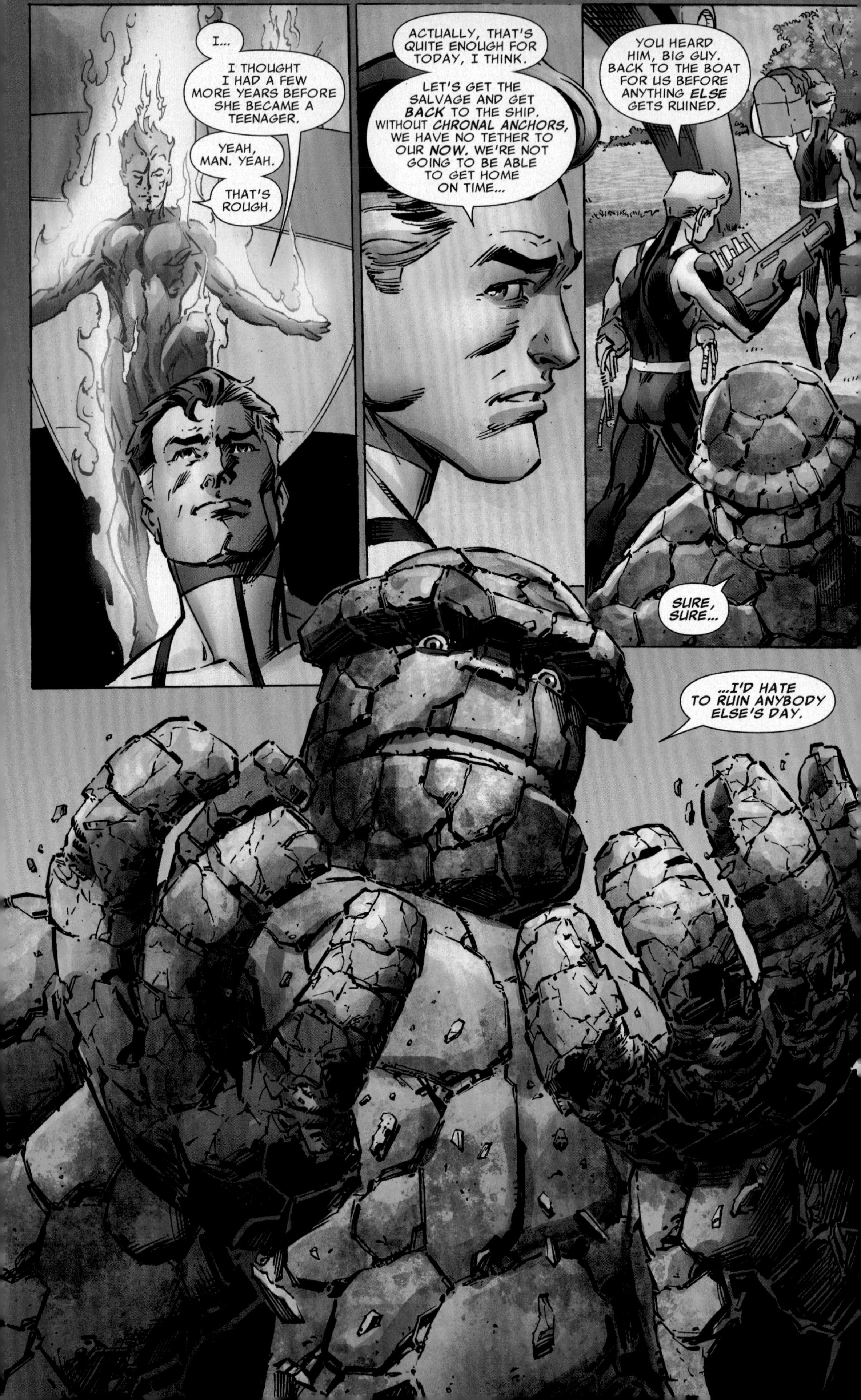
I...
I THOUGHT I HAD A FEW MORE YEARS BEFORE SHE BECAME A TEENAGER.
YEAH, MAN. YEAH.
THAT'S ROUGH.
ACTUALLY, THAT'S QUITE ENOUGH FOR TODAY, I THINK.
LET'S GET THE SALVAGE AND GET BACK TO THE SHIP. WITHOUT CHRONAL ANCHORS, WE HAVE NO TETHER TO OUR NOW. WE'RE NOT GOING TO BE ABLE TO GET HOME ON TIME...
YOU HEARD HIM, BIG GUY. BACK TO THE BOAT FOR US BEFORE ANYTHING ELSE GETS RUINED.
SURE, SURE...
...I'D HATE TO RUIN ANYBODY ELSE'S DAY.

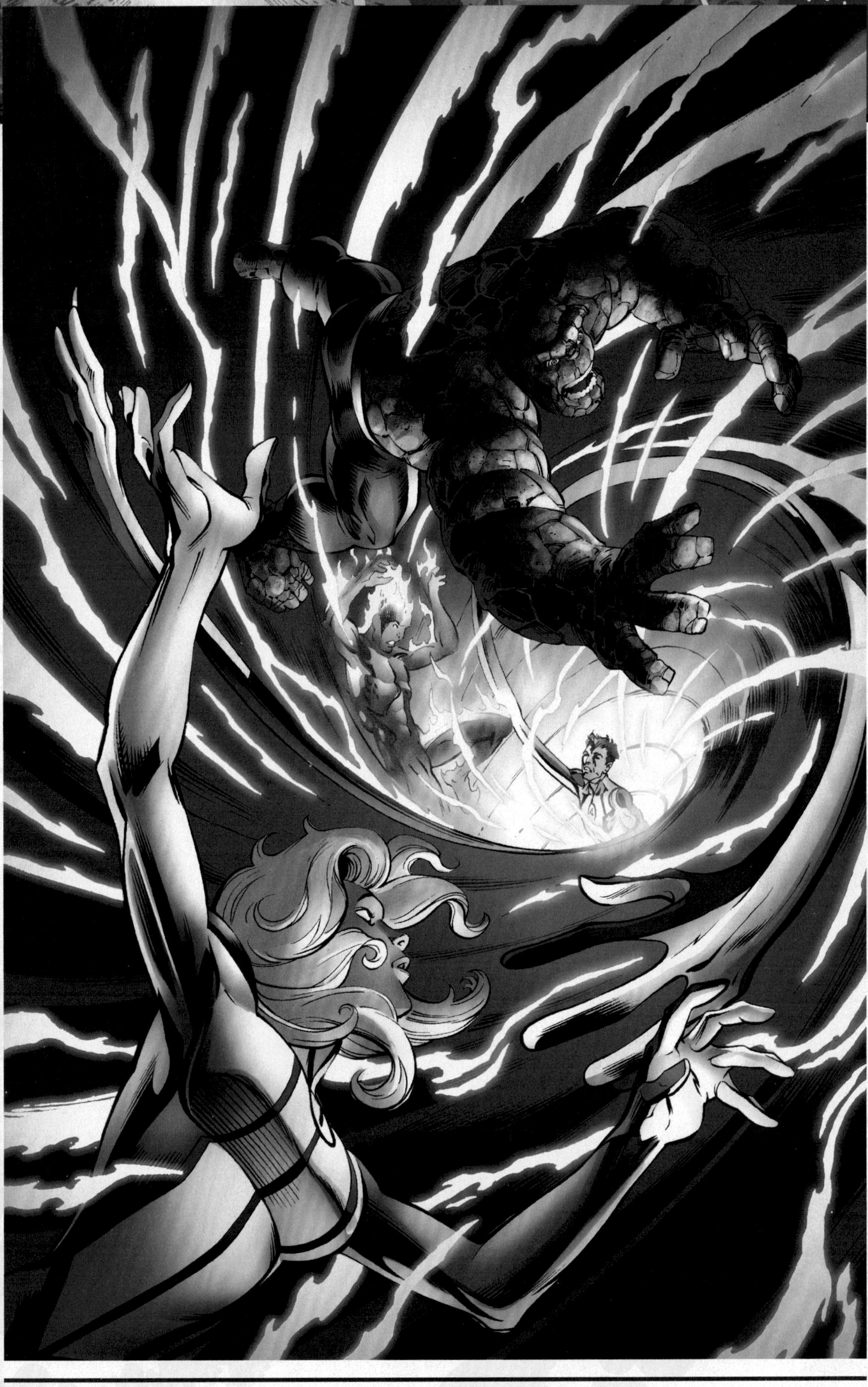

FANTASTIC FOUR #11 — “PLANET FUTURE PART 1”

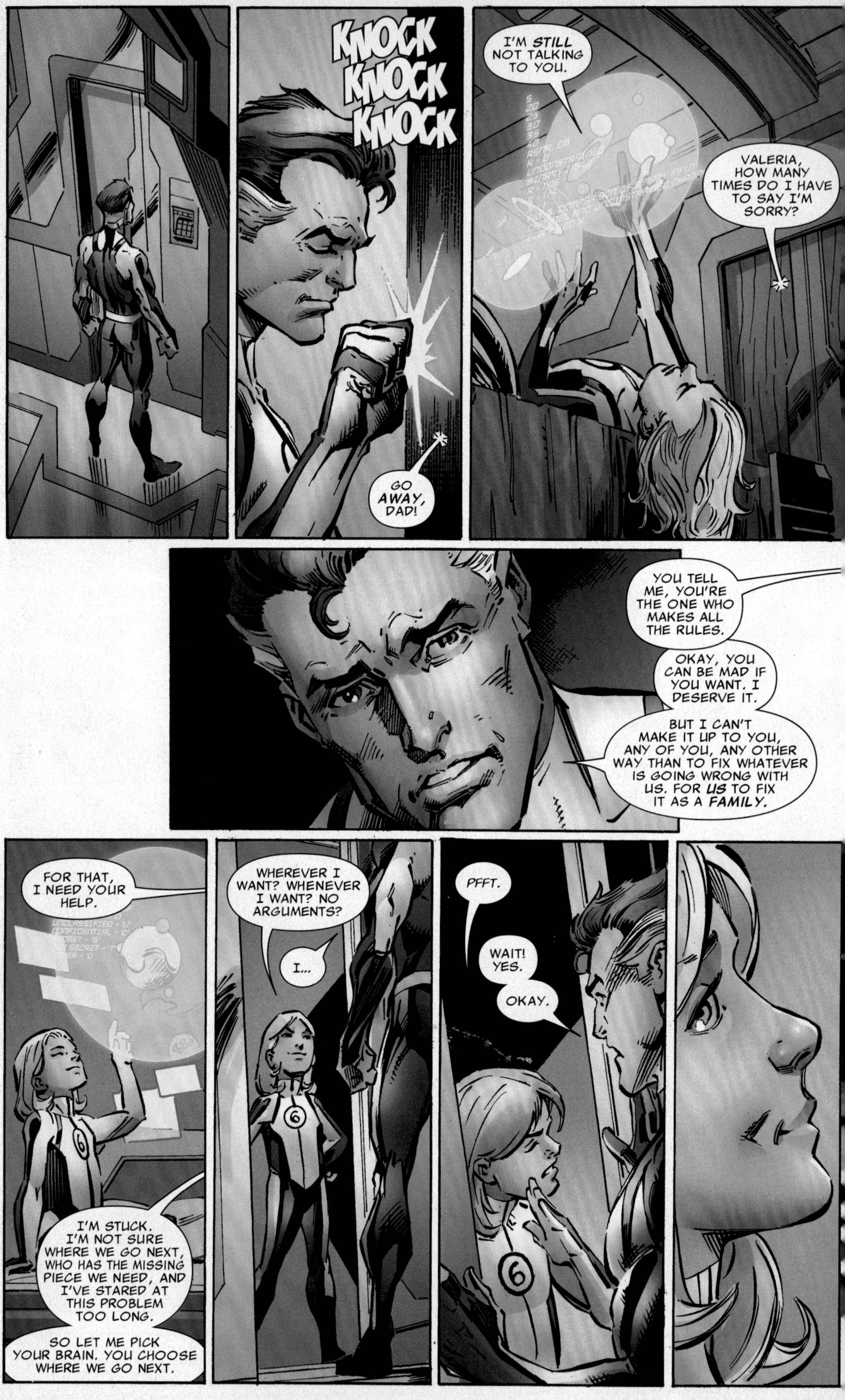
KNOCK KNOCK KNOCK
GO AWAY, DAD!
I'M STILL NOT TALKING TO YOU.
VALERIA, HOW MANY TIMES DO I HAVE TO SAY I'M SORRY?
YOU TELL ME, YOU'RE THE ONE WHO MAKES ALL THE RULES.
OKAY, YOU CAN BE MAD IF YOU WANT. I DESERVE IT.
BUT I CAN'T MAKE IT UP TO YOU, ANY OF YOU, ANY OTHER WAY THAN TO FIX WHATEVER IS GOING WRONG WITH US. FOR US TO FIX IT AS A FAMILY.
FOR THAT, I NEED YOUR HELP.
I'M STUCK. I'M NOT SURE WHERE WE GO NEXT, WHO HAS THE MISSING PIECE WE NEED, AND I'VE STARED AT THIS PROBLEM TOO LONG.
SO LET ME PICK YOUR BRAIN. YOU CHOOSE WHERE WE GO NEXT.
WHEREVER I WANT? WHENEVER I WANT? NO ARGUMENTS?
I...
PFFT.
WAIT! YES.
OKAY.

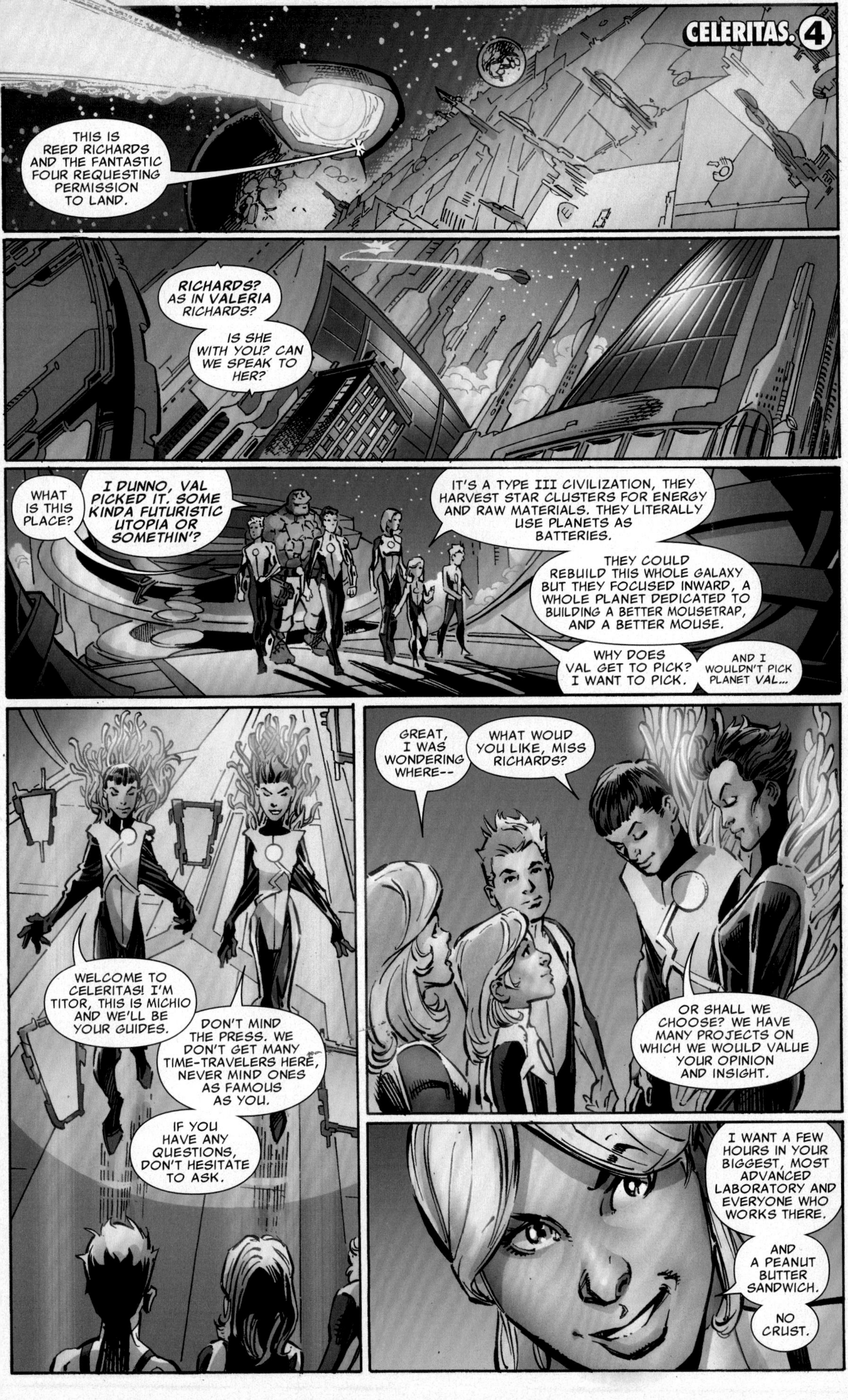
CELERITAS. 4
THIS IS REED RICHARDS AND THE FANTASTIC FOUR REQUESTING PERMISSION TO LAND.
RICHARDS? AS IN VALERIA RICHARDS?
IS SHE WITH YOU? CAN WE SPEAK TO HER?
WHAT IS THIS PLACE?
I DUNNO, VAL PICKED IT. SOME KINDA FUTURISTIC UTOPIA OR SOMETHIN'?
IT'S A TYPE III CIVILIZATION, THEY HARVEST STAR CLUSTERS FOR ENERGY AND RAW MATERIALS. THEY LITERALLY USE PLANETS AS BATTERIES.
THEY COULD REBUILD THIS WHOLE GALAXY BUT THEY FOCUSED INWARD, A WHOLE PLANET DEDICATED TO BUILDING A BETTER MOUSETRAP, AND A BETTER MOUSE.
WHY DOES VAL GET TO PICK? I WANT TO PICK.
AND I WOULDN'T PICK PLANET VAL...
WELCOME TO CELERITAS! I'M TITOR, THIS IS MICHIO AND WE'LL BE YOUR GUIDES.
DON'T MIND THE PRESS. WE DON'T GET MANY TIME-TRAVELERS HERE, NEVER MIND ONES AS FAMOUS AS YOU.
IF YOU HAVE ANY QUESTIONS, DON'T HESITATE TO ASK.
GREAT, I WAS WONDERING WHERE--
WHAT WOUD YOU LIKE, MISS RICHARDS?
OR SHALL WE CHOOSE? WE HAVE MANY PROJECTS ON WHICH WE WOULD VALUE YOUR OPINION AND INSIGHT.
I WANT A FEW HOURS IN YOUR BIGGEST, MOST ADVANCED LABORATORY AND EVERYONE WHO WORKS THERE.
AND A PEANUT BUTTER SANDWICH.
NO CRUST.

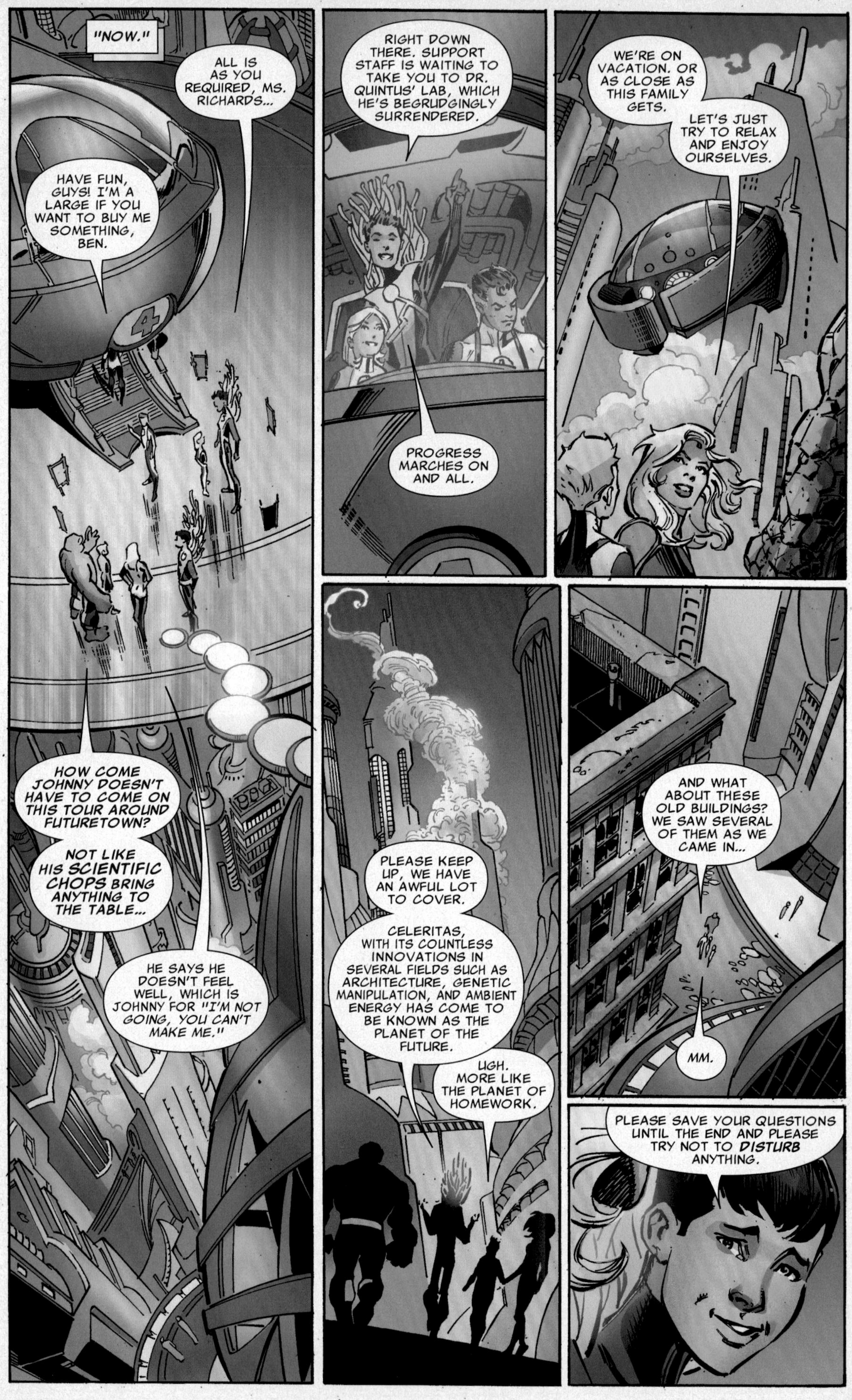

"NOW."
ALL IS AS YOU REQUIRED, MS. RICHARDS...
HAVE FUN, GUYS! I'M A LARGE IF YOU WANT TO BUY ME SOMETHING, BEN.
RIGHT DOWN THERE. SUPPORT STAFF IS WAITING TO TAKE YOU TO DR. QUINTUS' LAB, WHICH HE'S BEGRUDGINGLY SURRENDERED.
PROGRESS MARCHES ON AND ALL.
WE'RE ON VACATION. OR AS CLOSE AS THIS FAMILY GETS.
LET'S JUST TRY TO RELAX AND ENJOY OURSELVES.
HOW COME JOHNNY DOESN'T HAVE TO COME ON THIS TOUR AROUND FUTURETOWN?
NOT LIKE HIS SCIENTIFIC CHOPS BRING ANYTHING TO THE TABLE...
HE SAYS HE DOESN'T FEEL WELL, WHICH IS JOHNNY FOR "I'M NOT GOING, YOU CAN'T MAKE ME."
PLEASE KEEP UP, WE HAVE AN AWFUL LOT TO COVER.
CELERITAS, WITH ITS COUNTLESS INNOVATIONS IN SEVERAL FIELDS SUCH AS ARCHITECTURE, GENETIC MANIPULATION, AND AMBIENT ENERGY HAS COME TO BE KNOWN AS THE PLANET OF THE FUTURE.
UGH. MORE LIKE THE PLANET OF HOMEWORK.
AND WHAT ABOUT THESE OLD BUILDINGS? WE SAW SEVERAL OF THEM AS WE CAME IN...
MM.
PLEASE SAVE YOUR QUESTIONS UNTIL THE END AND PLEASE TRY NOT TO DISTURB ANYTHING.

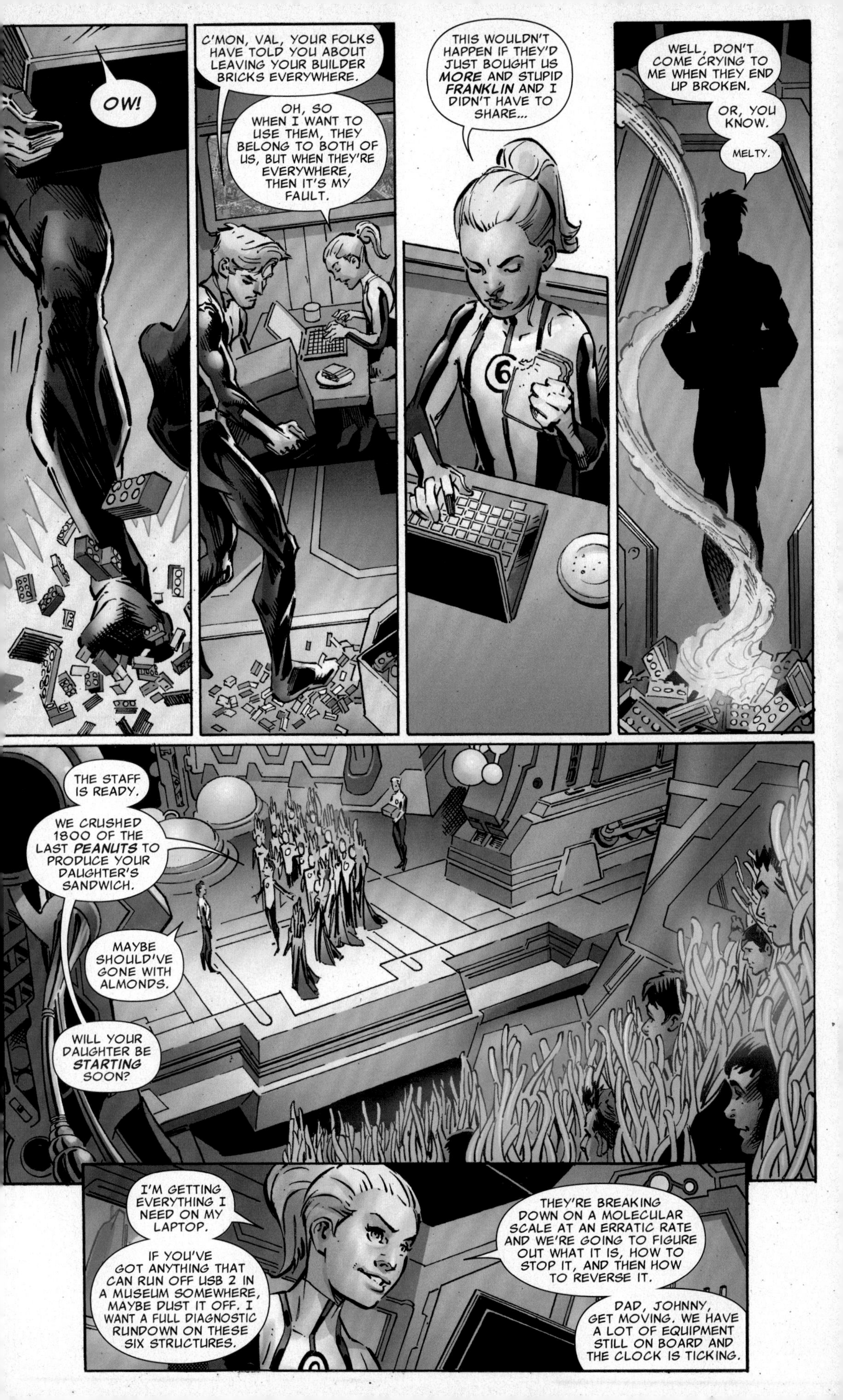
OW!
C'MON, VAL, YOUR FOLKS HAVE TOLD YOU ABOUT LEAVING YOUR BUILDER BRICKS EVERYWHERE.
OH, SO WHEN I WANT TO USE THEM, THEY BELONG TO BOTH OF US, BUT WHEN THEY'RE EVERYWHERE, THEN IT'S MY FAULT.
THIS WOULDN'T HAPPEN IF THEY'D JUST BOUGHT US MORE AND STUPID FRANKLIN AND I DIDN'T HAVE TO SHARE...
WELL, DON'T COME CRYING TO ME WHEN THEY END UP BROKEN.
OR, YOU KNOW.
MELTY.
THE STAFF IS READY.
WE CRUSHED 1800 OF THE LAST PEANUTS TO PRODUCE YOUR DAUGHTER'S SANDWICH.
MAYBE SHOULD'VE GONE WITH ALMONDS.
WILL YOUR DAUGHTER BE STARTING SOON?
I'M GETTING EVERYTHING I NEED ON MY LAPTOP.
IF YOU'VE GOT ANYTHING THAT CAN RUN OFF USB 2 IN A MUSEUM SOMEWHERE, MAYBE DUST IT OFF. I WANT A FULL DIAGNOSTIC RUNDOWN ON THESE SIX STRUCTURES.
THEY'RE BREAKING DOWN ON A MOLECULAR SCALE AT AN ERRATIC RATE AND WE'RE GOING TO FIGURE OUT WHAT IT IS, HOW TO STOP IT, AND THEN HOW TO REVERSE IT.
DAD, JOHNNY, GET MOVING. WE HAVE A LOT OF EQUIPMENT STILL ON BOARD AND THE CLOCK IS TICKING.

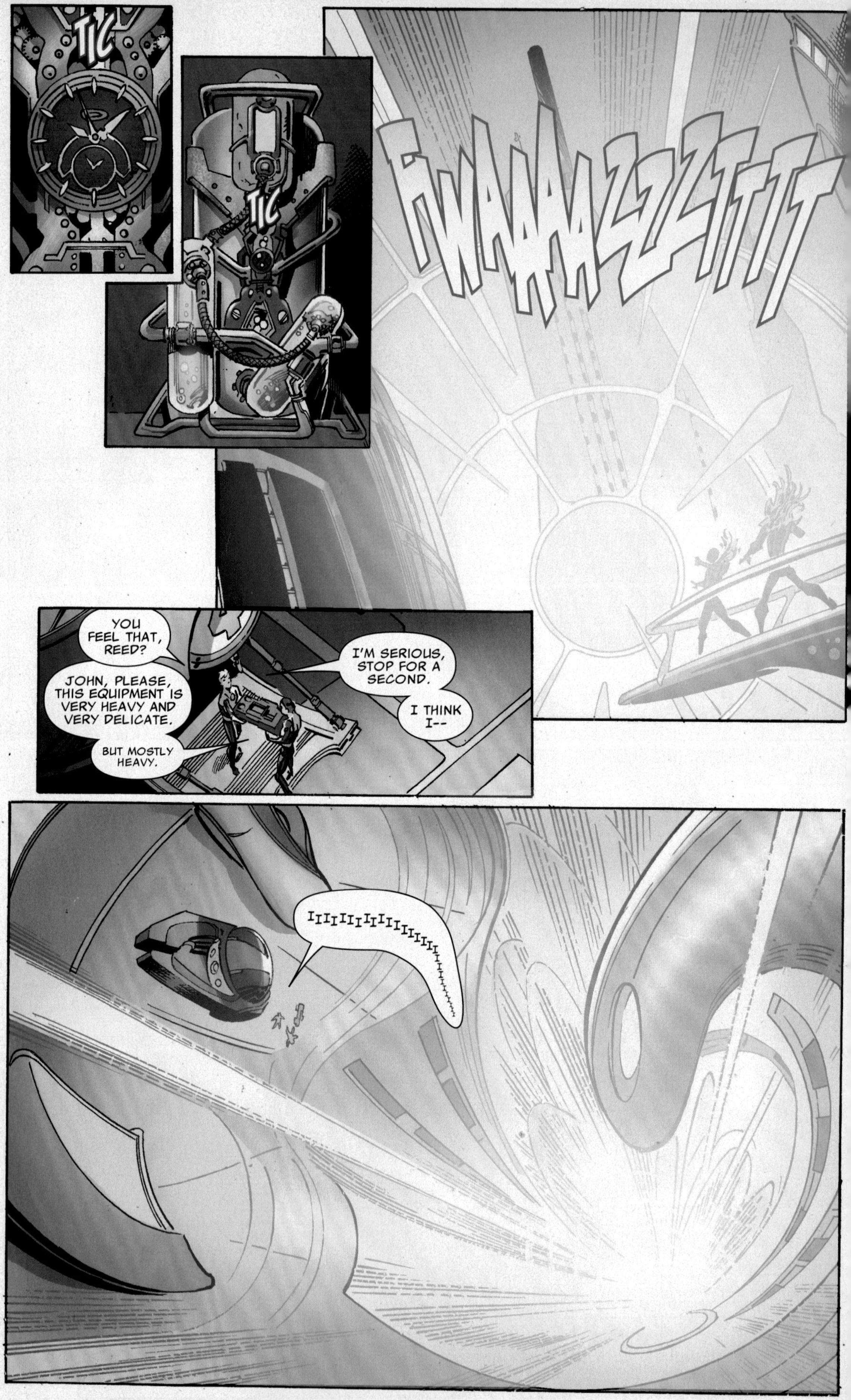

TIC
TIC
FWAAAAZZZTTTT
YOU FEEL THAT, REED?
JOHN, PLEASE, THIS EQUIPMENT IS VERY HEAVY AND VERY DELICATE.
BUT MOSTLY HEAVY.
I'M SERIOUS, STOP FOR A SECOND.
I THINK I--
IIIIIIIIIIIIIIIIIIIIIIIII

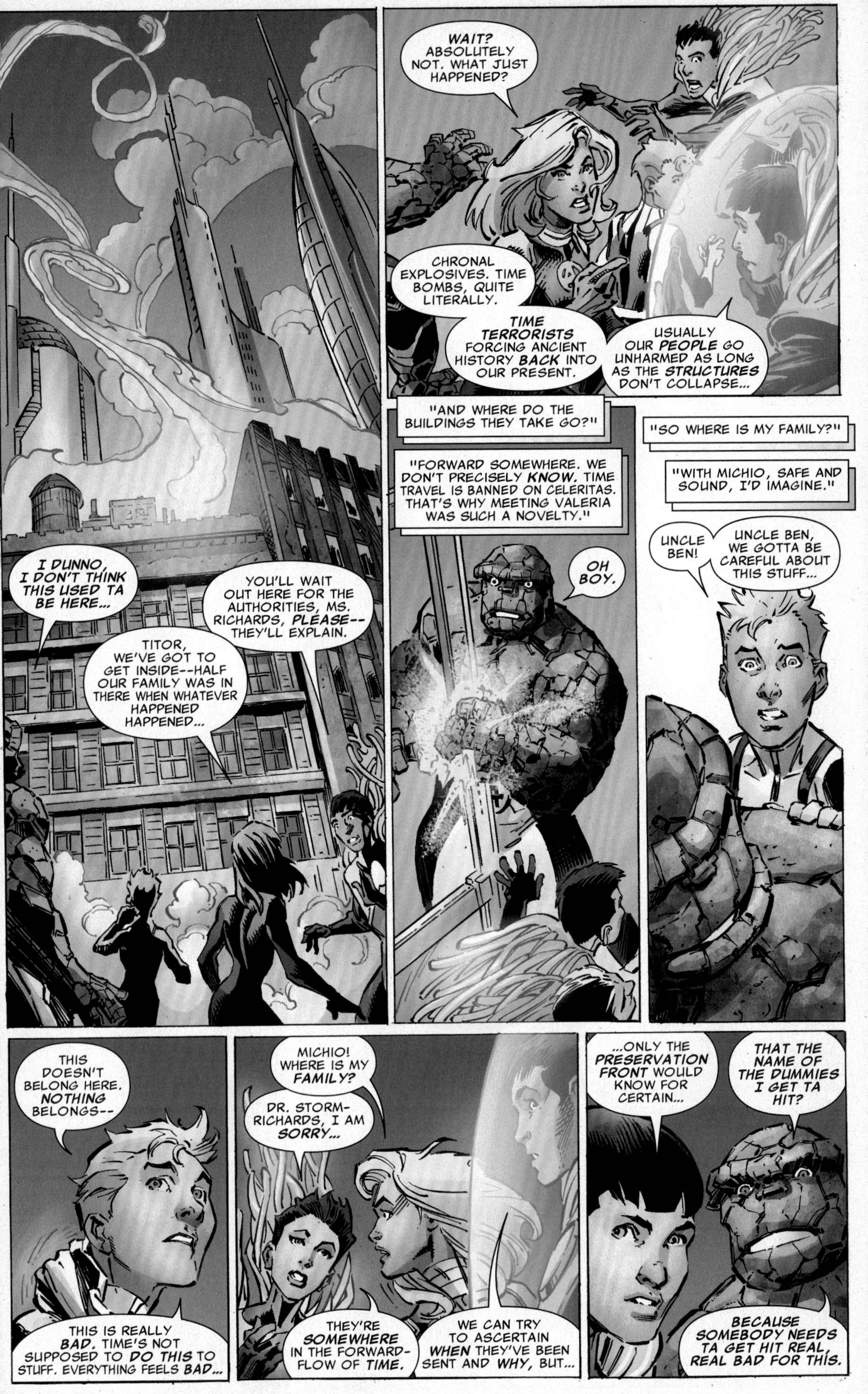
I DUNNO, I DON'T THINK THIS USED TA BE HERE...
YOU'LL WAIT OUT HERE FOR THE AUTHORITIES, MS. RICHARDS, PLEASE-- THEY'LL EXPLAIN.
TITOR, WE'VE GOT TO GET INSIDE--HALF OUR FAMILY WAS IN THERE WHEN WHATEVER HAPPENED HAPPENED...
WAIT? ABSOLUTELY NOT. WHAT JUST HAPPENED?
CHRONAL EXPLOSIVES. TIME BOMBS, QUITE LITERALLY.
TIME TERRORISTS FORCING ANCIENT HISTORY BACK INTO OUR PRESENT.
USUALLY OUR PEOPLE GO UNHARMED AS LONG AS THE STRUCTURES DON'T COLLAPSE...
"AND WHERE DO THE BUILDINGS THEY TAKE GO?"
"FORWARD SOMEWHERE. WE DON'T PRECISELY KNOW. TIME TRAVEL IS BANNED ON CELERITAS. THAT'S WHY MEETING VALERIA WAS SUCH A NOVELTY."
OH BOY.
"SO WHERE IS MY FAMILY?"
"WITH MICHIO, SAFE AND SOUND, I'D IMAGINE."
UNCLE BEN!
UNCLE BEN, WE GOTTA BE CAREFUL ABOUT THIS STUFF...
THIS DOESN'T BELONG HERE. NOTHING BELONGS--
THIS IS REALLY BAD. TIME'S NOT SUPPOSED TO DO THIS TO STUFF. EVERYTHING FEELS BAD...
MICHIO! WHERE IS MY FAMILY?
DR. STORM-RICHARDS, I AM SORRY...
THEY'RE SOMEWHERE IN THE FORWARD-FLOW OF TIME.
WE CAN TRY TO ASCERTAIN WHEN THEY'VE BEEN SENT AND WHY, BUT...
...ONLY THE PRESERVATION FRONT WOULD KNOW FOR CERTAIN...
THAT THE NAME OF THE DUMMIES I GET TA HIT?
BECAUSE SOMEBODY NEEDS TA GET HIT REAL, REAL BAD FOR THIS.

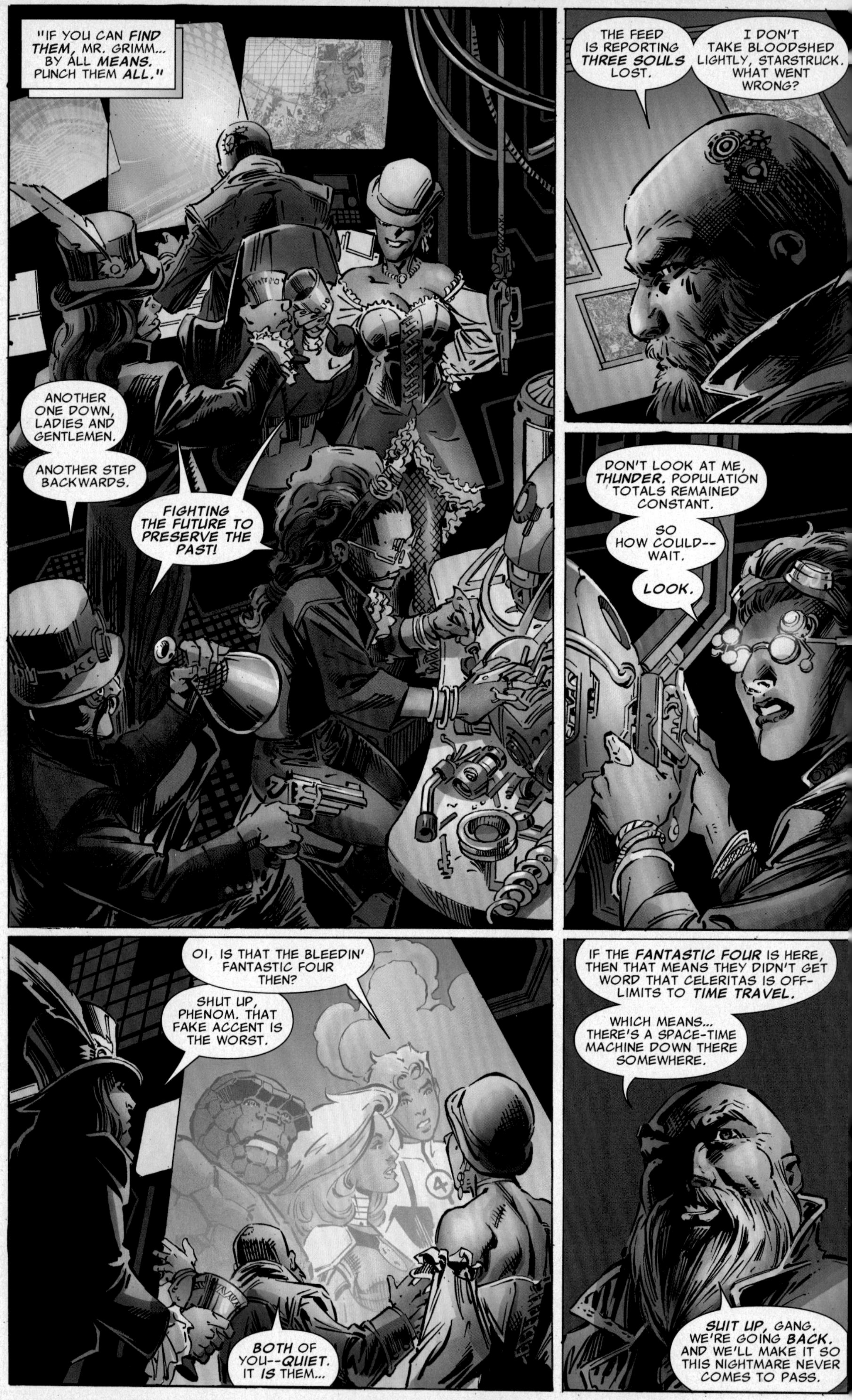
"IF YOU CAN FIND THEM, MR. GRIMM... BY ALL MEANS. PUNCH THEM ALL."
ANOTHER ONE DOWN, LADIES AND GENTLEMEN.
ANOTHER STEP BACKWARDS.
FIGHTING THE FUTURE TO PRESERVE THE PAST!
THE FEED IS REPORTING THREE SOULS LOST.
I DON'T TAKE BLOODSHED LIGHTLY, STARSTRUCK. WHAT WENT WRONG?
DON'T LOOK AT ME, THUNDER. POPULATION TOTALS REMAINED CONSTANT.
SO HOW COULD-- WAIT.
LOOK.
OI, IS THAT THE BLEEDIN' FANTASTIC FOUR THEN?
SHUT UP, PHENOM. THAT FAKE ACCENT IS THE WORST.
BOTH OF YOU--QUIET. IT IS THEM...
IF THE FANTASTIC FOUR IS HERE, THEN THAT MEANS THEY DIDN'T GET WORD THAT CELERITAS IS OFF-LIMITS TO TIME TRAVEL.
WHICH MEANS... THERE'S A SPACE-TIME MACHINE DOWN THERE SOMEWHERE.
SUIT UP, GANG. WE'RE GOING BACK. AND WE'LL MAKE IT SO THIS NIGHTMARE NEVER COMES TO PASS.

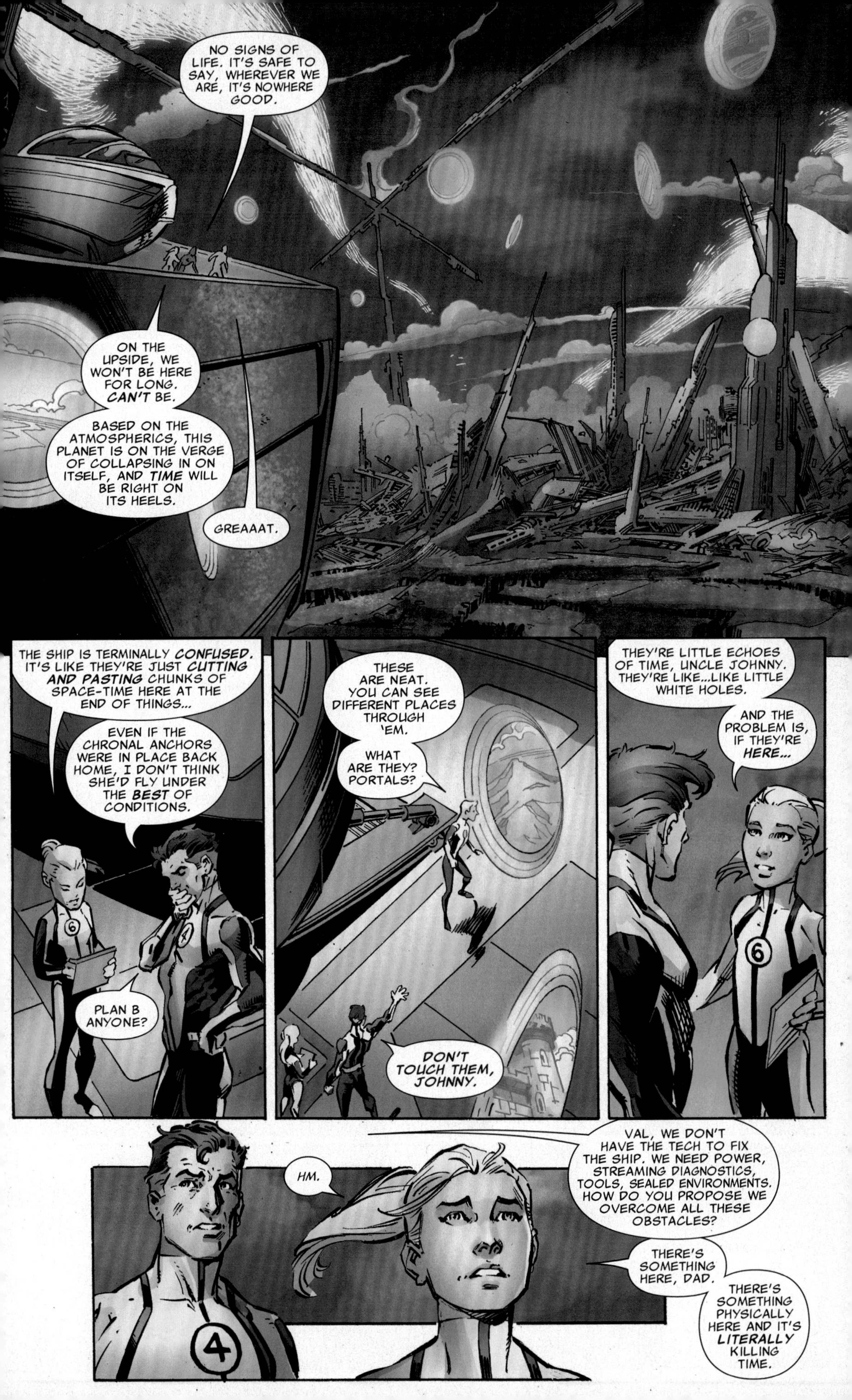
NO SIGNS OF LIFE. IT'S SAFE TO SAY, WHEREVER WE ARE, IT'S NOWHERE GOOD.
ON THE UPSIDE, WE WON'T BE HERE FOR LONG. *CAN'T* BE.
BASED ON THE ATMOSPHERICS, THIS PLANET IS ON THE VERGE OF COLLAPSING IN ON ITSELF, AND *TIME* WILL BE RIGHT ON ITS HEELS.
GREAAAT.
THE SHIP IS TERMINALLY *CONFUSED.* IT'S LIKE THEY'RE JUST *CUTTING AND PASTING* CHUNKS OF SPACE-TIME HERE AT THE END OF THINGS...
EVEN IF THE CHRONAL ANCHORS WERE IN PLACE BACK HOME, I DON'T THINK SHE'D FLY UNDER THE *BEST* OF CONDITIONS.
PLAN B ANYONE?
THESE ARE NEAT. YOU CAN SEE DIFFERENT PLACES THROUGH 'EM.
WHAT ARE THEY? PORTALS?
DON'T TOUCH THEM, JOHNNY.
THEY'RE LITTLE ECHOES OF TIME, UNCLE JOHNNY. THEY'RE LIKE...LIKE LITTLE WHITE HOLES.
AND THE PROBLEM IS, IF THEY'RE *HERE...*
VAL, WE DON'T HAVE THE TECH TO FIX THE SHIP. WE NEED POWER, STREAMING DIAGNOSTICS, TOOLS, SEALED ENVIRONMENTS. HOW DO YOU PROPOSE WE OVERCOME ALL THESE OBSTACLES?
HM.
THERE'S SOMETHING HERE, DAD.
THERE'S SOMETHING PHYSICALLY HERE AND IT'S *LITERALLY* KILLING TIME.

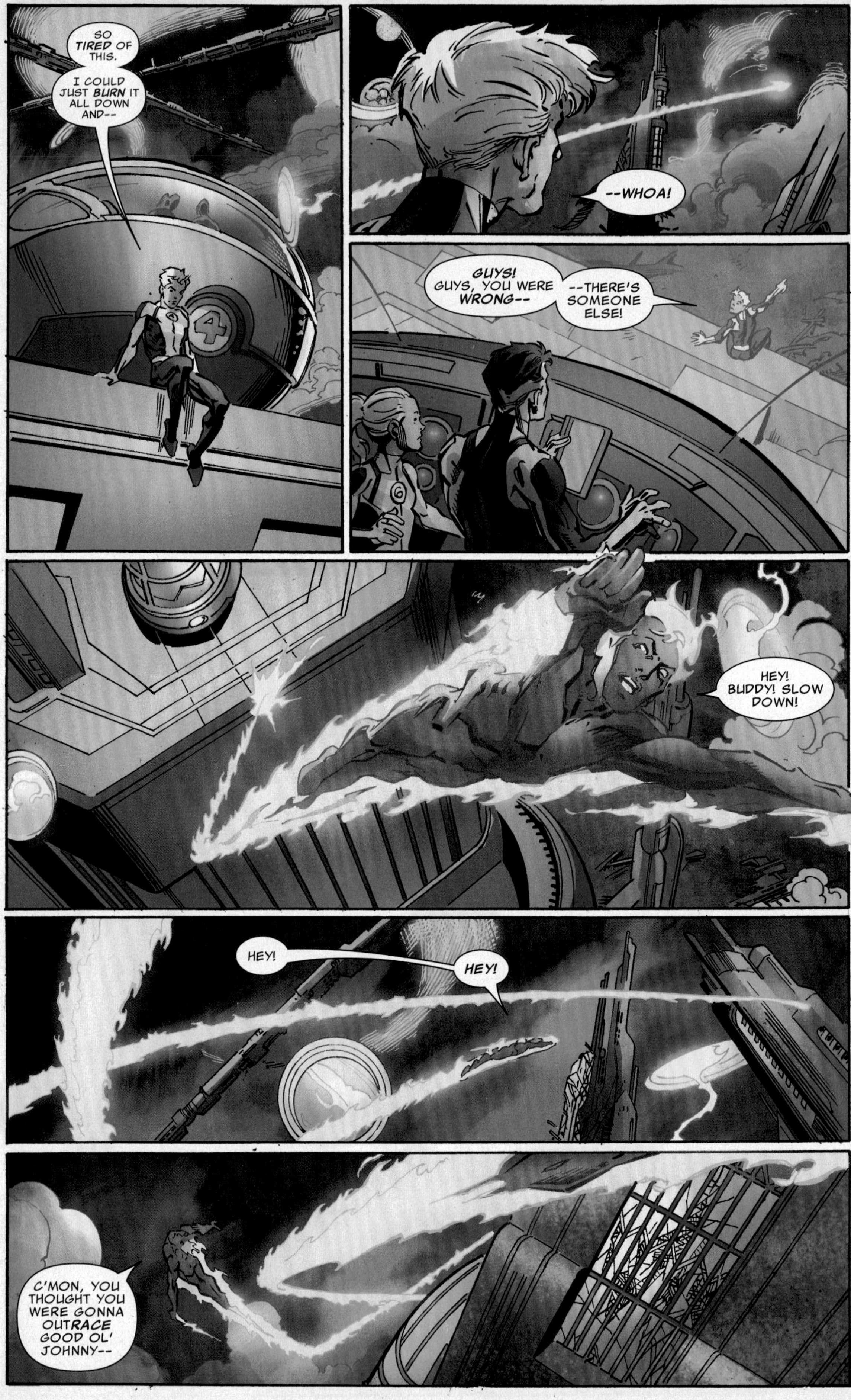
SO TIRED OF THIS.
I COULD JUST BURN IT ALL DOWN AND--
--WHOA!
GUYS! GUYS, YOU WERE WRONG--
--THERE'S SOMEONE ELSE!
HEY! BUDDY! SLOW DOWN!
HEY!
HEY!
C'MON, YOU THOUGHT YOU WERE GONNA OUTRACE GOOD OL' JOHNNY--

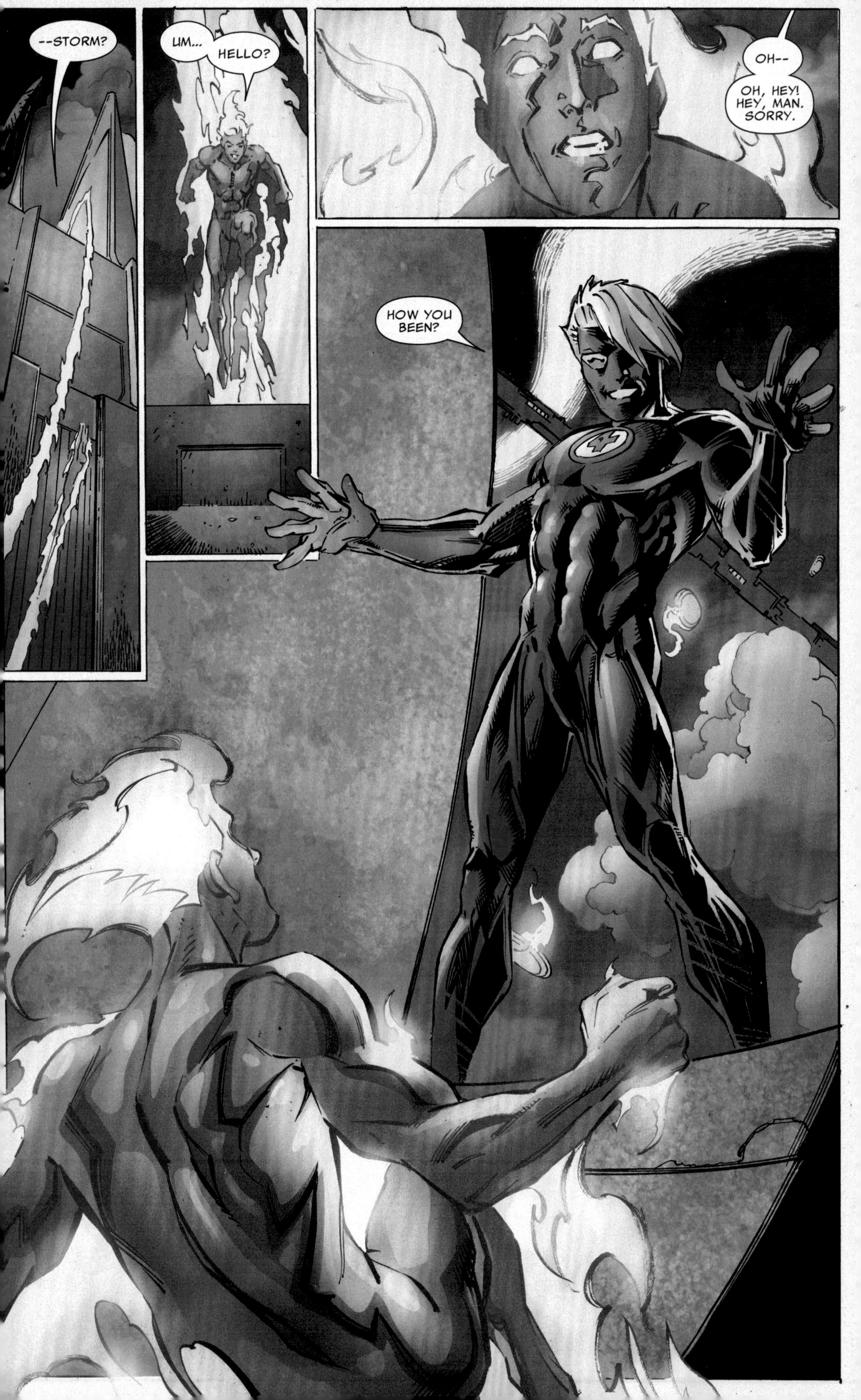
--STORM?
UM...
HELLO?
OH--
OH, HEY! HEY, MAN. SORRY.
HOW YOU BEEN?

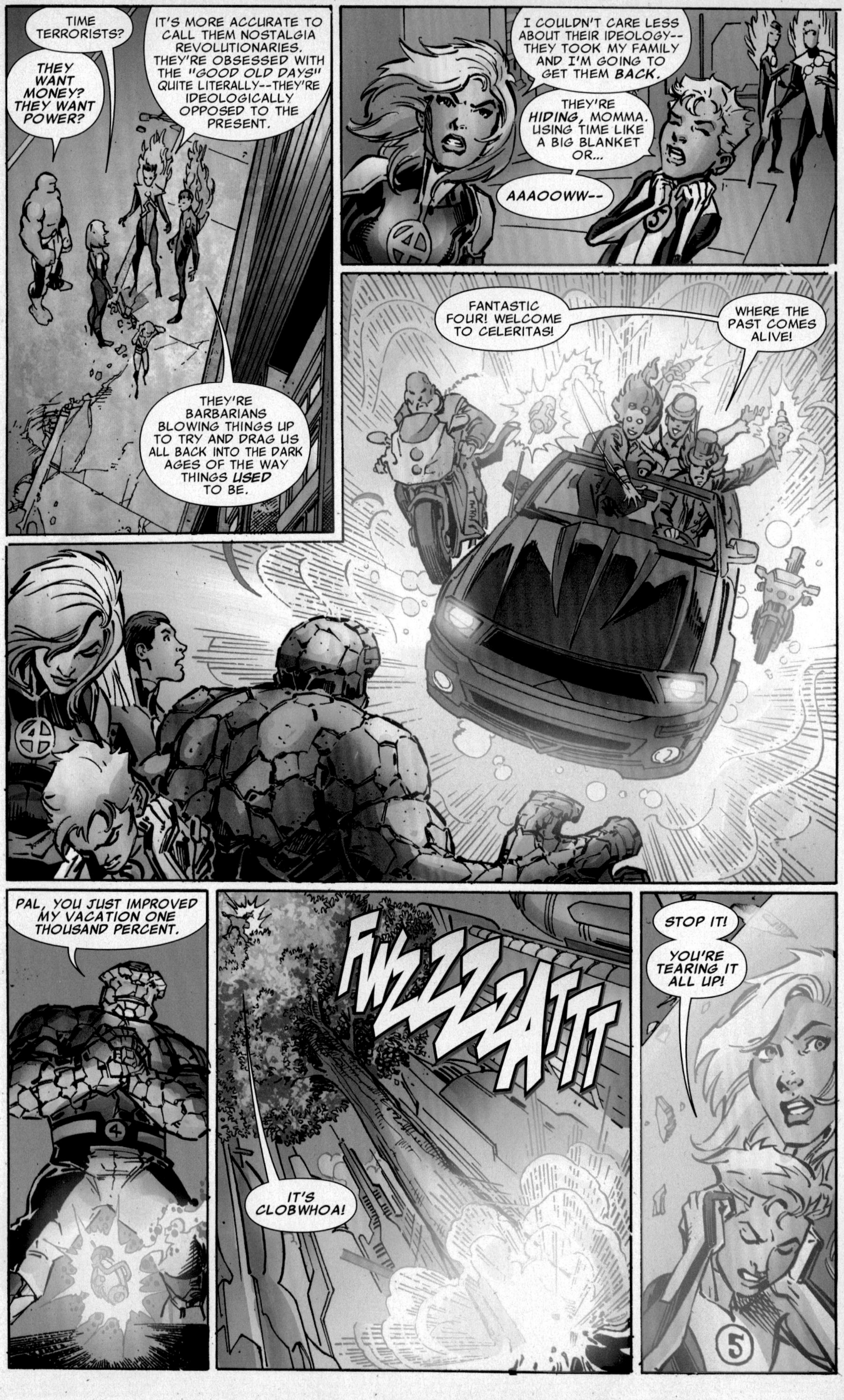
TIME TERRORISTS?
THEY WANT MONEY? THEY WANT POWER?
IT'S MORE ACCURATE TO CALL THEM NOSTALGIA REVOLUTIONARIES. THEY'RE OBSESSED WITH THE "GOOD OLD DAYS" QUITE LITERALLY--THEY'RE IDEOLOGICALLY OPPOSED TO THE PRESENT.
THEY'RE BARBARIANS BLOWING THINGS UP TO TRY AND DRAG US ALL BACK INTO THE DARK AGES OF THE WAY THINGS USED TO BE.
I COULDN'T CARE LESS ABOUT THEIR IDEOLOGY--THEY TOOK MY FAMILY AND I'M GOING TO GET THEM BACK.
THEY'RE HIDING, MOMMA. USING TIME LIKE A BIG BLANKET OR...
AAAOOWW--
FANTASTIC FOUR! WELCOME TO CELERITAS!
WHERE THE PAST COMES ALIVE!
PAL, YOU JUST IMPROVED MY VACATION ONE THOUSAND PERCENT.
FWZZZZATTT
IT'S CLOBWHOA!
STOP IT!
YOU'RE TEARING IT ALL UP!

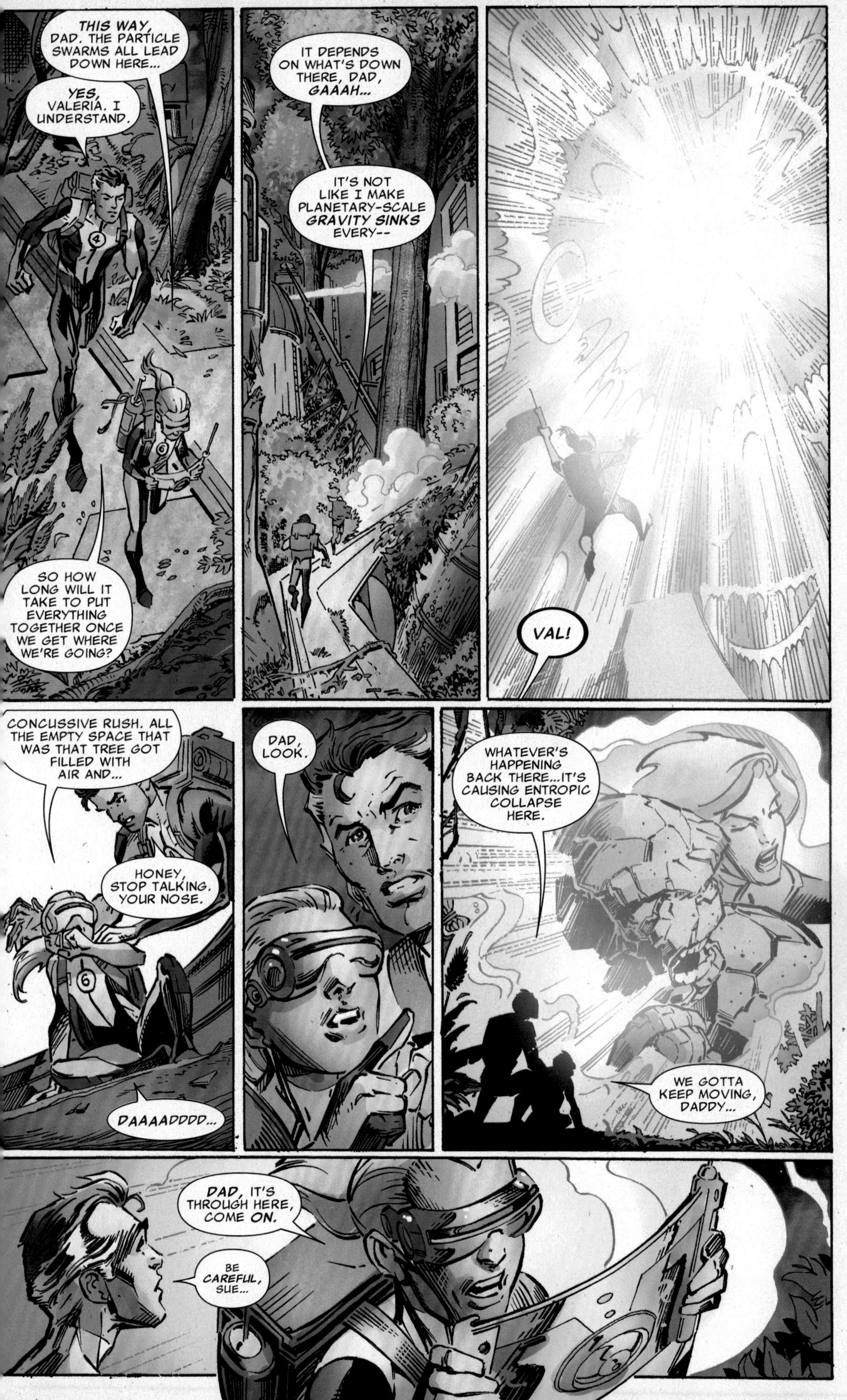
THIS WAY, DAD. THE PARTICLE SWARMS ALL LEAD DOWN HERE...
YES, VALERIA. I UNDERSTAND.
SO HOW LONG WILL IT TAKE TO PUT EVERYTHING TOGETHER ONCE WE GET WHERE WE'RE GOING?
IT DEPENDS ON WHAT'S DOWN THERE, DAD, GAAAH...
IT'S NOT LIKE I MAKE PLANETARY-SCALE GRAVITY SINKS EVERY--
VAL!
CONCUSSIVE RUSH. ALL THE EMPTY SPACE THAT WAS THAT TREE GOT FILLED WITH AIR AND...
HONEY, STOP TALKING. YOUR NOSE.
DAAAADDDD...
DAD, LOOK.
WHATEVER'S HAPPENING BACK THERE...IT'S CAUSING ENTROPIC COLLAPSE HERE.
WE GOTTA KEEP MOVING, DADDY...
DAD, IT'S THROUGH HERE, COME ON.
BE CAREFUL, SUE...

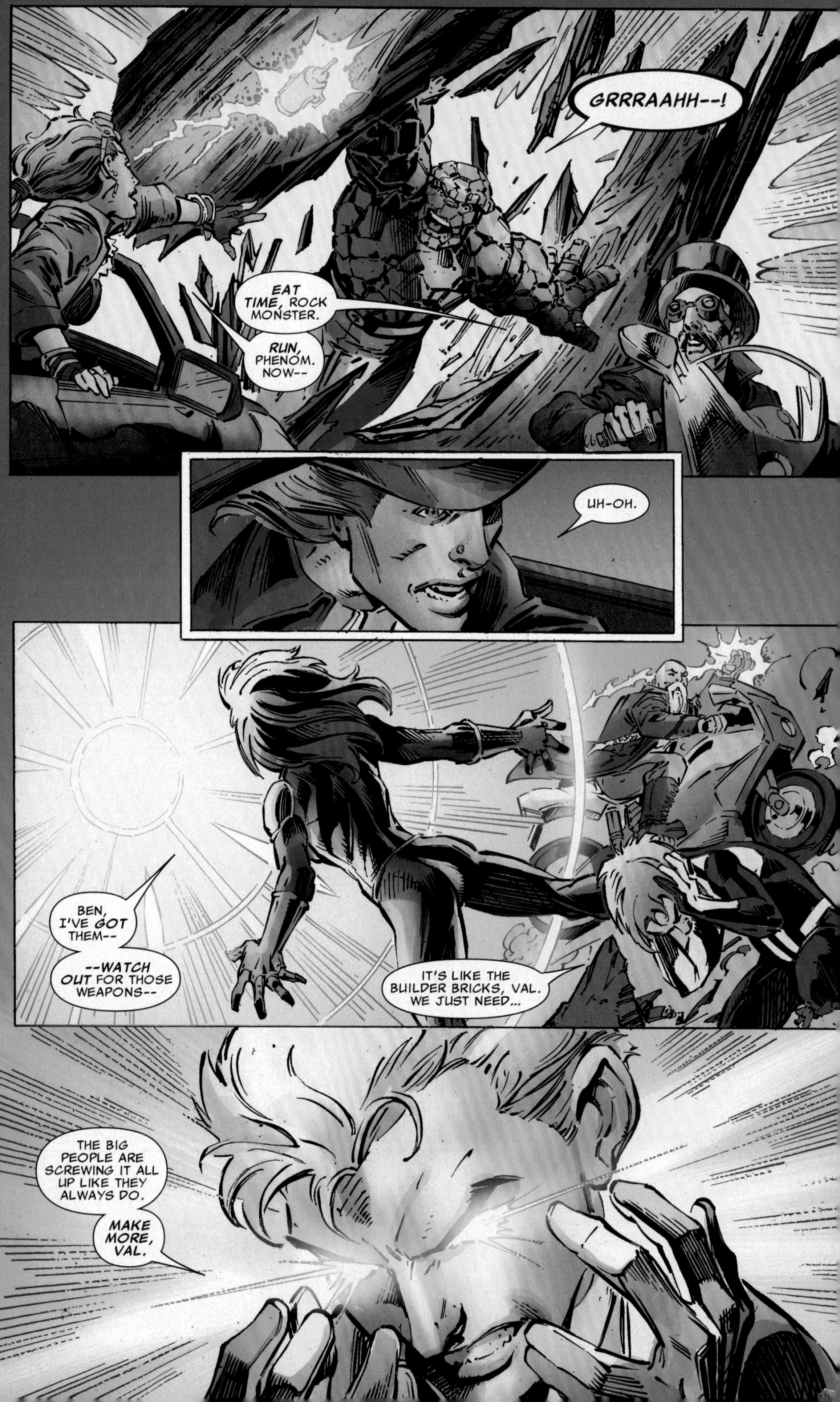
GRRRAAHH--!
EAT TIME, ROCK MONSTER.
RUN, PHENOM. NOW--
UH-OH.
BEN, I'VE GOT THEM--
--WATCH OUT FOR THOSE WEAPONS--
IT'S LIKE THE BUILDER BRICKS, VAL. WE JUST NEED...
THE BIG PEOPLE ARE SCREWING IT ALL UP LIKE THEY ALWAYS DO.
MAKE MORE, VAL.

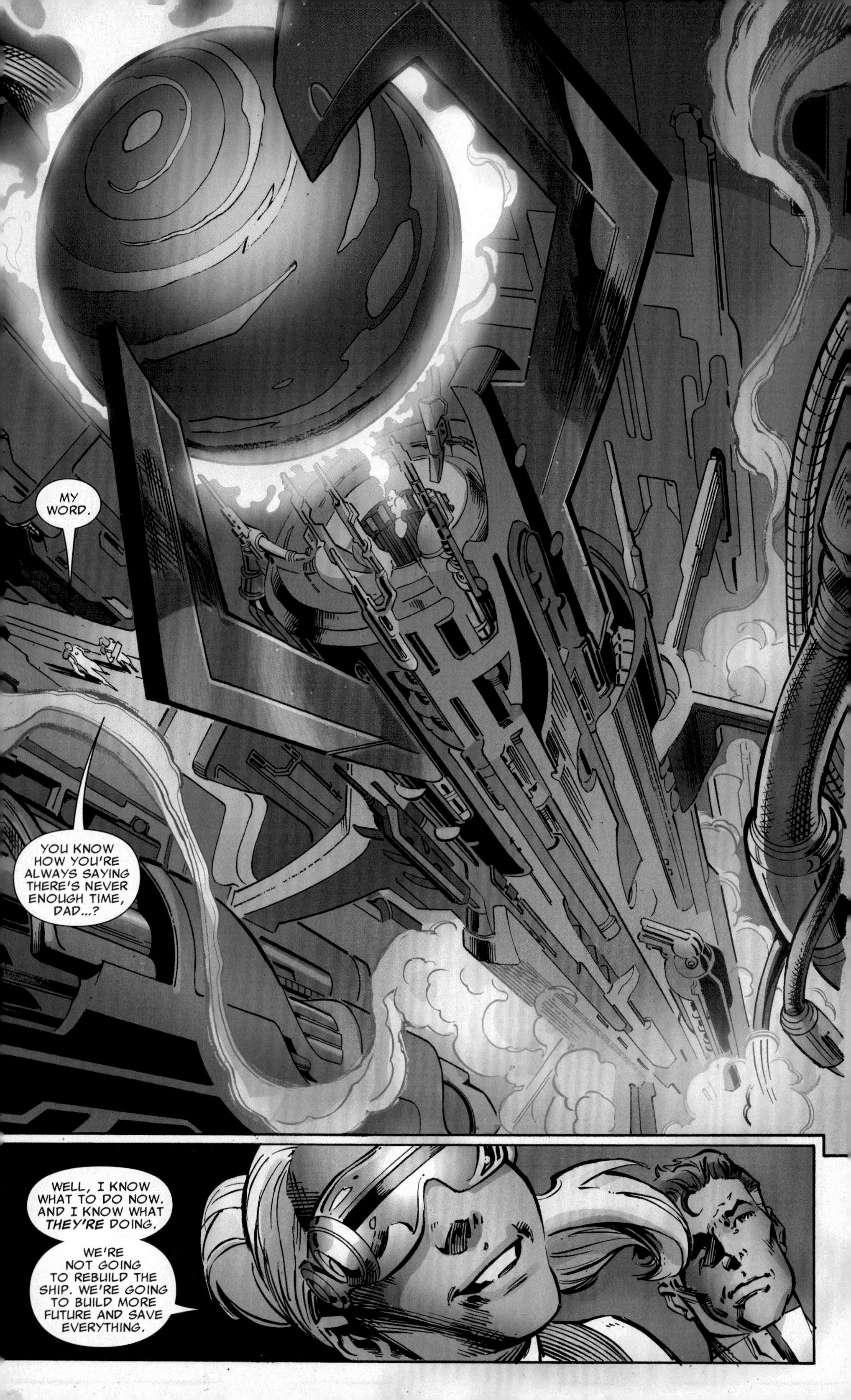
MY WORD.
YOU KNOW HOW YOU'RE ALWAYS SAYING THERE'S NEVER ENOUGH TIME, DAD...?
WELL, I KNOW WHAT TO DO NOW. AND I KNOW WHAT *THEY'RE* DOING.
WE'RE NOT GOING TO REBUILD THE SHIP. WE'RE GOING TO BUILD MORE FUTURE AND SAVE EVERYTHING.

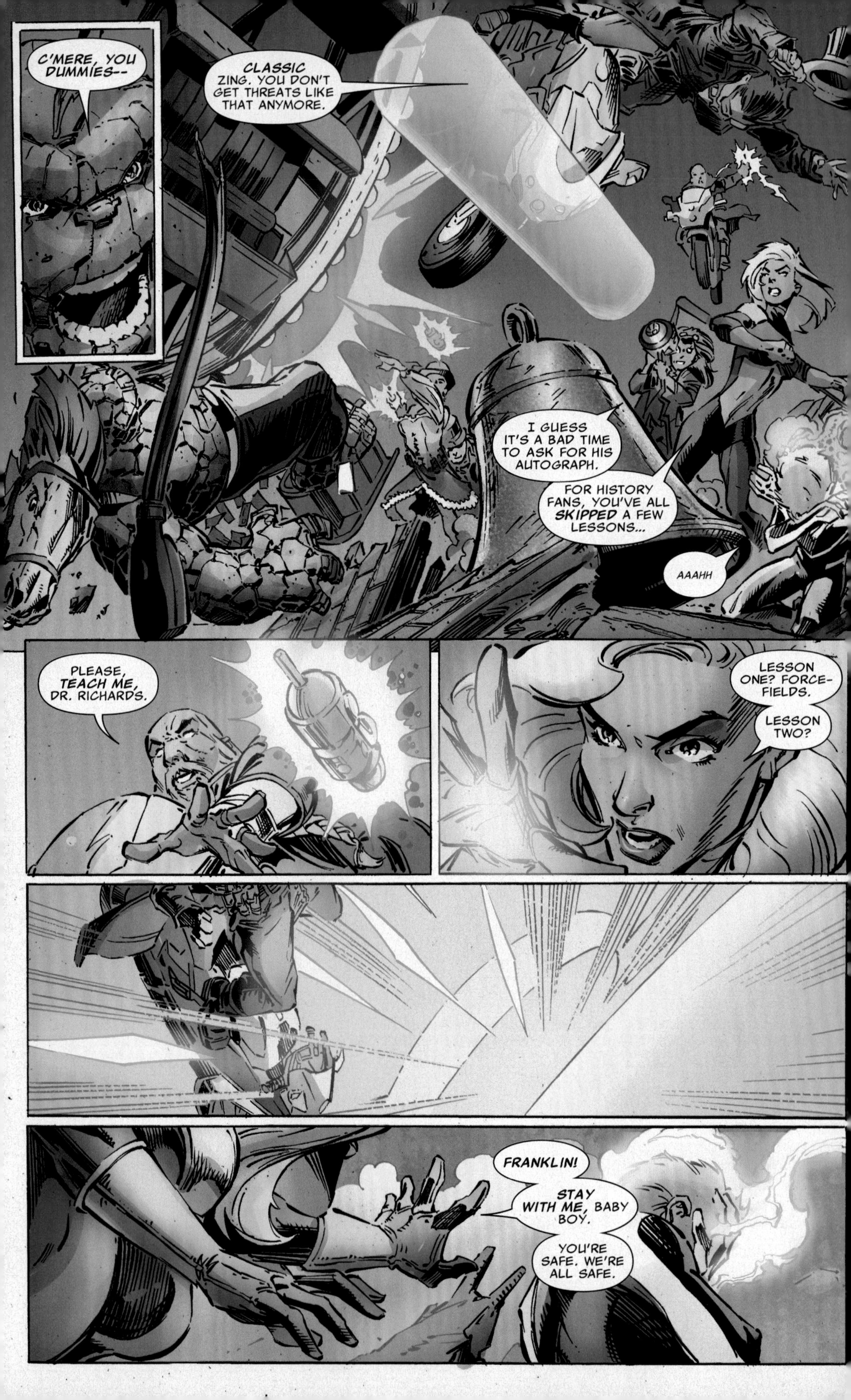
C'MERE, YOU DUMMIES--
CLASSIC ZING. YOU DON'T GET THREATS LIKE THAT ANYMORE.
I GUESS IT'S A BAD TIME TO ASK FOR HIS AUTOGRAPH.
FOR HISTORY FANS, YOU'VE ALL SKIPPED A FEW LESSONS...
AAAHH
PLEASE, TEACH ME, DR. RICHARDS.
LESSON ONE? FORCE-FIELDS.
LESSON TWO?
FRANKLIN!
STAY WITH ME, BABY BOY.
YOU'RE SAFE. WE'RE ALL SAFE.

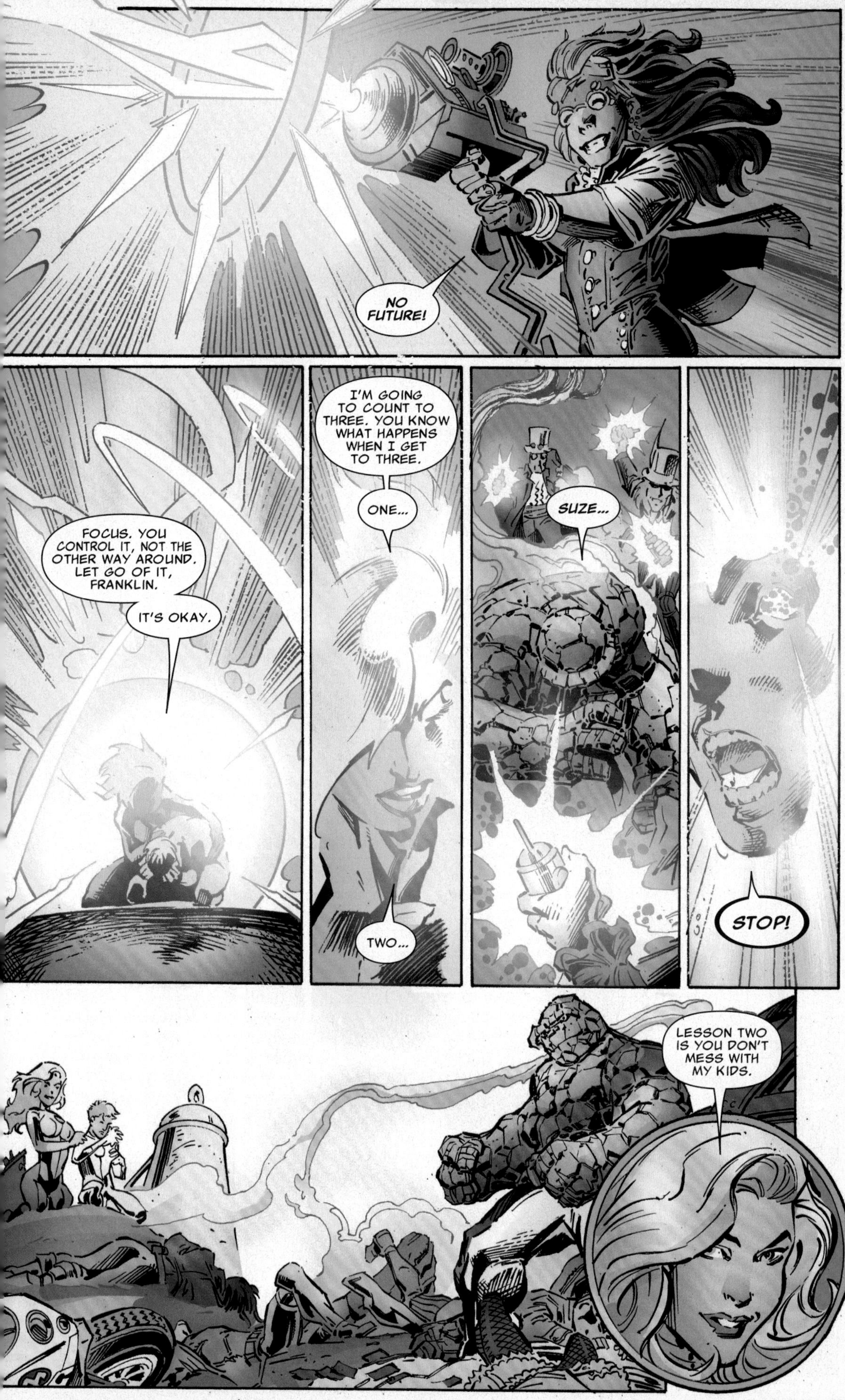
NO FUTURE!
FOCUS. YOU CONTROL IT, NOT THE OTHER WAY AROUND. LET GO OF IT, FRANKLIN.
IT'S OKAY.
I'M GOING TO COUNT TO THREE. YOU KNOW WHAT HAPPENS WHEN I GET TO THREE.
ONE...
TWO...
SUZE...
STOP!
LESSON TWO IS YOU DON'T MESS WITH MY KIDS.

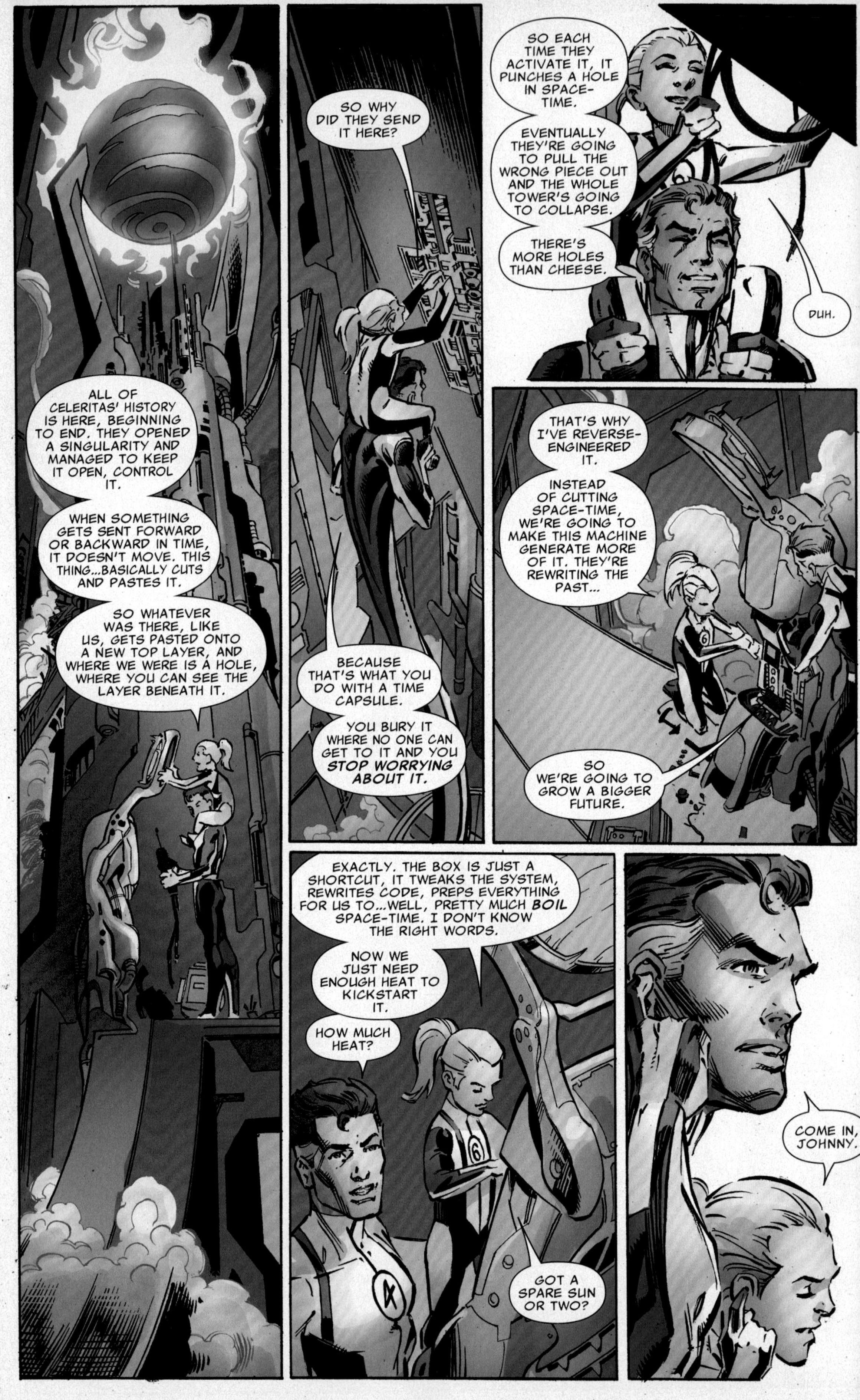
ALL OF CELERITAS' HISTORY IS HERE, BEGINNING TO END. THEY OPENED A SINGULARITY AND MANAGED TO KEEP IT OPEN, CONTROL IT.
WHEN SOMETHING GETS SENT FORWARD OR BACKWARD IN TIME, IT DOESN'T MOVE. THIS THING...BASICALLY CUTS AND PASTES IT.
SO WHATEVER WAS THERE, LIKE US, GETS PASTED ONTO A NEW TOP LAYER, AND WHERE WE WERE IS A HOLE, WHERE YOU CAN SEE THE LAYER BENEATH IT.
SO WHY DID THEY SEND IT HERE?
BECAUSE THAT'S WHAT YOU DO WITH A TIME CAPSULE.
YOU BURY IT WHERE NO ONE CAN GET TO IT AND YOU STOP WORRYING ABOUT IT.
SO EACH TIME THEY ACTIVATE IT, IT PUNCHES A HOLE IN SPACE-TIME.
EVENTUALLY THEY'RE GOING TO PULL THE WRONG PIECE OUT AND THE WHOLE TOWER'S GOING TO COLLAPSE.
THERE'S MORE HOLES THAN CHEESE.
DUH.
THAT'S WHY I'VE REVERSE-ENGINEERED IT.
INSTEAD OF CUTTING SPACE-TIME, WE'RE GOING TO MAKE THIS MACHINE GENERATE MORE OF IT. THEY'RE REWRITING THE PAST...
SO WE'RE GOING TO GROW A BIGGER FUTURE.
EXACTLY. THE BOX IS JUST A SHORTCUT, IT TWEAKS THE SYSTEM, REWRITES CODE, PREPS EVERYTHING FOR US TO...WELL, PRETTY MUCH BOIL SPACE-TIME. I DON'T KNOW THE RIGHT WORDS.
NOW WE JUST NEED ENOUGH HEAT TO KICKSTART IT.
HOW MUCH HEAT?
GOT A SPARE SUN OR TWO?
COME IN, JOHNNY.

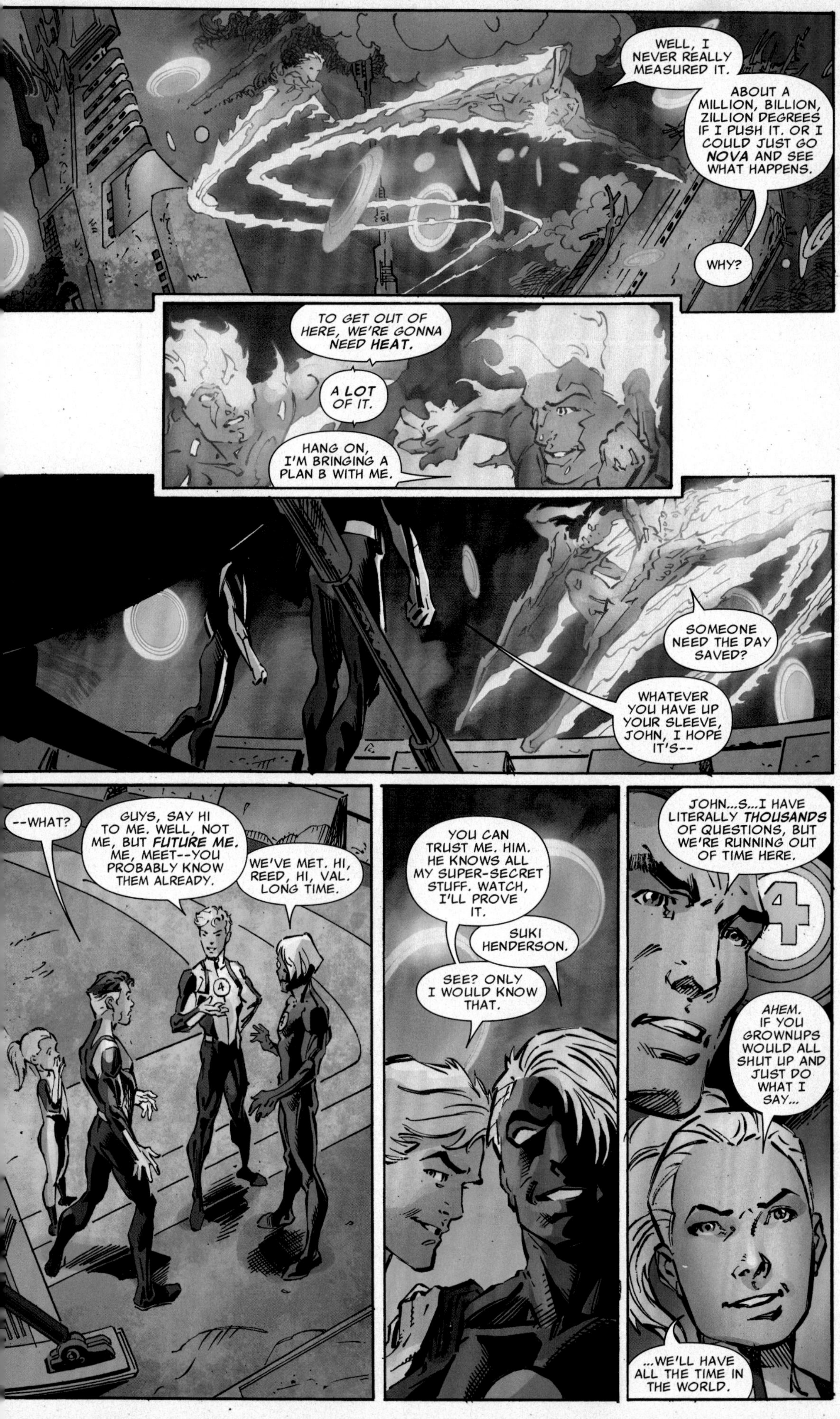
WELL, I NEVER REALLY MEASURED IT.
ABOUT A MILLION, BILLION, ZILLION DEGREES IF I PUSH IT. OR I COULD JUST GO NOVA AND SEE WHAT HAPPENS.
WHY?
TO GET OUT OF HERE, WE'RE GONNA NEED HEAT.
A LOT OF IT.
HANG ON, I'M BRINGING A PLAN B WITH ME.
SOMEONE NEED THE DAY SAVED?
WHATEVER YOU HAVE UP YOUR SLEEVE, JOHN, I HOPE IT'S--
--WHAT?
GUYS, SAY HI TO ME. WELL, NOT ME, BUT FUTURE ME. ME, MEET--YOU PROBABLY KNOW THEM ALREADY.
WE'VE MET. HI, REED, HI, VAL. LONG TIME.
YOU CAN TRUST ME. HIM. HE KNOWS ALL MY SUPER-SECRET STUFF. WATCH, I'LL PROVE IT.
SUKI HENDERSON.
SEE? ONLY I WOULD KNOW THAT.
JOHN...S...I HAVE LITERALLY THOUSANDS OF QUESTIONS, BUT WE'RE RUNNING OUT OF TIME HERE.
AHEM. IF YOU GROWNUPS WOULD ALL SHUT UP AND JUST DO WHAT I SAY...
...WE'LL HAVE ALL THE TIME IN THE WORLD.

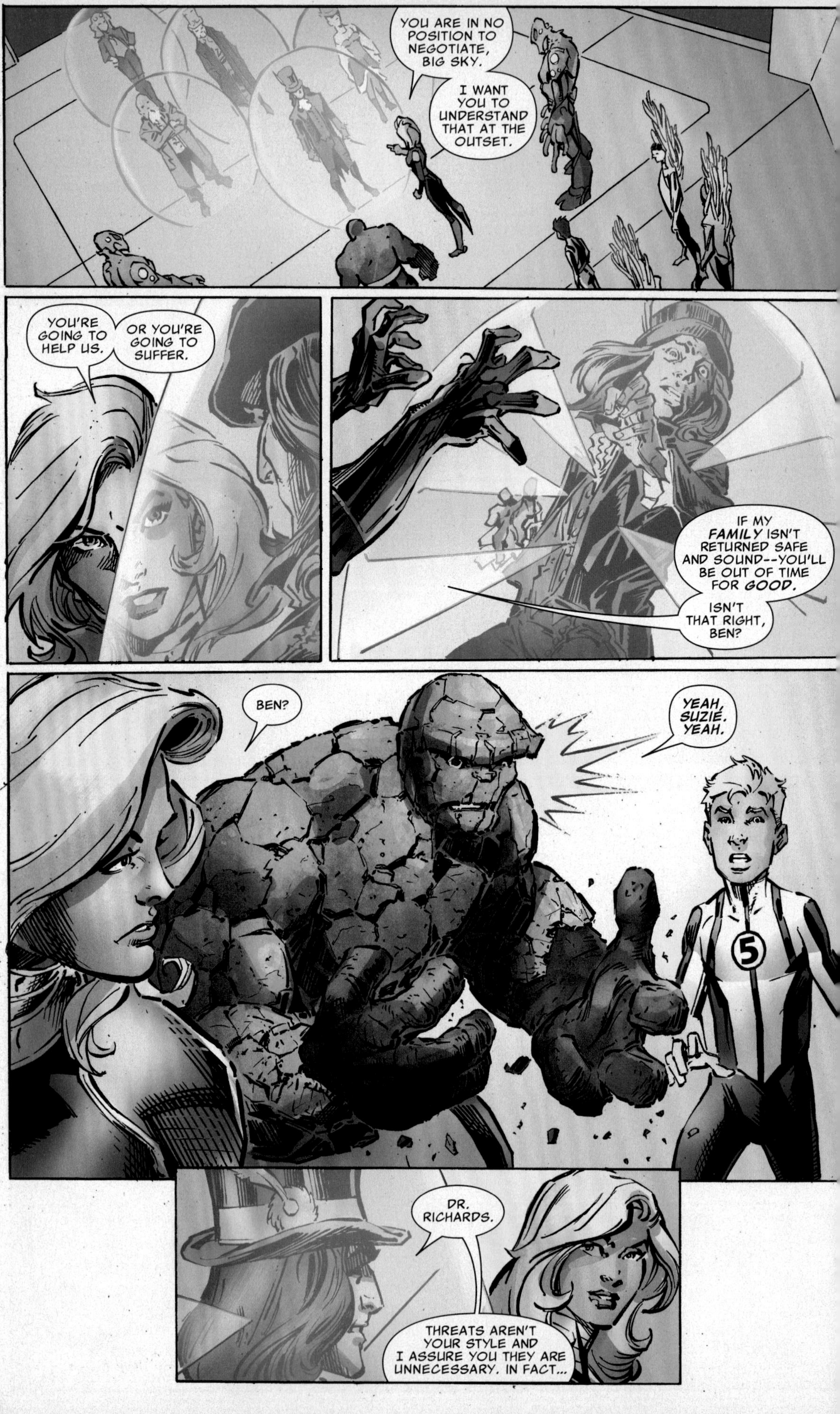

YOU ARE IN NO POSITION TO NEGOTIATE, BIG SKY.
I WANT YOU TO UNDERSTAND THAT AT THE OUTSET.
YOU'RE GOING TO HELP US.
OR YOU'RE GOING TO SUFFER.
IF MY FAMILY ISN'T RETURNED SAFE AND SOUND--YOU'LL BE OUT OF TIME FOR GOOD.
ISN'T THAT RIGHT, BEN?
BEN?
YEAH, SUZIE. YEAH.
DR. RICHARDS.
THREATS AREN'T YOUR STYLE AND I ASSURE YOU THEY ARE UNNECESSARY. IN FACT...

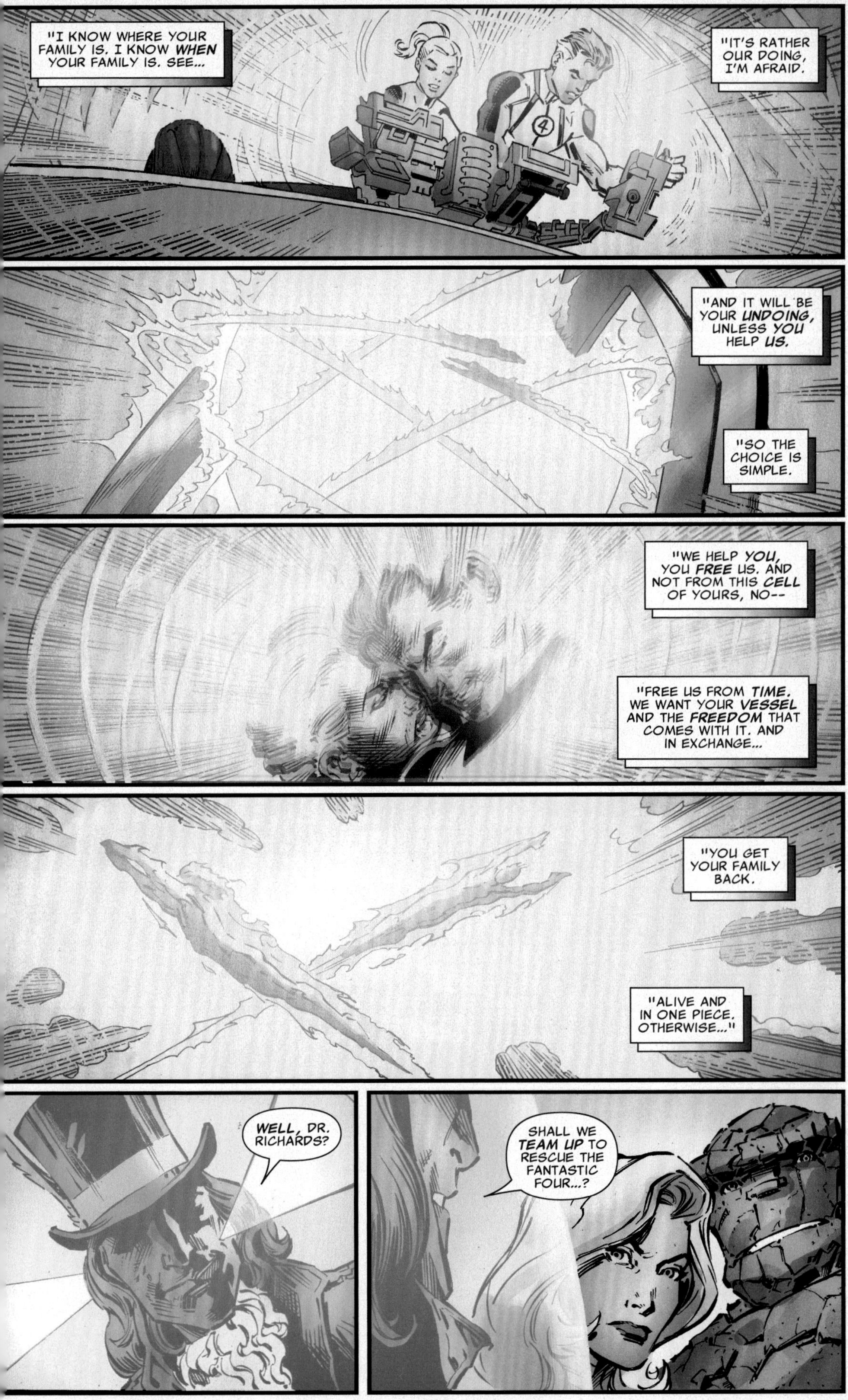
"I KNOW WHERE YOUR FAMILY IS. I KNOW *WHEN* YOUR FAMILY IS. SEE...
"IT'S RATHER OUR DOING, I'M AFRAID.
"AND IT WILL BE YOUR *UNDOING*, UNLESS *YOU* HELP *US*.
"SO THE CHOICE IS SIMPLE.
"WE HELP *YOU*, YOU *FREE* US. AND NOT FROM THIS *CELL* OF YOURS, NO--
"FREE US FROM *TIME*. WE WANT YOUR *VESSEL* AND THE *FREEDOM* THAT COMES WITH IT. AND IN EXCHANGE...
"YOU GET YOUR FAMILY BACK.
"ALIVE AND IN ONE PIECE. OTHERWISE..."
WELL, DR. RICHARDS?
SHALL WE *TEAM UP* TO RESCUE THE FANTASTIC FOUR...?

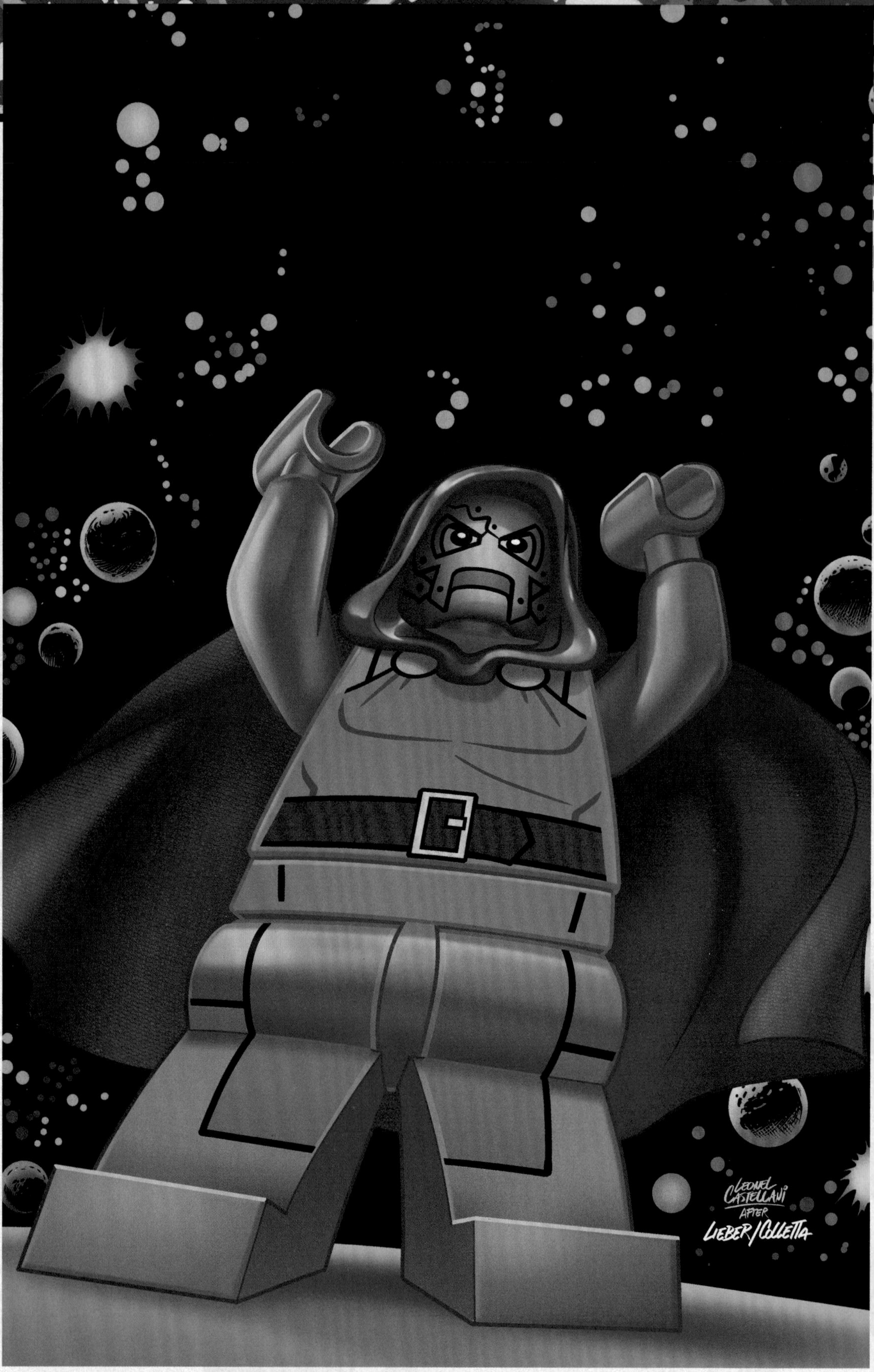
LEONEL CASTELLANI
AFTER
LIEBER/COLLETTA

FANTASTIC FOUR #13 LEGO VARIANT BY LEONEL CASTELLANI

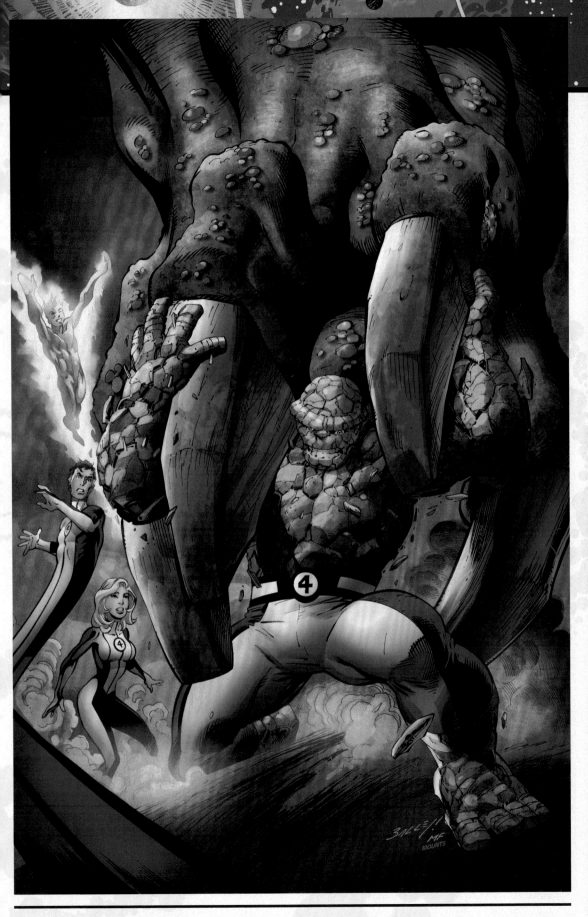

FANTASTIC FOUR #12 — "PLANET FUTURE PART 2"

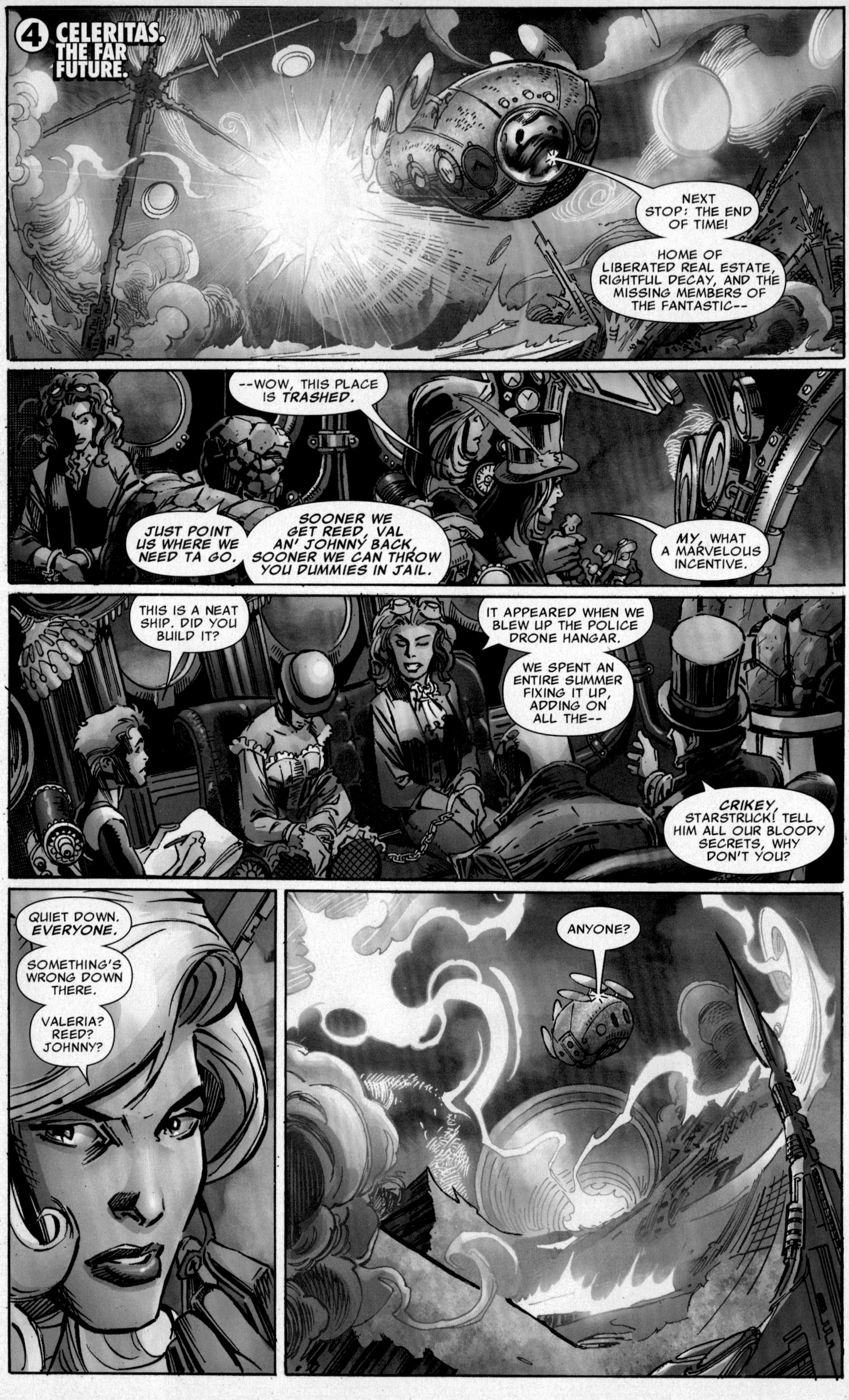
CELERITAS. THE FAR FUTURE.
NEXT STOP: THE END OF TIME!
HOME OF LIBERATED REAL ESTATE, RIGHTFUL DECAY, AND THE MISSING MEMBERS OF THE FANTASTIC--
--WOW, THIS PLACE IS TRASHED.
JUST POINT US WHERE WE NEED TA GO.
SOONER WE GET REED, VAL AN' JOHNNY BACK, SOONER WE CAN THROW YOU DUMMIES IN JAIL.
MY, WHAT A MARVELOUS INCENTIVE.
THIS IS A NEAT SHIP. DID YOU BUILD IT?
IT APPEARED WHEN WE BLEW UP THE POLICE DRONE HANGAR.
WE SPENT AN ENTIRE SUMMER FIXING IT UP, ADDING ON ALL THE--
CRIKEY, STARSTRUCK! TELL HIM ALL OUR BLOODY SECRETS, WHY DON'T YOU?
QUIET DOWN. EVERYONE.
SOMETHING'S WRONG DOWN THERE.
VALERIA? REED? JOHNNY?
ANYONE?

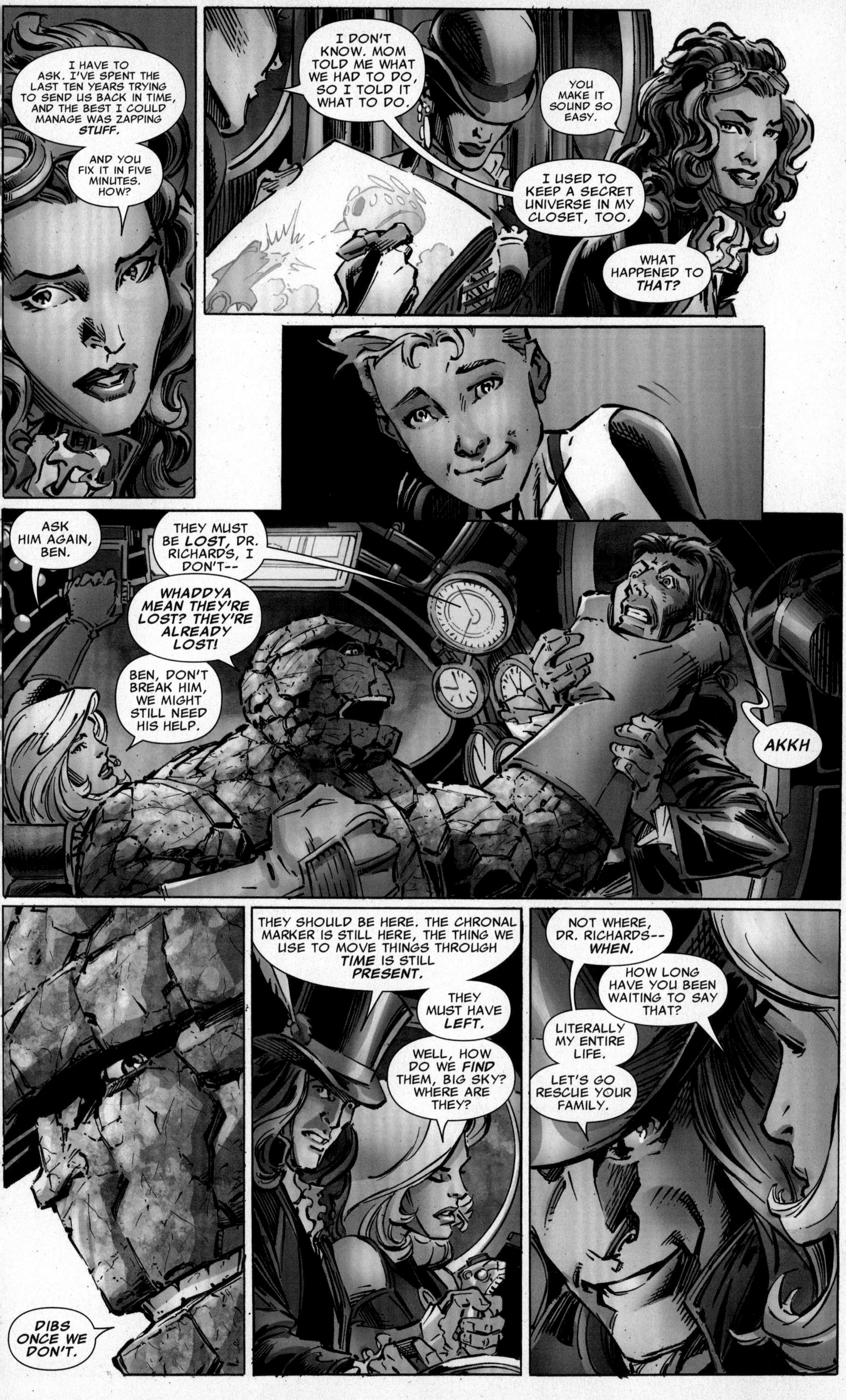
I HAVE TO ASK. I'VE SPENT THE LAST TEN YEARS TRYING TO SEND US BACK IN TIME, AND THE BEST I COULD MANAGE WAS ZAPPING STUFF.
AND YOU FIX IT IN FIVE MINUTES. HOW?
I DON'T KNOW. MOM TOLD ME WHAT WE HAD TO DO, SO I TOLD IT WHAT TO DO.
YOU MAKE IT SOUND SO EASY.
I USED TO KEEP A SECRET UNIVERSE IN MY CLOSET, TOO.
WHAT HAPPENED TO THAT?
ASK HIM AGAIN, BEN.
THEY MUST BE LOST, DR. RICHARDS, I DON'T--
WHADDYA MEAN THEY'RE LOST? THEY'RE ALREADY LOST!
BEN, DON'T BREAK HIM, WE MIGHT STILL NEED HIS HELP.
AKKH
THEY SHOULD BE HERE. THE CHRONAL MARKER IS STILL HERE, THE THING WE USE TO MOVE THINGS THROUGH TIME IS STILL PRESENT.
THEY MUST HAVE LEFT.
WELL, HOW DO WE FIND THEM, BIG SKY? WHERE ARE THEY?
DIBS ONCE WE DON'T.
NOT WHERE, DR. RICHARDS-- WHEN.
HOW LONG HAVE YOU BEEN WAITING TO SAY THAT?
LITERALLY MY ENTIRE LIFE.
LET'S GO RESCUE YOUR FAMILY.

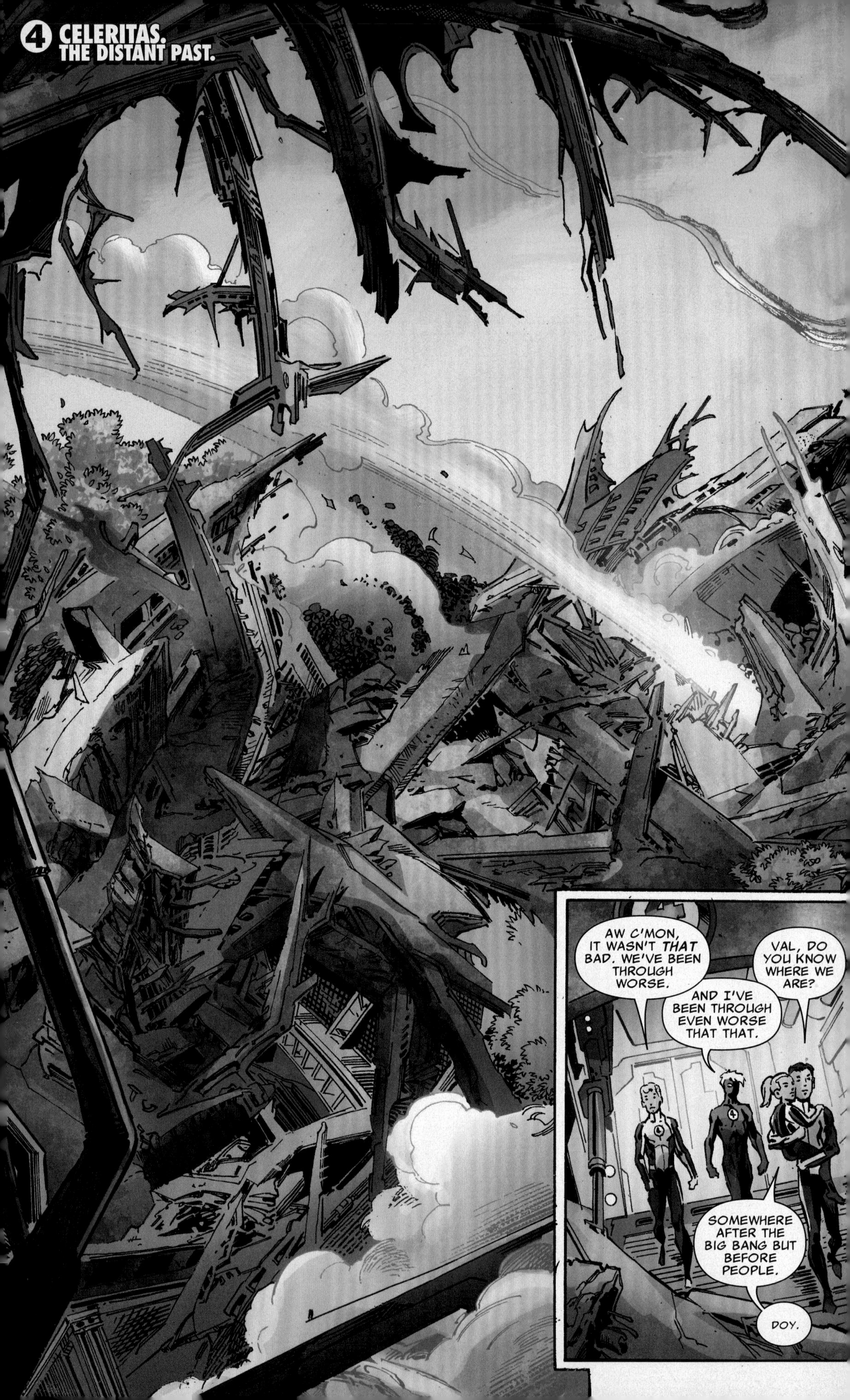
4 CELERITAS.
THE DISTANT PAST.
AW C'MON, IT WASN'T THAT BAD. WE'VE BEEN THROUGH WORSE.
AND I'VE BEEN THROUGH EVEN WORSE THAT THAT.
VAL, DO YOU KNOW WHERE WE ARE?
SOMEWHERE AFTER THE BIG BANG BUT BEFORE PEOPLE.
DOY.

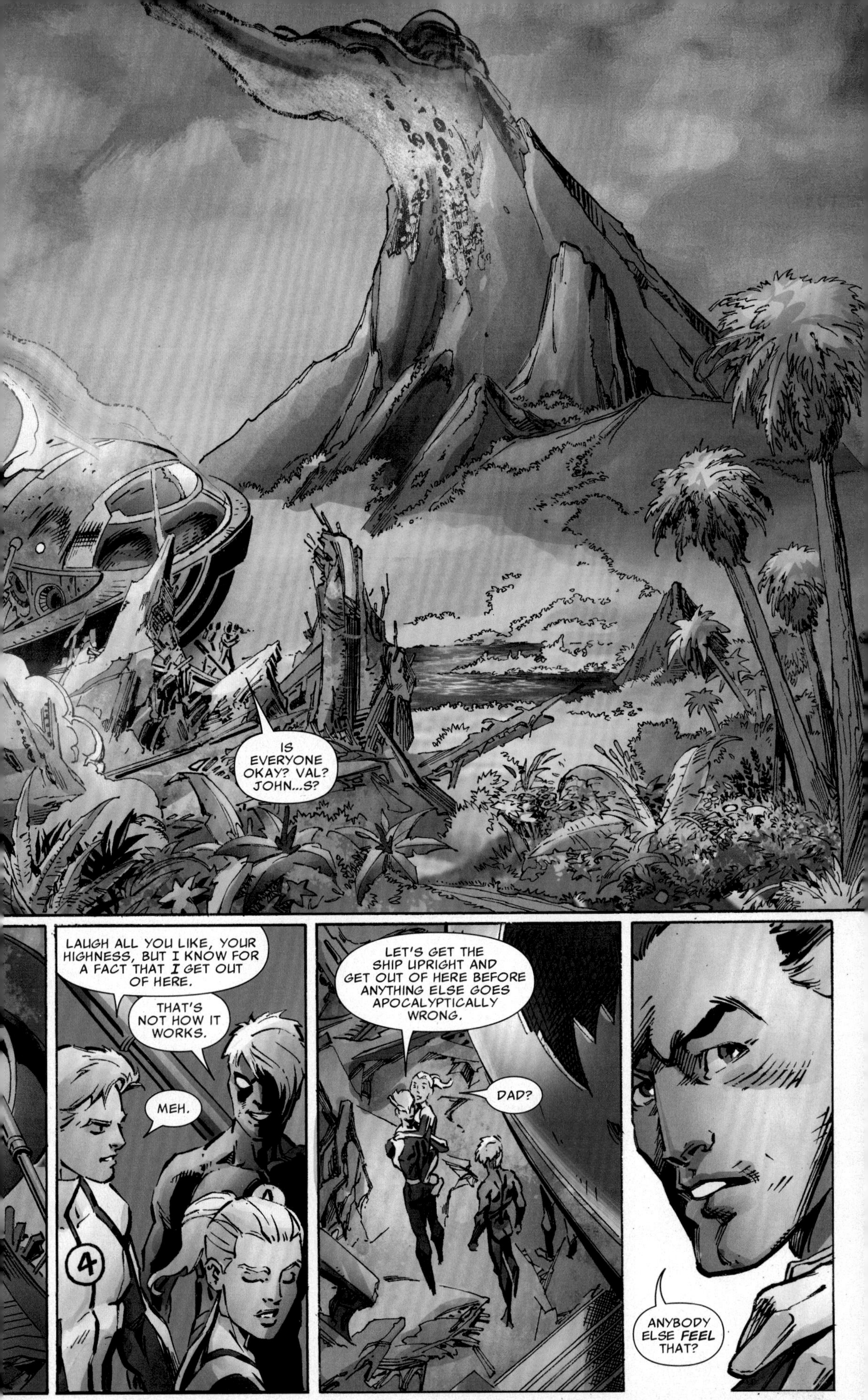
IS EVERYONE OKAY? VAL? JOHN...S?
LAUGH ALL YOU LIKE, YOUR HIGHNESS, BUT I KNOW FOR A FACT THAT I GET OUT OF HERE.
THAT'S NOT HOW IT WORKS.
MEH.
LET'S GET THE SHIP UPRIGHT AND GET OUT OF HERE BEFORE ANYTHING ELSE GOES APOCALYPTICALLY WRONG.
DAD?
ANYBODY ELSE FEEL THAT?

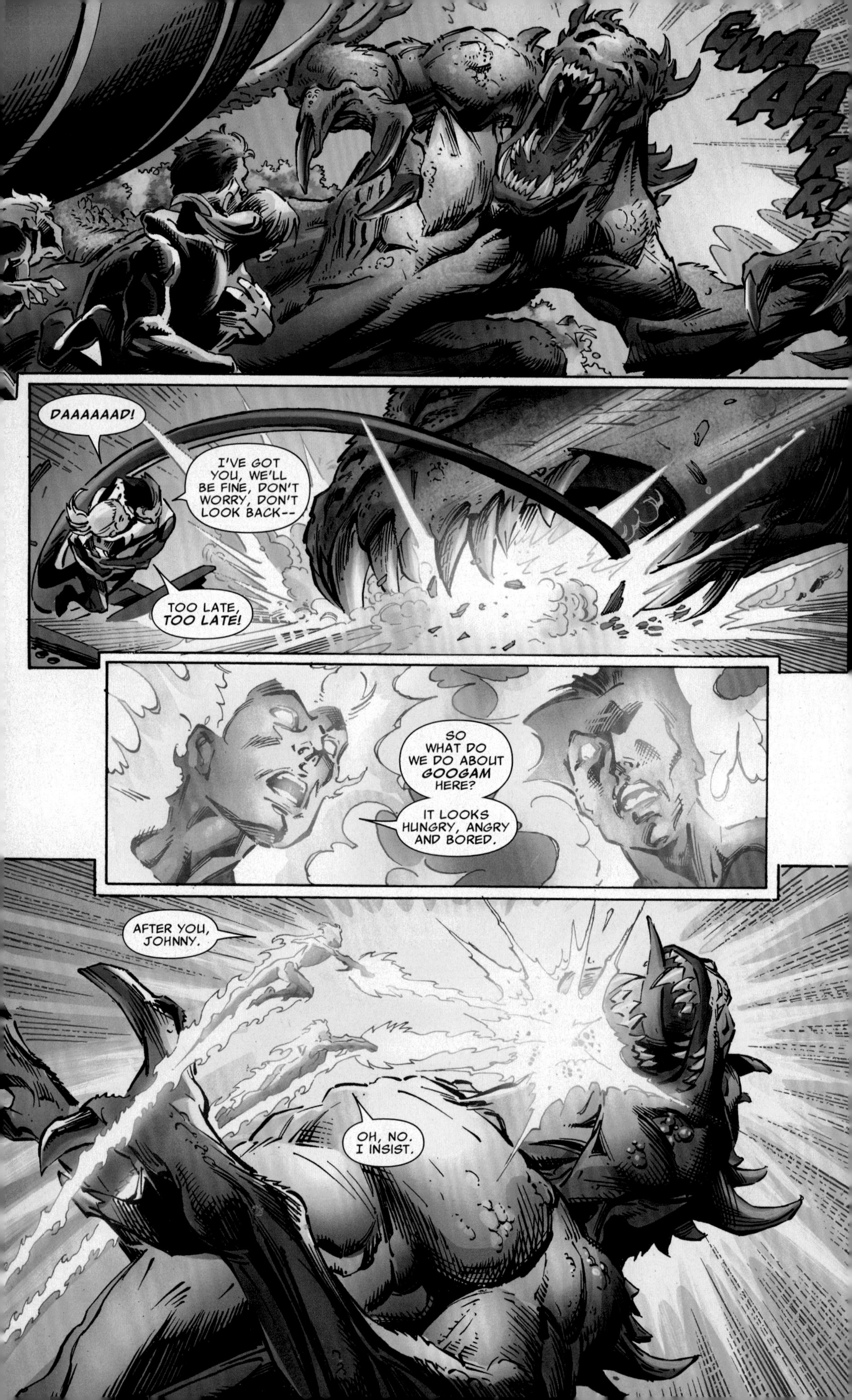
GWAAARRR!
DAAAAAAD!
I'VE GOT YOU, WE'LL BE FINE, DON'T WORRY, DON'T LOOK BACK--
TOO LATE, TOO LATE!
SO WHAT DO WE DO ABOUT GOOGAM HERE?
IT LOOKS HUNGRY, ANGRY AND BORED.
AFTER YOU, JOHNNY.
OH, NO. I INSIST.

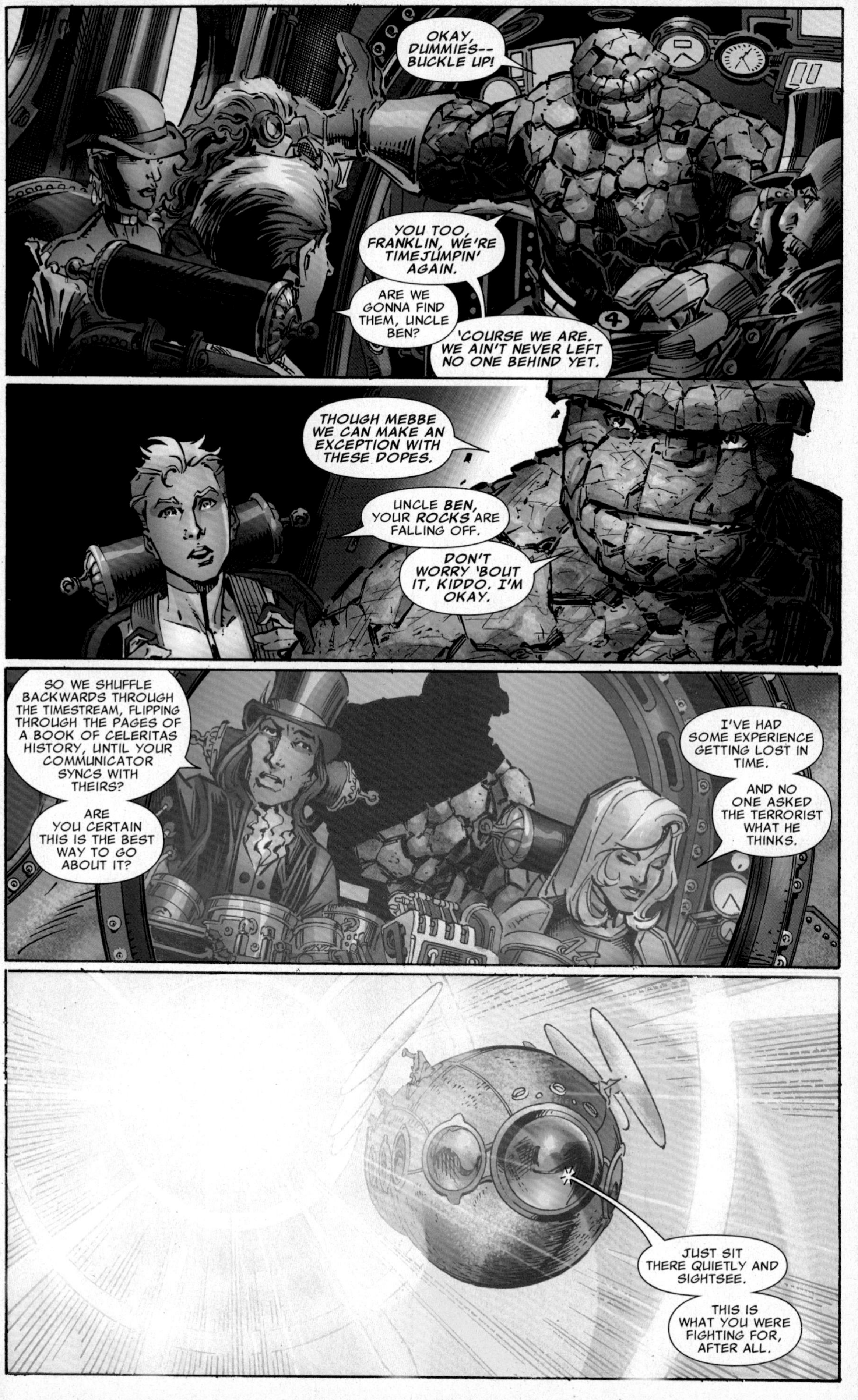
OKAY, DUMMIES-- BUCKLE UP!
YOU TOO, FRANKLIN, WE'RE TIMEJUMPIN' AGAIN.
ARE WE GONNA FIND THEM, UNCLE BEN?
'COURSE WE ARE. WE AIN'T NEVER LEFT NO ONE BEHIND YET.
THOUGH MEBBE WE CAN MAKE AN EXCEPTION WITH THESE DOPES.
UNCLE BEN, YOUR ROCKS ARE FALLING OFF.
DON'T WORRY 'BOUT IT, KIDDO. I'M OKAY.
SO WE SHUFFLE BACKWARDS THROUGH THE TIMESTREAM, FLIPPING THROUGH THE PAGES OF A BOOK OF CELERITAS HISTORY, UNTIL YOUR COMMUNICATOR SYNCS WITH THEIRS?
ARE YOU CERTAIN THIS IS THE BEST WAY TO GO ABOUT IT?
I'VE HAD SOME EXPERIENCE GETTING LOST IN TIME.
AND NO ONE ASKED THE TERRORIST WHAT HE THINKS.
JUST SIT THERE QUIETLY AND SIGHTSEE.
THIS IS WHAT YOU WERE FIGHTING FOR, AFTER ALL.

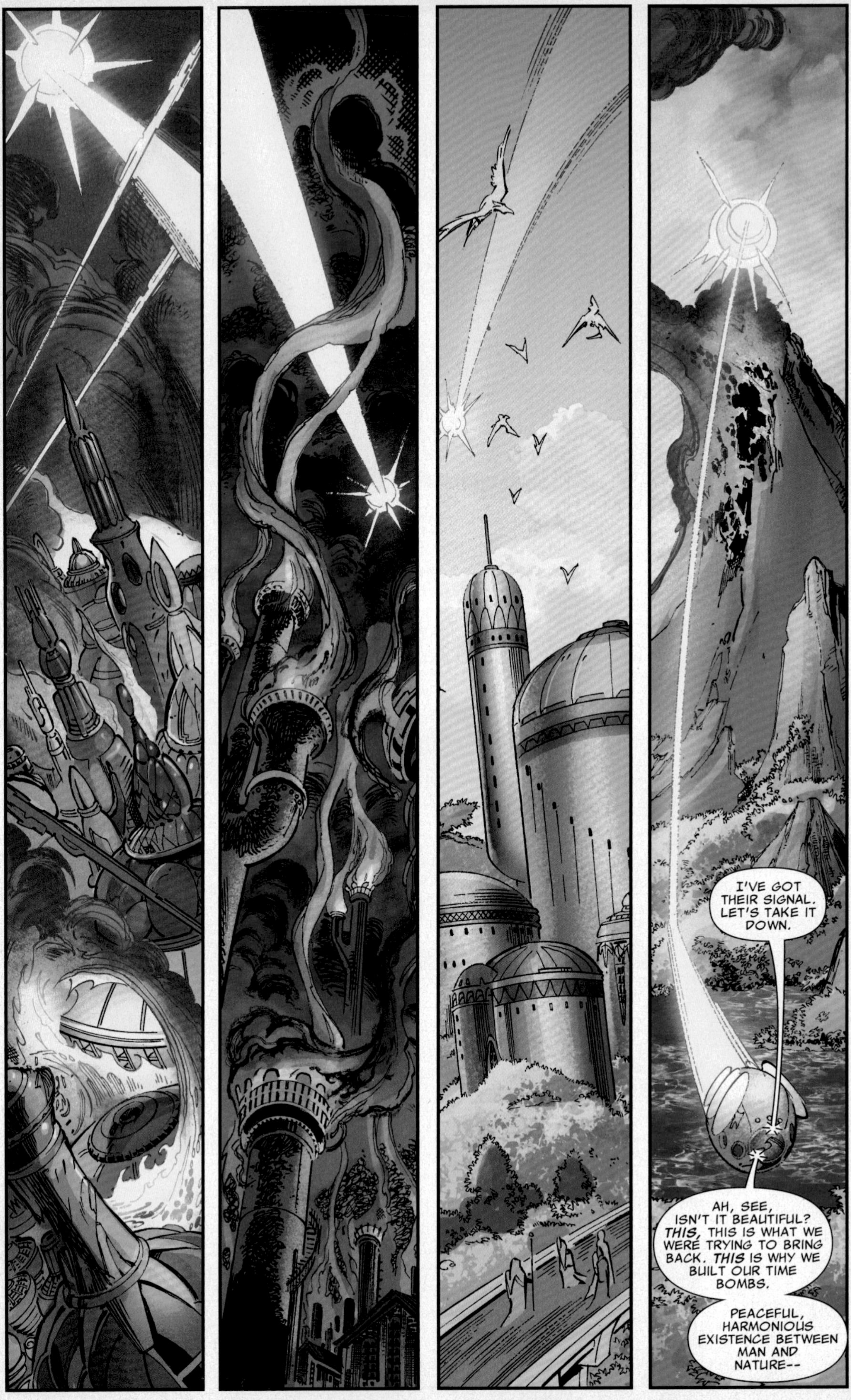
I'VE GOT THEIR SIGNAL. LET'S TAKE IT DOWN.
AH, SEE, ISN'T IT BEAUTIFUL? THIS, THIS IS WHAT WE WERE TRYING TO BRING BACK. THIS IS WHY WE BUILT OUR TIME BOMBS.
PEACEFUL, HARMONIOUS EXISTENCE BETWEEN MAN AND NATURE--

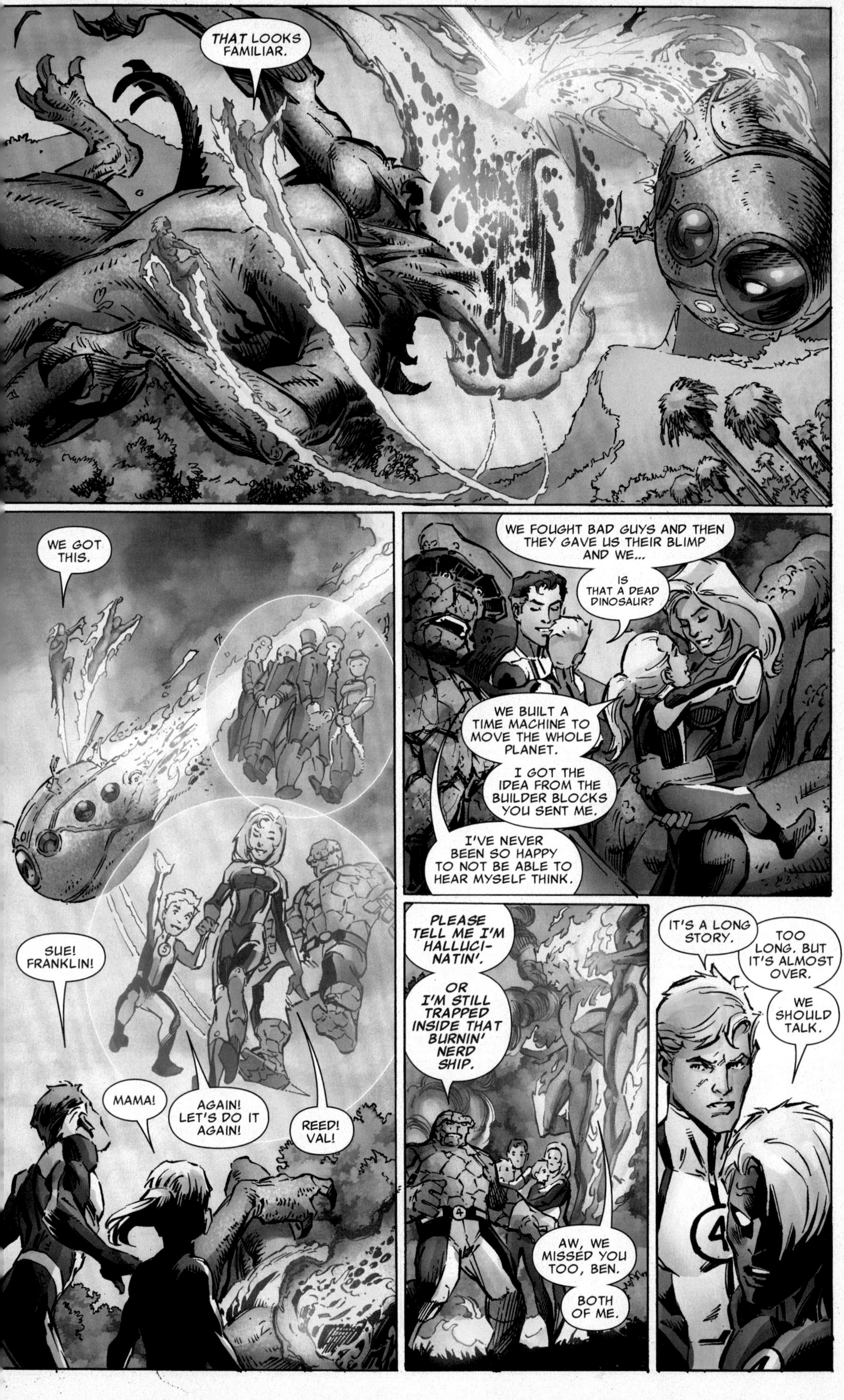

THAT LOOKS FAMILIAR.
WE GOT THIS.
SUE! FRANKLIN!
MAMA!
AGAIN! LET'S DO IT AGAIN!
REED! VAL!
WE FOUGHT BAD GUYS AND THEN THEY GAVE US THEIR BLIMP AND WE...
IS THAT A DEAD DINOSAUR?
WE BUILT A TIME MACHINE TO MOVE THE WHOLE PLANET.
I GOT THE IDEA FROM THE BUILDER BLOCKS YOU SENT ME.
I'VE NEVER BEEN SO HAPPY TO NOT BE ABLE TO HEAR MYSELF THINK.
PLEASE TELL ME I'M HALLUCI-NATIN'.
OR I'M STILL TRAPPED INSIDE THAT BURNIN' NERD SHIP.
AW, WE MISSED YOU TOO, BEN.
BOTH OF ME.
IT'S A LONG STORY.
TOO LONG. BUT IT'S ALMOST OVER.
WE SHOULD TALK.

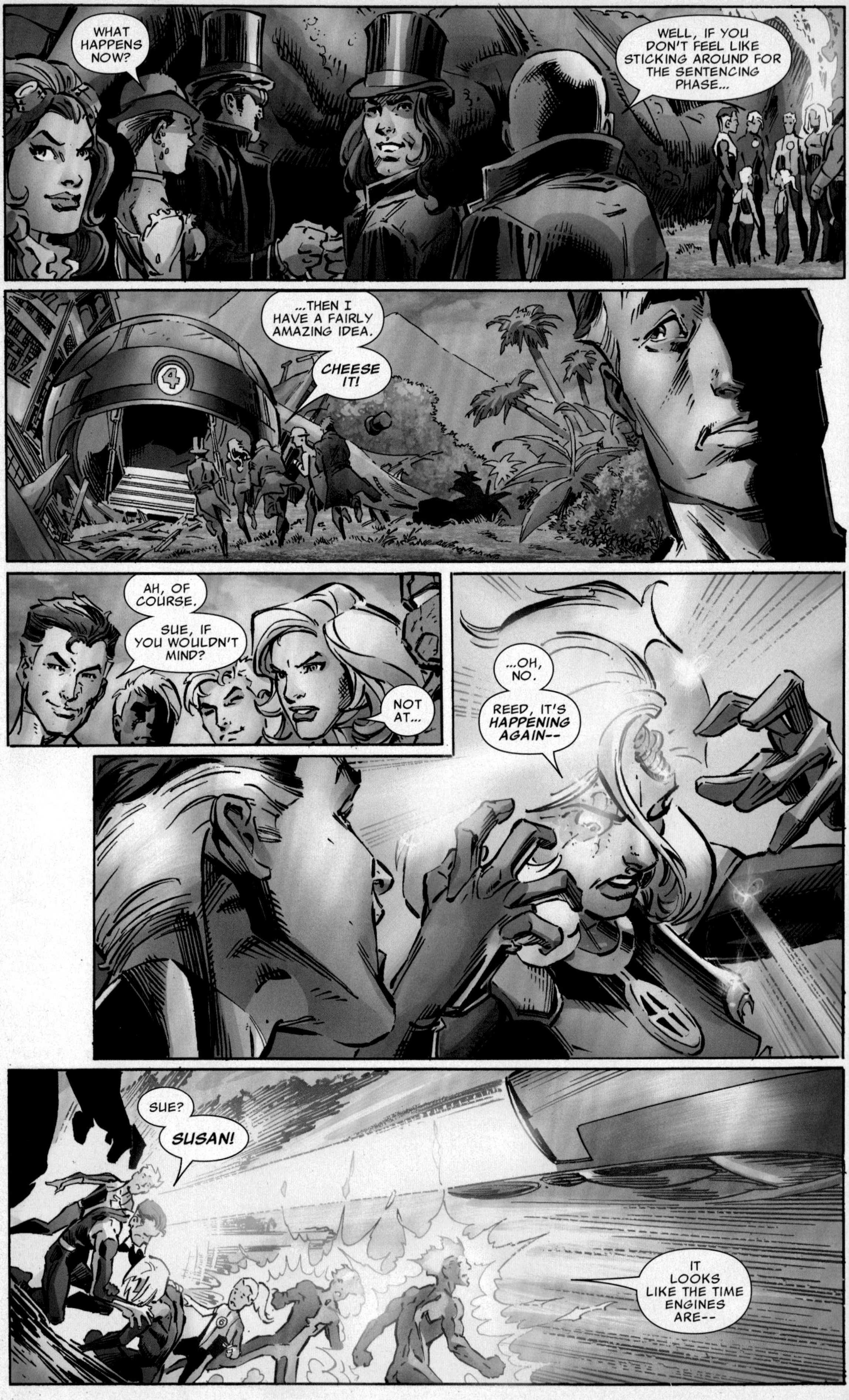
WHAT HAPPENS NOW?
WELL, IF YOU DON'T FEEL LIKE STICKING AROUND FOR THE SENTENCING PHASE...
...THEN I HAVE A FAIRLY AMAZING IDEA.
CHEESE IT!
AH, OF COURSE.
SUE, IF YOU WOULDN'T MIND?
NOT AT...
...OH, NO.
REED, IT'S HAPPENING AGAIN--
SUE?
SUSAN!
IT LOOKS LIKE THE TIME ENGINES ARE--

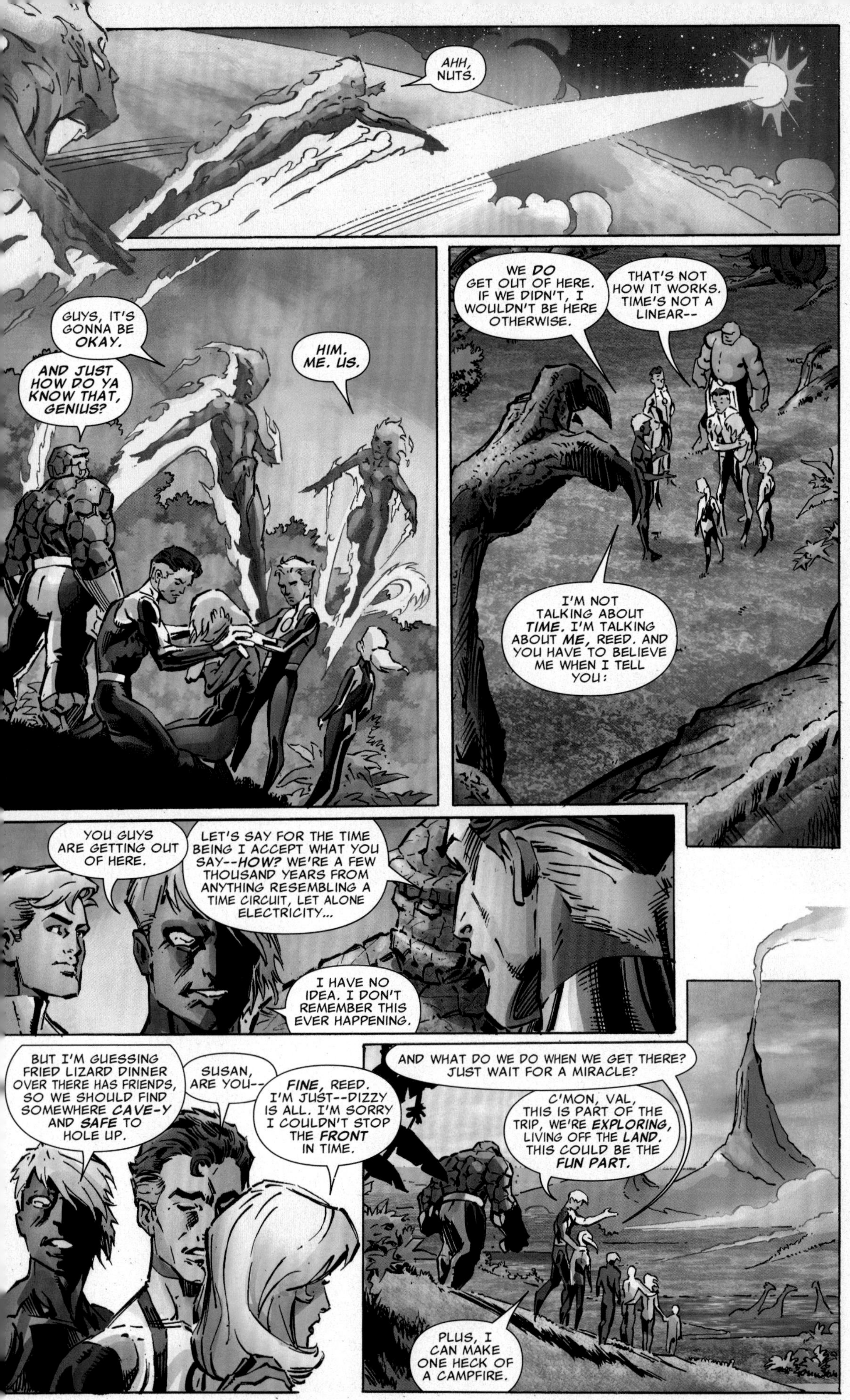
AHH, NUTS.
GUYS, IT'S GONNA BE OKAY.
AND JUST HOW DO YA KNOW THAT, GENIUS?
HIM. ME. US.
WE DO GET OUT OF HERE. IF WE DIDN'T, I WOULDN'T BE HERE OTHERWISE.
THAT'S NOT HOW IT WORKS. TIME'S NOT A LINEAR--
I'M NOT TALKING ABOUT TIME. I'M TALKING ABOUT ME, REED. AND YOU HAVE TO BELIEVE ME WHEN I TELL YOU:
YOU GUYS ARE GETTING OUT OF HERE.
LET'S SAY FOR THE TIME BEING I ACCEPT WHAT YOU SAY--HOW? WE'RE A FEW THOUSAND YEARS FROM ANYTHING RESEMBLING A TIME CIRCUIT, LET ALONE ELECTRICITY...
I HAVE NO IDEA. I DON'T REMEMBER THIS EVER HAPPENING.
BUT I'M GUESSING FRIED LIZARD DINNER OVER THERE HAS FRIENDS, SO WE SHOULD FIND SOMEWHERE CAVE-Y AND SAFE TO HOLE UP.
SUSAN, ARE YOU--
FINE, REED. I'M JUST--DIZZY IS ALL. I'M SORRY I COULDN'T STOP THE FRONT IN TIME.
AND WHAT DO WE DO WHEN WE GET THERE? JUST WAIT FOR A MIRACLE?
C'MON, VAL, THIS IS PART OF THE TRIP, WE'RE EXPLORING, LIVING OFF THE LAND. THIS COULD BE THE FUN PART.
PLUS, I CAN MAKE ONE HECK OF A CAMPFIRE.

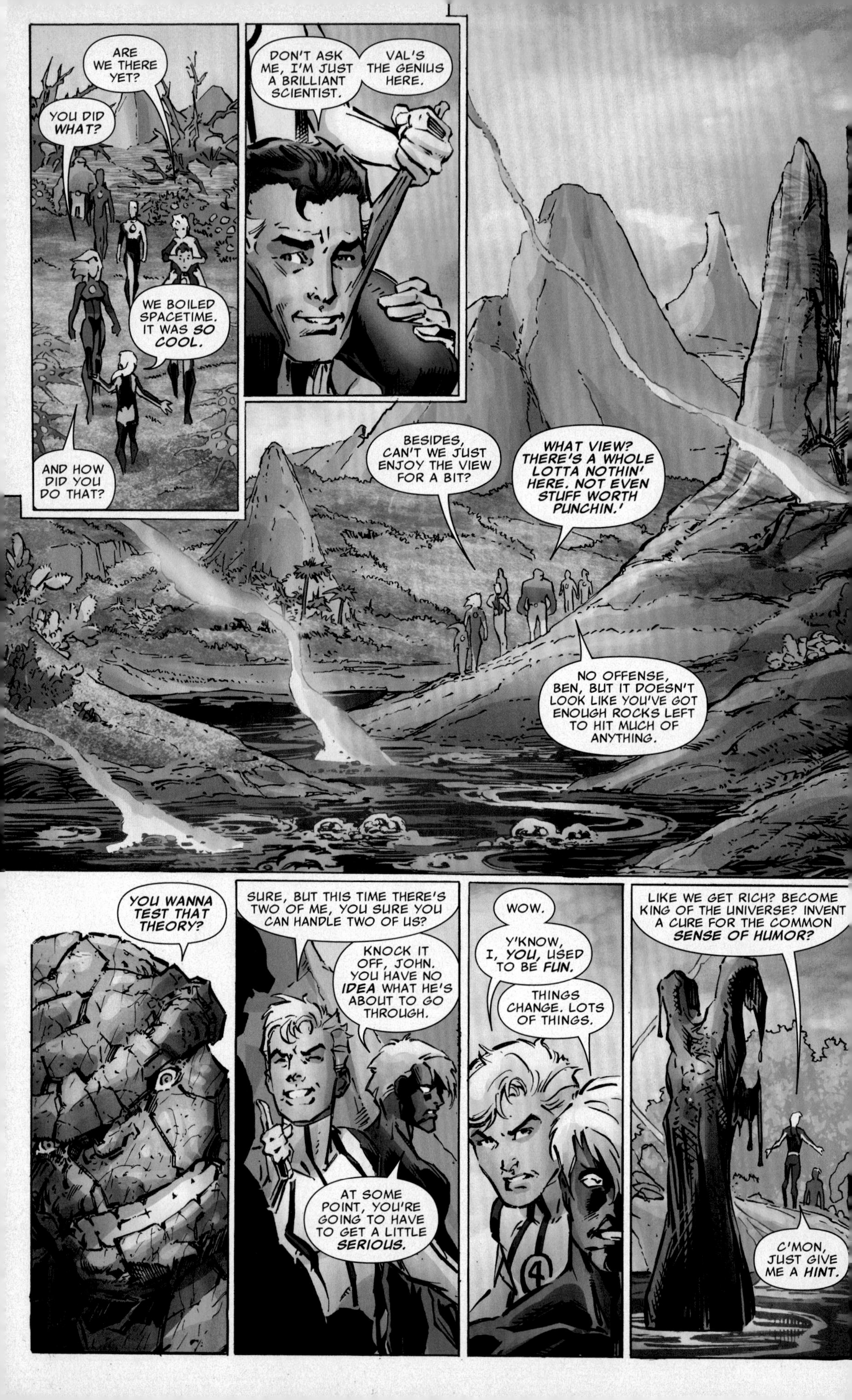
ARE WE THERE YET?
YOU DID WHAT?
WE BOILED SPACETIME. IT WAS SO COOL.
AND HOW DID YOU DO THAT?
DON'T ASK ME, I'M JUST A BRILLIANT SCIENTIST.
VAL'S THE GENIUS HERE.
BESIDES, CAN'T WE JUST ENJOY THE VIEW FOR A BIT?
WHAT VIEW? THERE'S A WHOLE LOTTA NOTHIN' HERE. NOT EVEN STUFF WORTH PUNCHIN.'
NO OFFENSE, BEN, BUT IT DOESN'T LOOK LIKE YOU'VE GOT ENOUGH ROCKS LEFT TO HIT MUCH OF ANYTHING.
YOU WANNA TEST THAT THEORY?
SURE, BUT THIS TIME THERE'S TWO OF ME, YOU SURE YOU CAN HANDLE TWO OF US?
KNOCK IT OFF, JOHN. YOU HAVE NO IDEA WHAT HE'S ABOUT TO GO THROUGH.
AT SOME POINT, YOU'RE GOING TO HAVE TO GET A LITTLE SERIOUS.
WOW.
Y'KNOW, I, YOU, USED TO BE FUN.
THINGS CHANGE. LOTS OF THINGS.
LIKE WE GET RICH? BECOME KING OF THE UNIVERSE? INVENT A CURE FOR THE COMMON SENSE OF HUMOR?
C'MON, JUST GIVE ME A HINT.

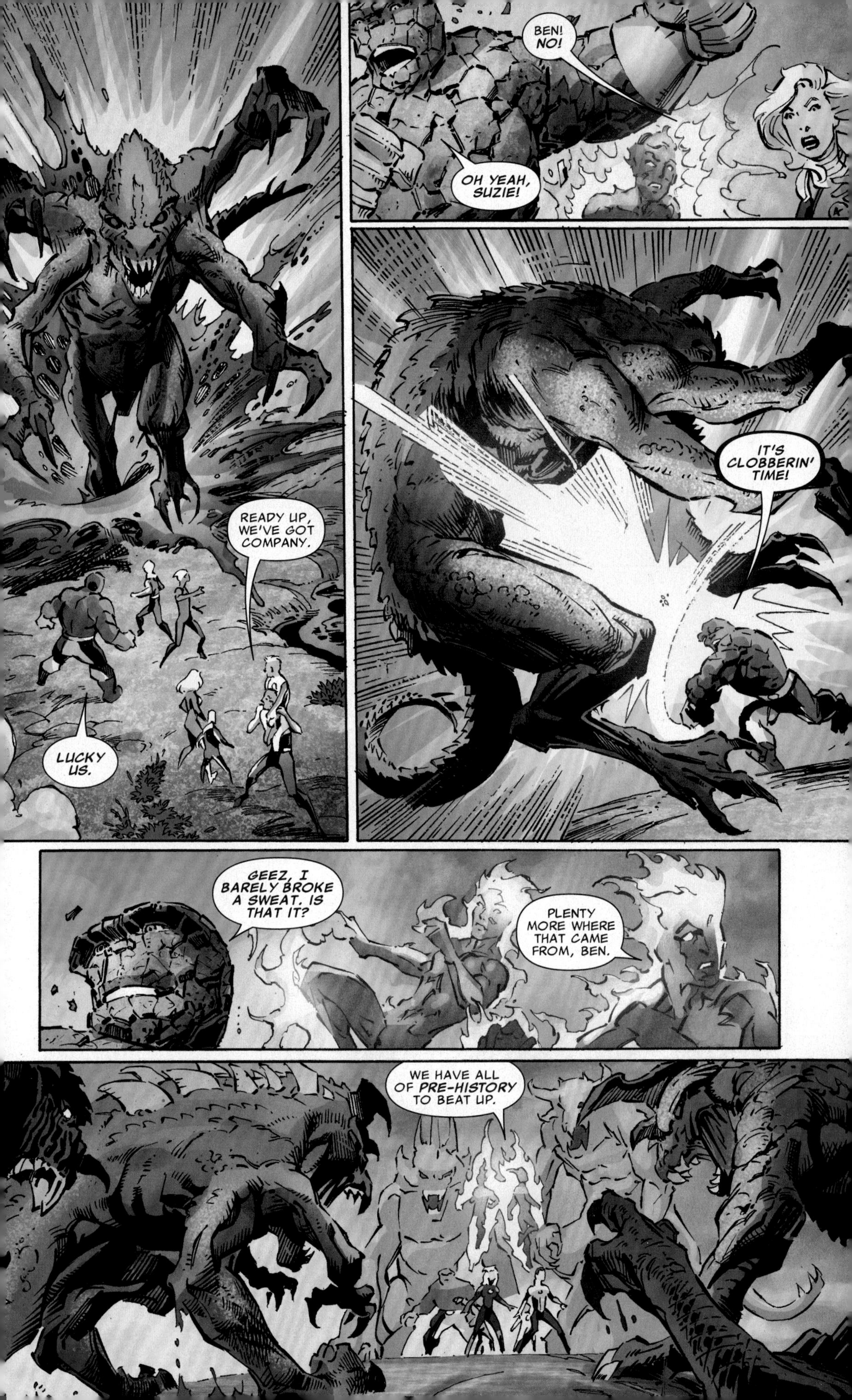
READY UP, WE'VE GOT COMPANY.
LUCKY US.
BEN! NO!
OH YEAH, SUZIE!
IT'S CLOBBERIN' TIME!
GEEZ, I BARELY BROKE A SWEAT. IS THAT IT?
PLENTY MORE WHERE THAT CAME FROM, BEN.
WE HAVE ALL OF PRE-HISTORY TO BEAT UP.

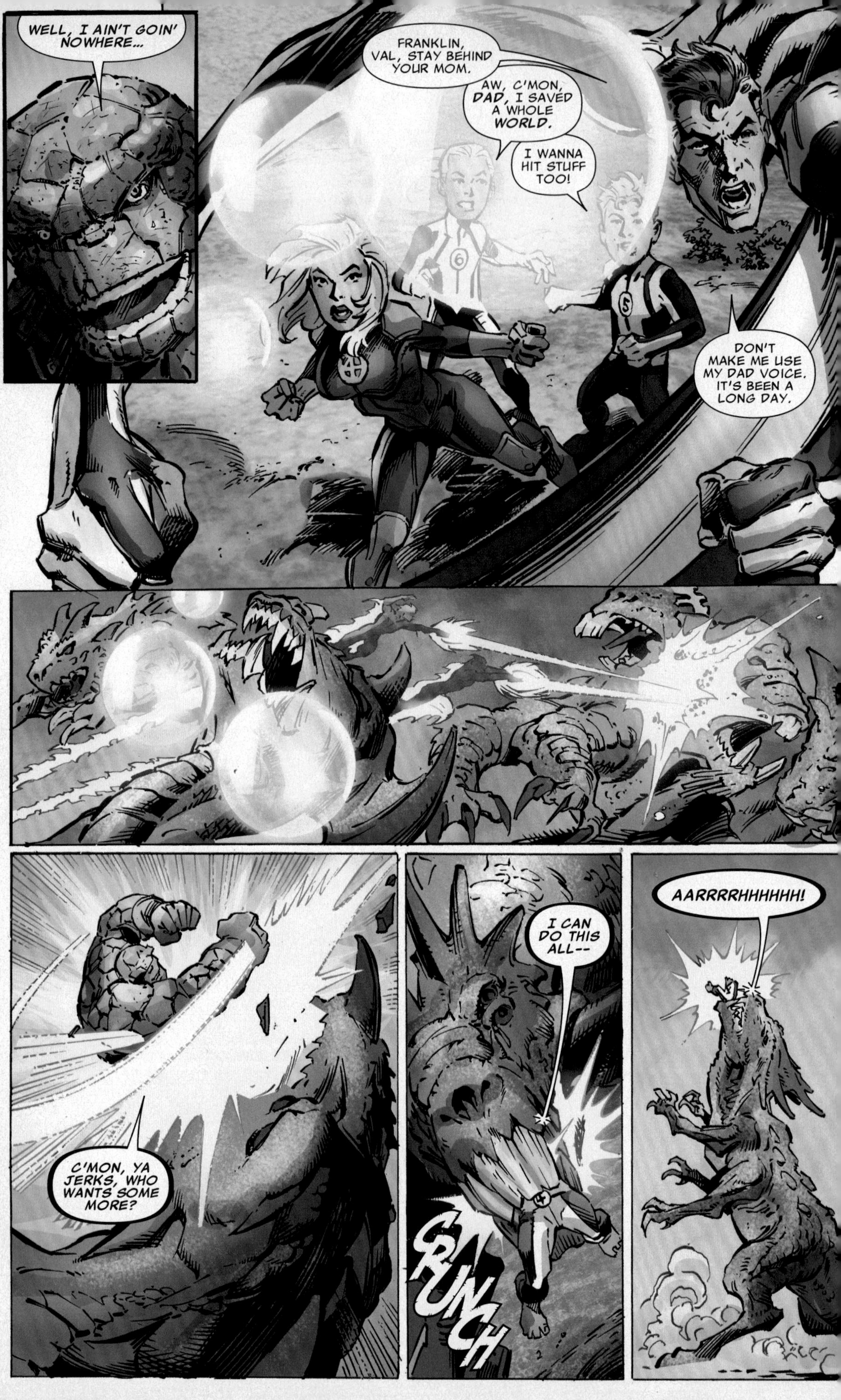
WELL, I AIN'T GOIN' NOWHERE...
FRANKLIN, VAL, STAY BEHIND YOUR MOM.
AW, C'MON, DAD, I SAVED A WHOLE WORLD.
I WANNA HIT STUFF TOO!
DON'T MAKE ME USE MY DAD VOICE. IT'S BEEN A LONG DAY.
C'MON, YA JERKS, WHO WANTS SOME MORE?
I CAN DO THIS ALL--
CRUNCH
AARRRRHHHHHH!

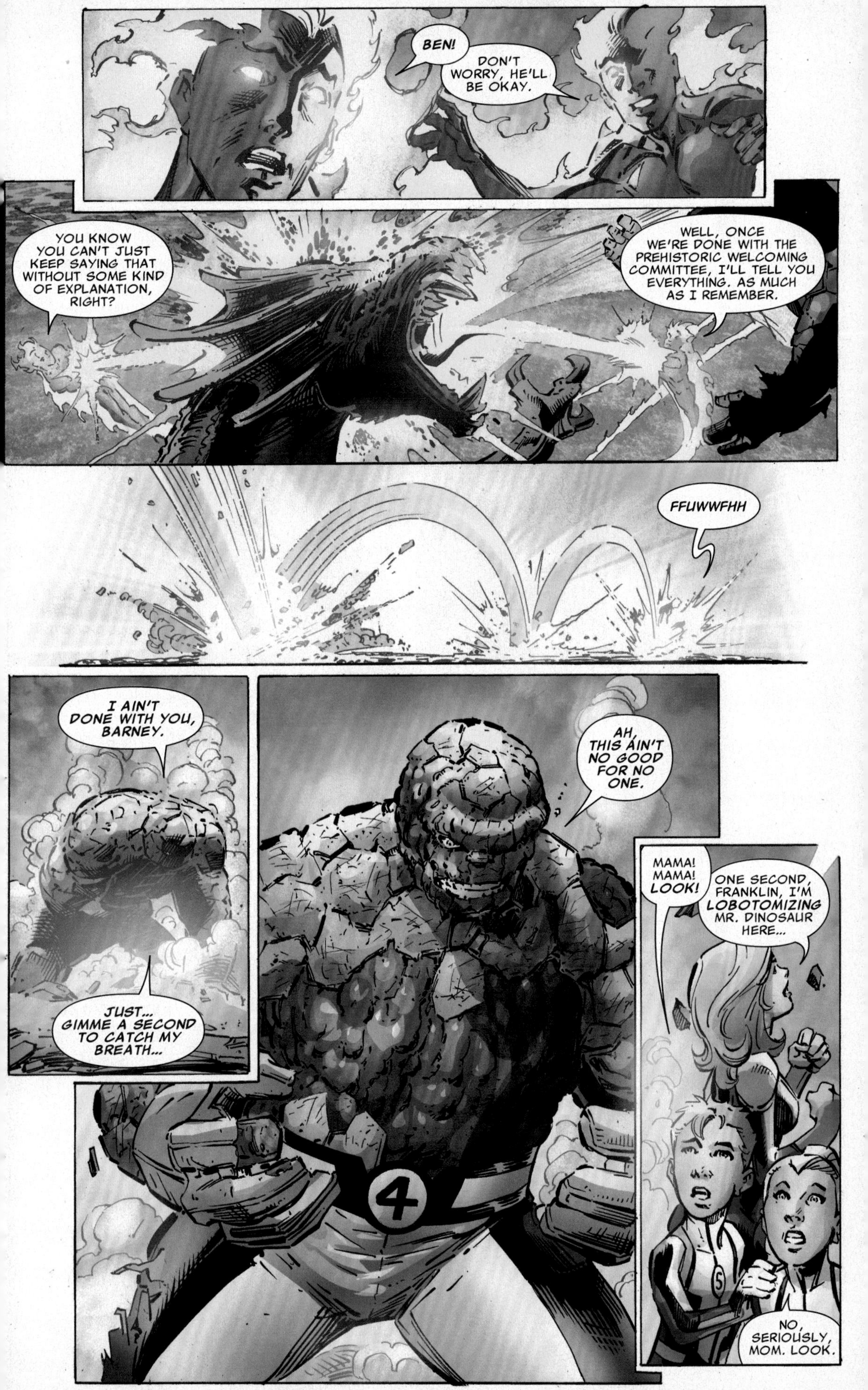

BEN!
DON'T WORRY, HE'LL BE OKAY.
YOU KNOW YOU CAN'T JUST KEEP SAYING THAT WITHOUT SOME KIND OF EXPLANATION, RIGHT?
WELL, ONCE WE'RE DONE WITH THE PREHISTORIC WELCOMING COMMITTEE, I'LL TELL YOU EVERYTHING. AS MUCH AS I REMEMBER.
FFUWWFHH
I AIN'T DONE WITH YOU, BARNEY.
JUST... GIMME A SECOND TO CATCH MY BREATH...
AH, THIS AIN'T NO GOOD FOR NO ONE.
MAMA! MAMA! LOOK!
ONE SECOND, FRANKLIN, I'M LOBOTOMIZING MR. DINOSAUR HERE...
NO, SERIOUSLY, MOM. LOOK.

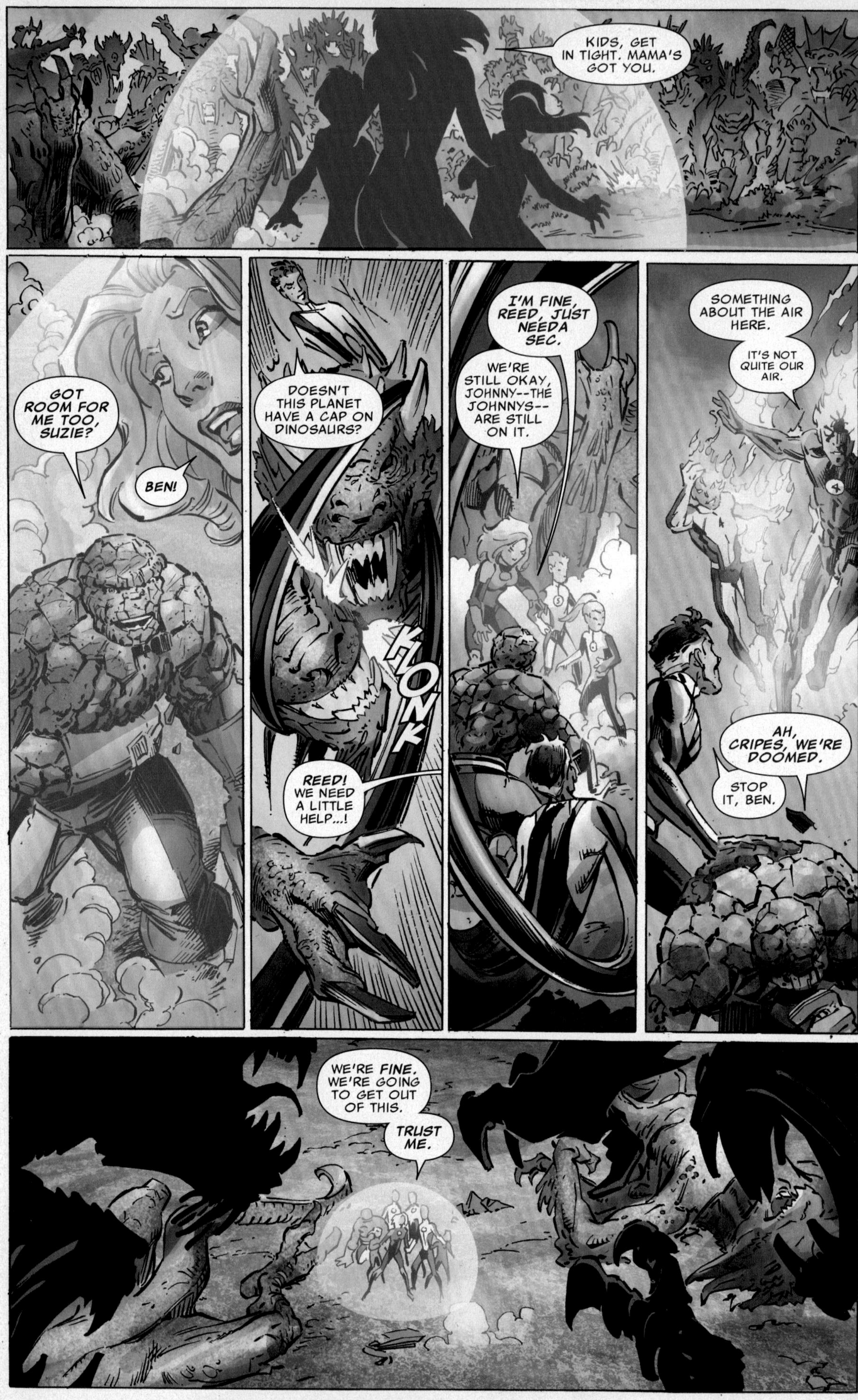
KIDS, GET IN TIGHT. MAMA'S GOT YOU.
GOT ROOM FOR ME TOO, SUZIE?
BEN!
DOESN'T THIS PLANET HAVE A CAP ON DINOSAURS?
KLONK
REED! WE NEED A LITTLE HELP...!
I'M FINE, REED, JUST NEEDA SEC.
WE'RE STILL OKAY, JOHNNY--THE JOHNNYS--ARE STILL ON IT.
SOMETHING ABOUT THE AIR HERE.
IT'S NOT QUITE OUR AIR.
AH, CRIPES, WE'RE DOOMED.
STOP IT, BEN.
WE'RE FINE. WE'RE GOING TO GET OUT OF THIS.
TRUST ME.

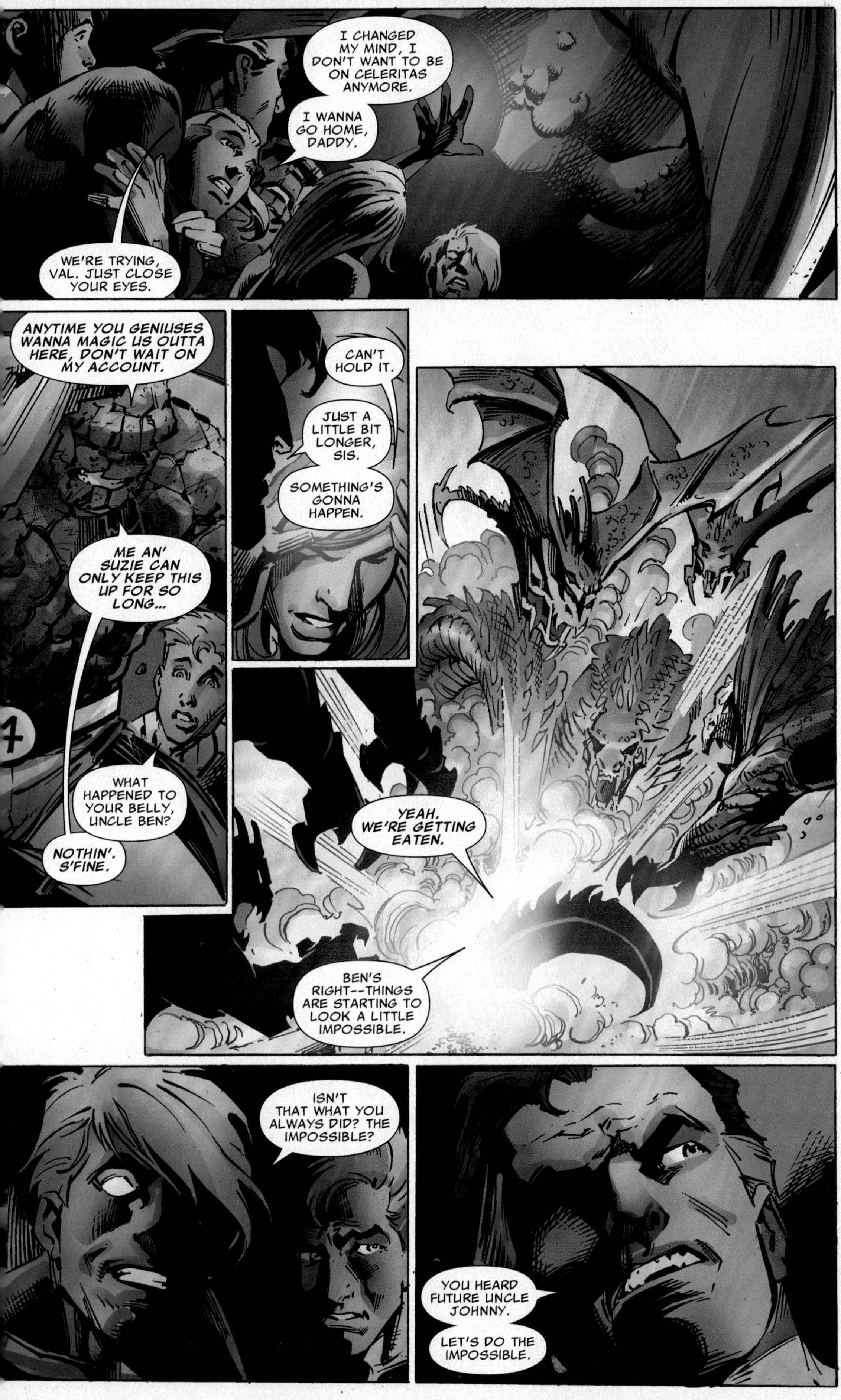

I CHANGED MY MIND, I DON'T WANT TO BE ON CELERITAS ANYMORE.
I WANNA GO HOME, DADDY.
WE'RE TRYING, VAL. JUST CLOSE YOUR EYES.
ANYTIME YOU GENIUSES WANNA MAGIC US OUTTA HERE, DON'T WAIT ON MY ACCOUNT.
ME AN' SUZIE CAN ONLY KEEP THIS UP FOR SO LONG...
WHAT HAPPENED TO YOUR BELLY, UNCLE BEN?
NOTHIN'. S'FINE.
CAN'T HOLD IT.
JUST A LITTLE BIT LONGER, SIS.
SOMETHING'S GONNA HAPPEN.
YEAH. WE'RE GETTING EATEN.
BEN'S RIGHT--THINGS ARE STARTING TO LOOK A LITTLE IMPOSSIBLE.
ISN'T THAT WHAT YOU ALWAYS DID? THE IMPOSSIBLE?
YOU HEARD FUTURE UNCLE JOHNNY.
LET'S DO THE IMPOSSIBLE.

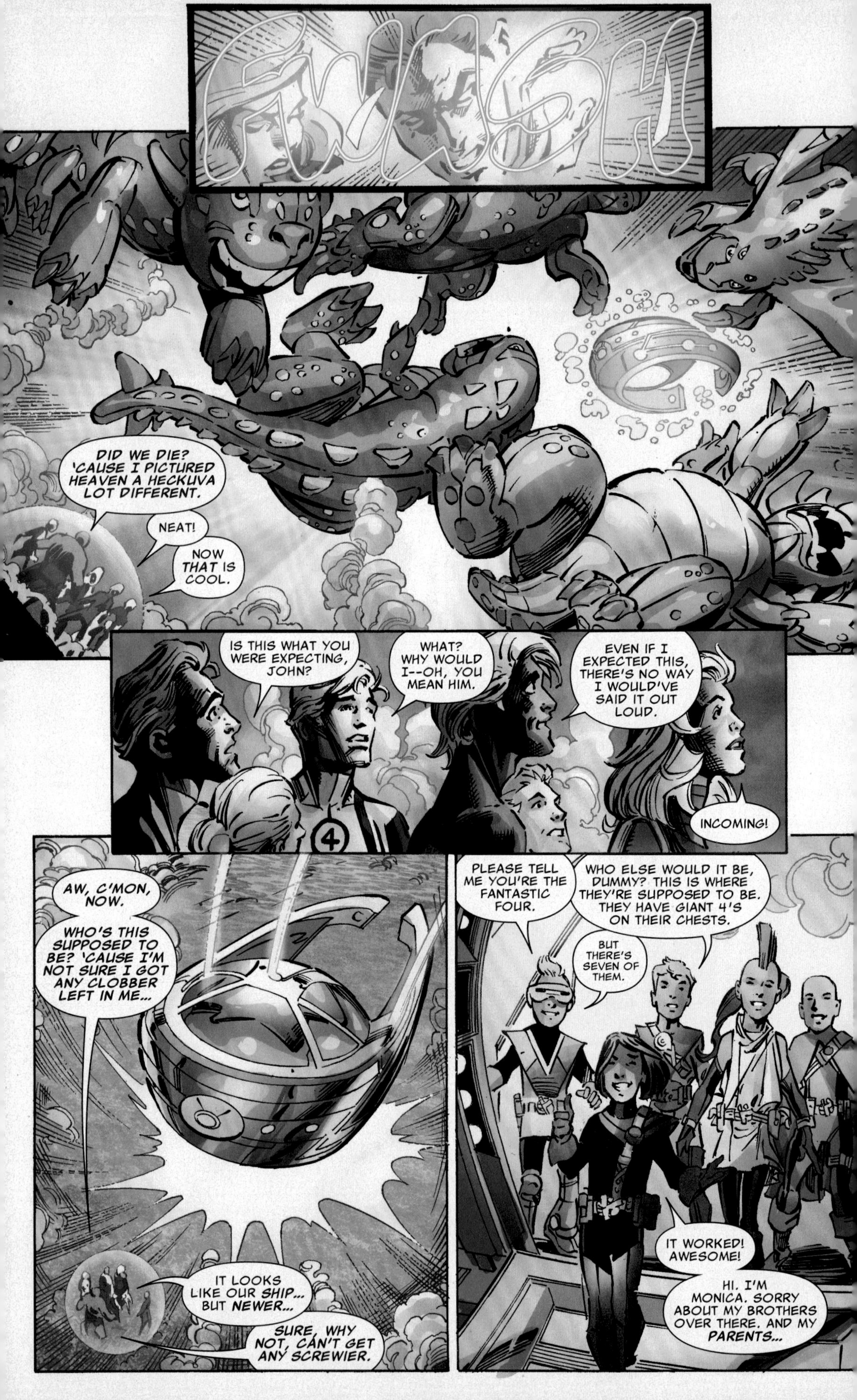
FWASH
DID WE DIE? 'CAUSE I PICTURED HEAVEN A HECKUVA LOT DIFFERENT.
NEAT!
NOW THAT IS COOL.
IS THIS WHAT YOU WERE EXPECTING, JOHN?
WHAT? WHY WOULD I--OH, YOU MEAN HIM.
EVEN IF I EXPECTED THIS, THERE'S NO WAY I WOULD'VE SAID IT OUT LOUD.
INCOMING!
AW, C'MON, NOW.
WHO'S THIS SUPPOSED TO BE? 'CAUSE I'M NOT SURE I GOT ANY CLOBBER LEFT IN ME...
IT LOOKS LIKE OUR SHIP... BUT NEWER...
SURE, WHY NOT, CAN'T GET ANY SCREWIER.
PLEASE TELL ME YOU'RE THE FANTASTIC FOUR.
WHO ELSE WOULD IT BE, DUMMY? THIS IS WHERE THEY'RE SUPPOSED TO BE. THEY HAVE GIANT 4'S ON THEIR CHESTS.
BUT THERE'S SEVEN OF THEM.
IT WORKED! AWESOME!
HI. I'M MONICA. SORRY ABOUT MY BROTHERS OVER THERE. AND MY PARENTS...

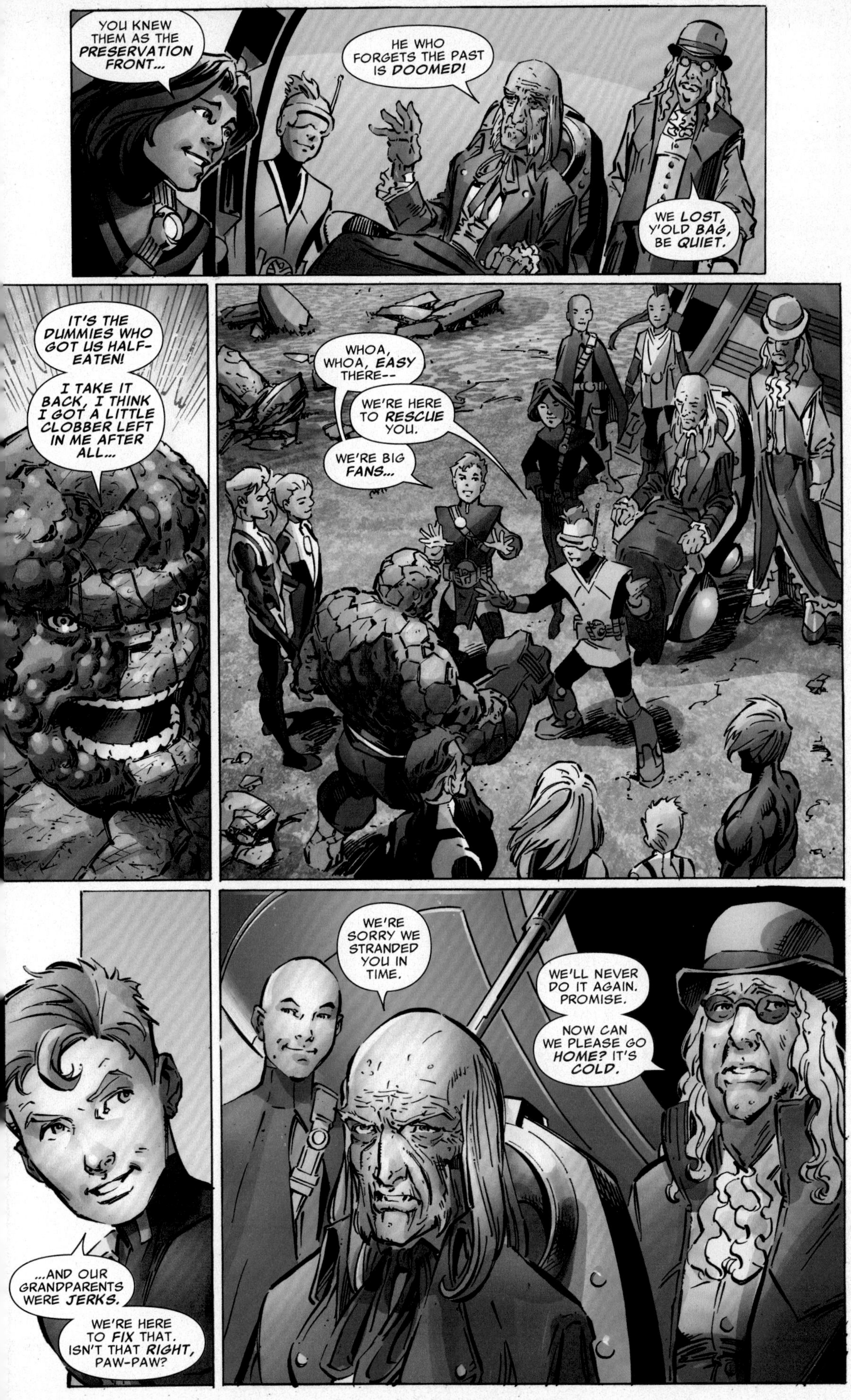
YOU KNEW THEM AS THE PRESERVATION FRONT...
HE WHO FORGETS THE PAST IS DOOMED!
WE LOST, Y'OLD BAG, BE QUIET.
IT'S THE DUMMIES WHO GOT US HALF-EATEN!
I TAKE IT BACK, I THINK I GOT A LITTLE CLOBBER LEFT IN ME AFTER ALL...
WHOA, WHOA, EASY THERE--
WE'RE HERE TO RESCUE YOU.
WE'RE BIG FANS...
...AND OUR GRANDPARENTS WERE JERKS.
WE'RE HERE TO FIX THAT. ISN'T THAT RIGHT, PAW-PAW?
WE'RE SORRY WE STRANDED YOU IN TIME.
WE'LL NEVER DO IT AGAIN. PROMISE.
NOW CAN WE PLEASE GO HOME? IT'S COLD.

THEY TOLD US THEY WERE GREAT ADVENTURERS, BUT WHEN WE GOT OLD ENOUGH TO SNOOP AROUND, WE FOUND OUT THEY WERE JUST THIEVES.

AND WORSE, THEY TRAPPED YOU GUYS HERE TO *DIE* TO DO IT.

HOW'D YOU GET THEM TO DO WHAT YOU WANTED, COME BACK HERE, ALL THAT STUFF?

LOCKED MYSELF IN MY ROOM, TOLD MY DAD I HATED HIM, STUFF LIKE THAT.

GOOD TO KNOW THE CLASSICS NEVER GO OUT OF STYLE...

VALERIA! HAVE YOU SEEN WHAT THEY'VE DONE TO THE SHIP?

WE'VE UPGRADED AND FIXED IT FOR YOU GUYS. SEEMED THE LEAST WE COULD DO.

SINCE MEE-MEE AND PAW-PAW TOOK OVER THE FUTURE, THE TIME TRAVEL RULES ARE WAY DIFFERENT. EVERYBODY DOES IT. IT'S PORTABLE NOW!

THAT SEEMS *EXTRAORDINARILY* DANGEROUS.

YOU SOUND JUST LIKE PAW-PAW BIG SKY...

THANKS AGAIN! WE OWE YOU! SAY HI TO THE SPACE MONSTERS WHEN THEY COME BACK?

SURE THING! GOOD LUCK IN THE DOOMED UNIVERSE!

DO WHAT NOW?

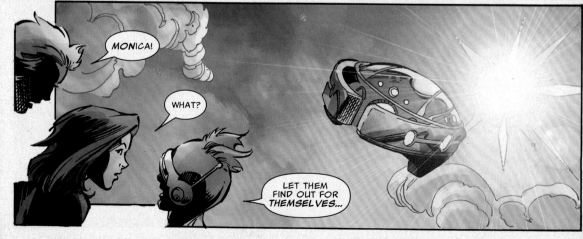

MONICA!

WHAT?

LET THEM FIND OUT FOR *THEMSELVES*...

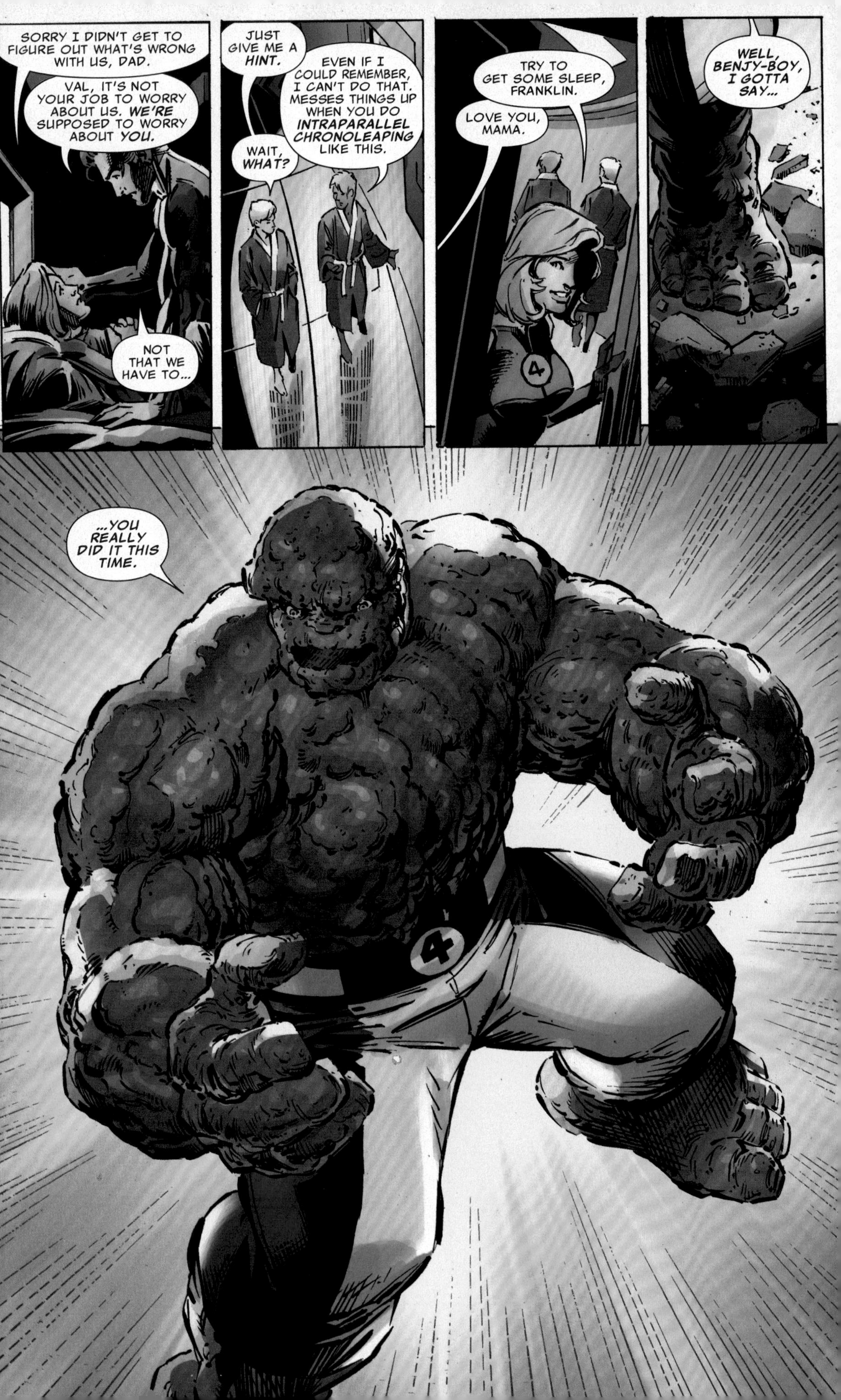
SORRY I DIDN'T GET TO FIGURE OUT WHAT'S WRONG WITH US, DAD.
VAL, IT'S NOT YOUR JOB TO WORRY ABOUT US. WE'RE SUPPOSED TO WORRY ABOUT YOU.
NOT THAT WE HAVE TO...
JUST GIVE ME A HINT.
EVEN IF I COULD REMEMBER, I CAN'T DO THAT. MESSES THINGS UP WHEN YOU DO INTRAPARALLEL CHRONOLEAPING LIKE THIS.
WAIT, WHAT?
TRY TO GET SOME SLEEP, FRANKLIN.
LOVE YOU, MAMA.
WELL, BENJY-BOY, I GOTTA SAY...
...YOU REALLY DID IT THIS TIME.

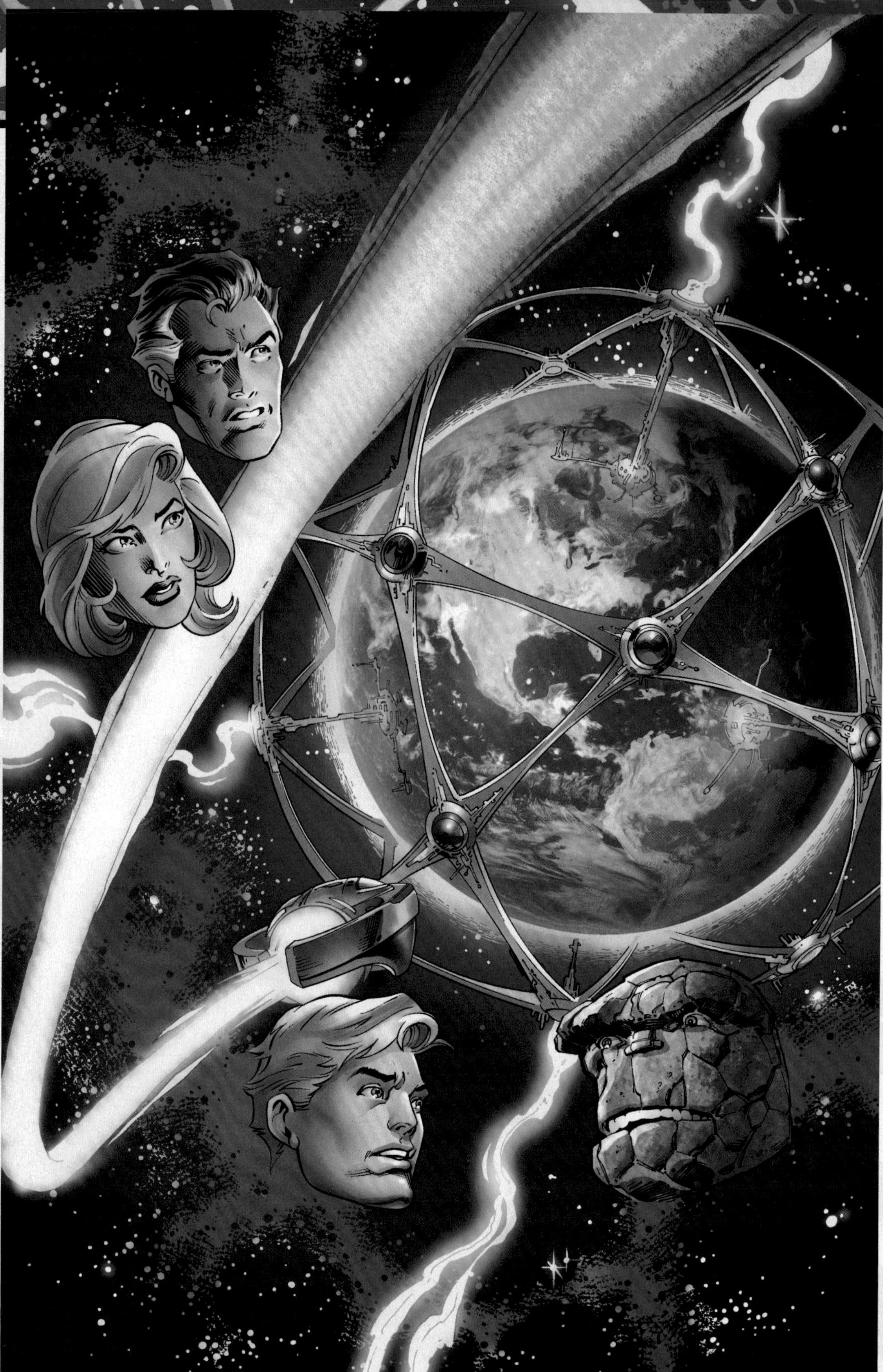

FANTASTIC FOUR #13 — “THE SCORCHED EARTH”

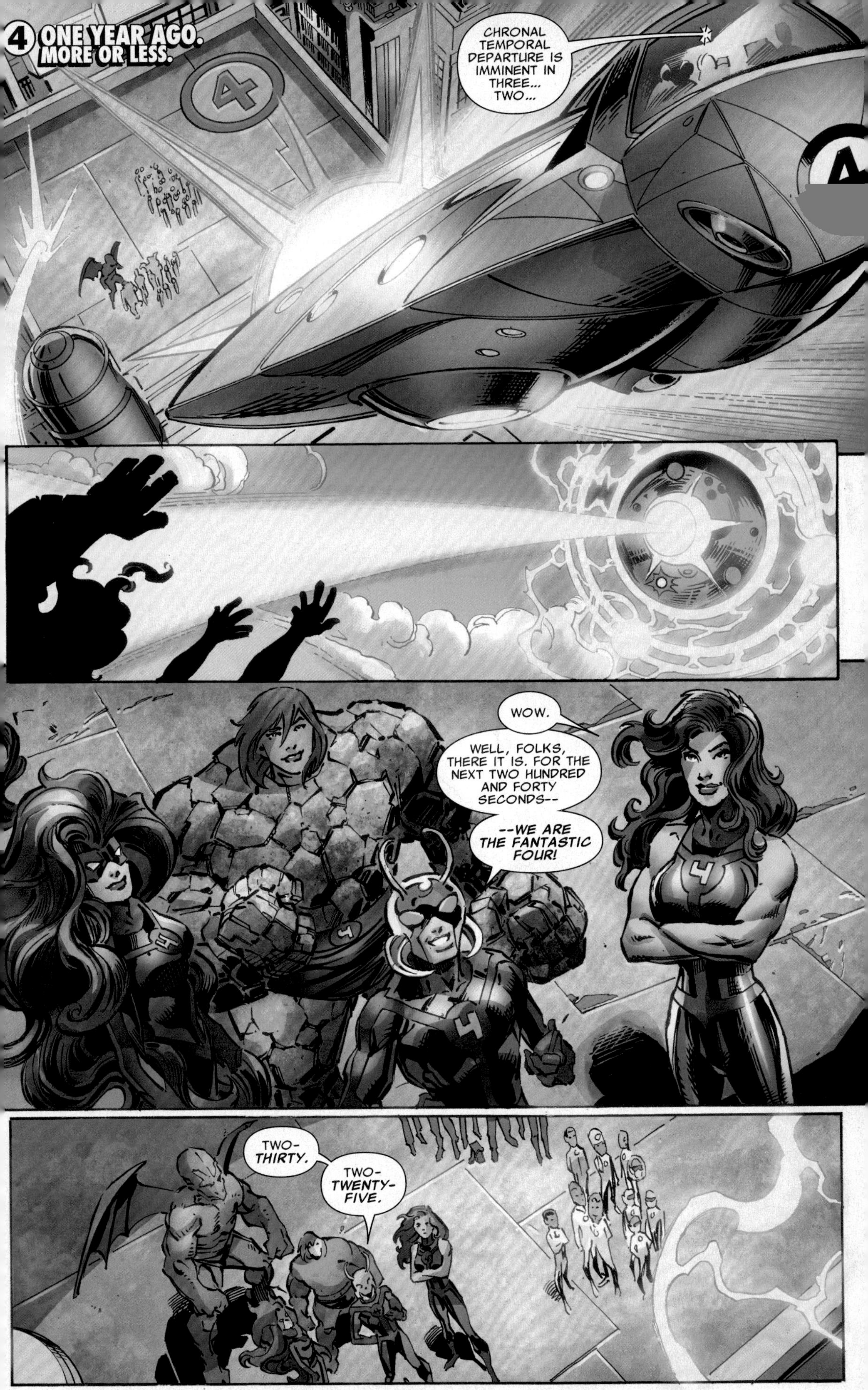
ONE YEAR AGO.
MORE OR LESS.
CHRONAL TEMPORAL DEPARTURE IS IMMINENT IN THREE... TWO...
WOW.
WELL, FOLKS, THERE IT IS. FOR THE NEXT TWO HUNDRED AND FORTY SECONDS--
--WE ARE THE FANTASTIC FOUR!
TWO-THIRTY.
TWO-TWENTY-FIVE.

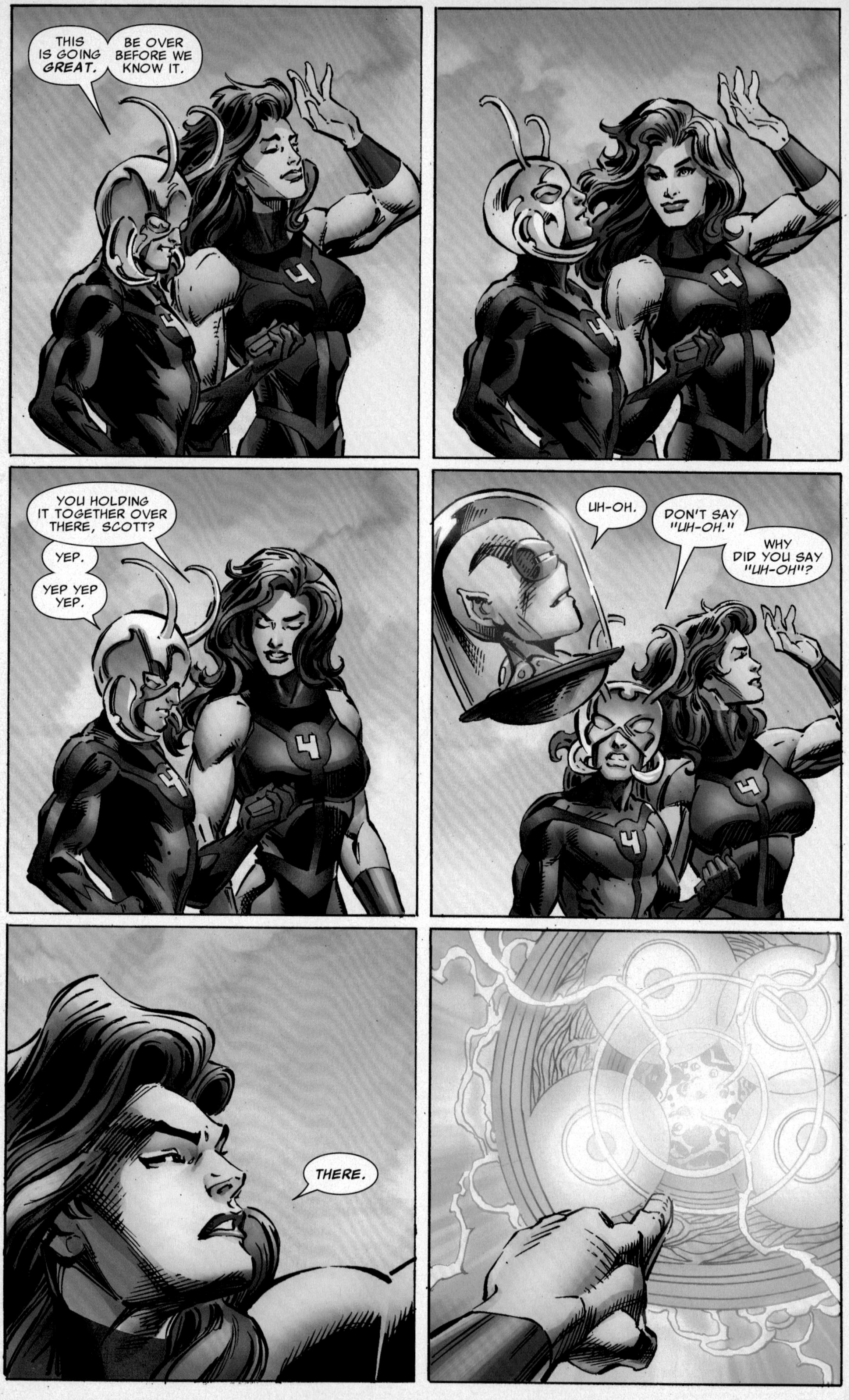
THIS IS GOING GREAT.
BE OVER BEFORE WE KNOW IT.
YOU HOLDING IT TOGETHER OVER THERE, SCOTT?
YEP.
YEP YEP YEP.
UH-OH.
DON'T SAY "UH-OH."
WHY DID YOU SAY "UH-OH"?
THERE.

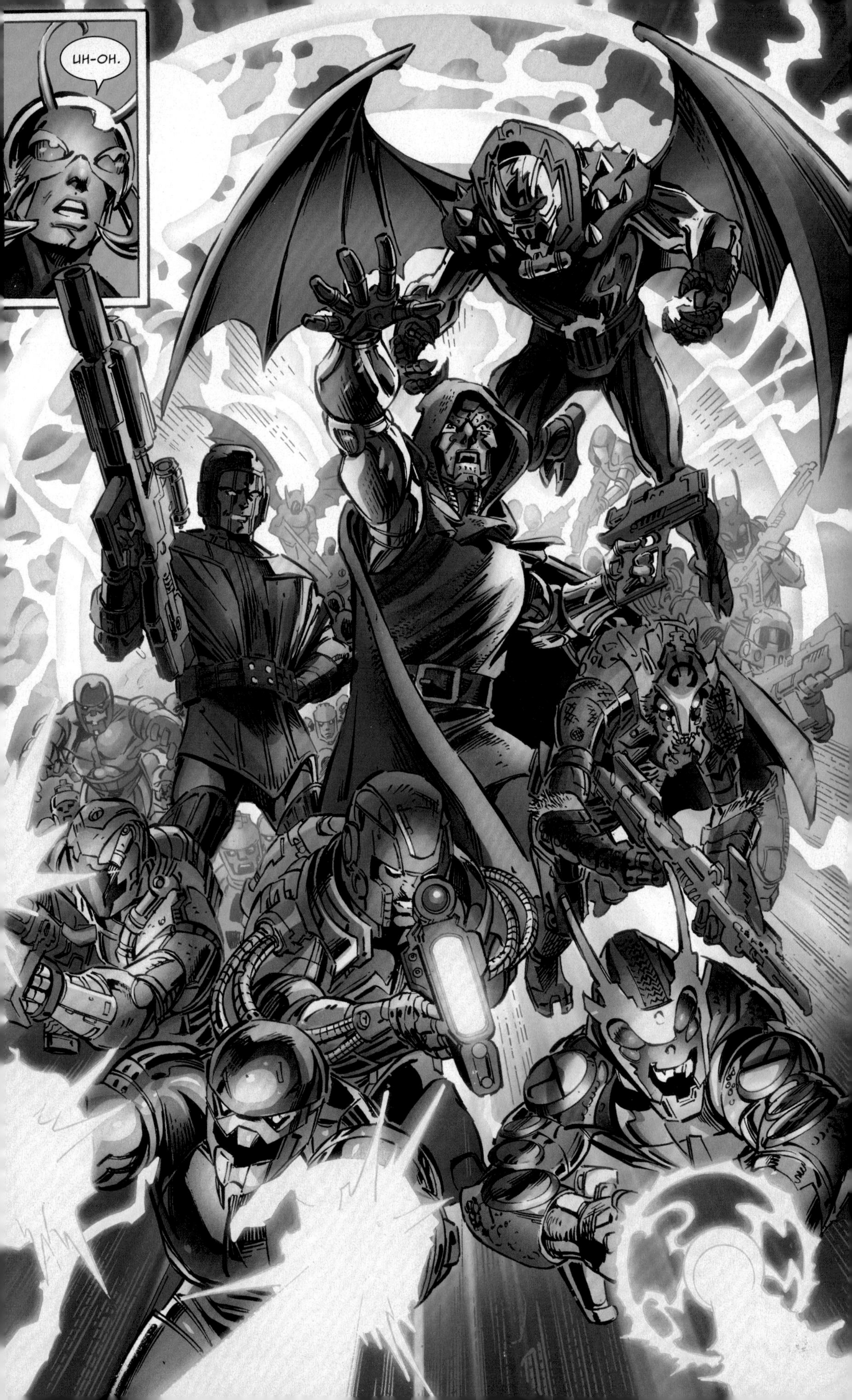
UH-OH.

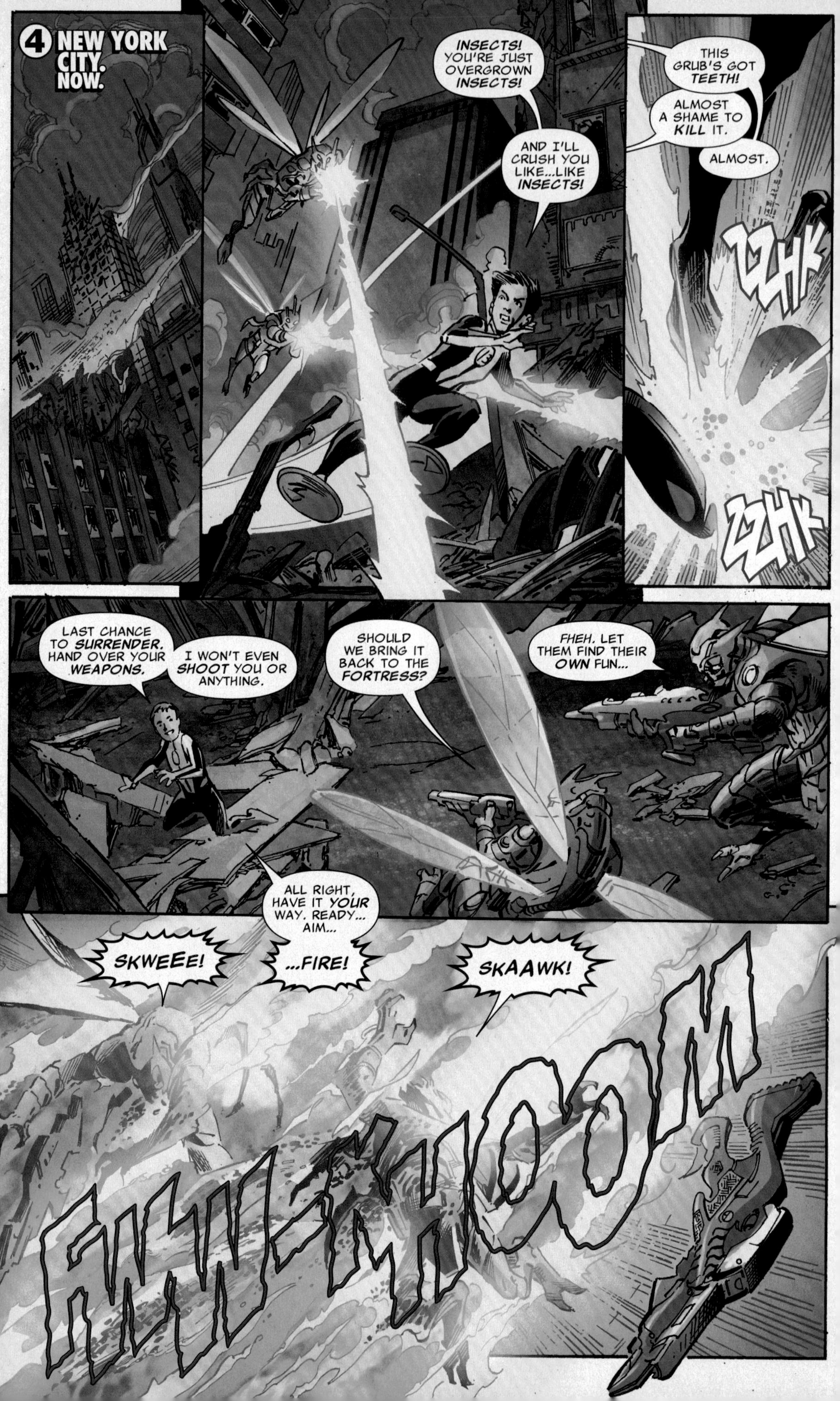
4 NEW YORK CITY. NOW.
INSECTS! YOU'RE JUST OVERGROWN INSECTS!
AND I'LL CRUSH YOU LIKE...LIKE INSECTS!
THIS GRUB'S GOT TEETH!
ALMOST A SHAME TO KILL IT.
ALMOST.
ZZHK
ZZHK
LAST CHANCE TO SURRENDER. HAND OVER YOUR WEAPONS.
I WON'T EVEN SHOOT YOU OR ANYTHING.
SHOULD WE BRING IT BACK TO THE FORTRESS?
FHEH. LET THEM FIND THEIR OWN FUN...
ALL RIGHT, HAVE IT YOUR WAY. READY... AIM...
SKWEEE!
...FIRE!
SKAAWK!

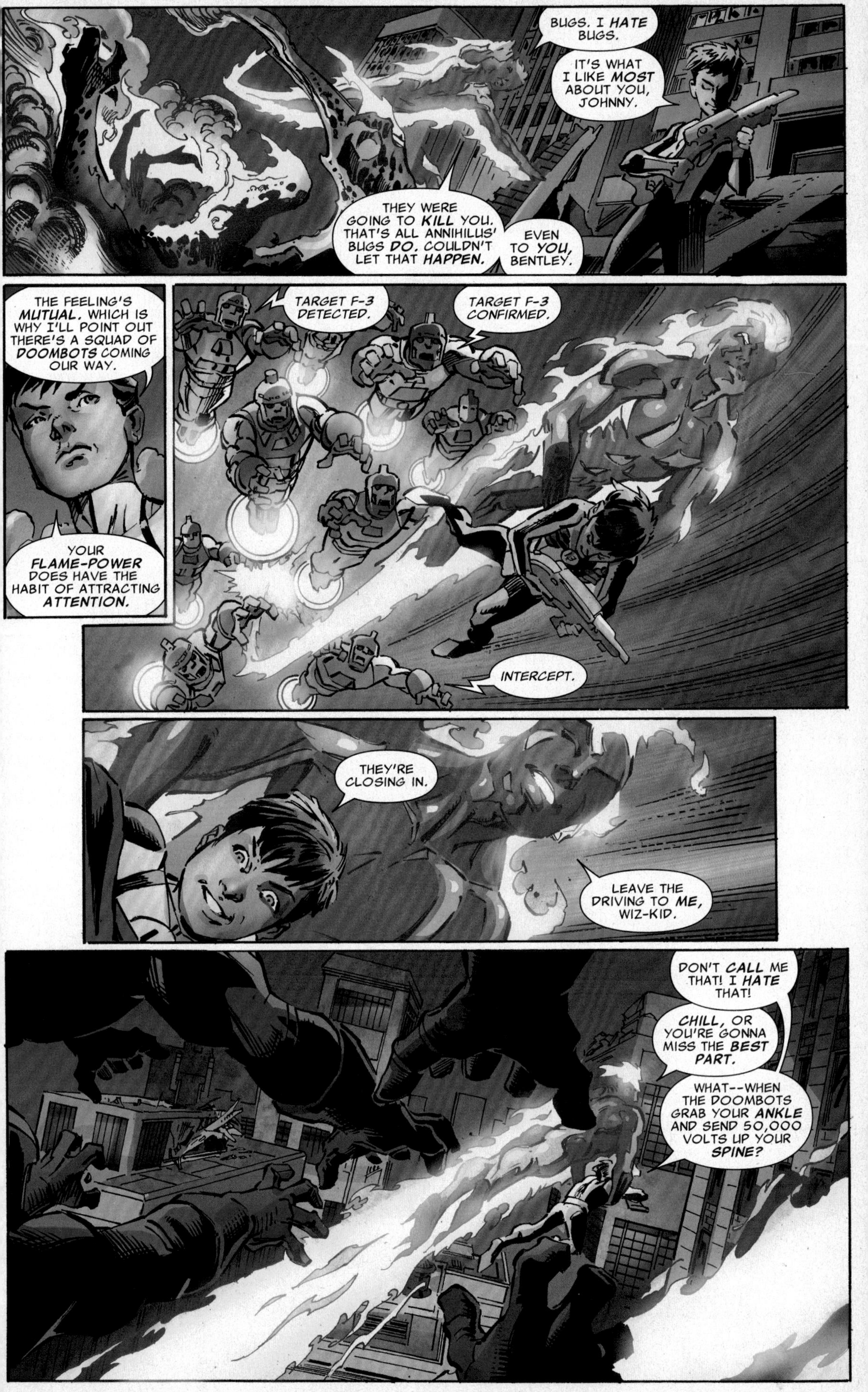
BUGS. I HATE BUGS.
IT'S WHAT I LIKE MOST ABOUT YOU, JOHNNY.
THEY WERE GOING TO KILL YOU. THAT'S ALL ANNIHILUS' BUGS DO. COULDN'T LET THAT HAPPEN.
EVEN TO YOU, BENTLEY.
THE FEELING'S MUTUAL. WHICH IS WHY I'LL POINT OUT THERE'S A SQUAD OF DOOMBOTS COMING OUR WAY.
YOUR FLAME-POWER DOES HAVE THE HABIT OF ATTRACTING ATTENTION.
TARGET F-3 DETECTED.
TARGET F-3 CONFIRMED.
INTERCEPT.
THEY'RE CLOSING IN.
LEAVE THE DRIVING TO ME, WIZ-KID.
DON'T CALL ME THAT! I HATE THAT!
CHILL, OR YOU'RE GONNA MISS THE BEST PART.
WHAT--WHEN THE DOOMBOTS GRAB YOUR ANKLE AND SEND 50,000 VOLTS UP YOUR SPINE?

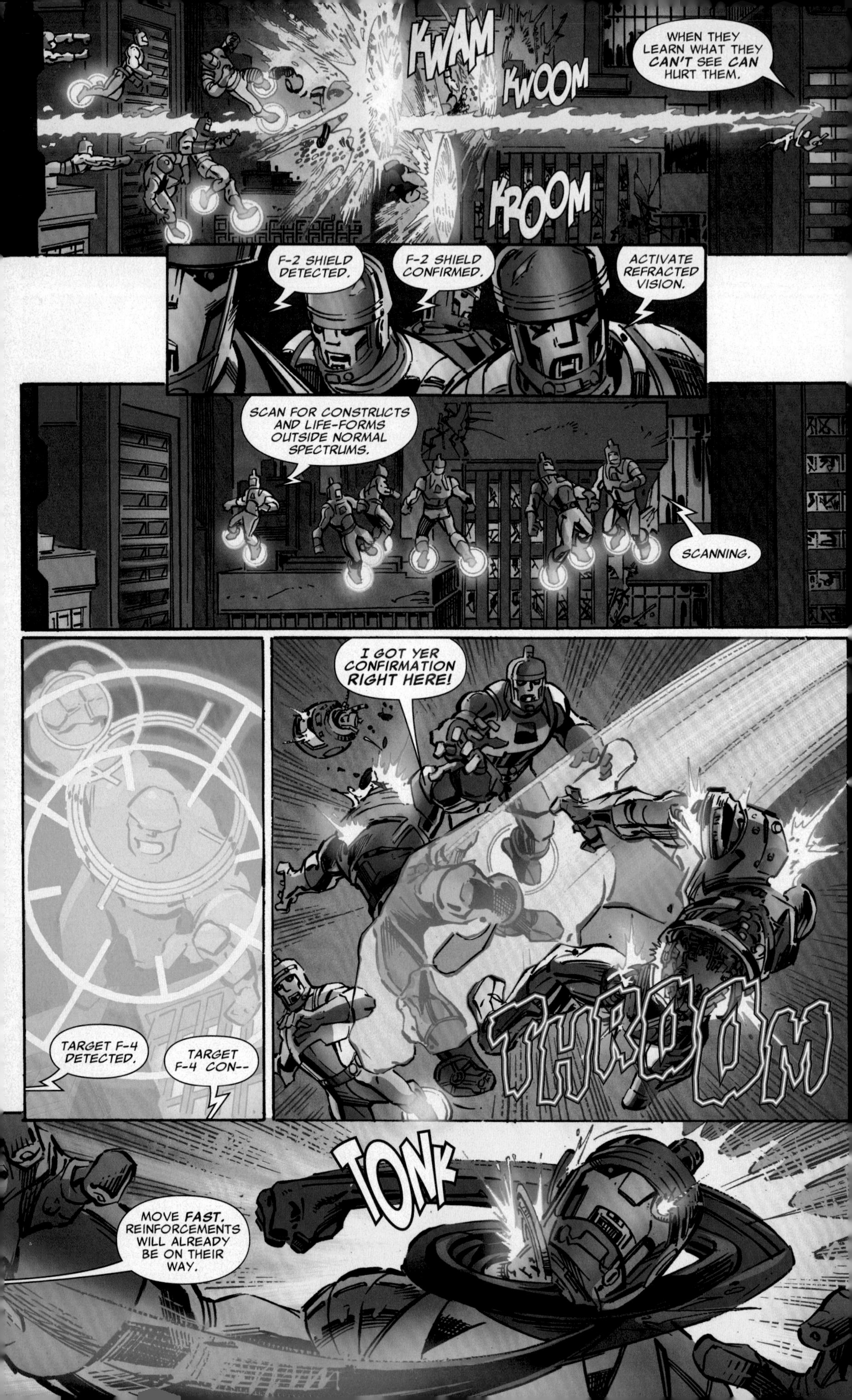
KWAM
KWOOM
WHEN THEY LEARN WHAT THEY CAN'T SEE CAN HURT THEM.
KROOM
F-2 SHIELD DETECTED.
F-2 SHIELD CONFIRMED.
ACTIVATE REFRACTED VISION.
SCAN FOR CONSTRUCTS AND LIFE-FORMS OUTSIDE NORMAL SPECTRUMS.
SCANNING.
TARGET F-4 DETECTED.
TARGET F-4 CON--
I GOT YER CONFIRMATION RIGHT HERE!
THROOM
TONK
MOVE FAST. REINFORCEMENTS WILL ALREADY BE ON THEIR WAY.

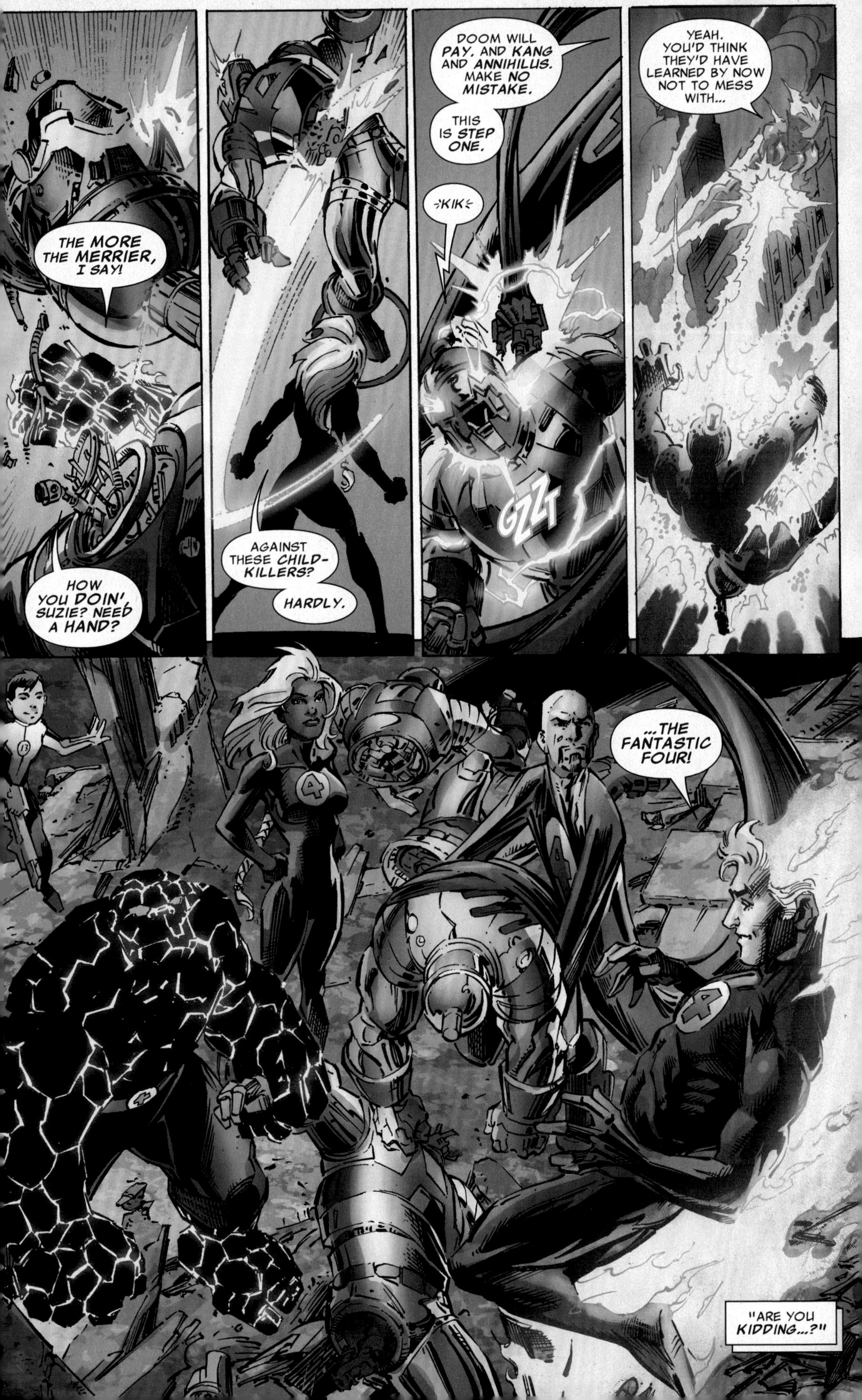
THE MORE THE MERRIER, I SAY!
HOW YOU DOIN' SUZIE? NEED A HAND?
AGAINST THESE CHILD-KILLERS?
HARDLY.
DOOM WILL PAY. AND KANG AND ANNIHILUS. MAKE NO MISTAKE.
THIS IS STEP ONE.
KIK
GZZZT
YEAH. YOU'D THINK THEY'D HAVE LEARNED BY NOW NOT TO MESS WITH...
...THE FANTASTIC FOUR!
"ARE YOU KIDDING...?"

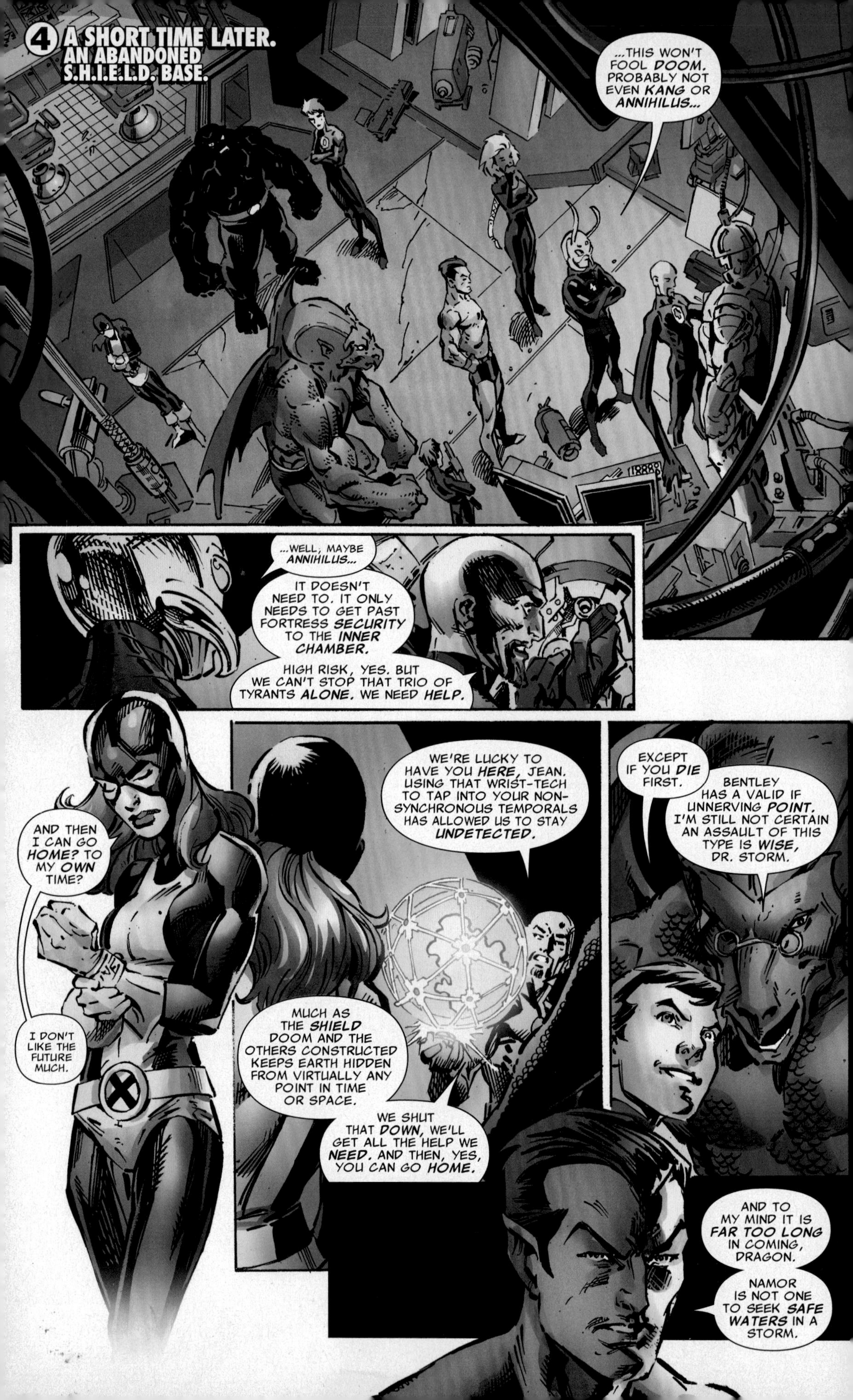

4 A SHORT TIME LATER. AN ABANDONED S.H.I.E.L.D. BASE.
...THIS WON'T FOOL DOOM. PROBABLY NOT EVEN KANG OR ANNIHILUS...
...WELL, MAYBE ANNIHILUS...
IT DOESN'T NEED TO. IT ONLY NEEDS TO GET PAST FORTRESS SECURITY TO THE INNER CHAMBER.
HIGH RISK, YES. BUT WE CAN'T STOP THAT TRIO OF TYRANTS ALONE. WE NEED HELP.
AND THEN I CAN GO HOME? TO MY OWN TIME?
I DON'T LIKE THE FUTURE MUCH.
WE'RE LUCKY TO HAVE YOU HERE, JEAN. USING THAT WRIST-TECH TO TAP INTO YOUR NON-SYNCHRONOUS TEMPORALS HAS ALLOWED US TO STAY UNDETECTED.
MUCH AS THE SHIELD DOOM AND THE OTHERS CONSTRUCTED KEEPS EARTH HIDDEN FROM VIRTUALLY ANY POINT IN TIME OR SPACE.
WE SHUT THAT DOWN, WE'LL GET ALL THE HELP WE NEED. AND THEN, YES, YOU CAN GO HOME.
EXCEPT IF YOU DIE FIRST.
BENTLEY HAS A VALID IF UNNERVING POINT. I'M STILL NOT CERTAIN AN ASSAULT OF THIS TYPE IS WISE, DR. STORM.
AND TO MY MIND IT IS FAR TOO LONG IN COMING, DRAGON.
NAMOR IS NOT ONE TO SEEK SAFE WATERS IN A STORM.

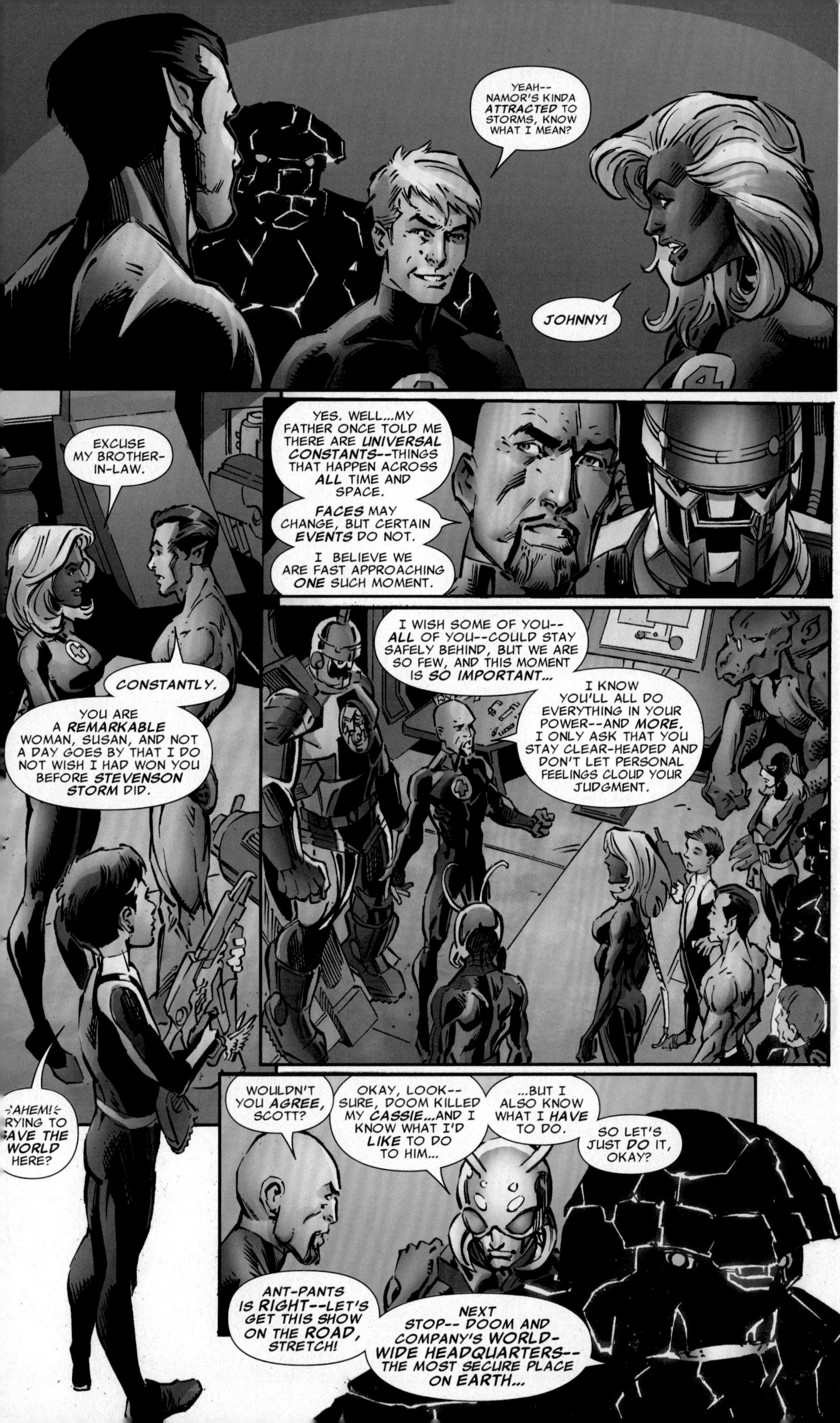
YEAH-- NAMOR'S KINDA ATTRACTED TO STORMS, KNOW WHAT I MEAN?
JOHNNY!
EXCUSE MY BROTHER-IN-LAW.
YES. WELL...MY FATHER ONCE TOLD ME THERE ARE UNIVERSAL CONSTANTS--THINGS THAT HAPPEN ACROSS ALL TIME AND SPACE.
FACES MAY CHANGE, BUT CERTAIN EVENTS DO NOT.
I BELIEVE WE ARE FAST APPROACHING ONE SUCH MOMENT.
CONSTANTLY.
YOU ARE A REMARKABLE WOMAN, SUSAN, AND NOT A DAY GOES BY THAT I DO NOT WISH I HAD WON YOU BEFORE STEVENSON STORM DID.
I WISH SOME OF YOU-- ALL OF YOU--COULD STAY SAFELY BEHIND, BUT WE ARE SO FEW, AND THIS MOMENT IS SO IMPORTANT...
I KNOW YOU'LL ALL DO EVERYTHING IN YOUR POWER--AND MORE. I ONLY ASK THAT YOU STAY CLEAR-HEADED AND DON'T LET PERSONAL FEELINGS CLOUD YOUR JUDGMENT.
AHEM! RYING TO AVE THE WORLD HERE?
WOULDN'T YOU AGREE, SCOTT?
OKAY, LOOK-- SURE, DOOM KILLED MY CASSIE...AND I KNOW WHAT I'D LIKE TO DO TO HIM...
...BUT I ALSO KNOW WHAT I HAVE TO DO.
SO LET'S JUST DO IT, OKAY?
ANT-PANTS IS RIGHT--LET'S GET THIS SHOW ON THE ROAD, STRETCH!
NEXT STOP-- DOOM AND COMPANY'S WORLD-WIDE HEADQUARTERS-- THE MOST SECURE PLACE ON EARTH...

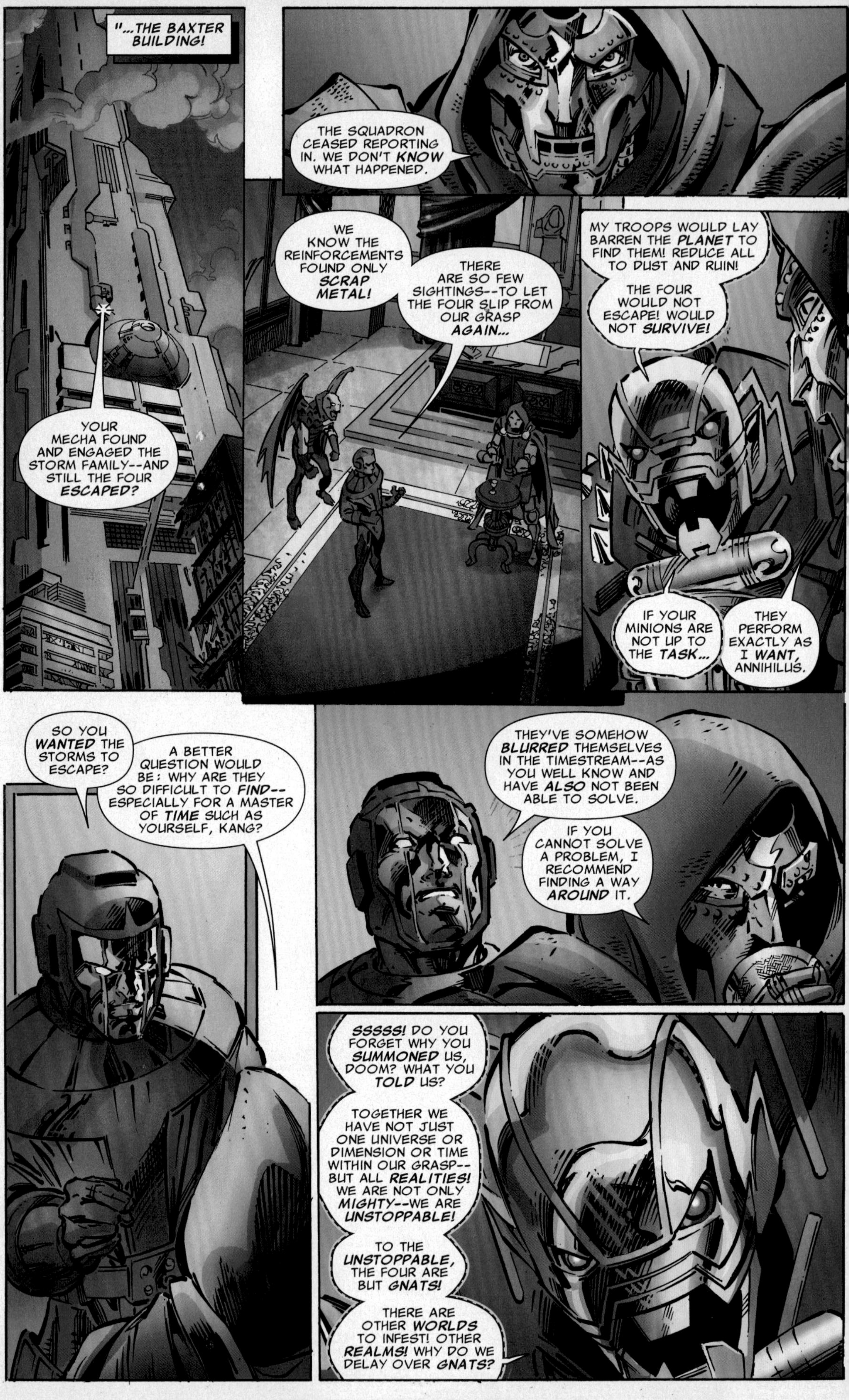
"...THE BAXTER BUILDING!
YOUR MECHA FOUND AND ENGAGED THE STORM FAMILY--AND STILL THE FOUR ESCAPED?
THE SQUADRON CEASED REPORTING IN. WE DON'T KNOW WHAT HAPPENED.
WE KNOW THE REINFORCEMENTS FOUND ONLY SCRAP METAL!
THERE ARE SO FEW SIGHTINGS--TO LET THE FOUR SLIP FROM OUR GRASP AGAIN...
MY TROOPS WOULD LAY BARREN THE PLANET TO FIND THEM! REDUCE ALL TO DUST AND RUIN!
THE FOUR WOULD NOT ESCAPE! WOULD NOT SURVIVE!
IF YOUR MINIONS ARE NOT UP TO THE TASK...
THEY PERFORM EXACTLY AS I WANT, ANNIHILUS.
SO YOU WANTED THE STORMS TO ESCAPE?
A BETTER QUESTION WOULD BE: WHY ARE THEY SO DIFFICULT TO FIND--ESPECIALLY FOR A MASTER OF TIME SUCH AS YOURSELF, KANG?
THEY'VE SOMEHOW BLURRED THEMSELVES IN THE TIMESTREAM--AS YOU WELL KNOW AND HAVE ALSO NOT BEEN ABLE TO SOLVE.
IF YOU CANNOT SOLVE A PROBLEM, I RECOMMEND FINDING A WAY AROUND IT.
SSSSS! DO YOU FORGET WHY YOU SUMMONED US, DOOM? WHAT YOU TOLD US?
TOGETHER WE HAVE NOT JUST ONE UNIVERSE OR DIMENSION OR TIME WITHIN OUR GRASP--BUT ALL REALITIES! WE ARE NOT ONLY MIGHTY--WE ARE UNSTOPPABLE!
TO THE UNSTOPPABLE, THE FOUR ARE BUT GNATS!
THERE ARE OTHER WORLDS TO INFEST! OTHER REALMS! WHY DO WE DELAY OVER GNATS?

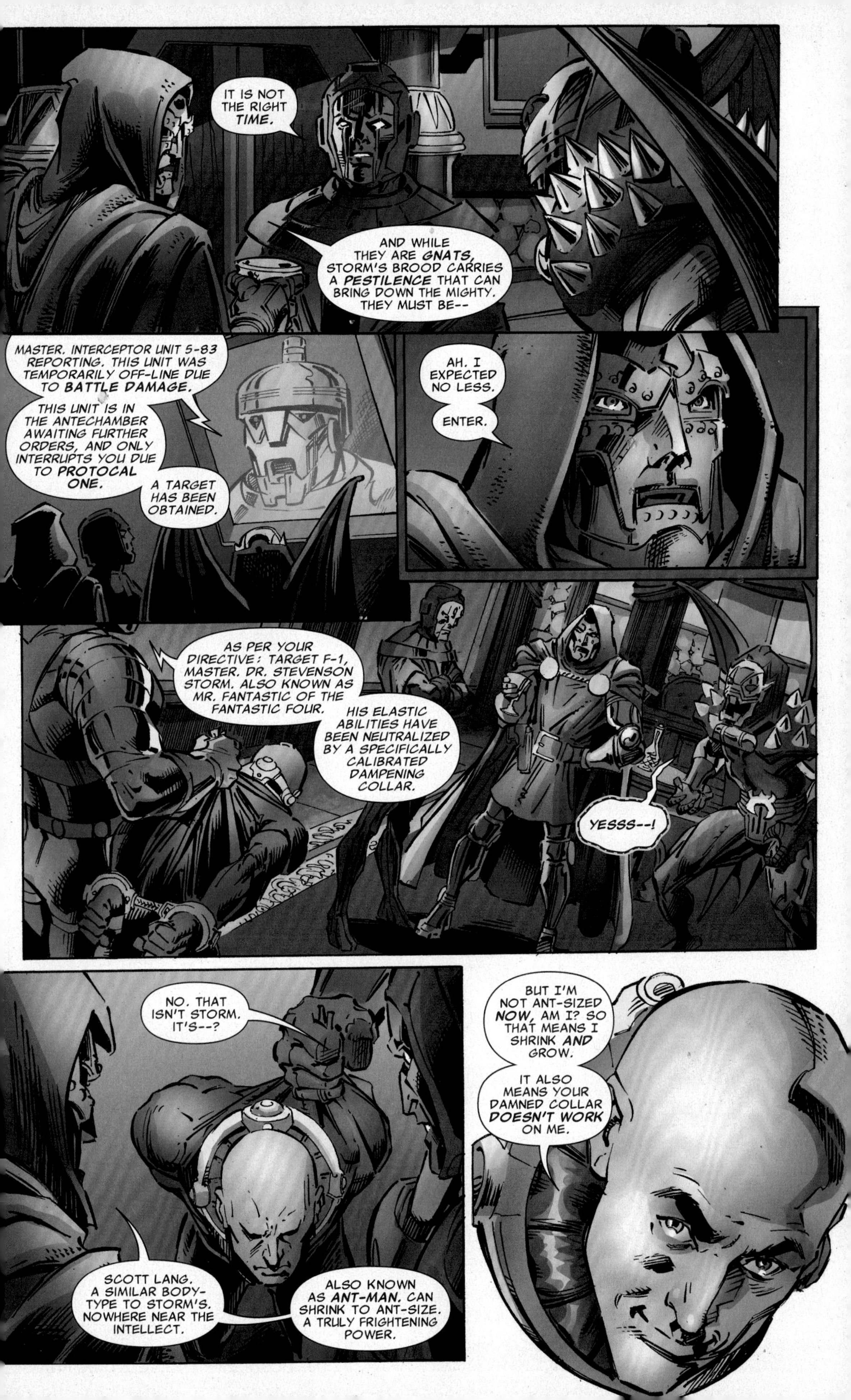
IT IS NOT THE RIGHT TIME.
AND WHILE THEY ARE GNATS, STORM'S BROOD CARRIES A PESTILENCE THAT CAN BRING DOWN THE MIGHTY. THEY MUST BE--
MASTER. INTERCEPTOR UNIT 5-83 REPORTING. THIS UNIT WAS TEMPORARILY OFF-LINE DUE TO BATTLE DAMAGE.
THIS UNIT IS IN THE ANTECHAMBER AWAITING FURTHER ORDERS, AND ONLY INTERRUPTS YOU DUE TO PROTOCAL ONE.
A TARGET HAS BEEN OBTAINED.
AH. I EXPECTED NO LESS.
ENTER.
AS PER YOUR DIRECTIVE: TARGET F-1, MASTER. DR. STEVENSON STORM. ALSO KNOWN AS MR. FANTASTIC OF THE FANTASTIC FOUR.
HIS ELASTIC ABILITIES HAVE BEEN NEUTRALIZED BY A SPECIFICALLY CALIBRATED DAMPENING COLLAR.
YESSS--!
NO. THAT ISN'T STORM. IT'S--?
SCOTT LANG. A SIMILAR BODY-TYPE TO STORM'S. NOWHERE NEAR THE INTELLECT.
ALSO KNOWN AS ANT-MAN. CAN SHRINK TO ANT-SIZE. A TRULY FRIGHTENING POWER.
BUT I'M NOT ANT-SIZED NOW, AM I? SO THAT MEANS I SHRINK AND GROW.
IT ALSO MEANS YOUR DAMNED COLLAR DOESN'T WORK ON ME.

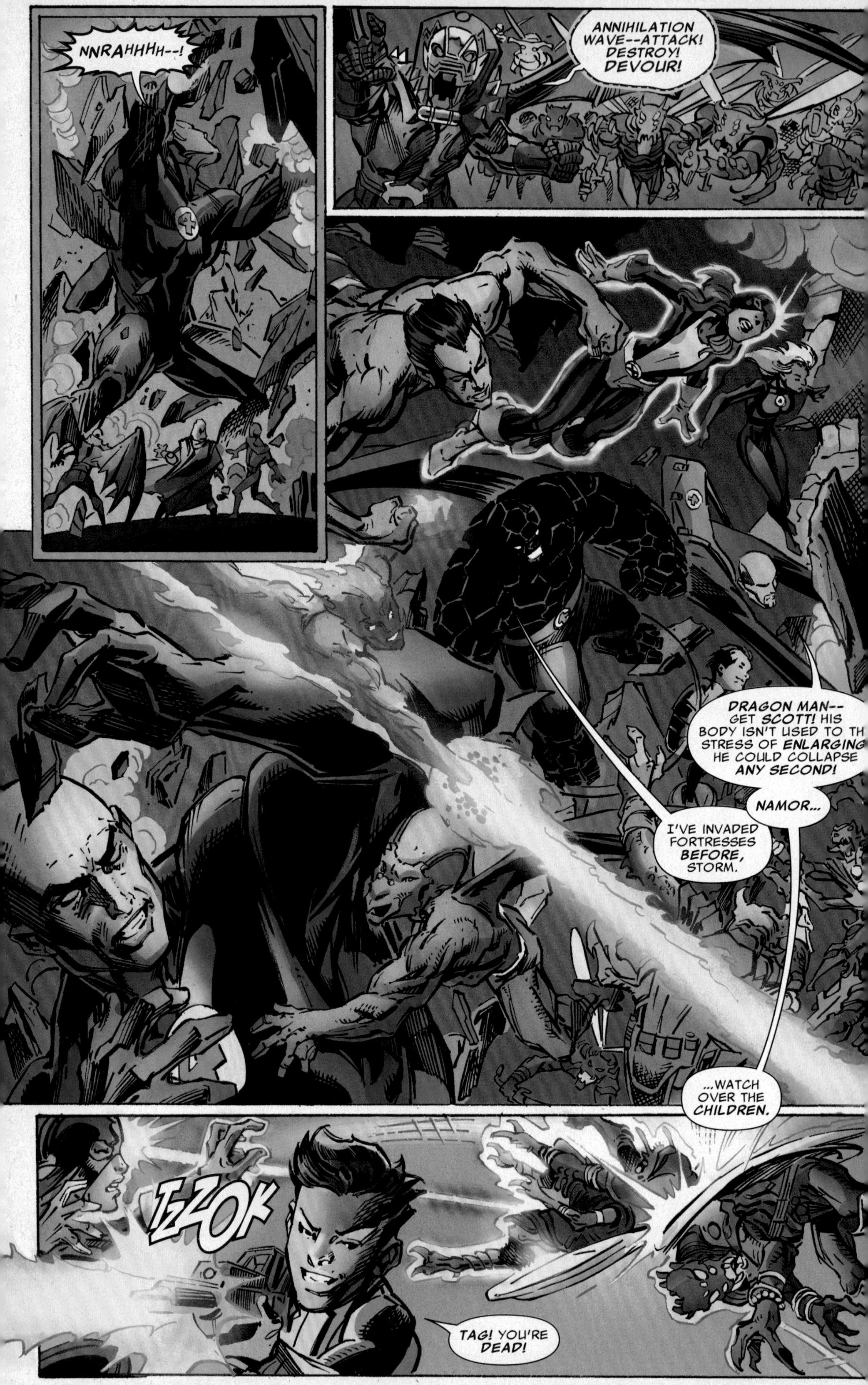
NNRAHHHH--!
ANNIHILATION WAVE--ATTACK! DESTROY! DEVOUR!
DRAGON MAN-- GET SCOTT! HIS BODY ISN'T USED TO TH STRESS OF ENLARGING HE COULD COLLAPSE ANY SECOND!
I'VE INVADED FORTRESSES BEFORE, STORM.
NAMOR...
...WATCH OVER THE CHILDREN.
TZZOK
TAG! YOU'RE DEAD!

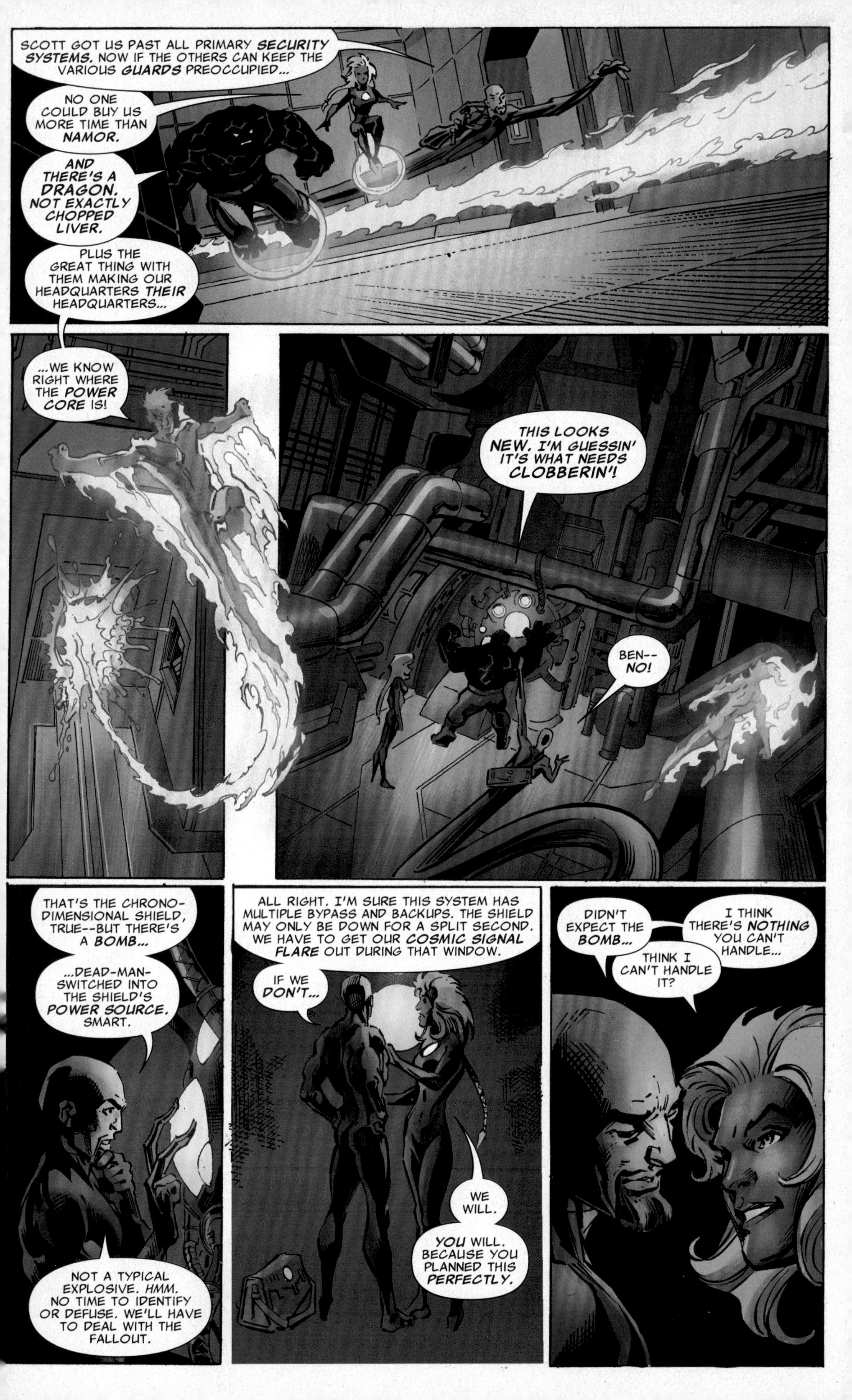

SCOTT GOT US PAST ALL PRIMARY SECURITY SYSTEMS. NOW IF THE OTHERS CAN KEEP THE VARIOUS GUARDS PREOCCUPIED...
NO ONE COULD BUY US MORE TIME THAN NAMOR.
AND THERE'S A DRAGON. NOT EXACTLY CHOPPED LIVER.
PLUS THE GREAT THING WITH THEM MAKING OUR HEADQUARTERS THEIR HEADQUARTERS...
...WE KNOW RIGHT WHERE THE POWER CORE IS!
THIS LOOKS NEW. I'M GUESSIN' IT'S WHAT NEEDS CLOBBERIN'!
BEN-- NO!
THAT'S THE CHRONO-DIMENSIONAL SHIELD, TRUE--BUT THERE'S A BOMB...
...DEAD-MAN-SWITCHED INTO THE SHIELD'S POWER SOURCE. SMART.
NOT A TYPICAL EXPLOSIVE. HMM. NO TIME TO IDENTIFY OR DEFUSE. WE'LL HAVE TO DEAL WITH THE FALLOUT.
ALL RIGHT. I'M SURE THIS SYSTEM HAS MULTIPLE BYPASS AND BACKUPS. THE SHIELD MAY ONLY BE DOWN FOR A SPLIT SECOND. WE HAVE TO GET OUR COSMIC SIGNAL FLARE OUT DURING THAT WINDOW.
IF WE DON'T...
WE WILL.
YOU WILL. BECAUSE YOU PLANNED THIS PERFECTLY.
DIDN'T EXPECT THE BOMB...
THINK I CAN'T HANDLE IT?
I THINK THERE'S NOTHING YOU CAN'T HANDLE...

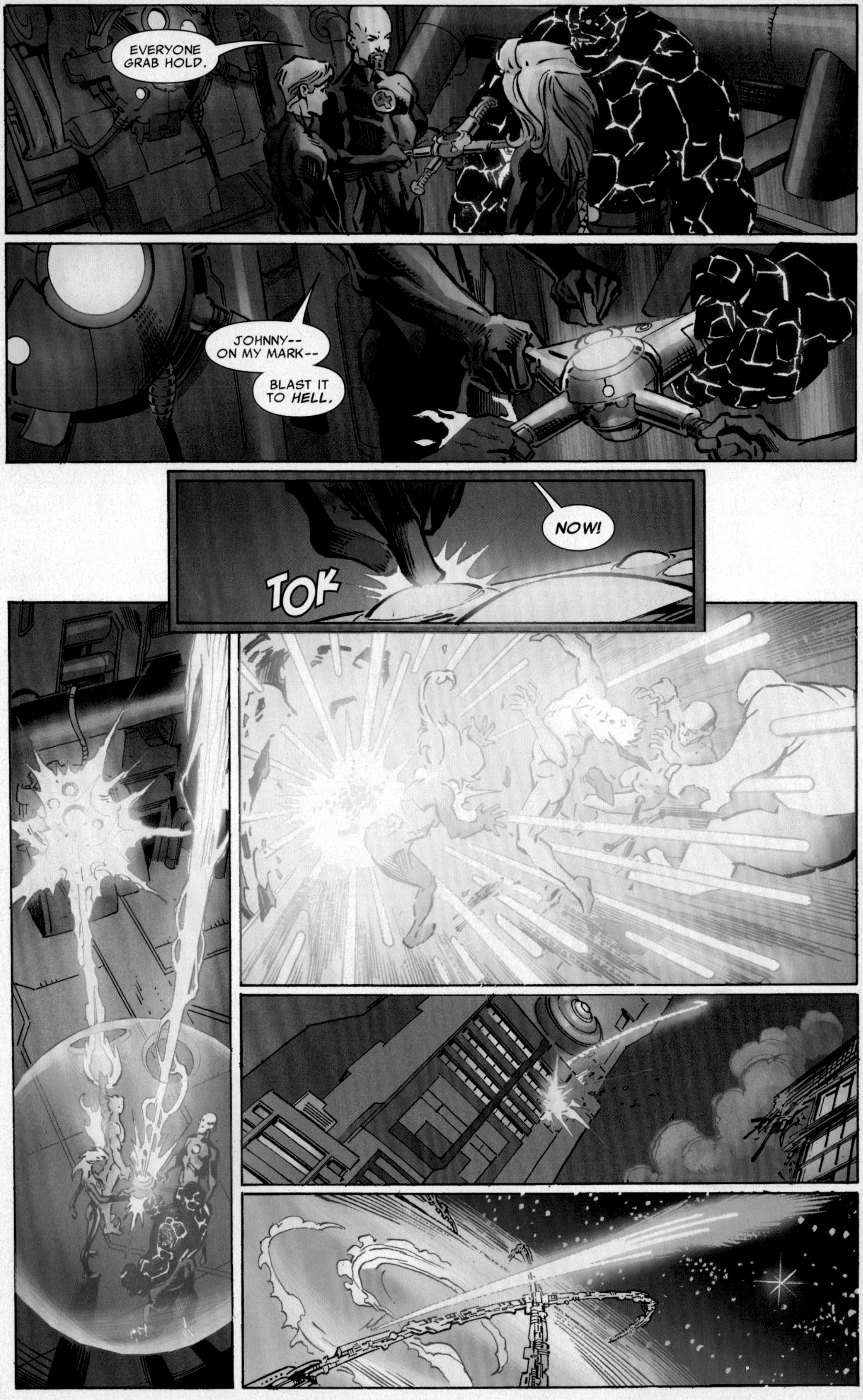
EVERYONE GRAB HOLD.
JOHNNY-- ON MY MARK--
BLAST IT TO HELL.
NOW!
TOK

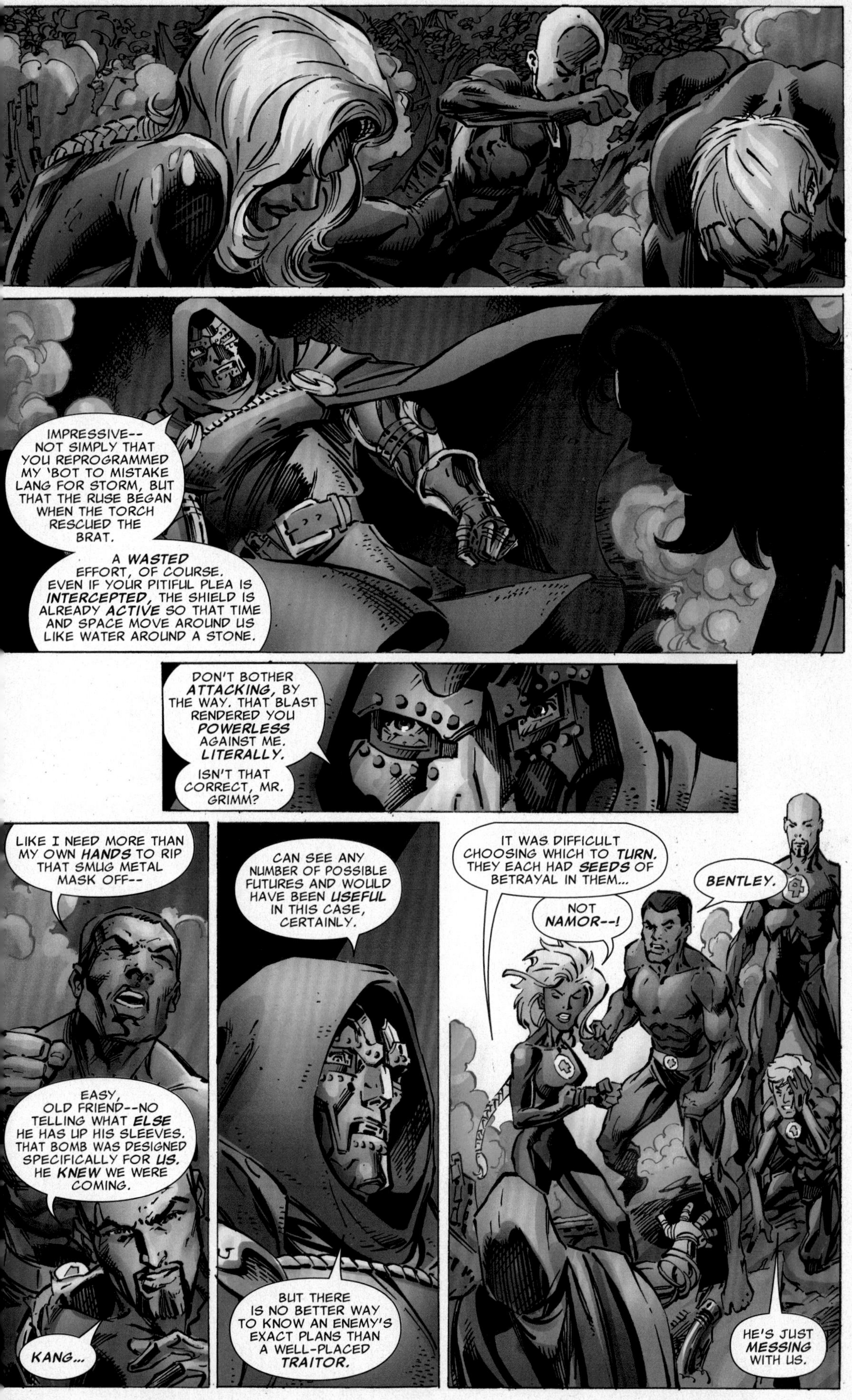
IMPRESSIVE-- NOT SIMPLY THAT YOU REPROGRAMMED MY 'BOT TO MISTAKE LANG FOR STORM, BUT THAT THE RUSE BEGAN WHEN THE TORCH RESCUED THE BRAT.
A WASTED EFFORT, OF COURSE. EVEN IF YOUR PITIFUL PLEA IS INTERCEPTED, THE SHIELD IS ALREADY ACTIVE SO THAT TIME AND SPACE MOVE AROUND US LIKE WATER AROUND A STONE.
DON'T BOTHER ATTACKING, BY THE WAY. THAT BLAST RENDERED YOU POWERLESS AGAINST ME. LITERALLY.
ISN'T THAT CORRECT, MR. GRIMM?
LIKE I NEED MORE THAN MY OWN HANDS TO RIP THAT SMUG METAL MASK OFF--
EASY, OLD FRIEND--NO TELLING WHAT ELSE HE HAS UP HIS SLEEVES. THAT BOMB WAS DESIGNED SPECIFICALLY FOR US. HE KNEW WE WERE COMING.
KANG...
CAN SEE ANY NUMBER OF POSSIBLE FUTURES AND WOULD HAVE BEEN USEFUL IN THIS CASE, CERTAINLY.
BUT THERE IS NO BETTER WAY TO KNOW AN ENEMY'S EXACT PLANS THAN A WELL-PLACED TRAITOR.
IT WAS DIFFICULT CHOOSING WHICH TO TURN. THEY EACH HAD SEEDS OF BETRAYAL IN THEM...
NOT NAMOR--!
BENTLEY.
HE'S JUST MESSING WITH US.

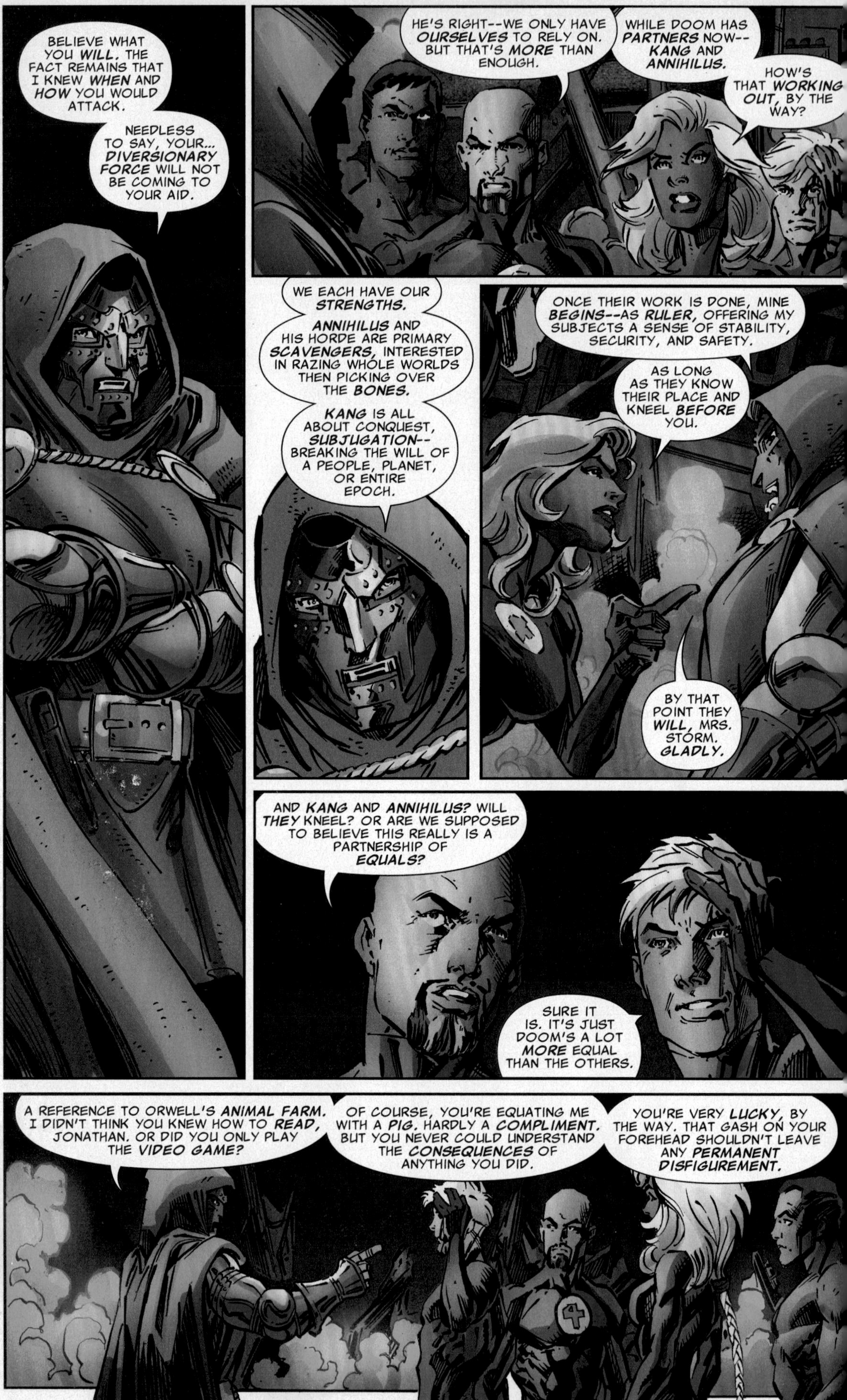
BELIEVE WHAT YOU WILL. THE FACT REMAINS THAT I KNEW WHEN AND HOW YOU WOULD ATTACK.
NEEDLESS TO SAY, YOUR... DIVERSIONARY FORCE WILL NOT BE COMING TO YOUR AID.
HE'S RIGHT--WE ONLY HAVE OURSELVES TO RELY ON. BUT THAT'S MORE THAN ENOUGH.
WHILE DOOM HAS PARTNERS NOW--KANG AND ANNIHILUS.
HOW'S THAT WORKING OUT, BY THE WAY?
WE EACH HAVE OUR STRENGTHS.
ANNIHILUS AND HIS HORDE ARE PRIMARY SCAVENGERS, INTERESTED IN RAZING WHOLE WORLDS THEN PICKING OVER THE BONES.
KANG IS ALL ABOUT CONQUEST, SUBJUGATION--BREAKING THE WILL OF A PEOPLE, PLANET, OR ENTIRE EPOCH.
ONCE THEIR WORK IS DONE, MINE BEGINS--AS RULER, OFFERING MY SUBJECTS A SENSE OF STABILITY, SECURITY, AND SAFETY.
AS LONG AS THEY KNOW THEIR PLACE AND KNEEL BEFORE YOU.
BY THAT POINT THEY WILL, MRS. STORM. GLADLY.
AND KANG AND ANNIHILUS? WILL THEY KNEEL? OR ARE WE SUPPOSED TO BELIEVE THIS REALLY IS A PARTNERSHIP OF EQUALS?
SURE IT IS. IT'S JUST DOOM'S A LOT MORE EQUAL THAN THE OTHERS.
A REFERENCE TO ORWELL'S ANIMAL FARM. I DIDN'T THINK YOU KNEW HOW TO READ, JONATHAN. OR DID YOU ONLY PLAY THE VIDEO GAME?
OF COURSE, YOU'RE EQUATING ME WITH A PIG. HARDLY A COMPLIMENT. BUT YOU NEVER COULD UNDERSTAND THE CONSEQUENCES OF ANYTHING YOU DID.
YOU'RE VERY LUCKY, BY THE WAY. THAT GASH ON YOUR FOREHEAD SHOULDN'T LEAVE ANY PERMANENT DISFIGUREMENT.

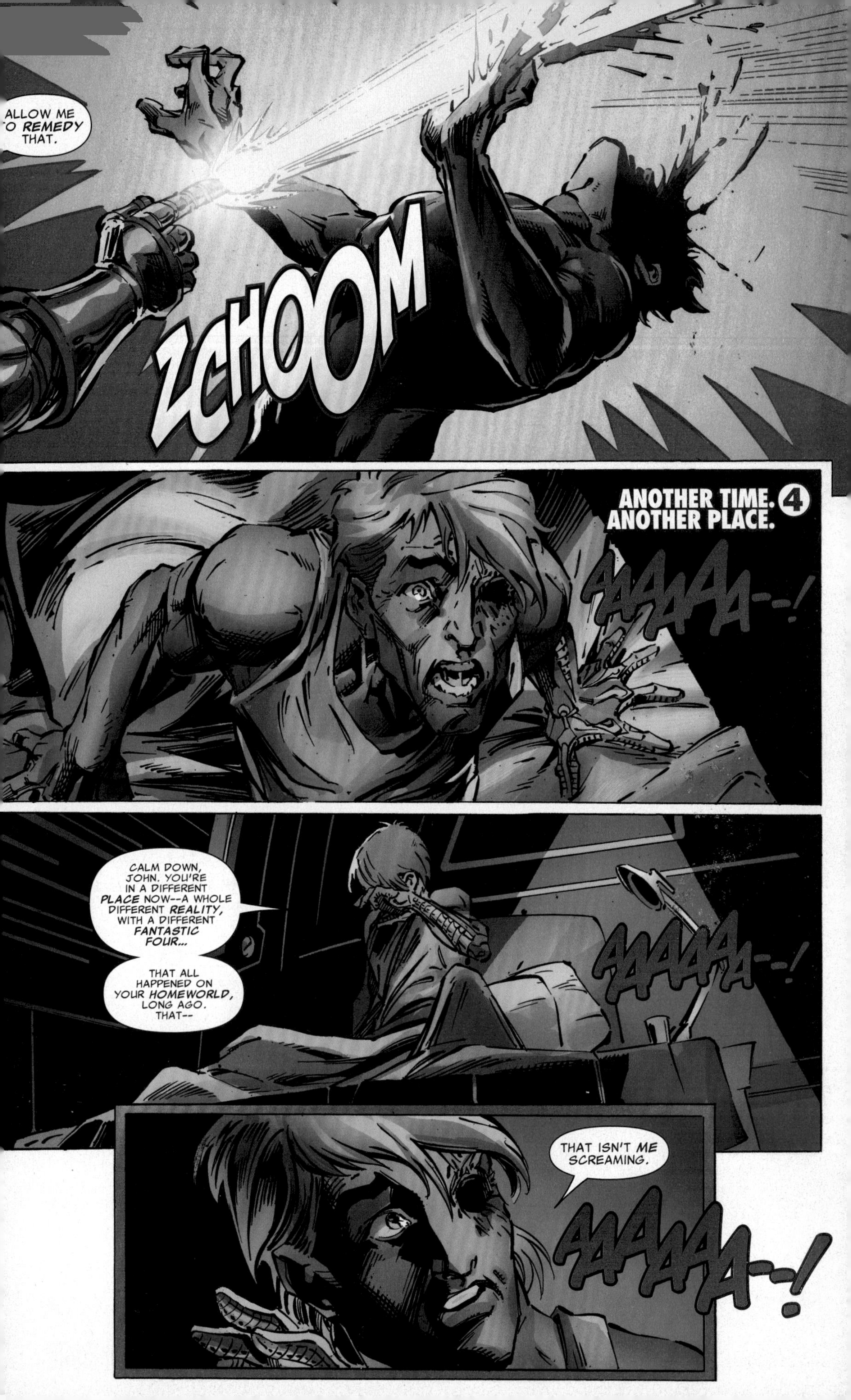
ALLOW ME TO REMEDY THAT.
ZCHOOM
ANOTHER TIME. ANOTHER PLACE.
AAAAAA---!
CALM DOWN, JOHN. YOU'RE IN A DIFFERENT PLACE NOW--A WHOLE DIFFERENT REALITY, WITH A DIFFERENT FANTASTIC FOUR...
THAT ALL HAPPENED ON YOUR HOMEWORLD, LONG AGO. THAT--
AAAAAA---!
THAT ISN'T ME SCREAMING.
AAAAAA---!

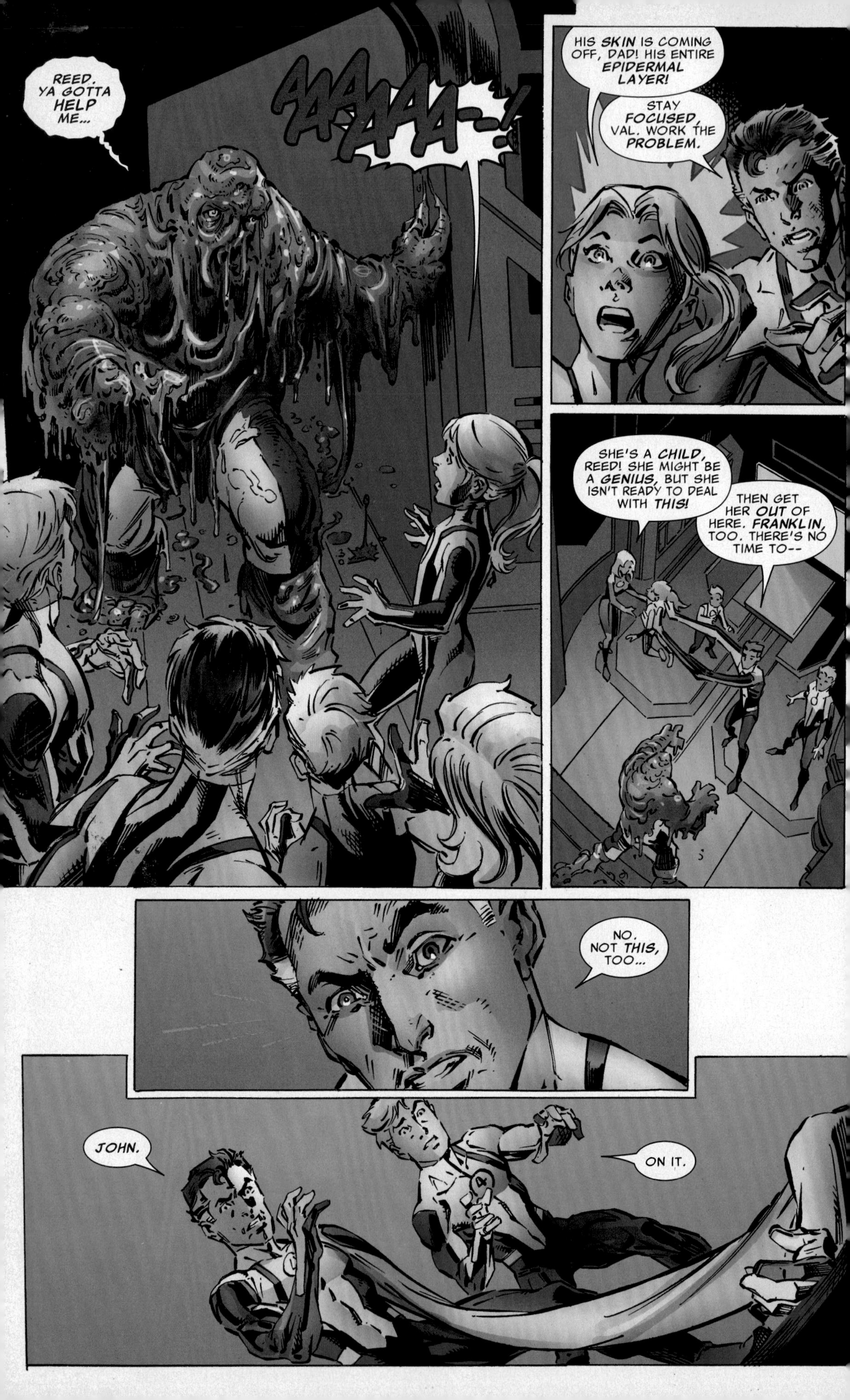
REED. YA GOTTA HELP ME...
AAAAAA--!
HIS SKIN IS COMING OFF, DAD! HIS ENTIRE EPIDERMAL LAYER!
STAY FOCUSED, VAL. WORK THE PROBLEM.
SHE'S A CHILD, REED! SHE MIGHT BE A GENIUS, BUT SHE ISN'T READY TO DEAL WITH THIS!
THEN GET HER OUT OF HERE. FRANKLIN, TOO. THERE'S NO TIME TO--
NO. NOT THIS, TOO...
JOHN.
ON IT.

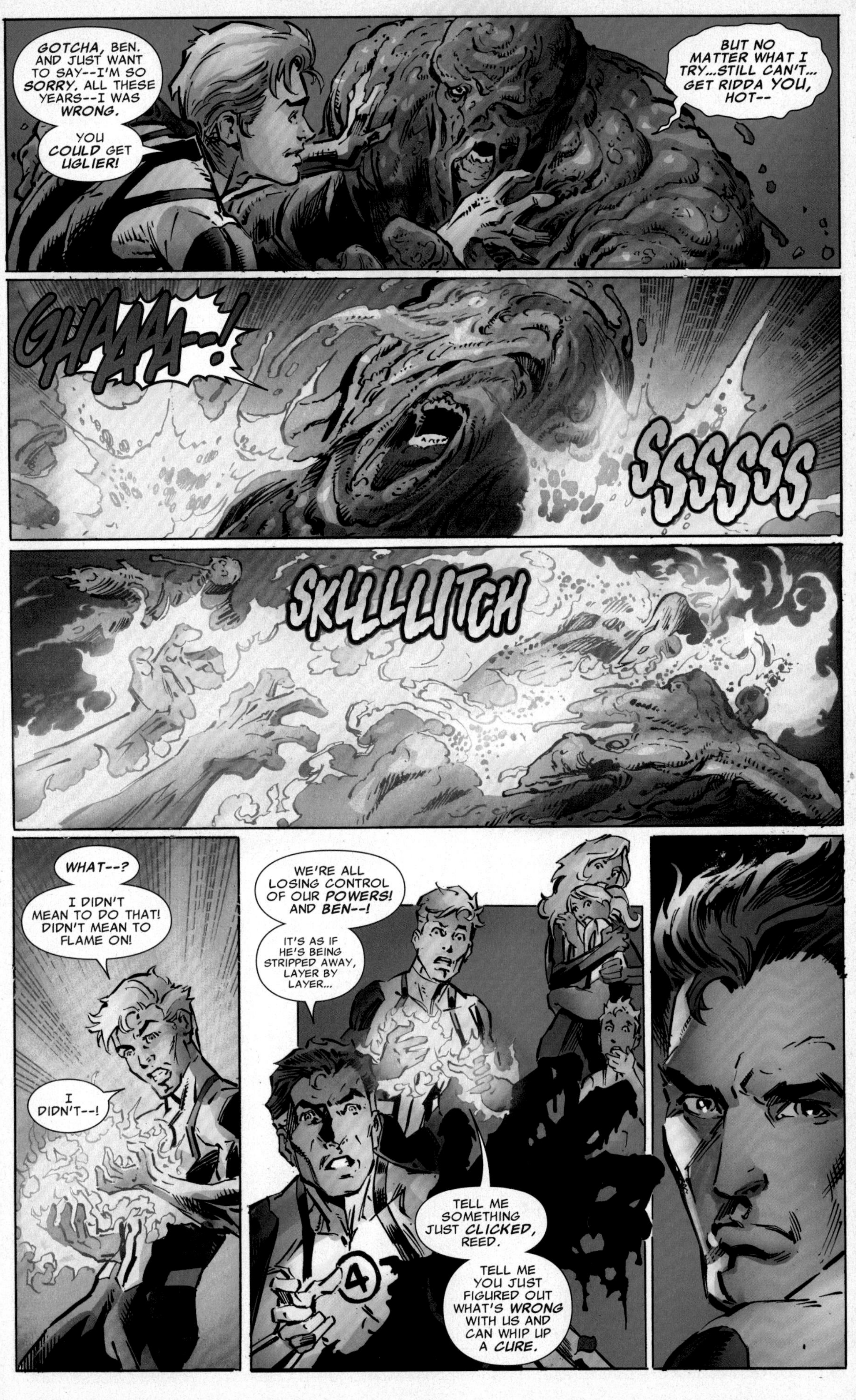

GOTCHA, BEN. AND JUST WANT TO SAY--I'M SO SORRY. ALL THESE YEARS--I WAS WRONG.
YOU COULD GET UGLIER!
BUT NO MATTER WHAT I TRY...STILL CAN'T... GET RIDDA YOU, HOT--
GHAAAA--!
SSSSSS
SKLLLLITCH
WHAT--?
I DIDN'T MEAN TO DO THAT! DIDN'T MEAN TO FLAME ON!
I DIDN'T--!
WE'RE ALL LOSING CONTROL OF OUR POWERS! AND BEN--!
IT'S AS IF HE'S BEING STRIPPED AWAY, LAYER BY LAYER...
TELL ME SOMETHING JUST CLICKED, REED.
TELL ME YOU JUST FIGURED OUT WHAT'S WRONG WITH US AND CAN WHIP UP A CURE.

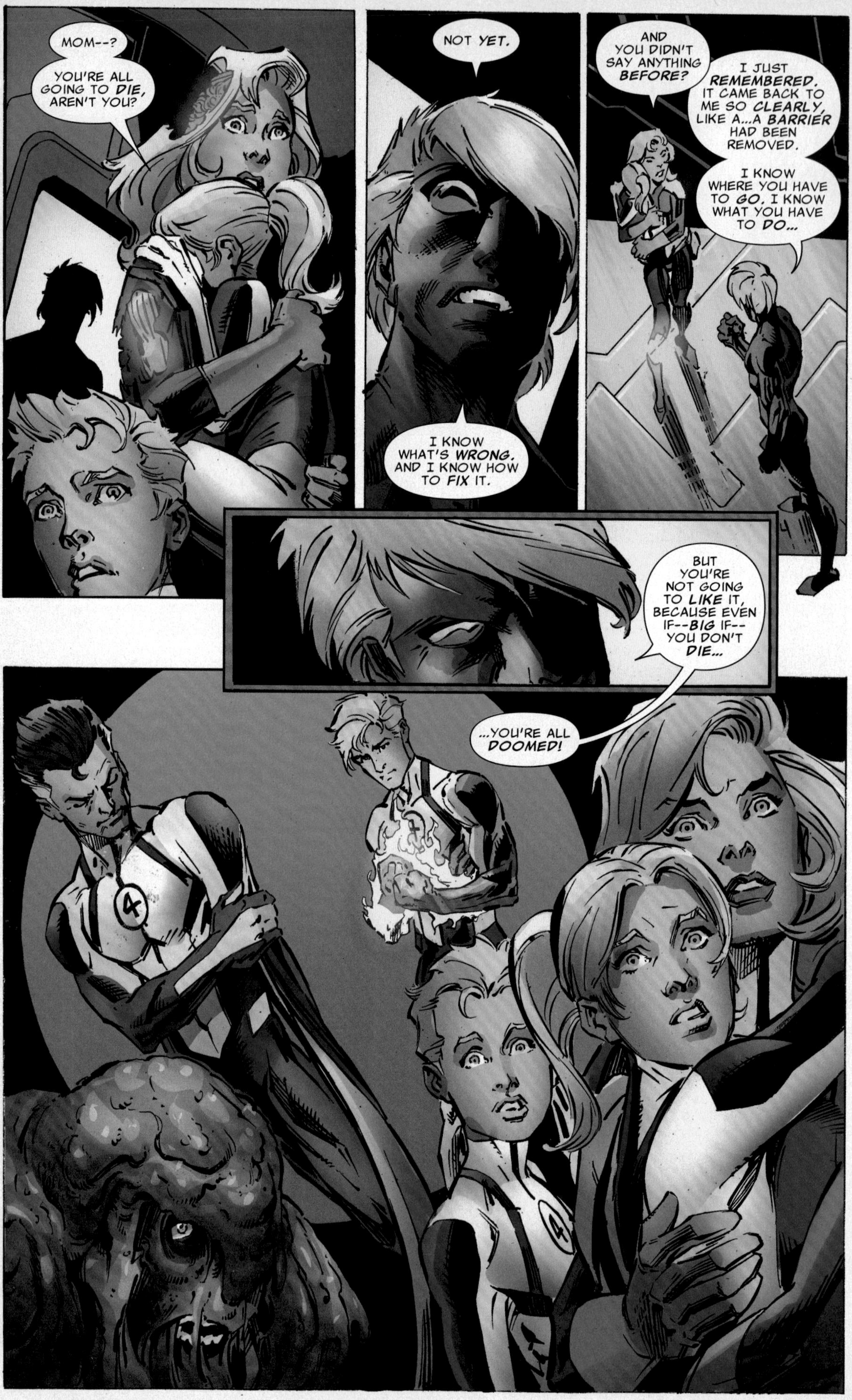
MOM--?
YOU'RE ALL GOING TO DIE, AREN'T YOU?
NOT YET.
I KNOW WHAT'S WRONG. AND I KNOW HOW TO FIX IT.
AND YOU DIDN'T SAY ANYTHING BEFORE?
I JUST REMEMBERED. IT CAME BACK TO ME SO CLEARLY, LIKE A...A BARRIER HAD BEEN REMOVED.
I KNOW WHERE YOU HAVE TO GO. I KNOW WHAT YOU HAVE TO DO...
BUT YOU'RE NOT GOING TO LIKE IT, BECAUSE EVEN IF--BIG IF--YOU DON'T DIE...
...YOU'RE ALL DOOMED!

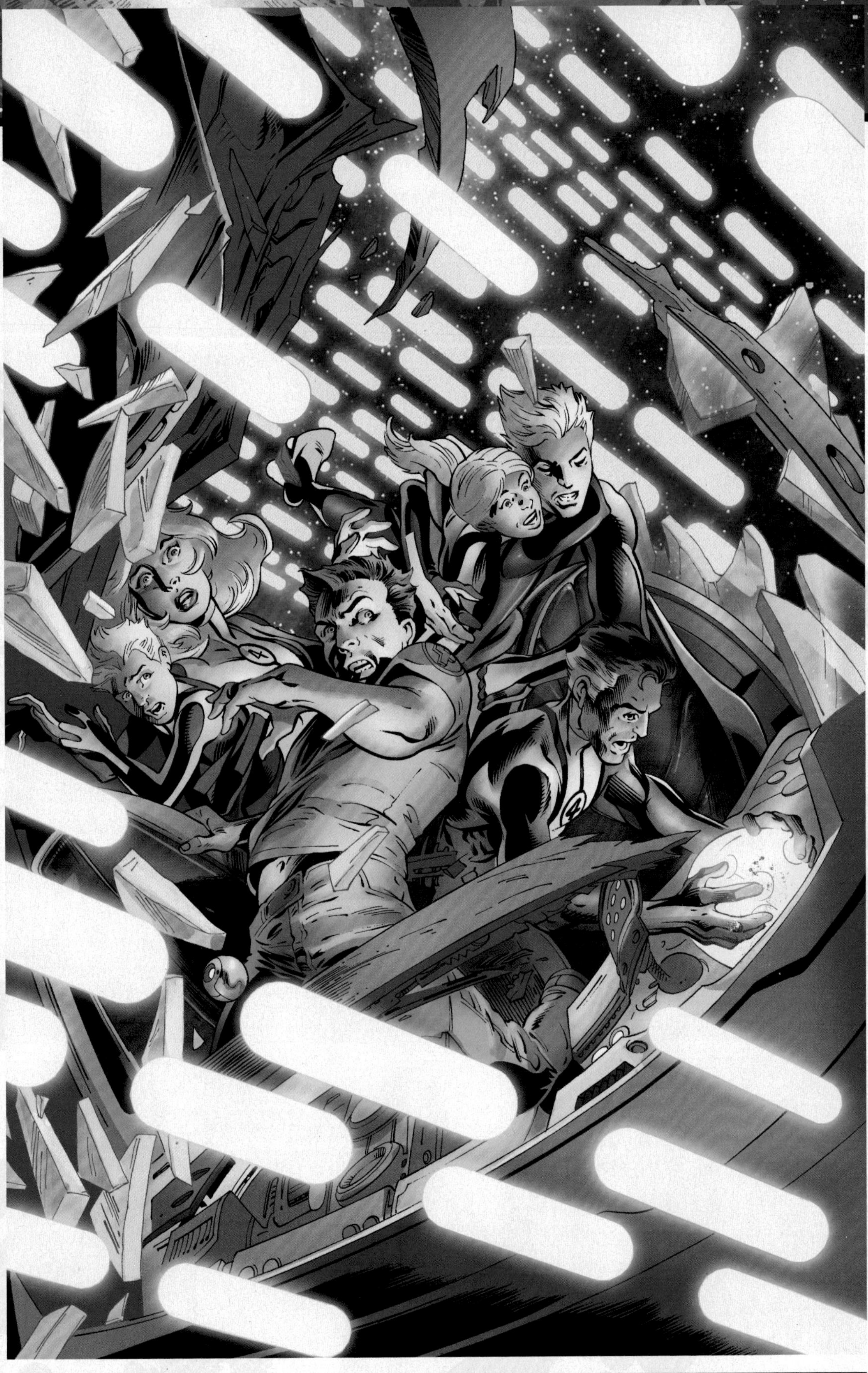

FANTASTIC FOUR #14 — "TRIAL BY FIRE"

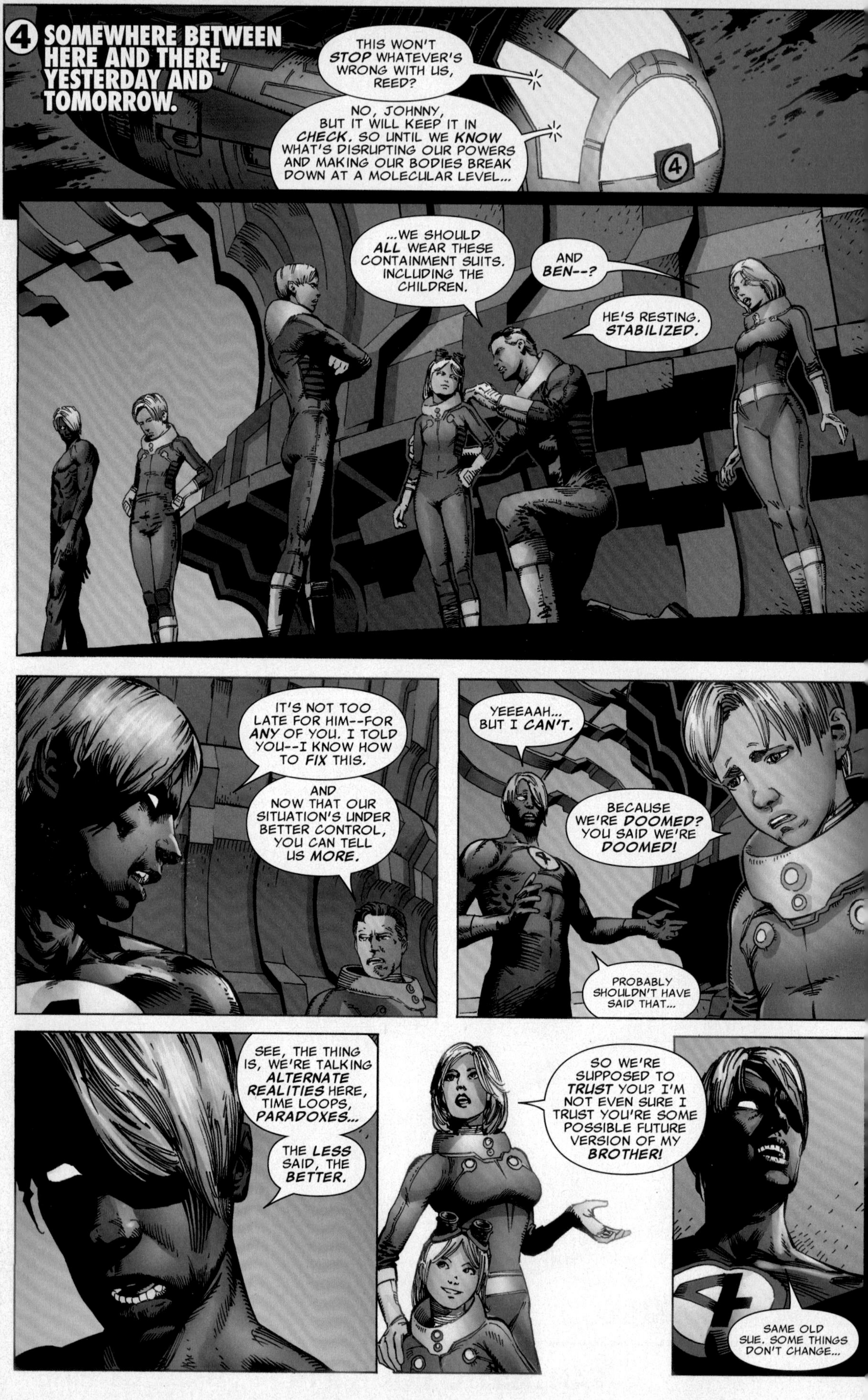
4 SOMEWHERE BETWEEN HERE AND THERE, YESTERDAY AND TOMORROW.
THIS WON'T STOP WHATEVER'S WRONG WITH US, REED?
NO, JOHNNY, BUT IT WILL KEEP IT IN CHECK. SO UNTIL WE KNOW WHAT'S DISRUPTING OUR POWERS AND MAKING OUR BODIES BREAK DOWN AT A MOLECULAR LEVEL...
4
...WE SHOULD ALL WEAR THESE CONTAINMENT SUITS. INCLUDING THE CHILDREN.
AND BEN--?
HE'S RESTING. STABILIZED.
IT'S NOT TOO LATE FOR HIM--FOR ANY OF YOU. I TOLD YOU--I KNOW HOW TO FIX THIS.
AND NOW THAT OUR SITUATION'S UNDER BETTER CONTROL, YOU CAN TELL US MORE.
YEEEAAH... BUT I CAN'T.
BECAUSE WE'RE DOOMED? YOU SAID WE'RE DOOMED!
PROBABLY SHOULDN'T HAVE SAID THAT...
SEE, THE THING IS, WE'RE TALKING ALTERNATE REALITIES HERE, TIME LOOPS, PARADOXES...
THE LESS SAID, THE BETTER.
SO WE'RE SUPPOSED TO TRUST YOU? I'M NOT EVEN SURE I TRUST YOU'RE SOME POSSIBLE FUTURE VERSION OF MY BROTHER!
SAME OLD SUE. SOME THINGS DON'T CHANGE...

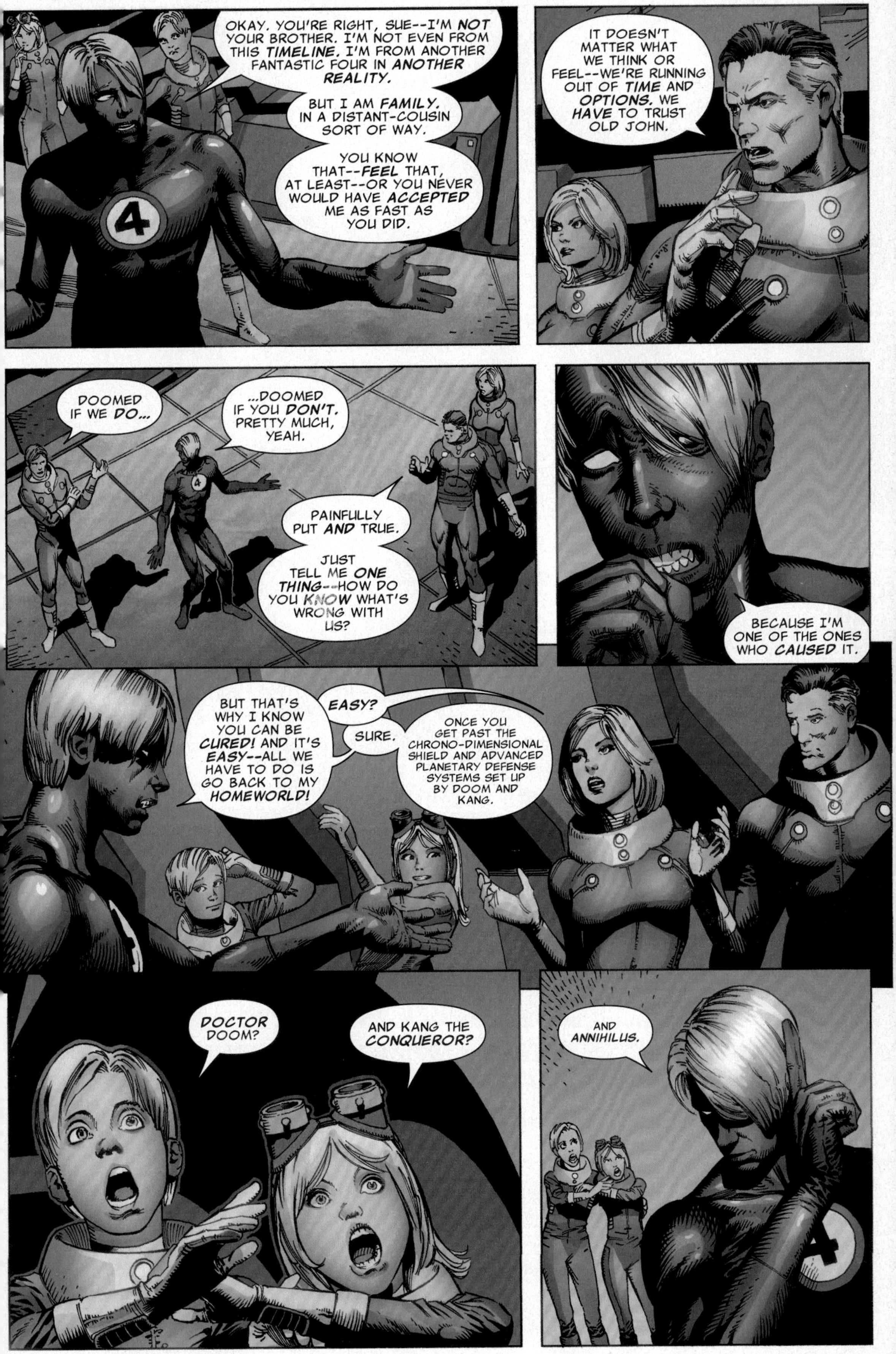
OKAY. YOU'RE RIGHT, SUE--I'M NOT YOUR BROTHER. I'M NOT EVEN FROM THIS TIMELINE. I'M FROM ANOTHER FANTASTIC FOUR IN ANOTHER REALITY.
BUT I AM FAMILY. IN A DISTANT-COUSIN SORT OF WAY.
YOU KNOW THAT--FEEL THAT, AT LEAST--OR YOU NEVER WOULD HAVE ACCEPTED ME AS FAST AS YOU DID.
IT DOESN'T MATTER WHAT WE THINK OR FEEL--WE'RE RUNNING OUT OF TIME AND OPTIONS. WE HAVE TO TRUST OLD JOHN.
DOOMED IF WE DO...
...DOOMED IF YOU DON'T. PRETTY MUCH, YEAH.
PAINFULLY PUT AND TRUE.
JUST TELL ME ONE THING--HOW DO YOU KNOW WHAT'S WRONG WITH US?
BECAUSE I'M ONE OF THE ONES WHO CAUSED IT.
BUT THAT'S WHY I KNOW YOU CAN BE CURED! AND IT'S EASY--ALL WE HAVE TO DO IS GO BACK TO MY HOMEWORLD!
EASY?
SURE.
ONCE YOU GET PAST THE CHRONO-DIMENSIONAL SHIELD AND ADVANCED PLANETARY DEFENSE SYSTEMS SET UP BY DOOM AND KANG.
DOCTOR DOOM?
AND KANG THE CONQUEROR?
AND ANNIHILUS.

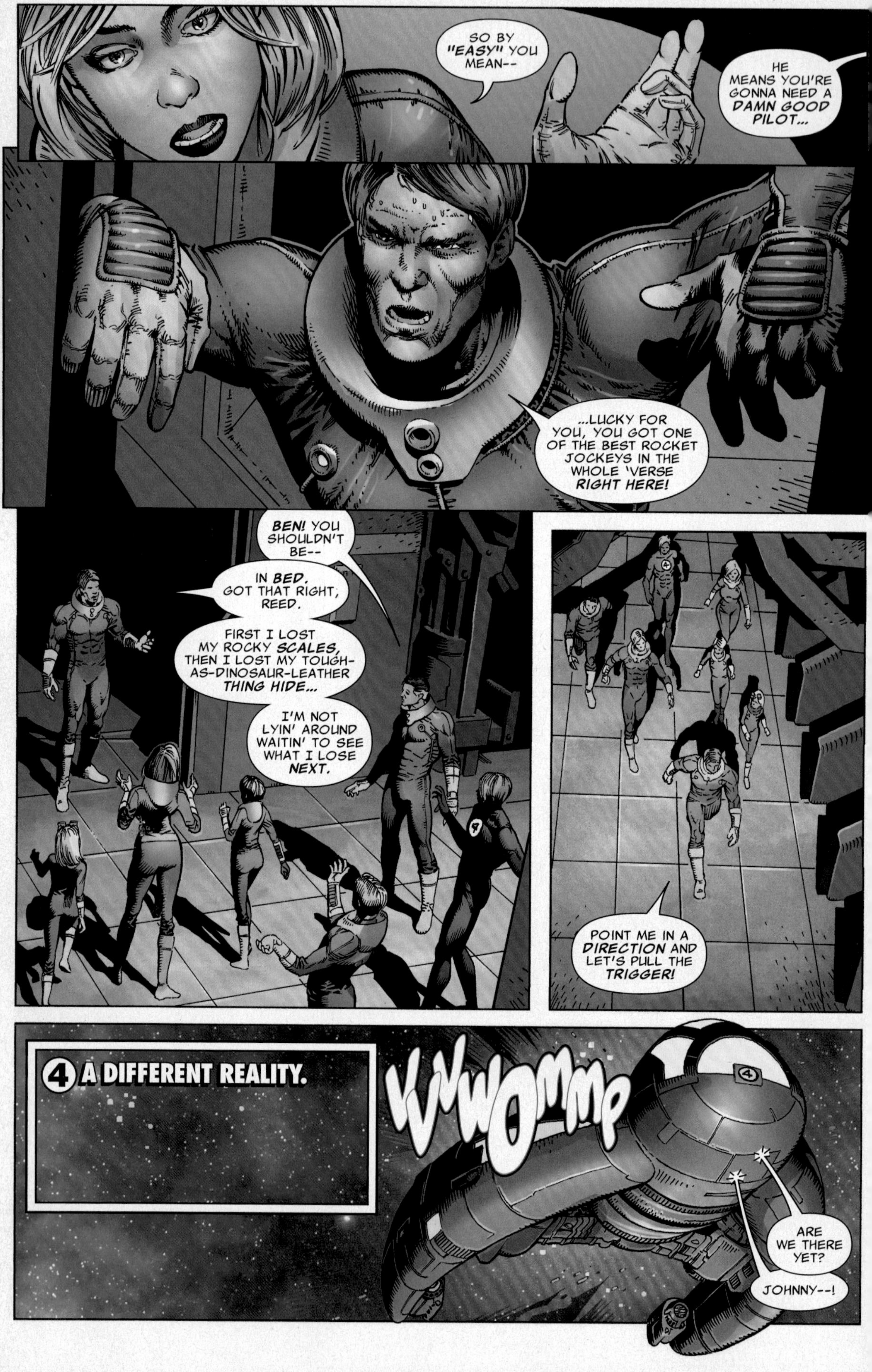
SO BY "EASY" YOU MEAN--
HE MEANS YOU'RE GONNA NEED A DAMN GOOD PILOT...
...LUCKY FOR YOU, YOU GOT ONE OF THE BEST ROCKET JOCKEYS IN THE WHOLE 'VERSE RIGHT HERE!
BEN! YOU SHOULDN'T BE--
IN BED. GOT THAT RIGHT, REED.
FIRST I LOST MY ROCKY SCALES, THEN I LOST MY TOUGH-AS-DINOSAUR-LEATHER THING HIDE...
I'M NOT LYIN' AROUND WAITIN' TO SEE WHAT I LOSE NEXT.
POINT ME IN A DIRECTION AND LET'S PULL THE TRIGGER!
4 A DIFFERENT REALITY.
VVVWOMMP
ARE WE THERE YET?
JOHNNY--!

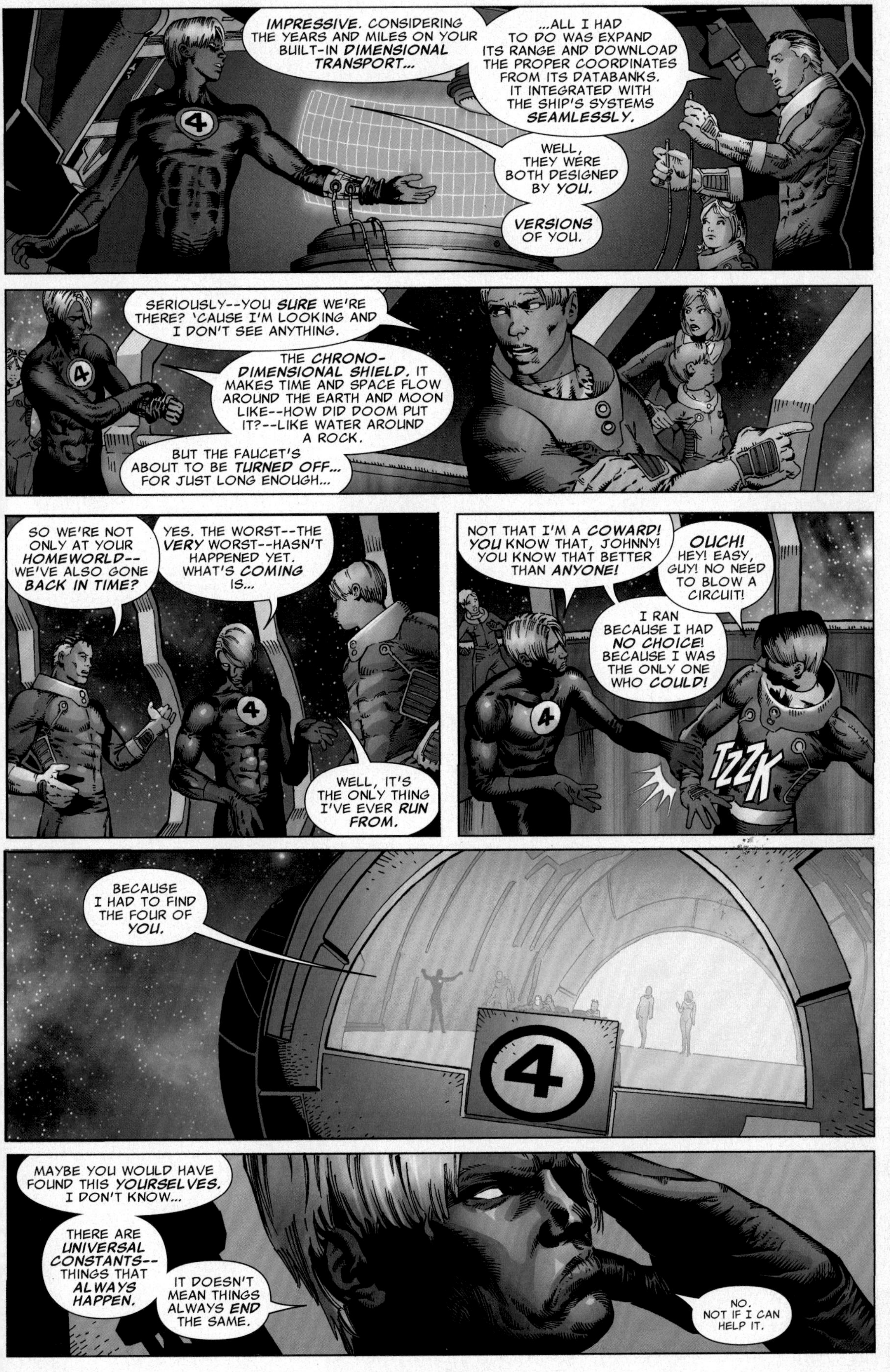
IMPRESSIVE. CONSIDERING THE YEARS AND MILES ON YOUR BUILT-IN DIMENSIONAL TRANSPORT...
...ALL I HAD TO DO WAS EXPAND ITS RANGE AND DOWNLOAD THE PROPER COORDINATES FROM ITS DATABANKS. IT INTEGRATED WITH THE SHIP'S SYSTEMS SEAMLESSLY.
WELL, THEY WERE BOTH DESIGNED BY YOU.
VERSIONS OF YOU.
SERIOUSLY--YOU SURE WE'RE THERE? 'CAUSE I'M LOOKING AND I DON'T SEE ANYTHING.
THE CHRONO-DIMENSIONAL SHIELD. IT MAKES TIME AND SPACE FLOW AROUND THE EARTH AND MOON LIKE--HOW DID DOOM PUT IT?--LIKE WATER AROUND A ROCK.
BUT THE FAUCET'S ABOUT TO BE TURNED OFF... FOR JUST LONG ENOUGH...
SO WE'RE NOT ONLY AT YOUR HOMEWORLD-- WE'VE ALSO GONE BACK IN TIME?
YES. THE WORST--THE VERY WORST--HASN'T HAPPENED YET. WHAT'S COMING IS...
WELL, IT'S THE ONLY THING I'VE EVER RUN FROM.
NOT THAT I'M A COWARD! YOU KNOW THAT, JOHNNY! YOU KNOW THAT BETTER THAN ANYONE!
OUCH! HEY! EASY, GUY! NO NEED TO BLOW A CIRCUIT!
I RAN BECAUSE I HAD NO CHOICE! BECAUSE I WAS THE ONLY ONE WHO COULD!
TZZK
BECAUSE I HAD TO FIND THE FOUR OF YOU.
4
MAYBE YOU WOULD HAVE FOUND THIS YOURSELVES. I DON'T KNOW...
THERE ARE UNIVERSAL CONSTANTS-- THINGS THAT ALWAYS HAPPEN.
IT DOESN'T MEAN THINGS ALWAYS END THE SAME.
NO. NOT IF I CAN HELP IT.

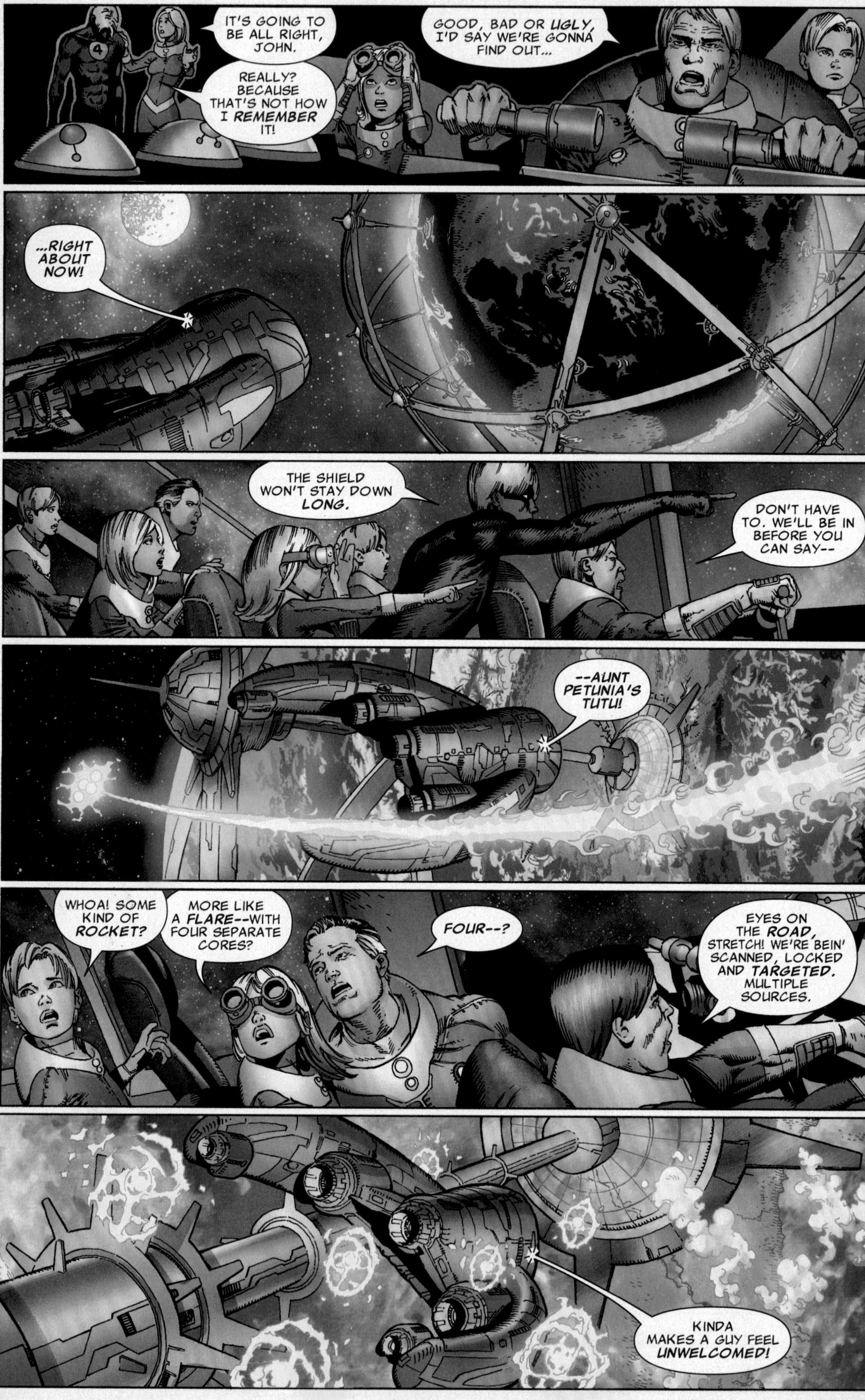
IT'S GOING TO BE ALL RIGHT, JOHN.
REALLY? BECAUSE THAT'S NOT HOW I REMEMBER IT!
GOOD, BAD OR UGLY, I'D SAY WE'RE GONNA FIND OUT...
...RIGHT ABOUT NOW!
THE SHIELD WON'T STAY DOWN LONG.
DON'T HAVE TO. WE'LL BE IN BEFORE YOU CAN SAY--
--AUNT PETUNIA'S TUTU!
WHOA! SOME KIND OF ROCKET?
MORE LIKE A FLARE--WITH FOUR SEPARATE CORES?
FOUR--?
EYES ON THE ROAD, STRETCH! WE'RE BEIN' SCANNED, LOCKED AND TARGETED. MULTIPLE SOURCES.
KINDA MAKES A GUY FEEL UNWELCOMED!

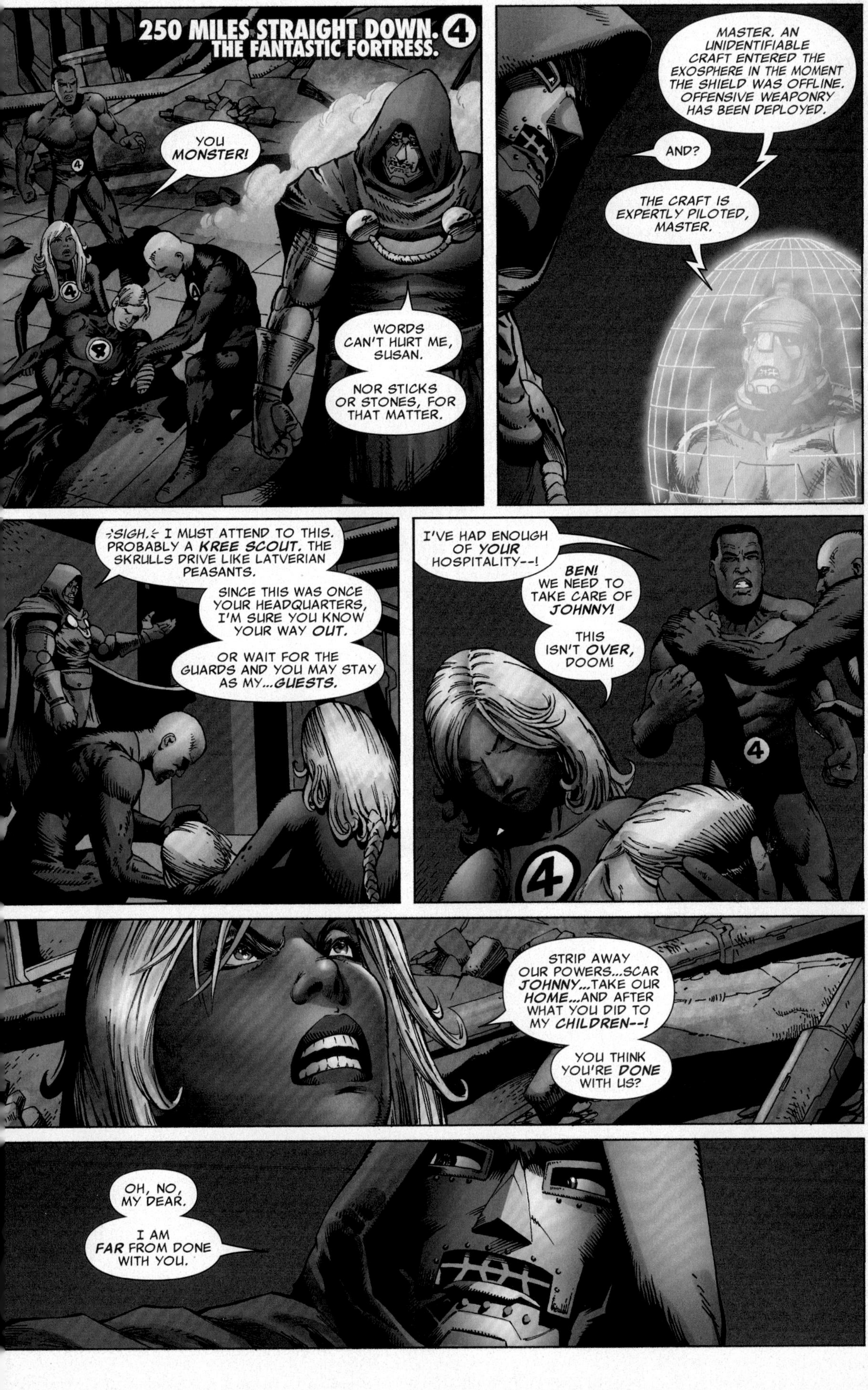
250 MILES STRAIGHT DOWN. THE FANTASTIC FORTRESS.
YOU MONSTER!
WORDS CAN'T HURT ME, SUSAN.
NOR STICKS OR STONES, FOR THAT MATTER.
MASTER. AN UNIDENTIFIABLE CRAFT ENTERED THE EXOSPHERE IN THE MOMENT THE SHIELD WAS OFFLINE. OFFENSIVE WEAPONRY HAS BEEN DEPLOYED.
AND?
THE CRAFT IS EXPERTLY PILOTED, MASTER.
SIGH. I MUST ATTEND TO THIS. PROBABLY A KREE SCOUT. THE SKRULLS DRIVE LIKE LATVERIAN PEASANTS.
SINCE THIS WAS ONCE YOUR HEADQUARTERS, I'M SURE YOU KNOW YOUR WAY OUT.
OR WAIT FOR THE GUARDS AND YOU MAY STAY AS MY...GUESTS.
I'VE HAD ENOUGH OF YOUR HOSPITALITY--!
BEN! WE NEED TO TAKE CARE OF JOHNNY!
THIS ISN'T OVER, DOOM!
STRIP AWAY OUR POWERS...SCAR JOHNNY...TAKE OUR HOME...AND AFTER WHAT YOU DID TO MY CHILDREN--!
YOU THINK YOU'RE DONE WITH US?
OH, NO, MY DEAR.
I AM FAR FROM DONE WITH YOU.

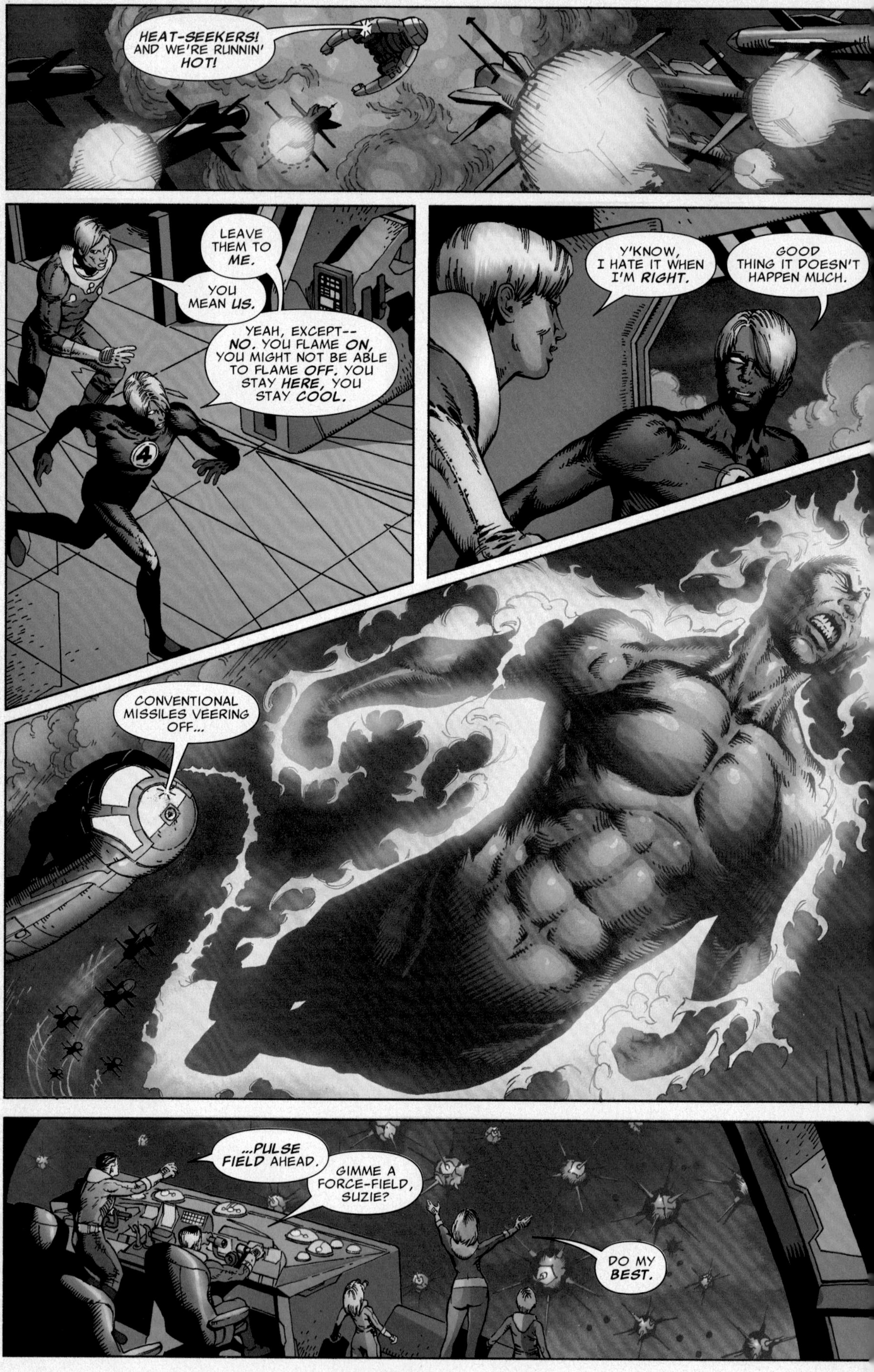
HEAT-SEEKERS! AND WE'RE RUNNIN' HOT!
LEAVE THEM TO ME.
YOU MEAN US.
YEAH, EXCEPT-- NO. YOU FLAME ON, YOU MIGHT NOT BE ABLE TO FLAME OFF. YOU STAY HERE, YOU STAY COOL.
Y'KNOW, I HATE IT WHEN I'M RIGHT.
GOOD THING IT DOESN'T HAPPEN MUCH.
CONVENTIONAL MISSILES VEERING OFF...
...PULSE FIELD AHEAD.
GIMME A FORCE-FIELD, SUZIE?
DO MY BEST.

AAA--!
MOM--!

ALMOST THROUGH...

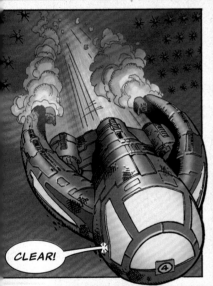

CLEAR!

÷NH÷ NICE FLYING... "ACE."

AW, YOU DID THE HEAVY LIFTIN', SUZIE, I WAS JUST KEEPIN' THIS RUST-BUCKET IN THE AIR...

...WHICH IT AIN'T GONNA BE MUCH LONGER!

I GOT NOTHIN' HERE! TALK TO ME, REED!

ELECTRO-MAGNETIC BARRAGE! ALL MECHANICS DEAD! ALL INSTRUMENTS OUT!

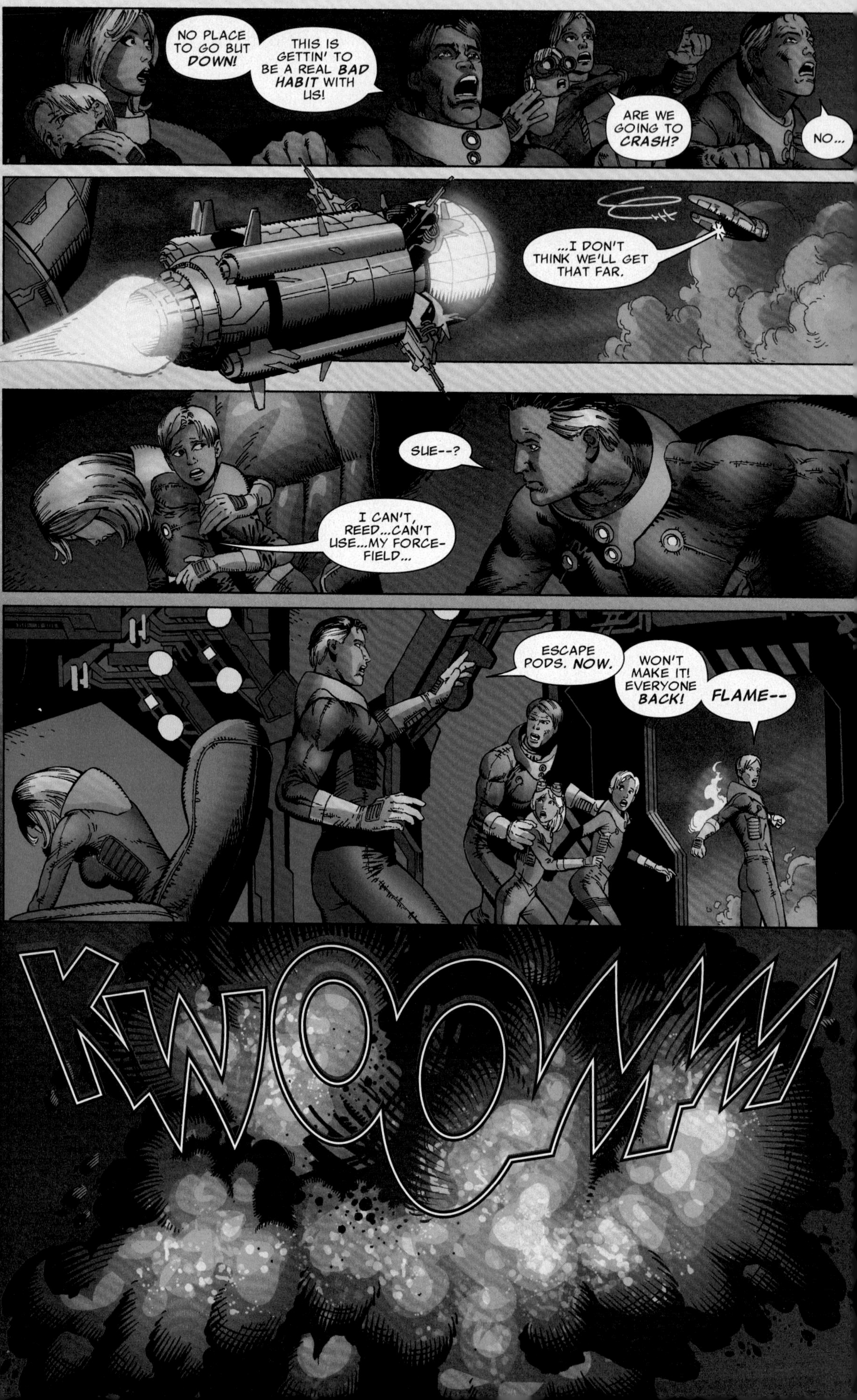
NO PLACE TO GO BUT DOWN!
THIS IS GETTIN' TO BE A REAL BAD HABIT WITH US!
ARE WE GOING TO CRASH?
NO...
...I DON'T THINK WE'LL GET THAT FAR.
SUE--?
I CAN'T, REED...CAN'T USE...MY FORCE-FIELD...
ESCAPE PODS. NOW.
WON'T MAKE IT! EVERYONE BACK!
FLAME--
KWOOMM

THE ELECTRO-MAGNETIC BARRAGE SHOULD BE YOUR *FIRST STRIKE*, FOLLOWED BY A *FATAL BLOW.*

THE E.M.B. PUTS A *DISPROPORTIONATE* STRAIN ON THE POWER RESERVES, MASTER.

AH. THEN I CAN SEE WHY IT WOULD BE OF *CONCERN*--TO *OTHERS.*

YES, MASTER.

FIRST STRIKE. *ALWAYS.*

INCOMING PROJECTILE, MASTER. IT APPEARS TO BE THE HUMAN TORCH, ALTHOUGH WITH *LEFT*-SIDED CYBERNETICS.

SSSTORM--!

KILLERS! *MURDERERS!*

YOU DIDN'T KILL ME *YESTERDAY!* YOU WON'T KILL ME *TOMORROW!* JUST TRY KILLING ME *TODAY!* *JUST TRY!*

WHERE DID THAT GNAT COME FROM? AND WITH *CYBERNETICS*--?

THE BETTER QUESTION IS, "*WHEN* DID HE COME FROM?"

AH. THE FUTURE. TAKES ONE TO KNOW ONE, I SUPPOSE.

FULL DIAGNOSTICS.

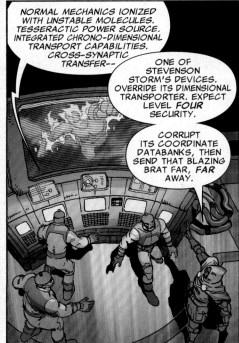

NORMAL MECHANICS IONIZED WITH UNSTABLE MOLECULES. TESSERACTIC POWER SOURCE. INTEGRATED CHRONO-DIMENSIONAL TRANSPORT CAPABILITIES. CROSS-SYNAPTIC TRANSFER--

ONE OF STEVENSON STORM'S DEVICES. OVERRIDE ITS DIMENSIONAL TRANSPORTER. EXPECT LEVEL *FOUR* SECURITY.

CORRUPT ITS COORDINATE DATABANKS, THEN SEND THAT BLAZING BRAT FAR, *FAR* AWAY.

NO! DESTROY HIM! *OBLITERATE* HIM!

IT'S CLEARLY A *SUICIDE* RUN. I WON'T GIVE HIM THAT *SATISFACTION.*

EXECUTE COMMAND.

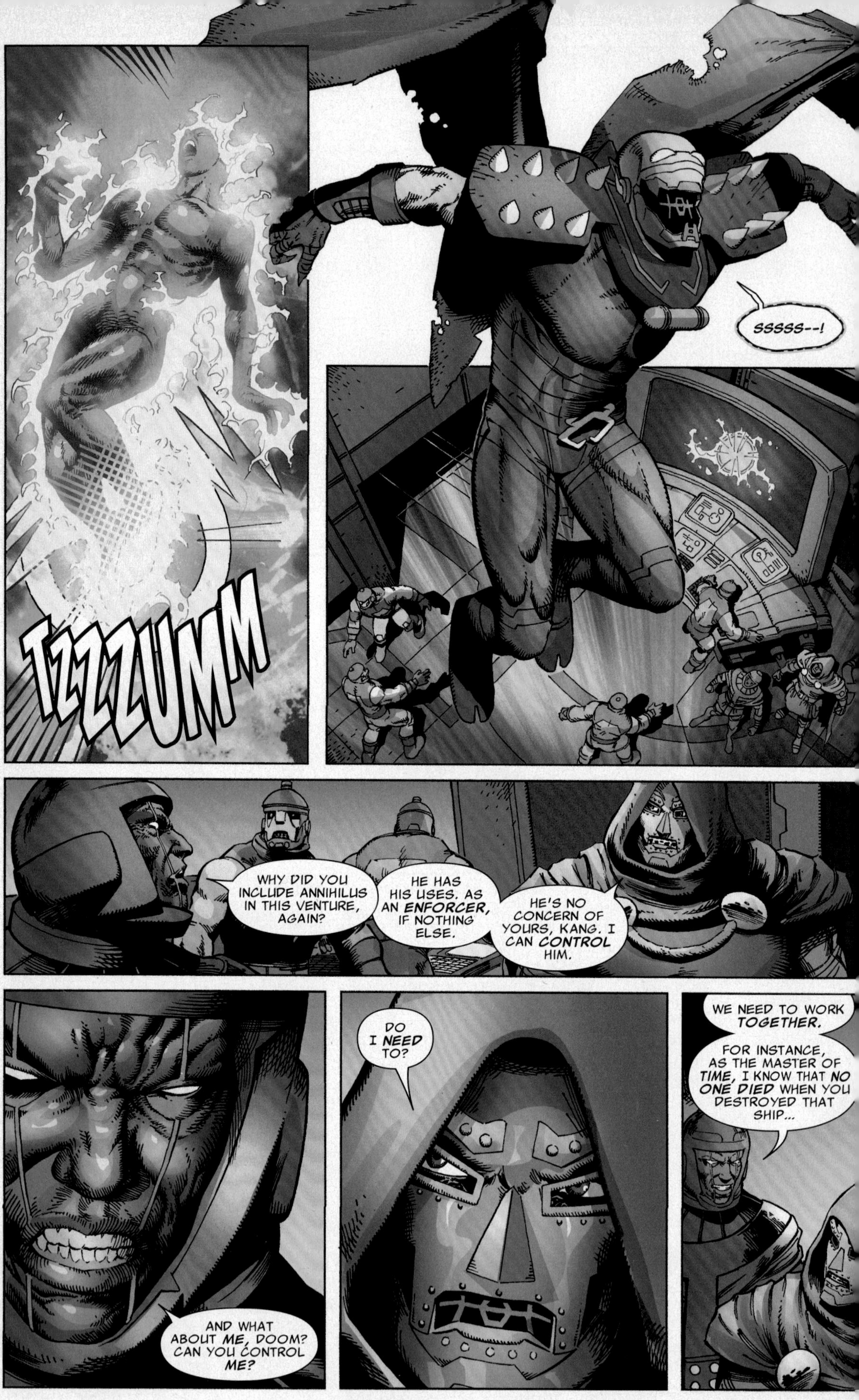
SSSSS--!
TZZZUMM
WHY DID YOU INCLUDE ANNIHILUS IN THIS VENTURE, AGAIN?
HE HAS HIS USES. AS AN ENFORCER, IF NOTHING ELSE.
HE'S NO CONCERN OF YOURS, KANG. I CAN CONTROL HIM.
AND WHAT ABOUT ME, DOOM? CAN YOU CONTROL ME?
DO I NEED TO?
WE NEED TO WORK TOGETHER.
FOR INSTANCE, AS THE MASTER OF TIME, I KNOW THAT NO ONE DIED WHEN YOU DESTROYED THAT SHIP...

"...FIVE MINUTES AGO."

SUE--?

I CAN'T, REED...CAN'T USE...

...MY FORCE-FIELD...

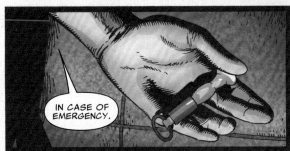

IN CASE OF EMERGENCY.

IT'S A *VACATION*, MEDUSA. I'M *MOSTLY* WORRIED THE KIDS WILL BE *BORED* WITHOUT *INTERNET* ACCESS.

IF *THAT* IS DIRE ENOUGH TO WARRANT *THIS*, THEN USE IT WITH MY BLESSING, SUSAN.

ESCAPE PODS. NOW.

WON'T MAKE IT! EVERYONE *BACK!*

FLAME--

WELL, THEY DO LOVE THAT *DOG...*

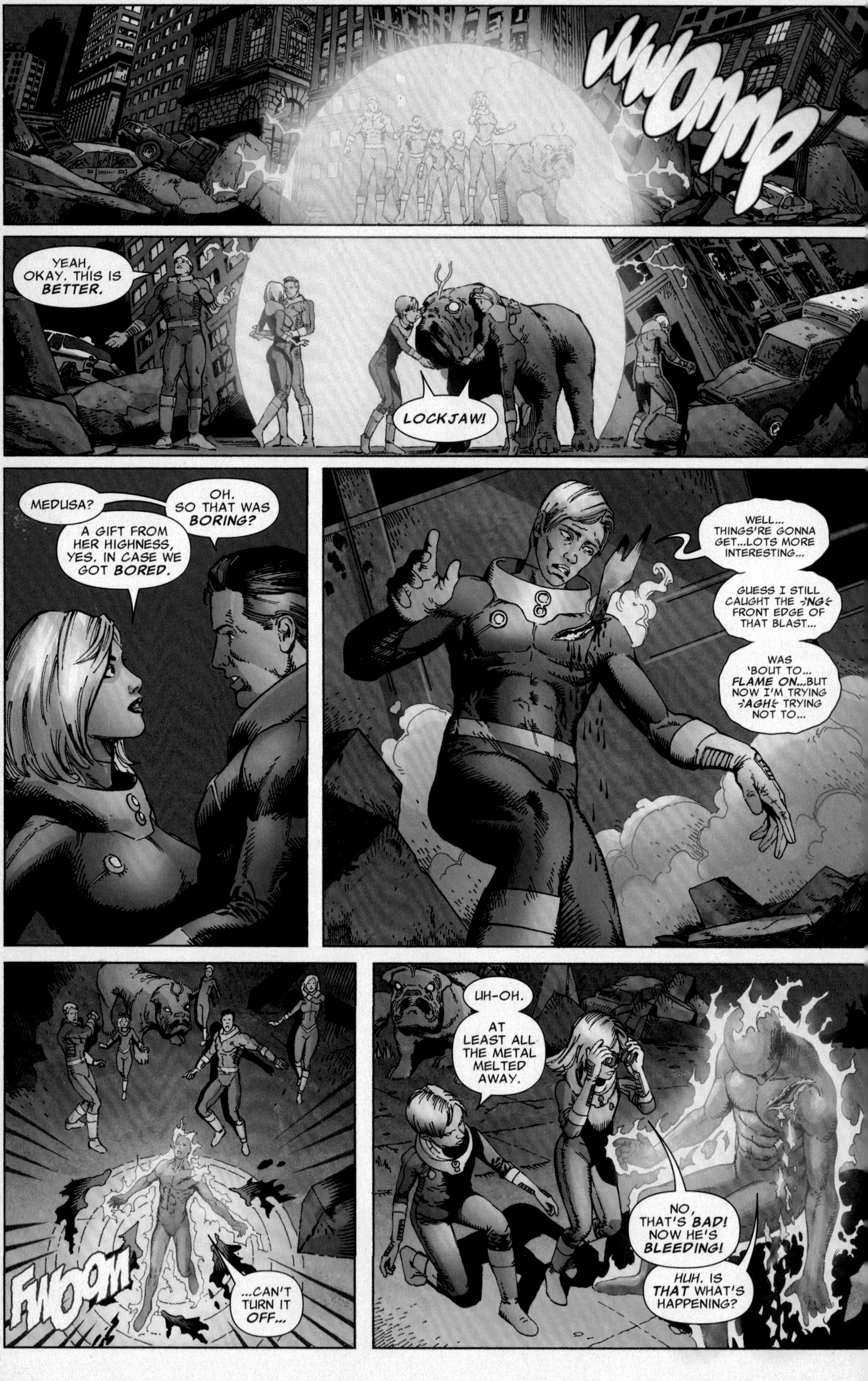
VWOMMP
YEAH, OKAY. THIS IS BETTER.
LOCKJAW!
MEDUSA?
A GIFT FROM HER HIGHNESS, YES. IN CASE WE GOT BORED.
OH. SO THAT WAS BORING?
WELL... THINGS'RE GONNA GET...LOTS MORE INTERESTING...
GUESS I STILL CAUGHT THE -NG- FRONT EDGE OF THAT BLAST...
WAS 'BOUT TO... FLAME ON...BUT NOW I'M TRYING -AGH- TRYING NOT TO...
FWOOM
...CAN'T TURN IT OFF...
UH-OH.
AT LEAST ALL THE METAL MELTED AWAY.
NO, THAT'S BAD! NOW HE'S BLEEDING!
HUH. IS THAT WHAT'S HAPPENING?

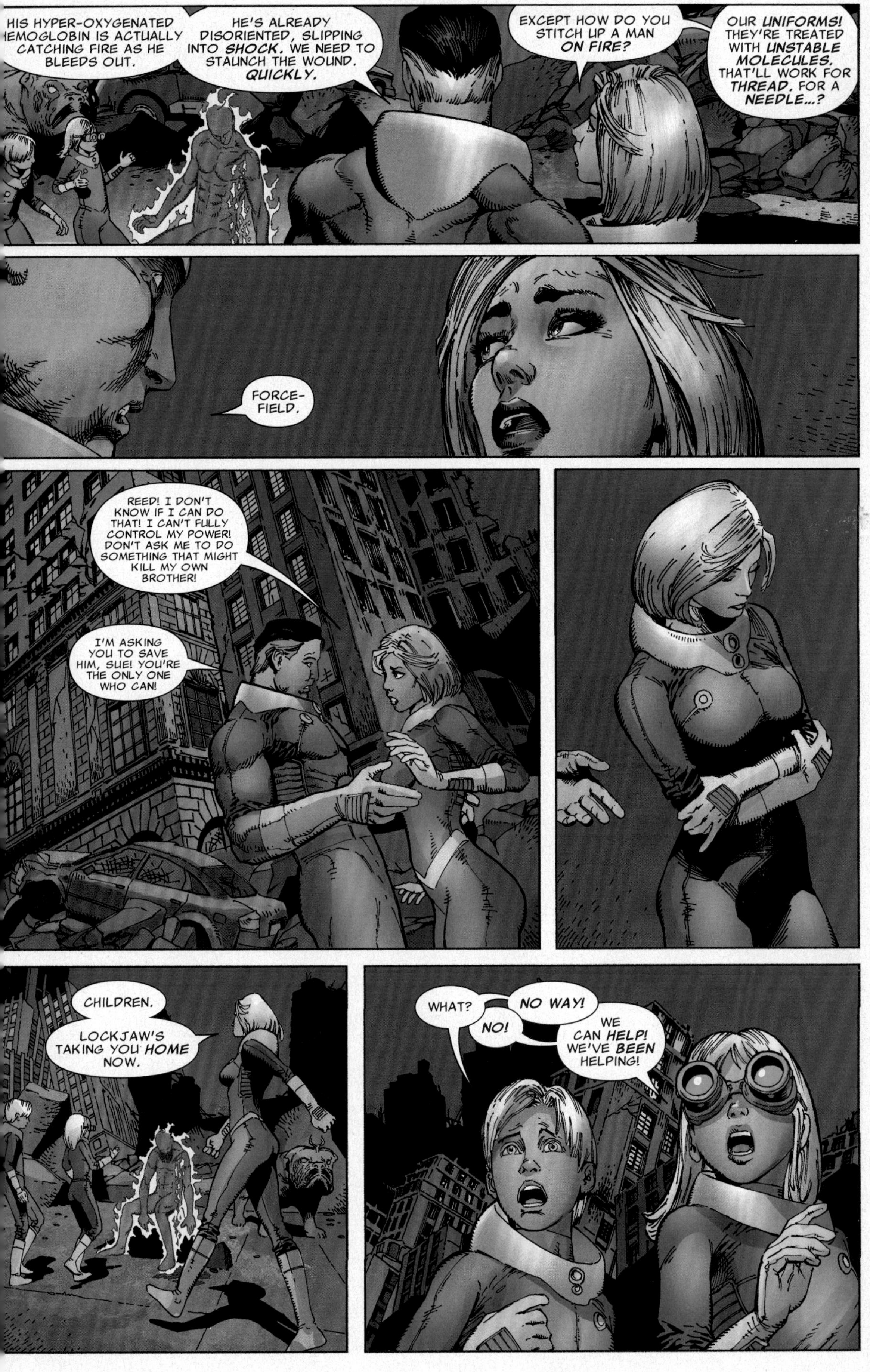
HIS HYPER-OXYGENATED HEMOGLOBIN IS ACTUALLY CATCHING FIRE AS HE BLEEDS OUT.
HE'S ALREADY DISORIENTED, SLIPPING INTO SHOCK. WE NEED TO STAUNCH THE WOUND. QUICKLY.
EXCEPT HOW DO YOU STITCH UP A MAN ON FIRE?
OUR UNIFORMS! THEY'RE TREATED WITH UNSTABLE MOLECULES. THAT'LL WORK FOR THREAD. FOR A NEEDLE...?
FORCE-FIELD.
REED! I DON'T KNOW IF I CAN DO THAT! I CAN'T FULLY CONTROL MY POWER! DON'T ASK ME TO DO SOMETHING THAT MIGHT KILL MY OWN BROTHER!
I'M ASKING YOU TO SAVE HIM, SUE! YOU'RE THE ONLY ONE WHO CAN!
CHILDREN.
LOCKJAW'S TAKING YOU HOME NOW.
WHAT?
NO WAY!
NO!
WE CAN HELP! WE'VE BEEN HELPING!

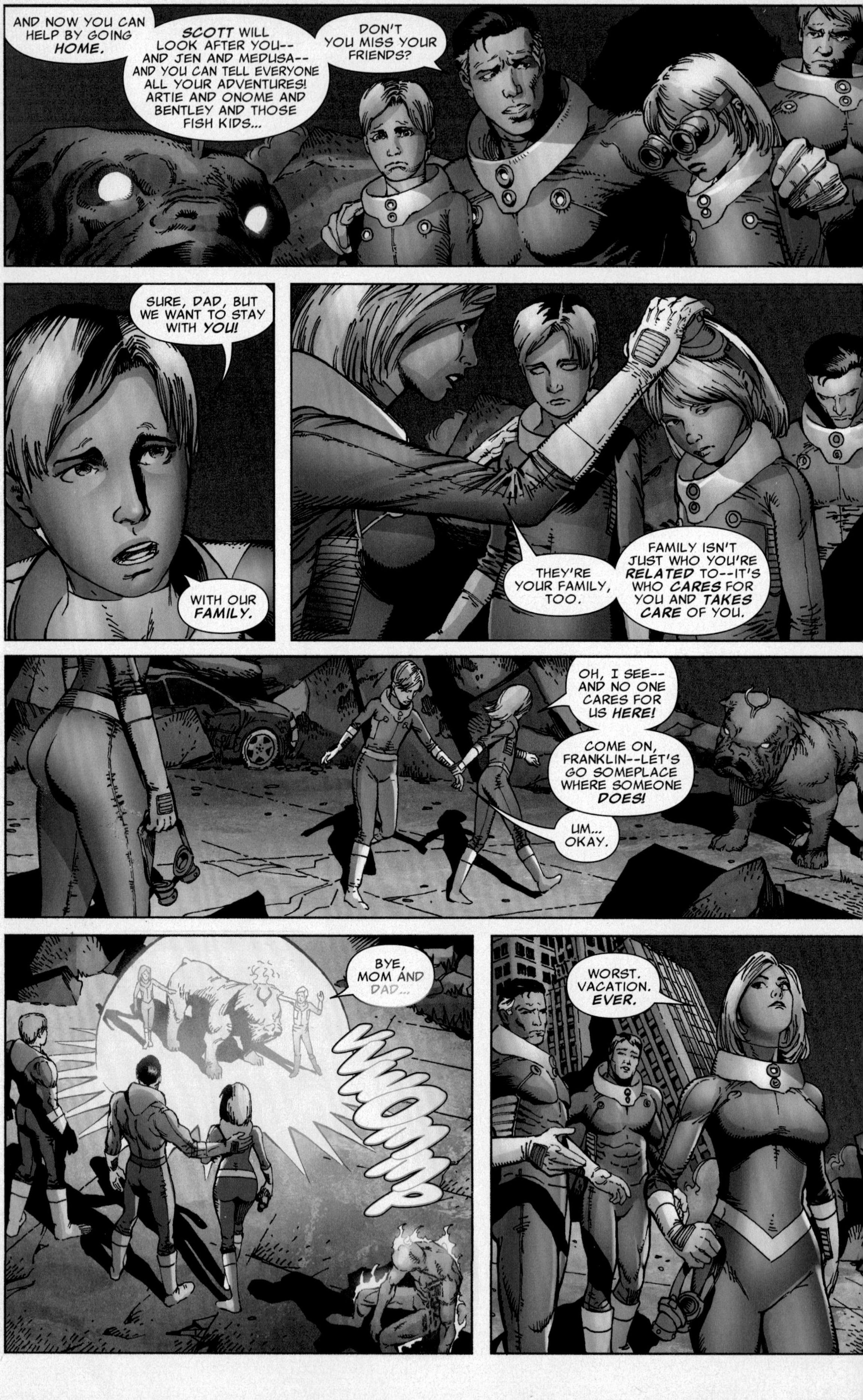

AND NOW YOU CAN HELP BY GOING HOME.
SCOTT WILL LOOK AFTER YOU-- AND JEN AND MEDUSA-- AND YOU CAN TELL EVERYONE ALL YOUR ADVENTURES! ARTIE AND ONOME AND BENTLEY AND THOSE FISH KIDS...
DON'T YOU MISS YOUR FRIENDS?
SURE, DAD, BUT WE WANT TO STAY WITH YOU!
WITH OUR FAMILY.
THEY'RE YOUR FAMILY, TOO.
FAMILY ISN'T JUST WHO YOU'RE RELATED TO--IT'S WHO CARES FOR YOU AND TAKES CARE OF YOU.
OH, I SEE-- AND NO ONE CARES FOR US HERE!
COME ON, FRANKLIN--LET'S GO SOMEPLACE WHERE SOMEONE DOES!
UM... OKAY.
BYE, MOM AND DAD...
WWOMMP
WORST. VACATION. EVER.

OKAY. HOW DO WE DO THIS?

YOU AND I HOLD HIM *DOWN,* BEN. THE UNSTABLE MOLECULES IN OUR UNIFORMS WILL GIVE US... *SOME* PROTECTION. *ENOUGH,* HOPEFULLY.

NEEDLESS TO SAY, WE DON'T HAVE AN *ANESTHETIC.*

YOU CAN *DO* THIS, SUE.

SURE. EASY.

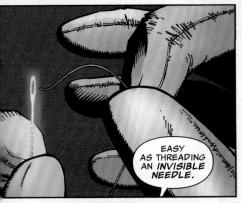

EASY AS THREADING AN *INVISIBLE* NEEDLE.

SIS... IF IT HELPS... I...

...I THINK I COULD PASS OUT...

JOHNNY! WILL YOU--

NOW I *HAVE* TO SAVE YOU!

THOSE CAN'T BE YOUR *LAST* WORDS!

I'LL TRY TO SHIELD US FROM THE HEAT, TOO. BUT JOHNNY COMES FIRST.

ABSOLUTELY.

UNDERSTOOD.

HOLD HIM.

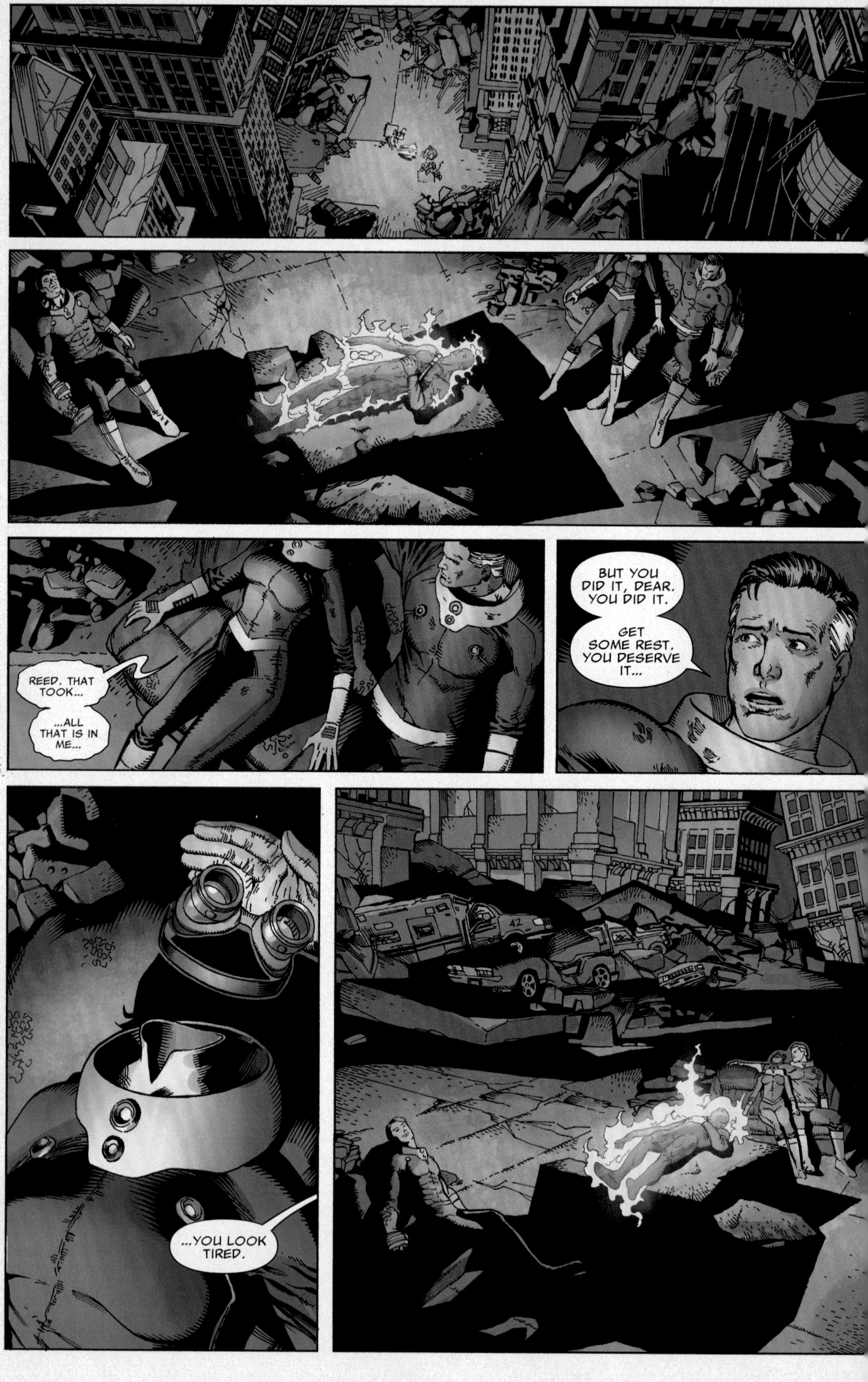
REED. THAT TOOK...
...ALL THAT IS IN ME...
BUT YOU DID IT, DEAR. YOU DID IT.
GET SOME REST. YOU DESERVE IT...
...YOU LOOK TIRED.

AT LEAST WE KNOW THE WOUND'S STERILE.

AND I THINK THE KID'LL *PULL THROUGH.* NASTY *SCAR,* BUT HE'LL *LIVE.*

I WISH THAT WAS THE WORST OF IT.

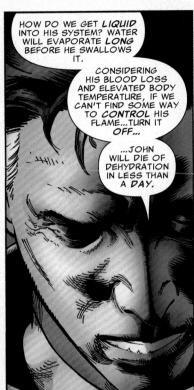

HOW DO WE GET *LIQUID* INTO HIS SYSTEM? WATER WILL EVAPORATE *LONG* BEFORE HE SWALLOWS IT.

CONSIDERING HIS BLOOD LOSS AND ELEVATED BODY TEMPERATURE, IF WE CAN'T FIND SOME WAY TO *CONTROL* HIS FLAME...TURN IT *OFF...*

...JOHN WILL DIE OF DEHYDRATION IN LESS THAN A *DAY.*

MAYBE *WE* CAN HELP...

...WE'RE THE *FANTASTIC FOUR.*

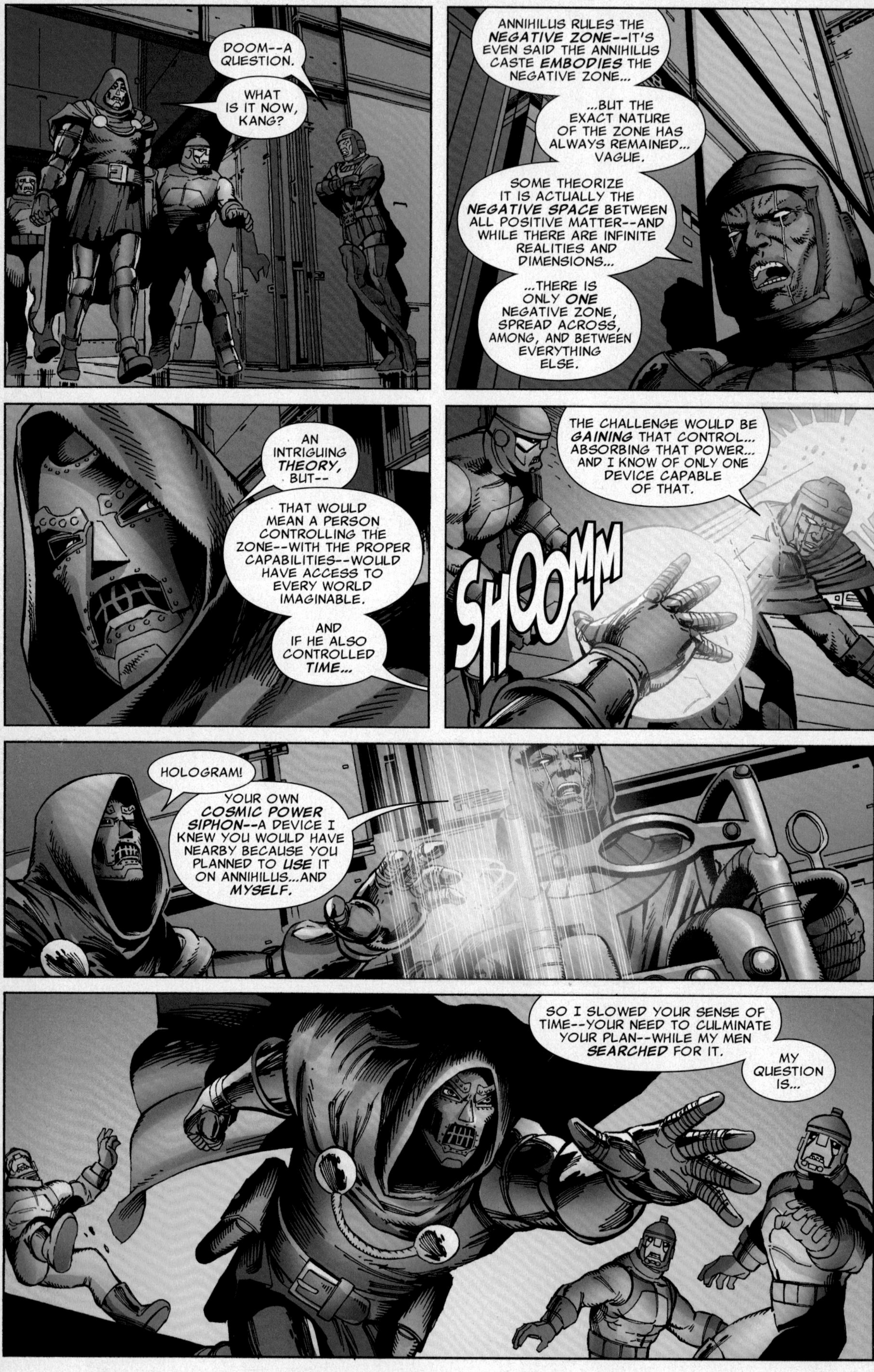
DOOM--A QUESTION.
WHAT IS IT NOW, KANG?
ANNIHILUS RULES THE NEGATIVE ZONE--IT'S EVEN SAID THE ANNIHILUS CASTE EMBODIES THE NEGATIVE ZONE...
...BUT THE EXACT NATURE OF THE ZONE HAS ALWAYS REMAINED... VAGUE.
SOME THEORIZE IT IS ACTUALLY THE NEGATIVE SPACE BETWEEN ALL POSITIVE MATTER--AND WHILE THERE ARE INFINITE REALITIES AND DIMENSIONS...
...THERE IS ONLY ONE NEGATIVE ZONE, SPREAD ACROSS, AMONG, AND BETWEEN EVERYTHING ELSE.
AN INTRIGUING THEORY, BUT--
THAT WOULD MEAN A PERSON CONTROLLING THE ZONE--WITH THE PROPER CAPABILITIES--WOULD HAVE ACCESS TO EVERY WORLD IMAGINABLE.
AND IF HE ALSO CONTROLLED TIME...
THE CHALLENGE WOULD BE GAINING THAT CONTROL... ABSORBING THAT POWER... AND I KNOW OF ONLY ONE DEVICE CAPABLE OF THAT.
SHOOMM
HOLOGRAM!
YOUR OWN COSMIC POWER SIPHON--A DEVICE I KNEW YOU WOULD HAVE NEARBY BECAUSE YOU PLANNED TO USE IT ON ANNIHILUS...AND MYSELF.
SO I SLOWED YOUR SENSE OF TIME--YOUR NEED TO CULMINATE YOUR PLAN--WHILE MY MEN SEARCHED FOR IT.
MY QUESTION IS...

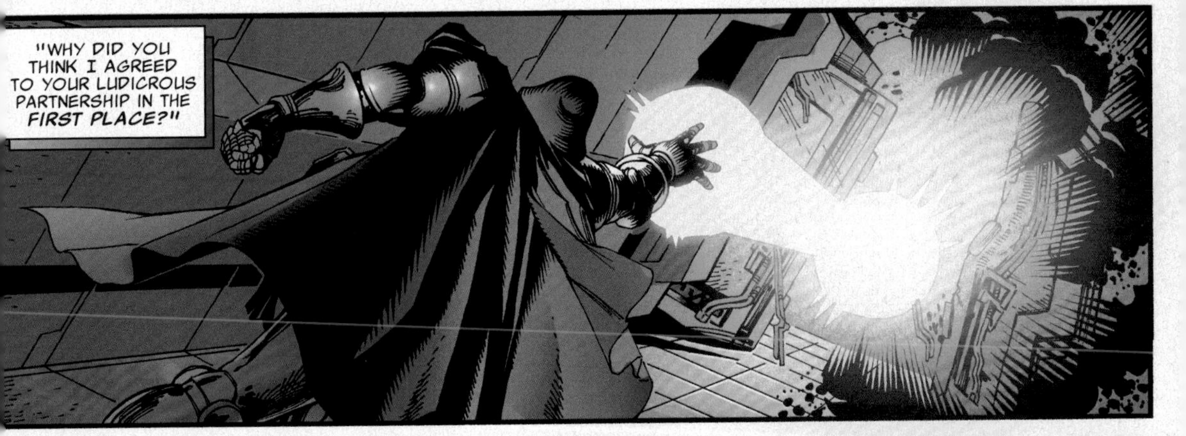
"WHY DID YOU THINK I AGREED TO YOUR LUDICROUS PARTNERSHIP IN THE *FIRST PLACE?*"

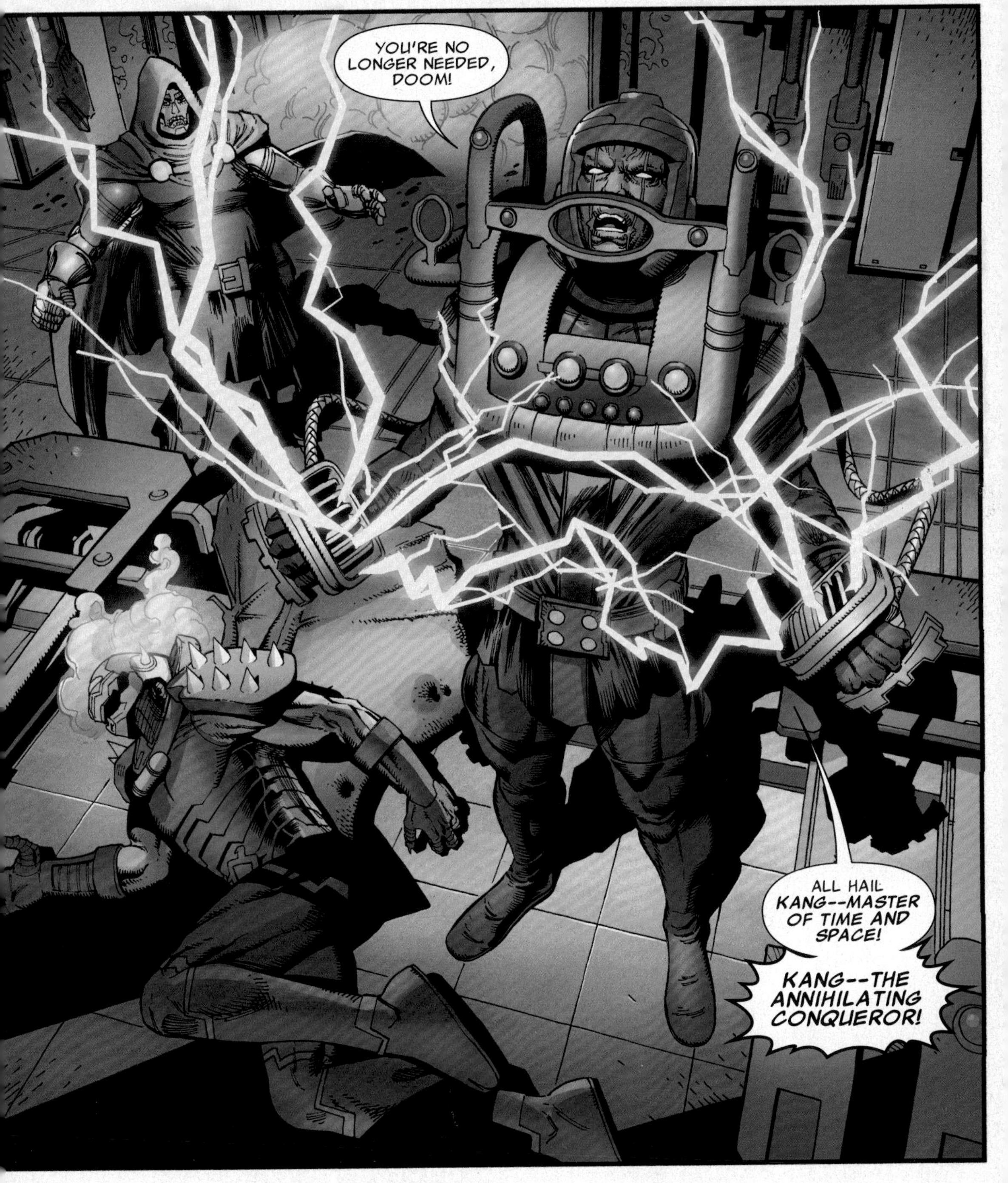
YOU'RE NO LONGER NEEDED, DOOM!
ALL HAIL KANG--MASTER OF TIME AND SPACE!
KANG--THE ANNIHILATING CONQUEROR!

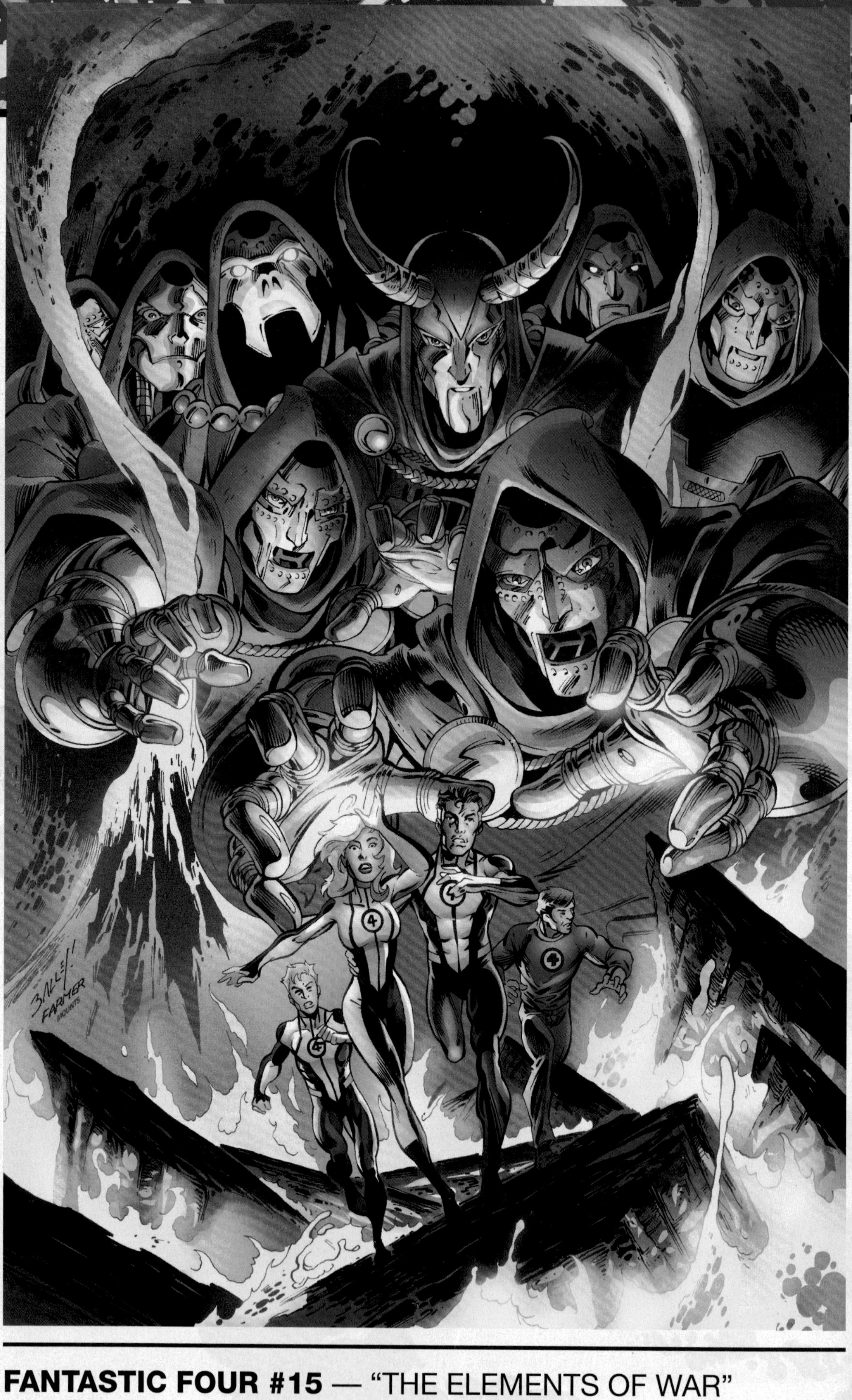

FANTASTIC FOUR #15 — “THE ELEMENTS OF WAR”

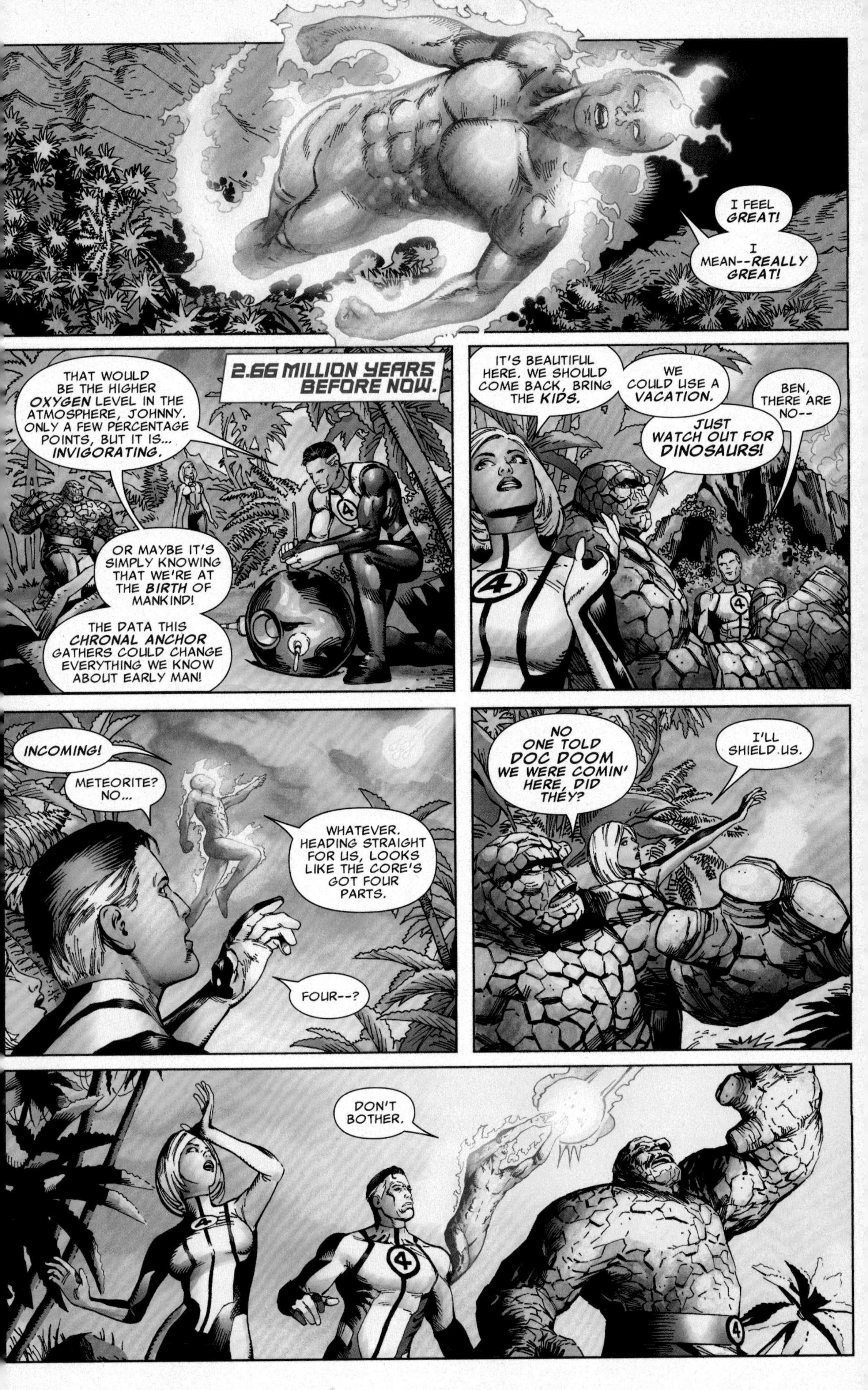
I FEEL GREAT!
I MEAN--REALLY GREAT!
2.66 MILLION YEARS BEFORE NOW.
THAT WOULD BE THE HIGHER OXYGEN LEVEL IN THE ATMOSPHERE, JOHNNY. ONLY A FEW PERCENTAGE POINTS, BUT IT IS... INVIGORATING.
OR MAYBE IT'S SIMPLY KNOWING THAT WE'RE AT THE BIRTH OF MANKIND!
THE DATA THIS CHRONAL ANCHOR GATHERS COULD CHANGE EVERYTHING WE KNOW ABOUT EARLY MAN!
IT'S BEAUTIFUL HERE. WE SHOULD COME BACK, BRING THE KIDS.
WE COULD USE A VACATION.
JUST WATCH OUT FOR DINOSAURS!
BEN, THERE ARE NO--
INCOMING!
METEORITE? NO...
WHATEVER. HEADING STRAIGHT FOR US, LOOKS LIKE THE CORE'S GOT FOUR PARTS.
FOUR--?
NO ONE TOLD DOC DOOM WE WERE COMIN' HERE, DID THEY?
I'LL SHIELD US.
DON'T BOTHER.

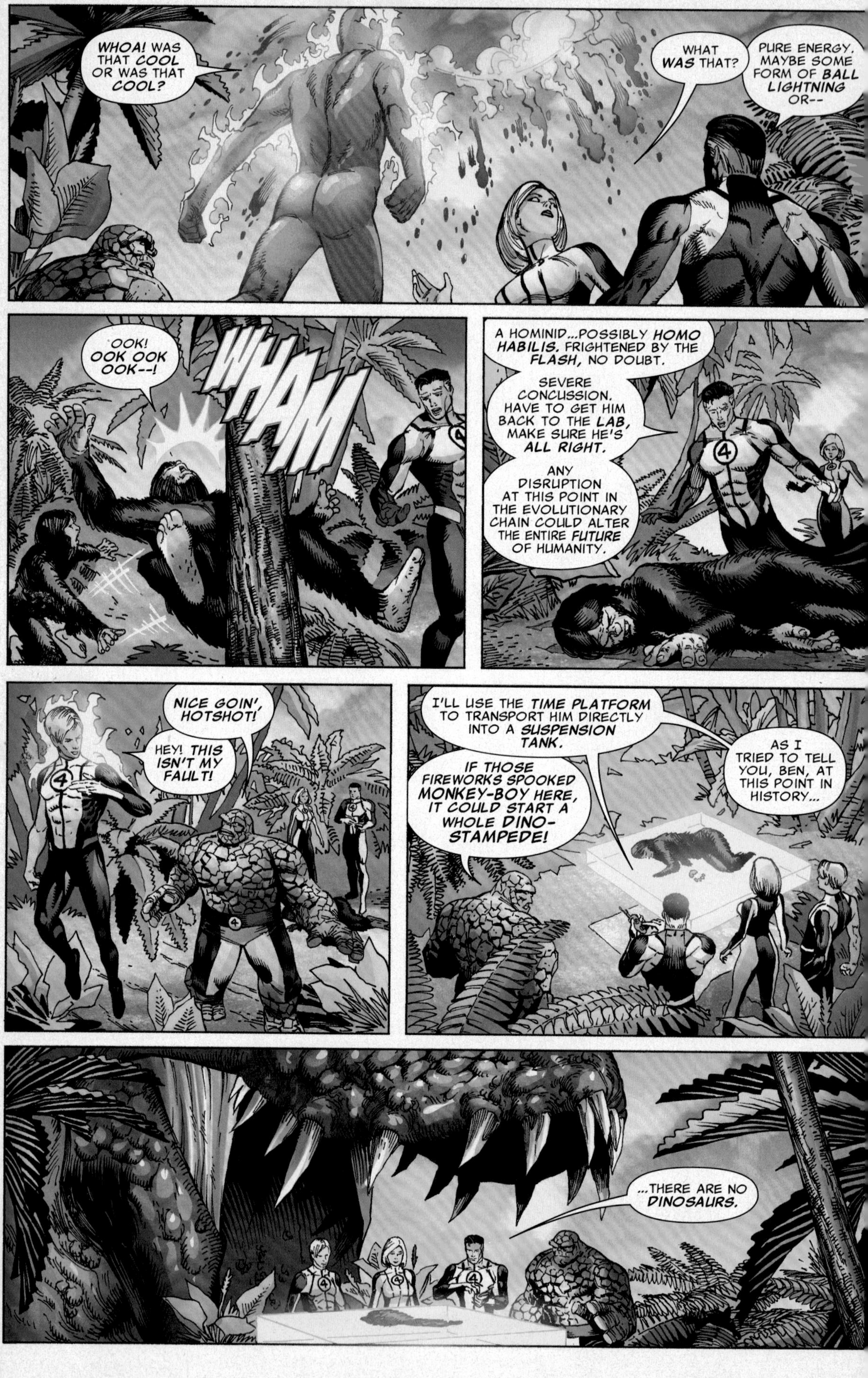
WHOA! WAS THAT COOL OR WAS THAT COOL?
WHAT WAS THAT?
PURE ENERGY. MAYBE SOME FORM OF BALL LIGHTNING OR--
OOK! OOK OOK OOK--!
WHAM
A HOMINID...POSSIBLY HOMO HABILIS. FRIGHTENED BY THE FLASH, NO DOUBT.
SEVERE CONCUSSION. HAVE TO GET HIM BACK TO THE LAB, MAKE SURE HE'S ALL RIGHT.
ANY DISRUPTION AT THIS POINT IN THE EVOLUTIONARY CHAIN COULD ALTER THE ENTIRE FUTURE OF HUMANITY.
NICE GOIN', HOTSHOT!
HEY! THIS ISN'T MY FAULT!
I'LL USE THE TIME PLATFORM TO TRANSPORT HIM DIRECTLY INTO A SUSPENSION TANK.
IF THOSE FIREWORKS SPOOKED MONKEY-BOY HERE, IT COULD START A WHOLE DINO-STAMPEDE!
AS I TRIED TO TELL YOU, BEN, AT THIS POINT IN HISTORY...
...THERE ARE NO DINOSAURS.

AGHHH!

NO...THAT'S WRONG...

REED GOT BIT... NOT ME. I WASN'T HURT...

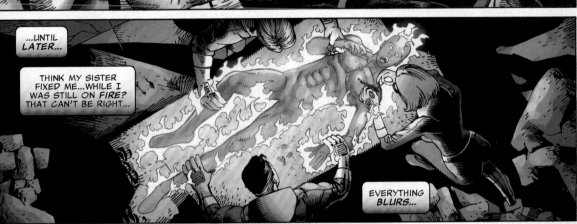

...UNTIL LATER...

THINK MY SISTER FIXED ME...WHILE I WAS STILL ON FIRE? THAT CAN'T BE RIGHT...

EVERYTHING BLURS...

I'M SEEING DOUBLE...

MY NAME'S STEVENSON STORM.

REED RICHARDS.

FASCINATING. MY WIFE'S MAIDEN NAME WAS RICHARDS.

THIS IS MY BROTHER, JOHNNY.

WAIT. THAT'S NOT ME. THAT'S...

THAT'S THE OTHER JOHNNY, FROM...

I'M FROM ANOTHER FANTASTIC FOUR IN ANOTHER REALITY.

ALL THE TIME TRAVEL AND DIMENSION-HOPPING WE'VE BEEN DOING...

EVERYTHING'S JUMBLED...

DOOM HAS JOINED FORCES WITH KANG AND ANNIHILUS, AND STRIPPED US OF OUR POWERS. WE *KNEW* THIS WOULD HAPPEN.

IT'S A *UNIVERSAL CONSTANT* ACROSS ALL REALITIES. IT *ALWAYS* HAPPENS.

SO YOU SENT OUT THE *FLARE* WE SAW ESCAPE THE SHIELD.

THE SAME FLARE THAT EXPLODED OVER US IN *PREHISTORIC TIMES.*

ONLY IT'S *MORE* THAN A FLARE--IT CONTAINED THE *ESSENCE* OF OUR POWERS. IT MOVED ACROSS TIME AND SPACE SEEKING OUT SIMILARLY GROUPED ENERGIES, THEN GRAFTED ONTO THEM.

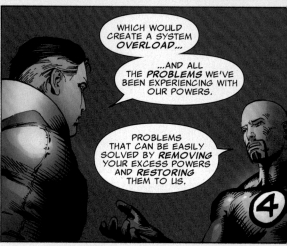

WHICH WOULD CREATE A SYSTEM *OVERLOAD...*

...AND ALL THE *PROBLEMS* WE'VE BEEN EXPERIENCING WITH OUR POWERS.

PROBLEMS THAT CAN BE EASILY SOLVED BY *REMOVING* YOUR EXCESS POWERS AND *RESTORING* THEM TO US.

SORRY TO HAVE DONE THIS, BUT WE HAD *NO CHOICE.* WE NEED YOUR *HELP.*

AGAINST DOOM?

AGAINST *DOOM THE ANNIHILATING CONQUEROR.*

DOOM, KANG AND ANNIHILUS ARE DESTINED TO MERGE THEIR POWERS *TOGETHER.* ONLY *OUR COMBINED TEAMS* CAN STOP THEM.

IF WE DON'T, THIS ENTIRE UNIVERSE IS... *DOOMED.*

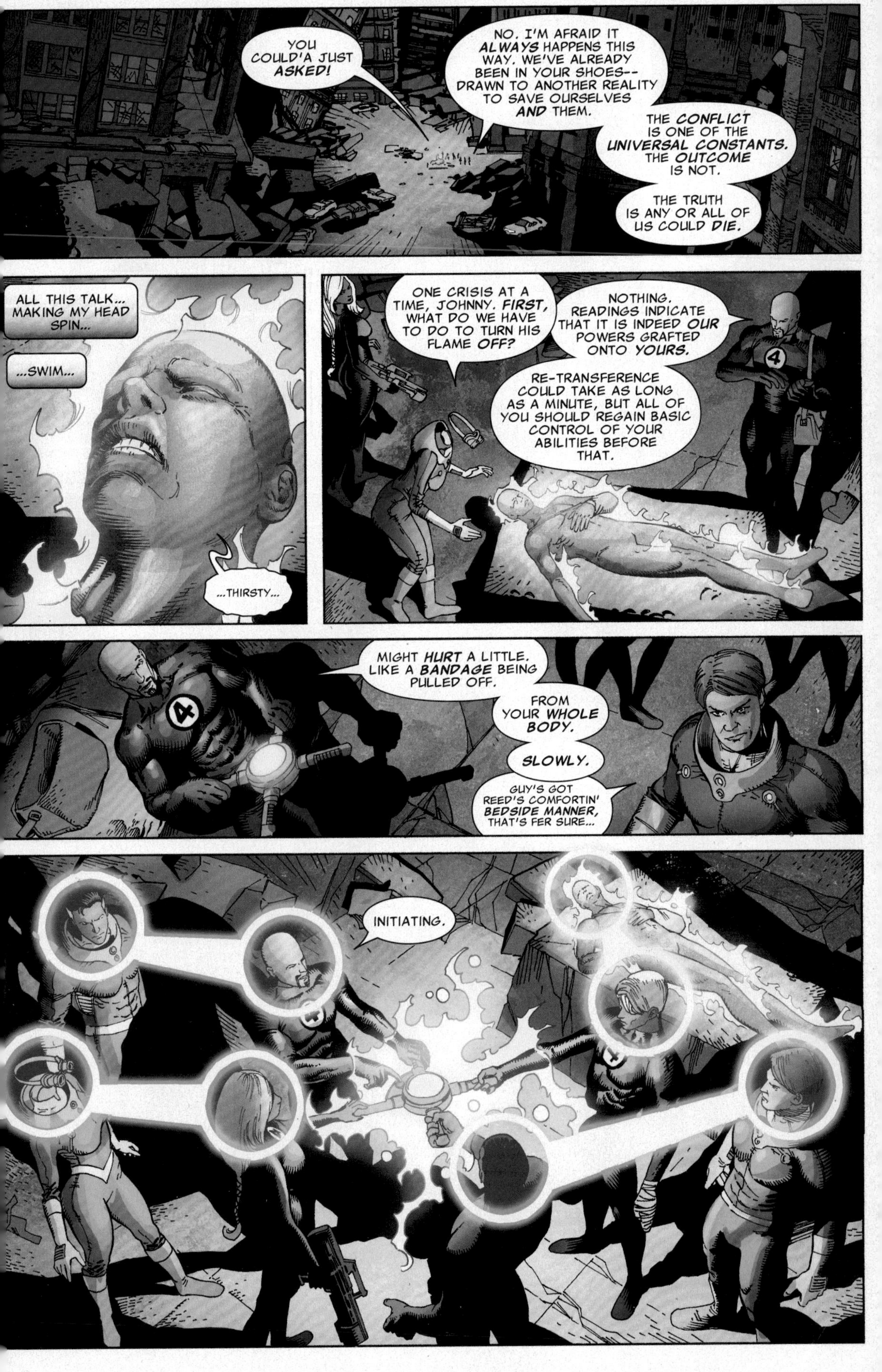
YOU COULD'A JUST ASKED!
NO. I'M AFRAID IT ALWAYS HAPPENS THIS WAY. WE'VE ALREADY BEEN IN YOUR SHOES-- DRAWN TO ANOTHER REALITY TO SAVE OURSELVES AND THEM.
THE CONFLICT IS ONE OF THE UNIVERSAL CONSTANTS. THE OUTCOME IS NOT.
THE TRUTH IS ANY OR ALL OF US COULD DIE.
ALL THIS TALK... MAKING MY HEAD SPIN...
...SWIM...
...THIRSTY...
ONE CRISIS AT A TIME, JOHNNY. FIRST, WHAT DO WE HAVE TO DO TO TURN HIS FLAME OFF?
NOTHING. READINGS INDICATE THAT IT IS INDEED OUR POWERS GRAFTED ONTO YOURS.
RE-TRANSFERENCE COULD TAKE AS LONG AS A MINUTE, BUT ALL OF YOU SHOULD REGAIN BASIC CONTROL OF YOUR ABILITIES BEFORE THAT.
MIGHT HURT A LITTLE. LIKE A BANDAGE BEING PULLED OFF.
FROM YOUR WHOLE BODY.
SLOWLY.
GUY'S GOT REED'S COMFORTIN' BEDSIDE MANNER, THAT'S FER SURE...
INITIATING.

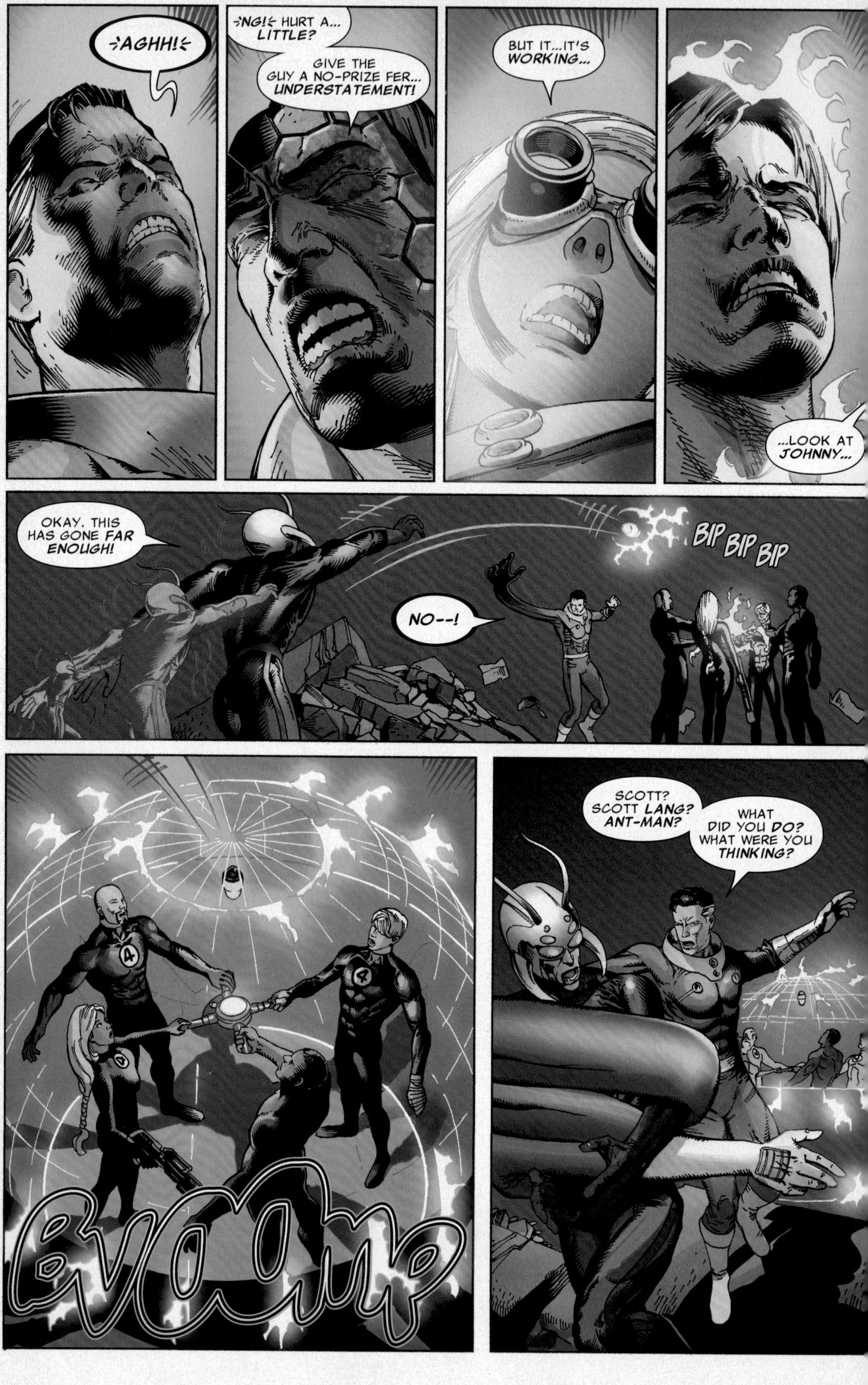
AGHH!
NG! HURT A... LITTLE?
GIVE THE GUY A NO-PRIZE FER... UNDERSTATEMENT!
BUT IT...IT'S WORKING...
...LOOK AT JOHNNY...
OKAY. THIS HAS GONE FAR ENOUGH!
BIP BIP BIP
NO--!
SCOTT? SCOTT LANG? ANT-MAN?
WHAT DID YOU DO? WHAT WERE YOU THINKING?

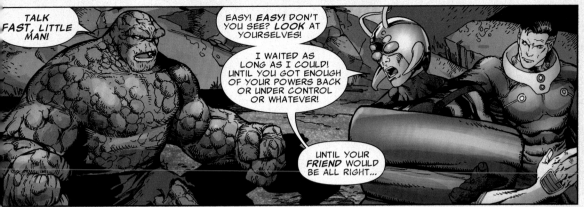

TALK FAST, LITTLE MAN!

EASY! *EASY!* DON'T YOU SEE? *LOOK* AT YOURSELVES!

I WAITED AS LONG AS I COULD! UNTIL YOU GOT ENOUGH OF YOUR POWERS BACK OR UNDER CONTROL OR WHATEVER!

UNTIL YOUR *FRIEND* WOULD BE ALL RIGHT...

...'HANKS...

SHH, JOHNNY. DRINK THIS.

WE NEED TO GET HIM INTO HIS *SPARE UNIFORM* AS SOON AS POSSIBLE. KEEP HIM WARM, PROTECT THE *WOUND* BETTER.

MIGHT AS WELL *ALL* DO THAT--SHOW SOME PEOPLE WE MEAN *BUSINESS!*

LOOK--YOUR POWERS HAVE *STABILIZED*, RIGHT? THINGS COULD BE WORSE.

AND I SUSPECT THEY WILL BE...

SUE-- FORCE FIELD.

KLONK

HEY!

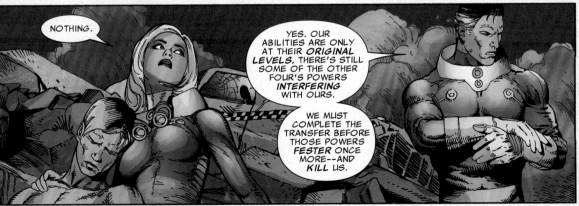

NOTHING.

YES. OUR ABILITIES ARE ONLY AT THEIR *ORIGINAL* LEVELS. THERE'S STILL SOME OF THE OTHER FOUR'S POWERS *INTERFERING* WITH OURS.

WE MUST COMPLETE THE TRANSFER BEFORE THOSE POWERS *FESTER* ONCE MORE--AND *KILL* US.

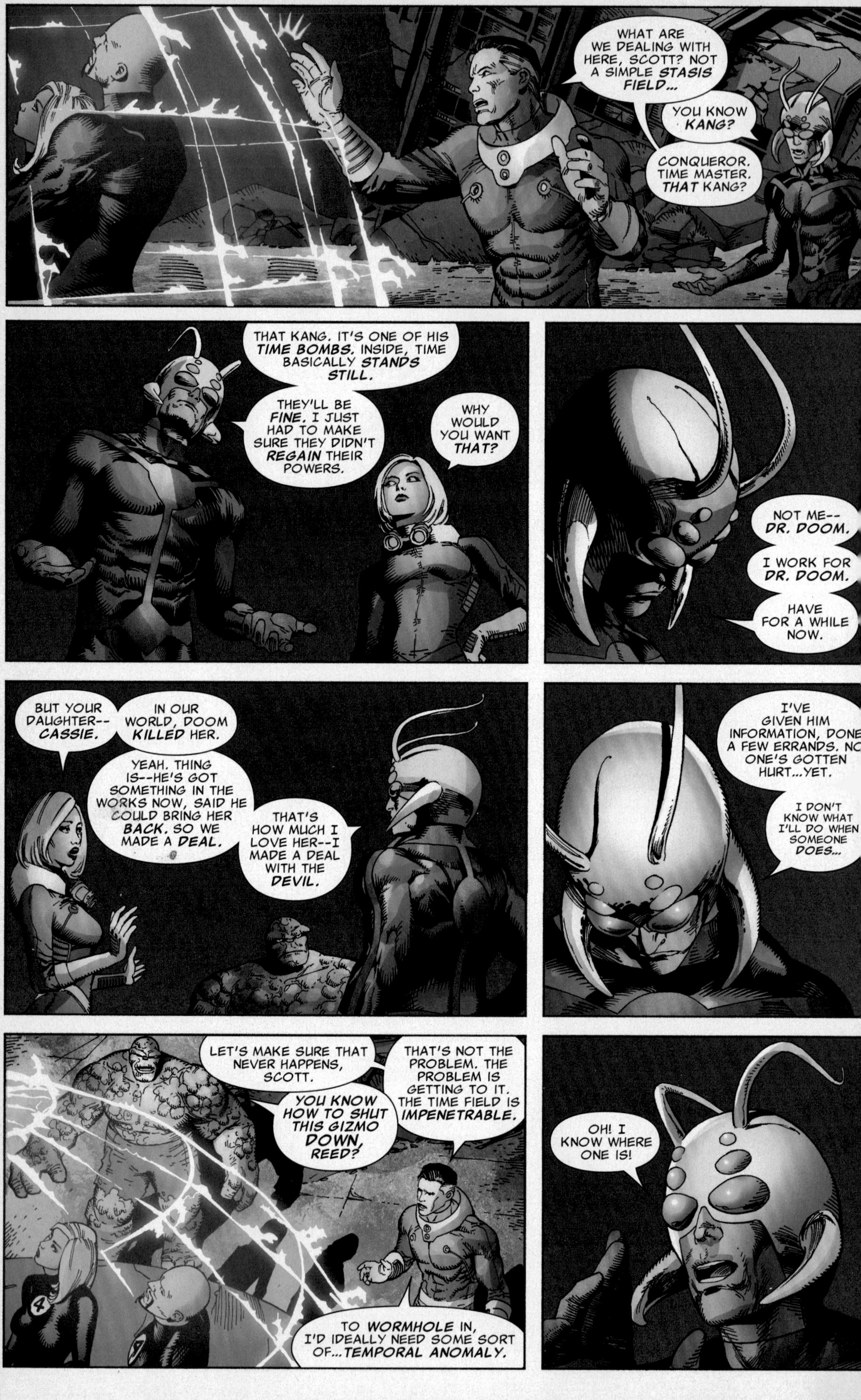
WHAT ARE WE DEALING WITH HERE, SCOTT? NOT A SIMPLE STASIS FIELD...
YOU KNOW KANG?
CONQUEROR. TIME MASTER. THAT KANG?
THAT KANG. IT'S ONE OF HIS TIME BOMBS. INSIDE, TIME BASICALLY STANDS STILL.
THEY'LL BE FINE. I JUST HAD TO MAKE SURE THEY DIDN'T REGAIN THEIR POWERS.
WHY WOULD YOU WANT THAT?
NOT ME-- DR. DOOM.
I WORK FOR DR. DOOM.
HAVE FOR A WHILE NOW.
BUT YOUR DAUGHTER-- CASSIE.
IN OUR WORLD, DOOM KILLED HER.
YEAH. THING IS--HE'S GOT SOMETHING IN THE WORKS NOW, SAID HE COULD BRING HER BACK. SO WE MADE A DEAL.
THAT'S HOW MUCH I LOVE HER--I MADE A DEAL WITH THE DEVIL.
I'VE GIVEN HIM INFORMATION, DONE A FEW ERRANDS. NO ONE'S GOTTEN HURT...YET.
I DON'T KNOW WHAT I'LL DO WHEN SOMEONE DOES...
LET'S MAKE SURE THAT NEVER HAPPENS, SCOTT.
YOU KNOW HOW TO SHUT THIS GIZMO DOWN, REED?
THAT'S NOT THE PROBLEM. THE PROBLEM IS GETTING TO IT. THE TIME FIELD IS IMPENETRABLE.
TO WORMHOLE IN, I'D IDEALLY NEED SOME SORT OF...TEMPORAL ANOMALY.
OH! I KNOW WHERE ONE IS!

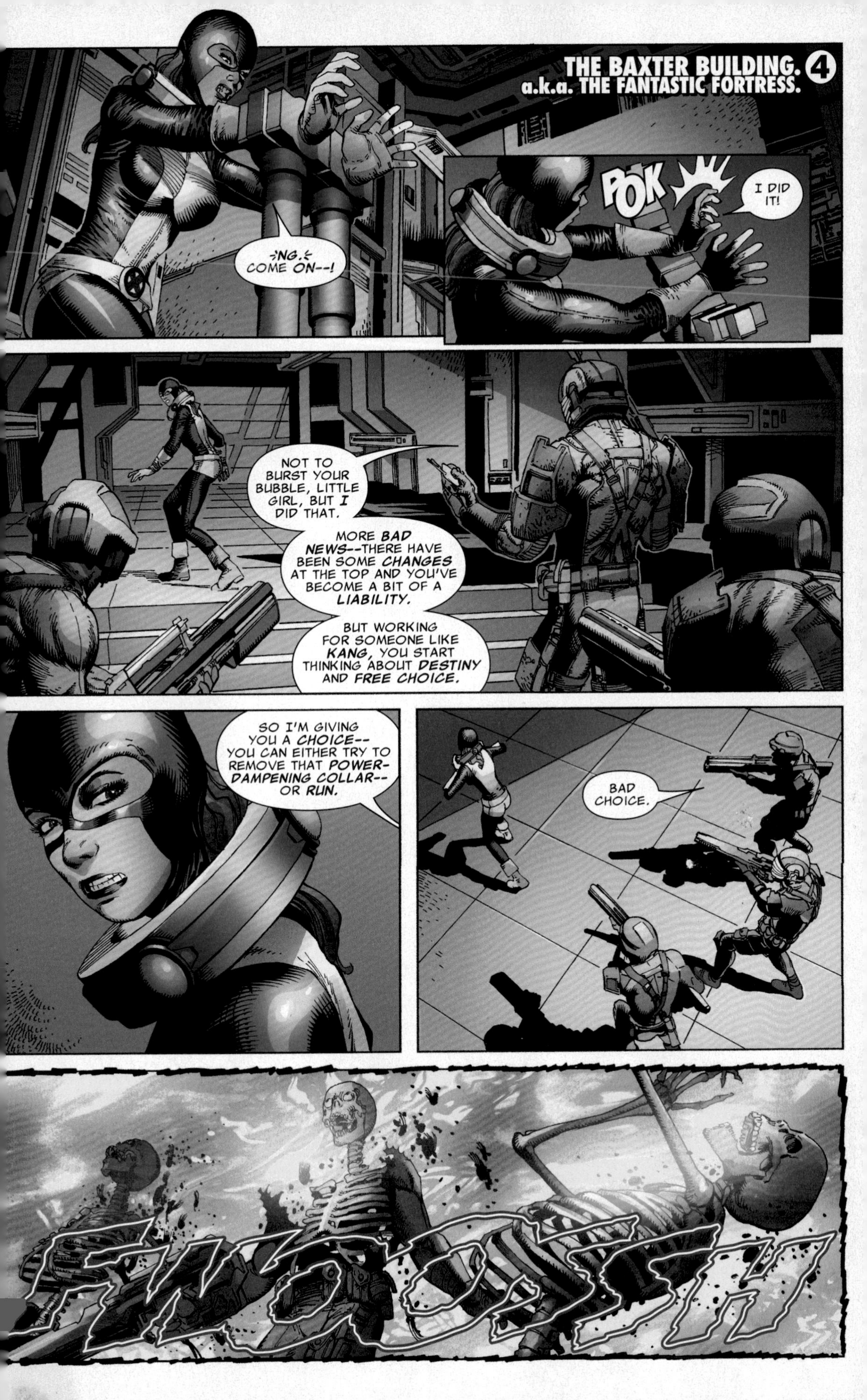
THE BAXTER BUILDING. 4
a.k.a. THE FANTASTIC FORTRESS.
:NG.: COME ON--!
POK
I DID IT!
NOT TO BURST YOUR BUBBLE, LITTLE GIRL, BUT I DID THAT.
MORE BAD NEWS--THERE HAVE BEEN SOME CHANGES AT THE TOP AND YOU'VE BECOME A BIT OF A LIABILITY.
BUT WORKING FOR SOMEONE LIKE KANG, YOU START THINKING ABOUT DESTINY AND FREE CHOICE.
SO I'M GIVING YOU A CHOICE--YOU CAN EITHER TRY TO REMOVE THAT POWER-DAMPENING COLLAR--OR RUN.
BAD CHOICE.
FWOOSH

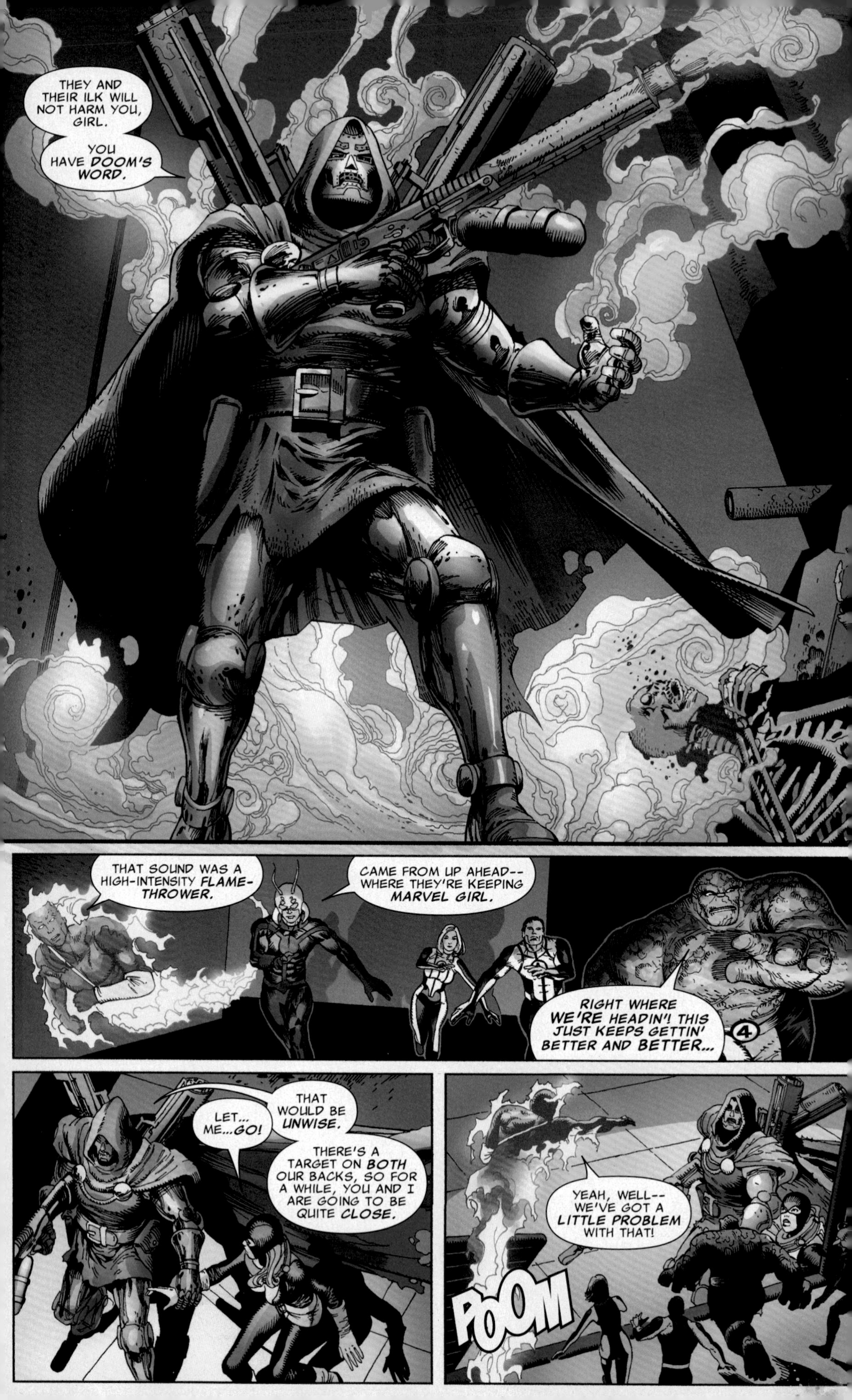
THEY AND THEIR ILK WILL NOT HARM YOU, GIRL.
YOU HAVE DOOM'S WORD.
THAT SOUND WAS A HIGH-INTENSITY FLAME-THROWER.
CAME FROM UP AHEAD-- WHERE THEY'RE KEEPING MARVEL GIRL.
RIGHT WHERE WE'RE HEADIN'! THIS JUST KEEPS GETTIN' BETTER AND BETTER...
LET... ME...GO!
THAT WOULD BE UNWISE.
THERE'S A TARGET ON BOTH OUR BACKS, SO FOR A WHILE, YOU AND I ARE GOING TO BE QUITE CLOSE.
YEAH, WELL-- WE'VE GOT A LITTLE PROBLEM WITH THAT!
POOM

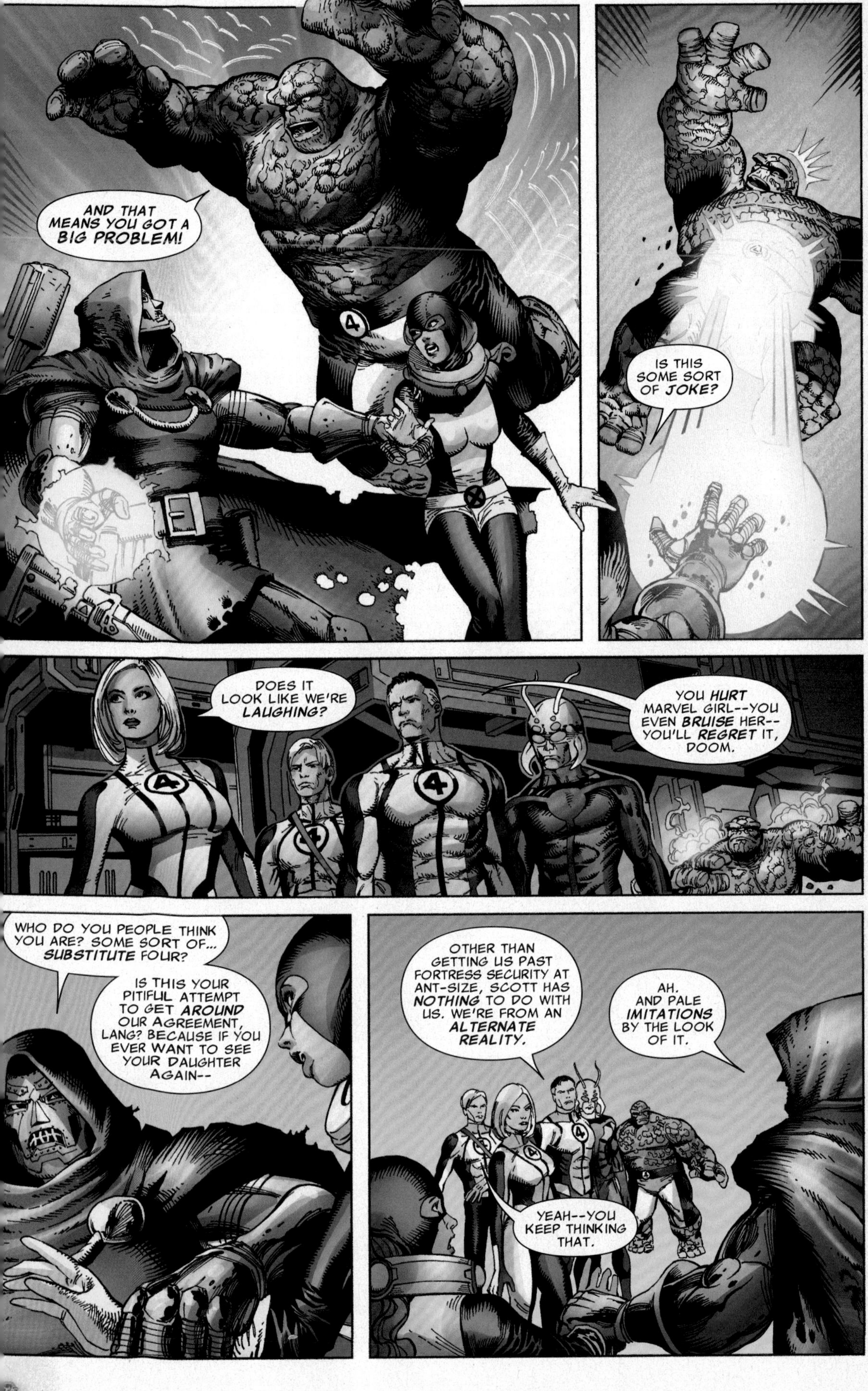
AND THAT MEANS YOU GOT A BIG PROBLEM!
IS THIS SOME SORT OF JOKE?
DOES IT LOOK LIKE WE'RE LAUGHING?
YOU HURT MARVEL GIRL--YOU EVEN BRUISE HER--YOU'LL REGRET IT, DOOM.
WHO DO YOU PEOPLE THINK YOU ARE? SOME SORT OF... SUBSTITUTE FOUR?
IS THIS YOUR PITIFUL ATTEMPT TO GET AROUND OUR AGREEMENT, LANG? BECAUSE IF YOU EVER WANT TO SEE YOUR DAUGHTER AGAIN--
OTHER THAN GETTING US PAST FORTRESS SECURITY AT ANT-SIZE, SCOTT HAS NOTHING TO DO WITH US. WE'RE FROM AN ALTERNATE REALITY.
AH. AND PALE IMITATIONS BY THE LOOK OF IT.
YEAH--YOU KEEP THINKING THAT.

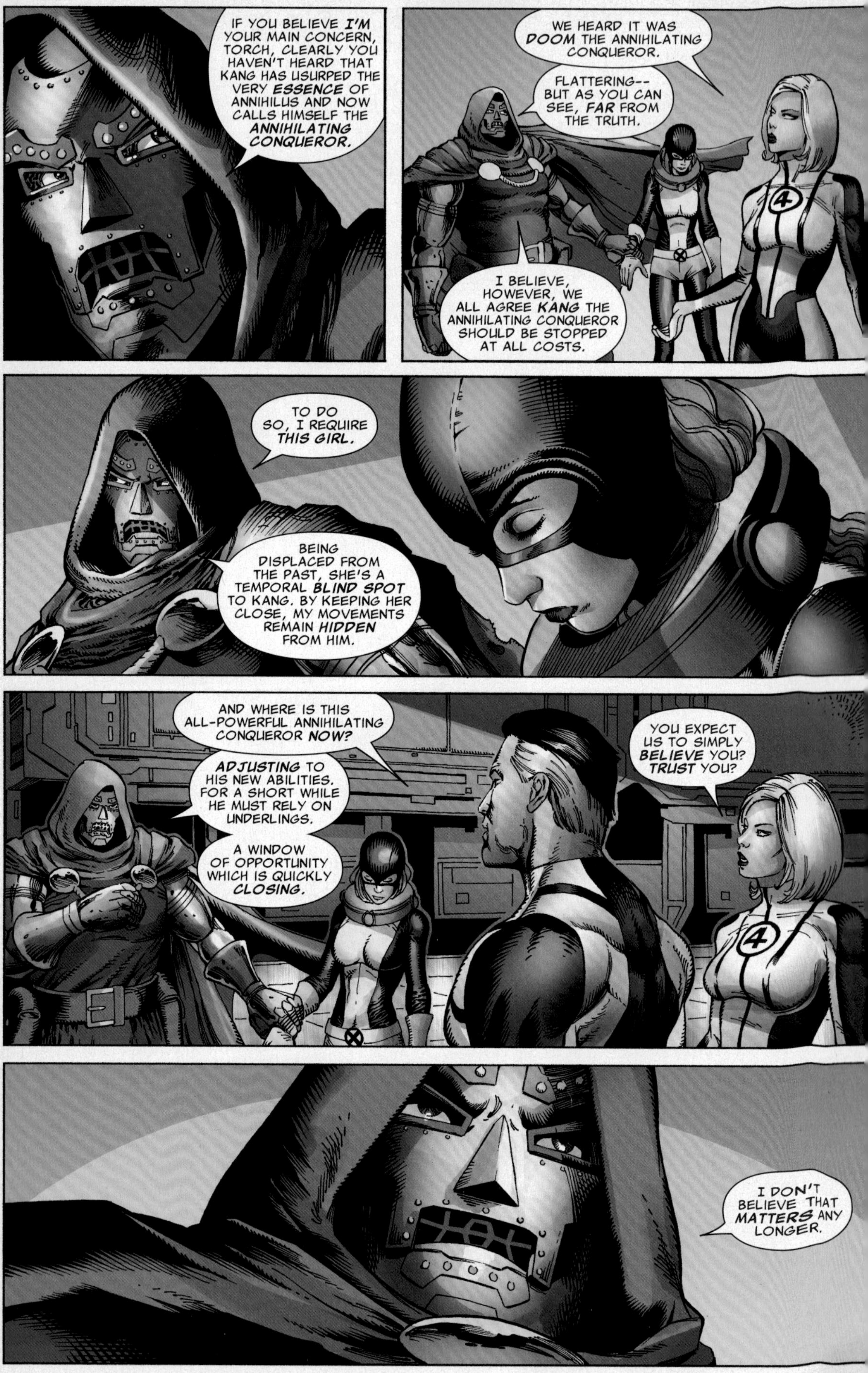
IF YOU BELIEVE I'M YOUR MAIN CONCERN, TORCH, CLEARLY YOU HAVEN'T HEARD THAT KANG HAS USURPED THE VERY ESSENCE OF ANNIHILUS AND NOW CALLS HIMSELF THE ANNIHILATING CONQUEROR.
WE HEARD IT WAS DOOM THE ANNIHILATING CONQUEROR.
FLATTERING-- BUT AS YOU CAN SEE, FAR FROM THE TRUTH.
I BELIEVE, HOWEVER, WE ALL AGREE KANG THE ANNIHILATING CONQUEROR SHOULD BE STOPPED AT ALL COSTS.
TO DO SO, I REQUIRE THIS GIRL.
BEING DISPLACED FROM THE PAST, SHE'S A TEMPORAL BLIND SPOT TO KANG. BY KEEPING HER CLOSE, MY MOVEMENTS REMAIN HIDDEN FROM HIM.
AND WHERE IS THIS ALL-POWERFUL ANNIHILATING CONQUEROR NOW?
ADJUSTING TO HIS NEW ABILITIES. FOR A SHORT WHILE HE MUST RELY ON UNDERLINGS.
A WINDOW OF OPPORTUNITY WHICH IS QUICKLY CLOSING.
YOU EXPECT US TO SIMPLY BELIEVE YOU? TRUST YOU?
I DON'T BELIEVE THAT MATTERS ANY LONGER.

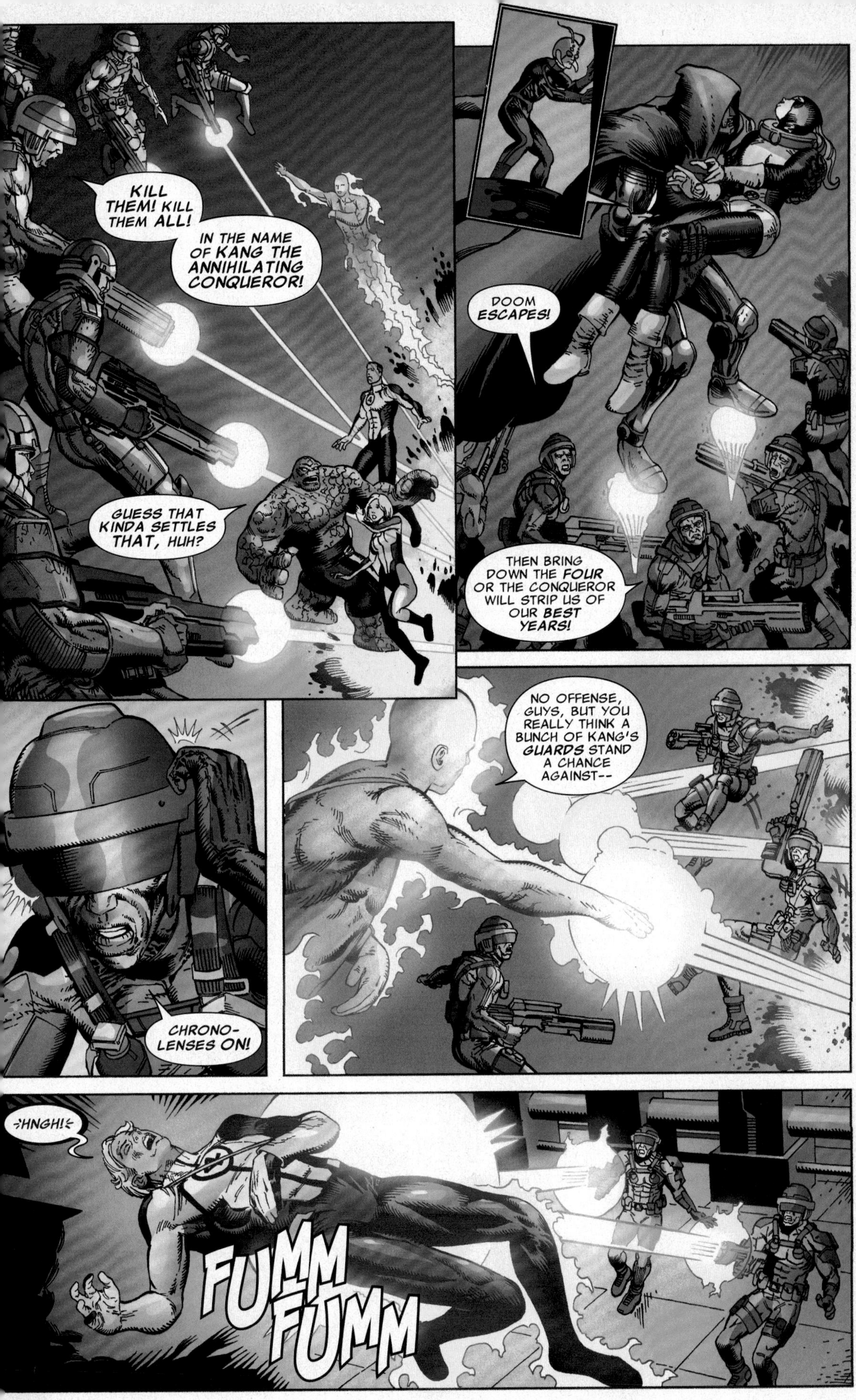
KILL THEM! KILL THEM ALL!
IN THE NAME OF KANG THE ANNIHILATING CONQUEROR!
GUESS THAT KINDA SETTLES THAT, HUH?
DOOM ESCAPES!
THEN BRING DOWN THE FOUR OR THE CONQUEROR WILL STRIP US OF OUR BEST YEARS!
CHRONO-LENSES ON!
NO OFFENSE, GUYS, BUT YOU REALLY THINK A BUNCH OF KANG'S GUARDS STAND A CHANCE AGAINST--
HNGH!
FUMM FUMM

THEY'RE HITTIN' ME ÷NG÷ EVERY PLACE I TURN!

SKROOM SKROOM

THEY...THEY CAN *SEE* WHAT WE'RE GOING TO DO BEFORE-- GHAH!

TZOKK

TZEKK

TZOKK

WHERE'S THE *WOMAN?* SHE COULDN'T HAVE *ESCAPED.*

WAIT. THAT SOUNDS LIKE OUR WEAPONS ARE--

VVVVVVOOOOOOOOO--

TZCHROOM

REACHING *CRITICAL MASS* AFTER SOMEONE SHUT OFF THEIR *VENTING?*

GOLD STAR.

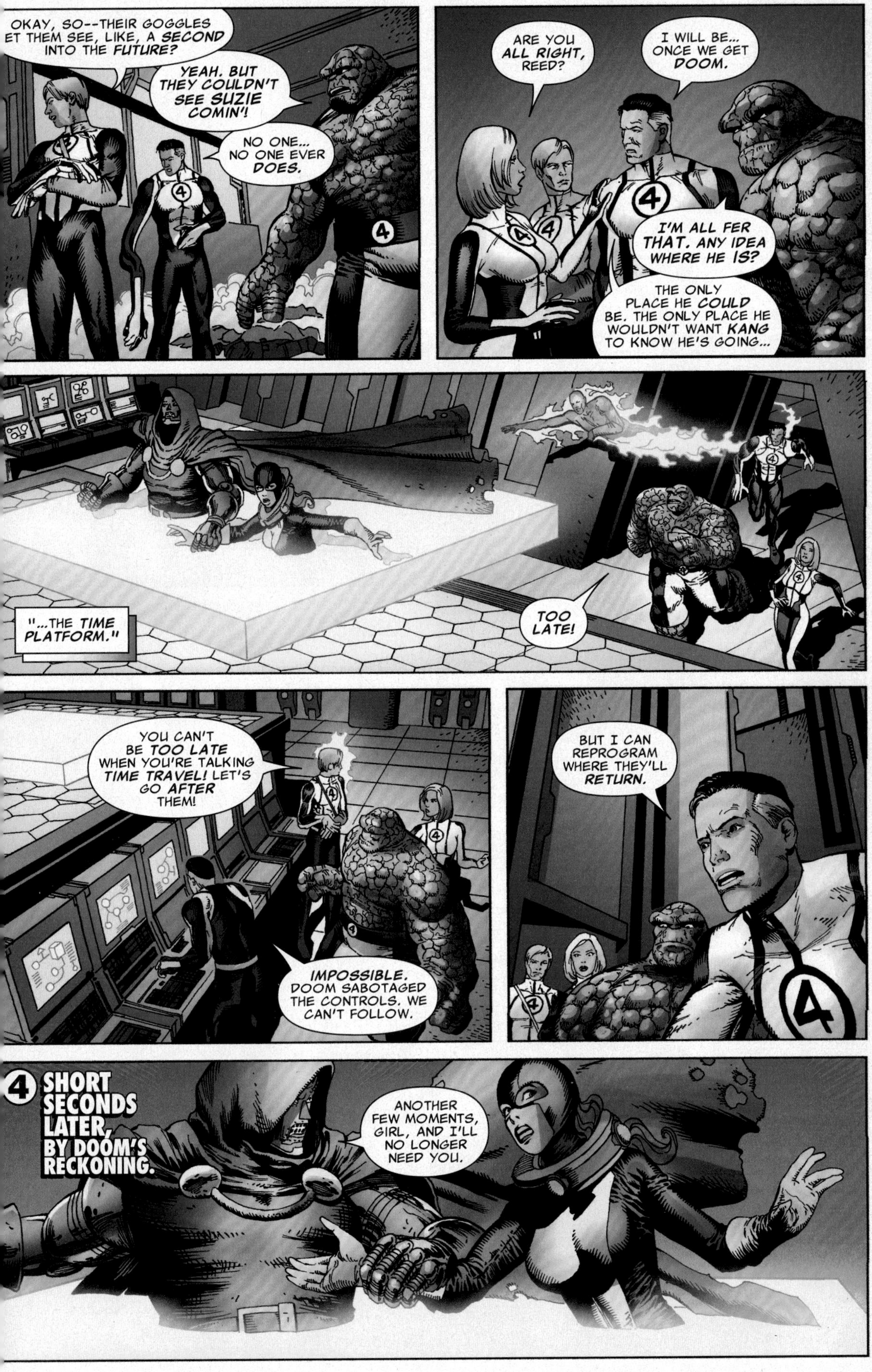

OKAY, SO--THEIR GOGGLES ET THEM SEE, LIKE, A SECOND INTO THE FUTURE?
YEAH. BUT THEY COULDN'T SEE SUZIE COMIN'!
NO ONE... NO ONE EVER DOES.
ARE YOU ALL RIGHT, REED?
I WILL BE... ONCE WE GET DOOM.
I'M ALL FER THAT. ANY IDEA WHERE HE IS?
THE ONLY PLACE HE COULD BE. THE ONLY PLACE HE WOULDN'T WANT KANG TO KNOW HE'S GOING...
"...THE TIME PLATFORM."
TOO LATE!
YOU CAN'T BE TOO LATE WHEN YOU'RE TALKING TIME TRAVEL! LET'S GO AFTER THEM!
IMPOSSIBLE. DOOM SABOTAGED THE CONTROLS. WE CAN'T FOLLOW.
BUT I CAN REPROGRAM WHERE THEY'LL RETURN.
4 SHORT SECONDS LATER, BY DOOM'S RECKONING.
ANOTHER FEW MOMENTS, GIRL, AND I'LL NO LONGER NEED YOU.

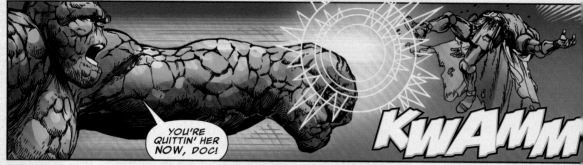

YOU'RE QUITTIN' HER NOW, DOC!

KWAMM

DID HE *HURT* YOU, MARVEL GIRL?

NO. IT WAS LIKE I WASN'T EVEN THERE. ALL HE DID WAS PUNCH BUTTONS ON SOME *MACHINE.*

SOUNDS LIKE DOOM.

AND IN CASE YOU DIDN'T NOTICE-- IF HE TRIED TO CHANGE THE *PAST,* IT *DIDN'T WORK.*

DOOM WOULDN'T. HE KNOWS BETTER.

THERE. YOUR TELEKINETIC ABILITIES SHOULD BE FULLY *RESTORED.*

ABILITIES THAT ARE AS USEFUL AGAINST A TIME-FIELD AS YOUR ANOMALOUS *TEMPORAL AURA* IS, SO...

...IF YOU WOULDN'T MIND USING THEM TO TURN THAT DEVICE OFF?

LIKE THIS?

TEK

OH, MY!

IS... IS THIS A *GOOD* THING?

IT IS FOR *THEM.*

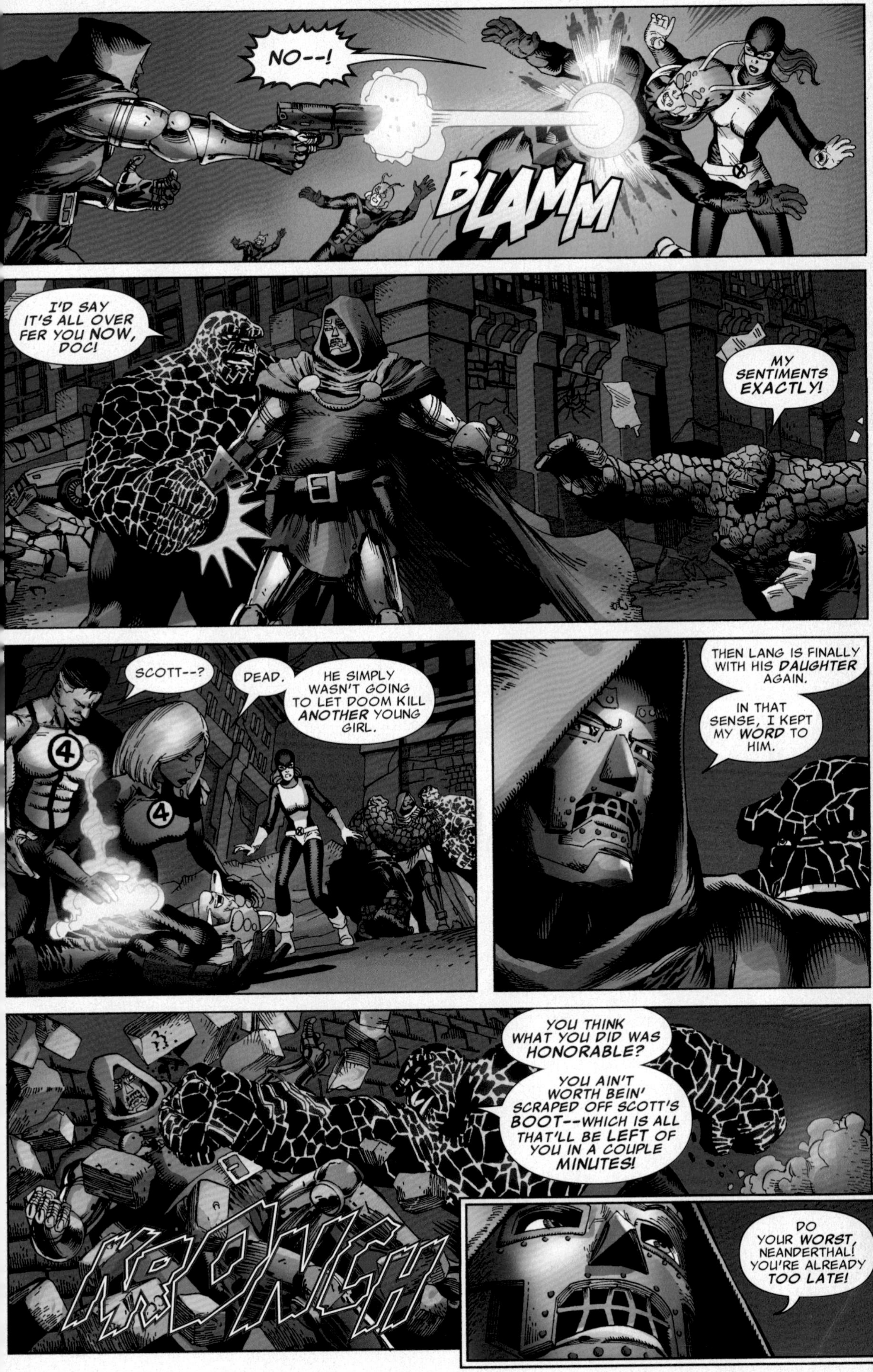
NO--!
BLAMM
I'D SAY IT'S ALL OVER FER YOU NOW, DOC!
MY SENTIMENTS EXACTLY!
SCOTT--?
DEAD.
HE SIMPLY WASN'T GOING TO LET DOOM KILL ANOTHER YOUNG GIRL.
THEN LANG IS FINALLY WITH HIS DAUGHTER AGAIN.
IN THAT SENSE, I KEPT MY WORD TO HIM.
YOU THINK WHAT YOU DID WAS HONORABLE?
YOU AIN'T WORTH BEIN' SCRAPED OFF SCOTT'S BOOT--WHICH IS ALL THAT'LL BE LEFT OF YOU IN A COUPLE MINUTES!
KRONCH
DO YOUR WORST, NEANDERTHAL! YOU'RE ALREADY TOO LATE!

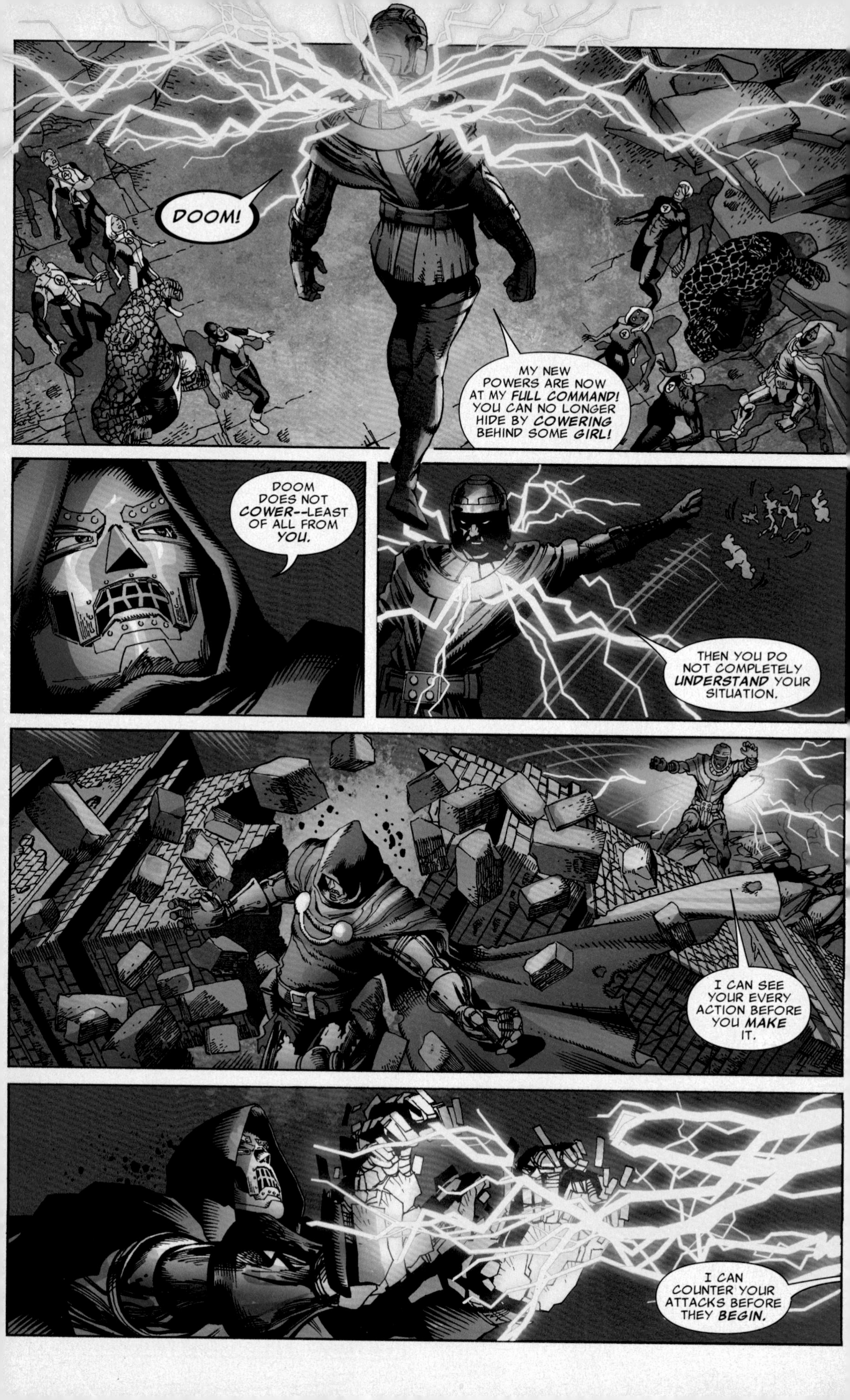
DOOM!
MY NEW POWERS ARE NOW AT MY FULL COMMAND! YOU CAN NO LONGER HIDE BY COWERING BEHIND SOME GIRL!
DOOM DOES NOT COWER--LEAST OF ALL FROM YOU.
THEN YOU DO NOT COMPLETELY UNDERSTAND YOUR SITUATION.
I CAN SEE YOUR EVERY ACTION BEFORE YOU MAKE IT.
I CAN COUNTER YOUR ATTACKS BEFORE THEY BEGIN.

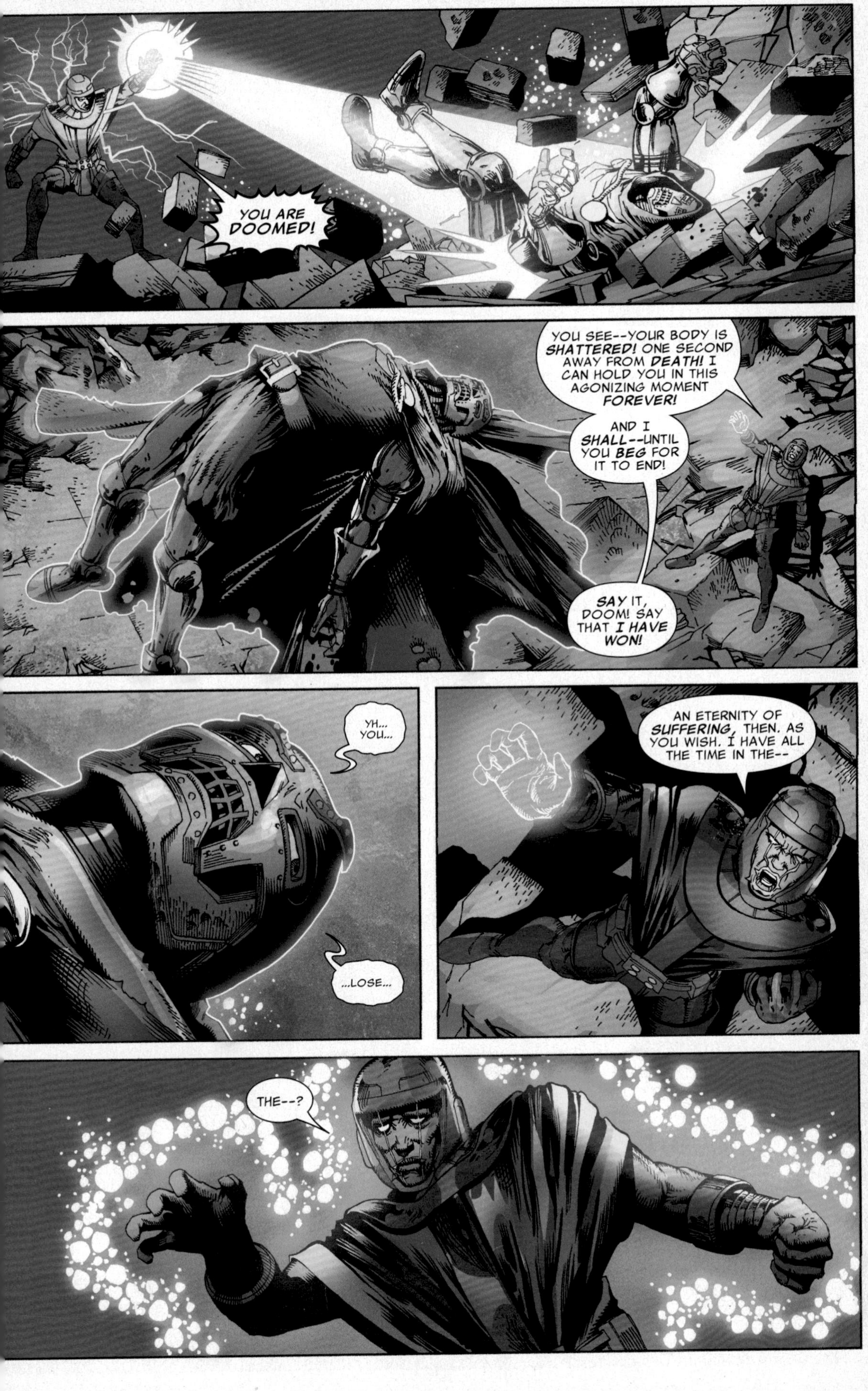
YOU ARE DOOMED!
YOU SEE--YOUR BODY IS SHATTERED! ONE SECOND AWAY FROM DEATH! I CAN HOLD YOU IN THIS AGONIZING MOMENT FOREVER!
AND I SHALL--UNTIL YOU BEG FOR IT TO END!
SAY IT, DOOM! SAY THAT I HAVE WON!
YH... YOU...
...LOSE...
AN ETERNITY OF SUFFERING, THEN. AS YOU WISH. I HAVE ALL THE TIME IN THE--
THE--?

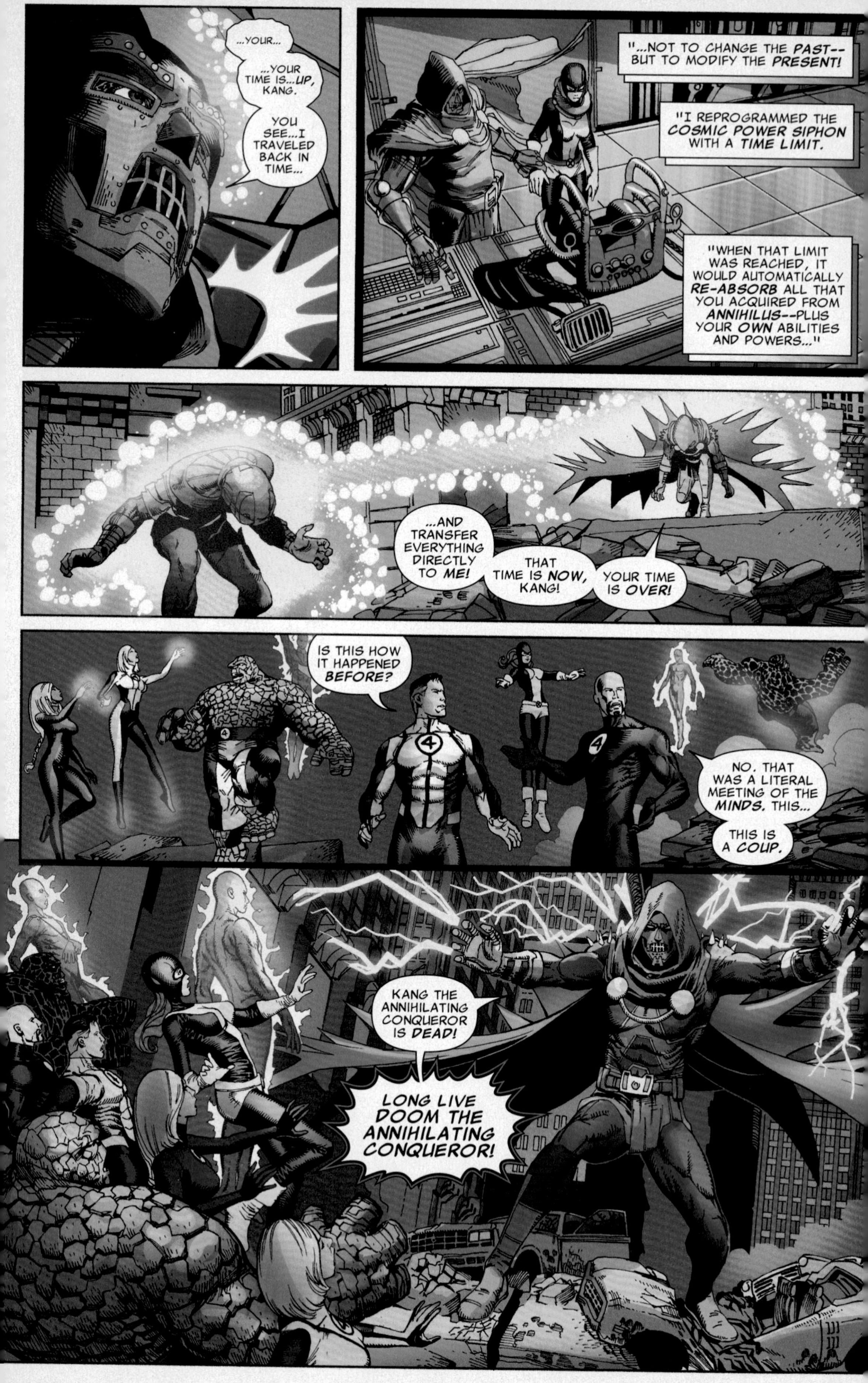
...YOUR...
...YOUR TIME IS...UP, KANG.
YOU SEE...I TRAVELED BACK IN TIME...
"...NOT TO CHANGE THE PAST--BUT TO MODIFY THE PRESENT!
"I REPROGRAMMED THE COSMIC POWER SIPHON WITH A TIME LIMIT.
"WHEN THAT LIMIT WAS REACHED, IT WOULD AUTOMATICALLY RE-ABSORB ALL THAT YOU ACQUIRED FROM ANNIHILUS--PLUS YOUR OWN ABILITIES AND POWERS..."
...AND TRANSFER EVERYTHING DIRECTLY TO ME!
THAT TIME IS NOW, KANG!
YOUR TIME IS OVER!
IS THIS HOW IT HAPPENED BEFORE?
NO. THAT WAS A LITERAL MEETING OF THE MINDS. THIS...
THIS IS A COUP.
KANG THE ANNIHILATING CONQUEROR IS DEAD!
LONG LIVE DOOM THE ANNIHILATING CONQUEROR!

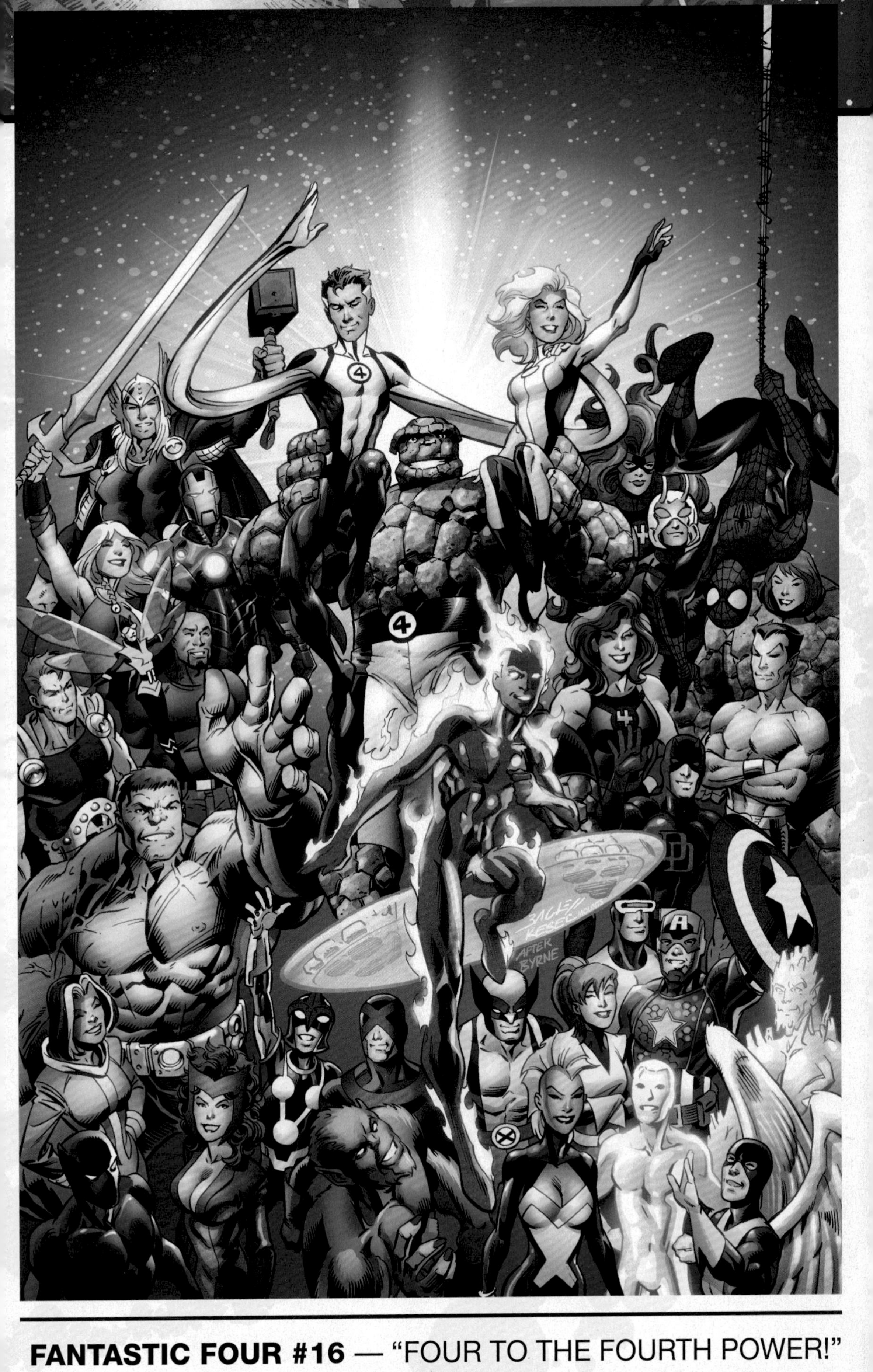

FANTASTIC FOUR #16 — "FOUR TO THE FOURTH POWER!"

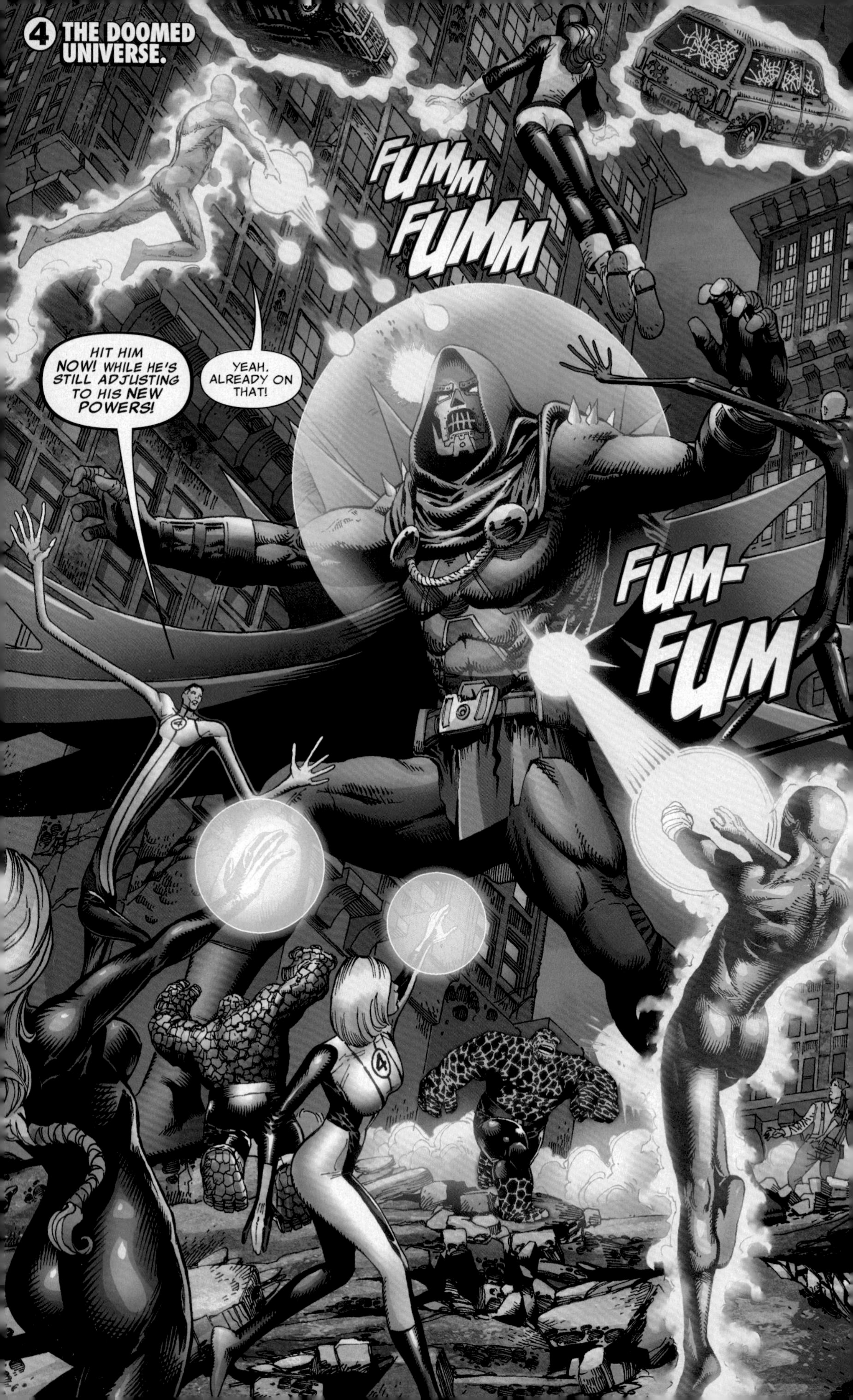
4 THE DOOMED UNIVERSE.
FUMM FUMM
HIT HIM NOW! WHILE HE'S STILL ADJUSTING TO HIS NEW POWERS!
YEAH. ALREADY ON THAT!
FUM-FUM

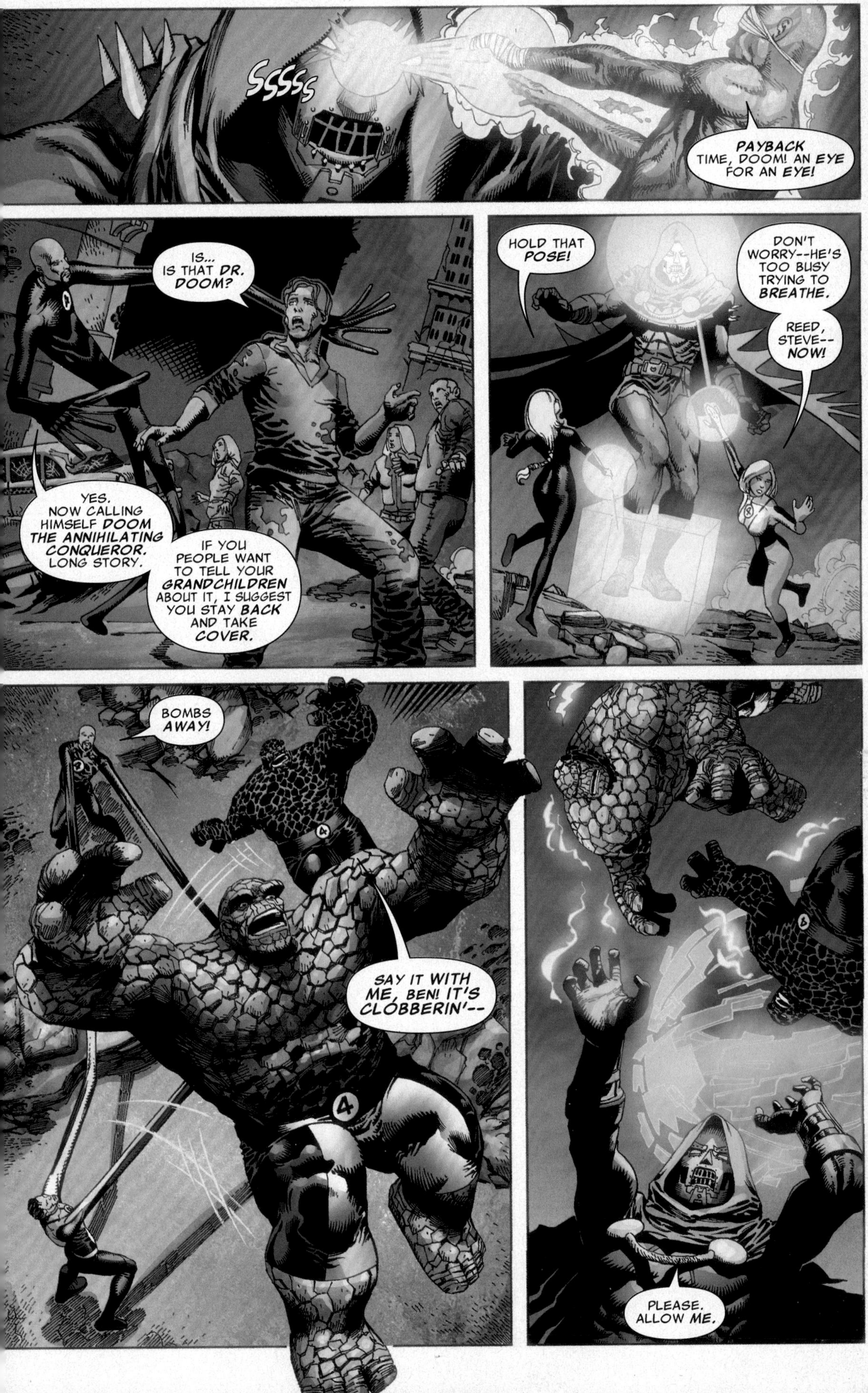
SSSSS
PAYBACK TIME, DOOM! AN EYE FOR AN EYE!
IS... IS THAT DR. DOOM?
YES. NOW CALLING HIMSELF DOOM THE ANNIHILATING CONQUEROR. LONG STORY.
IF YOU PEOPLE WANT TO TELL YOUR GRANDCHILDREN ABOUT IT, I SUGGEST YOU STAY BACK AND TAKE COVER.
HOLD THAT POSE!
DON'T WORRY--HE'S TOO BUSY TRYING TO BREATHE.
REED, STEVE-- NOW!
BOMBS AWAY!
SAY IT WITH ME, BEN! IT'S CLOBBERIN'--
PLEASE. ALLOW ME.

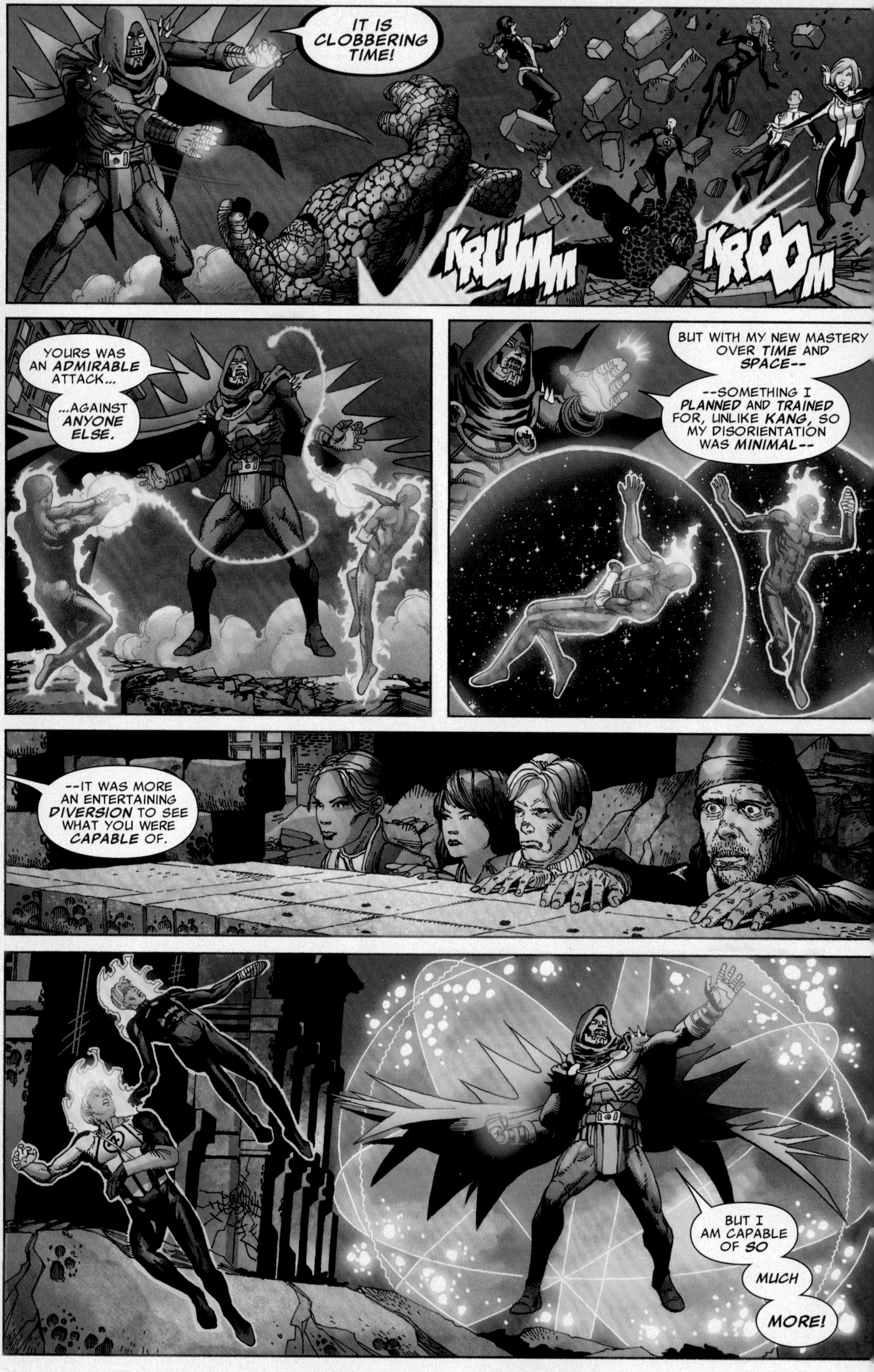
IT IS CLOBBERING TIME!
KRUMMM
KROOOM
YOURS WAS AN ADMIRABLE ATTACK...
...AGAINST ANYONE ELSE.
BUT WITH MY NEW MASTERY OVER TIME AND SPACE--
--SOMETHING I PLANNED AND TRAINED FOR, UNLIKE KANG, SO MY DISORIENTATION WAS MINIMAL--
--IT WAS MORE AN ENTERTAINING DIVERSION TO SEE WHAT YOU WERE CAPABLE OF.
BUT I AM CAPABLE OF SO
MUCH
MORE!

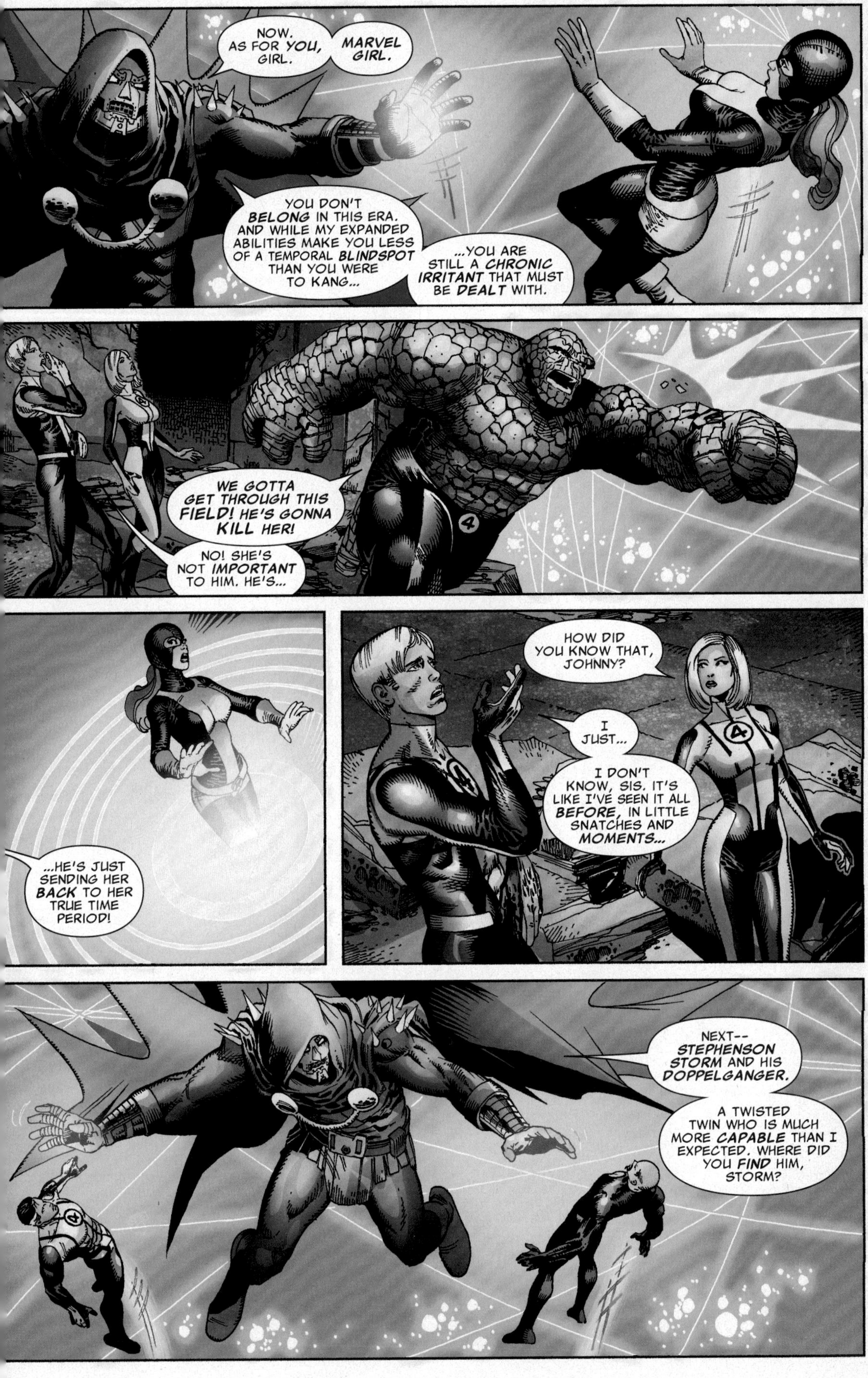
NOW. AS FOR YOU, GIRL.
MARVEL GIRL.
YOU DON'T BELONG IN THIS ERA. AND WHILE MY EXPANDED ABILITIES MAKE YOU LESS OF A TEMPORAL BLINDSPOT THAN YOU WERE TO KANG...
...YOU ARE STILL A CHRONIC IRRITANT THAT MUST BE DEALT WITH.
WE GOTTA GET THROUGH THIS FIELD! HE'S GONNA KILL HER!
NO! SHE'S NOT IMPORTANT TO HIM. HE'S...
...HE'S JUST SENDING HER BACK TO HER TRUE TIME PERIOD!
HOW DID YOU KNOW THAT, JOHNNY?
I JUST...
I DON'T KNOW, SIS. IT'S LIKE I'VE SEEN IT ALL BEFORE, IN LITTLE SNATCHES AND MOMENTS...
NEXT-- STEPHENSON STORM AND HIS DOPPELGANGER.
A TWISTED TWIN WHO IS MUCH MORE CAPABLE THAN I EXPECTED. WHERE DID YOU FIND HIM, STORM?

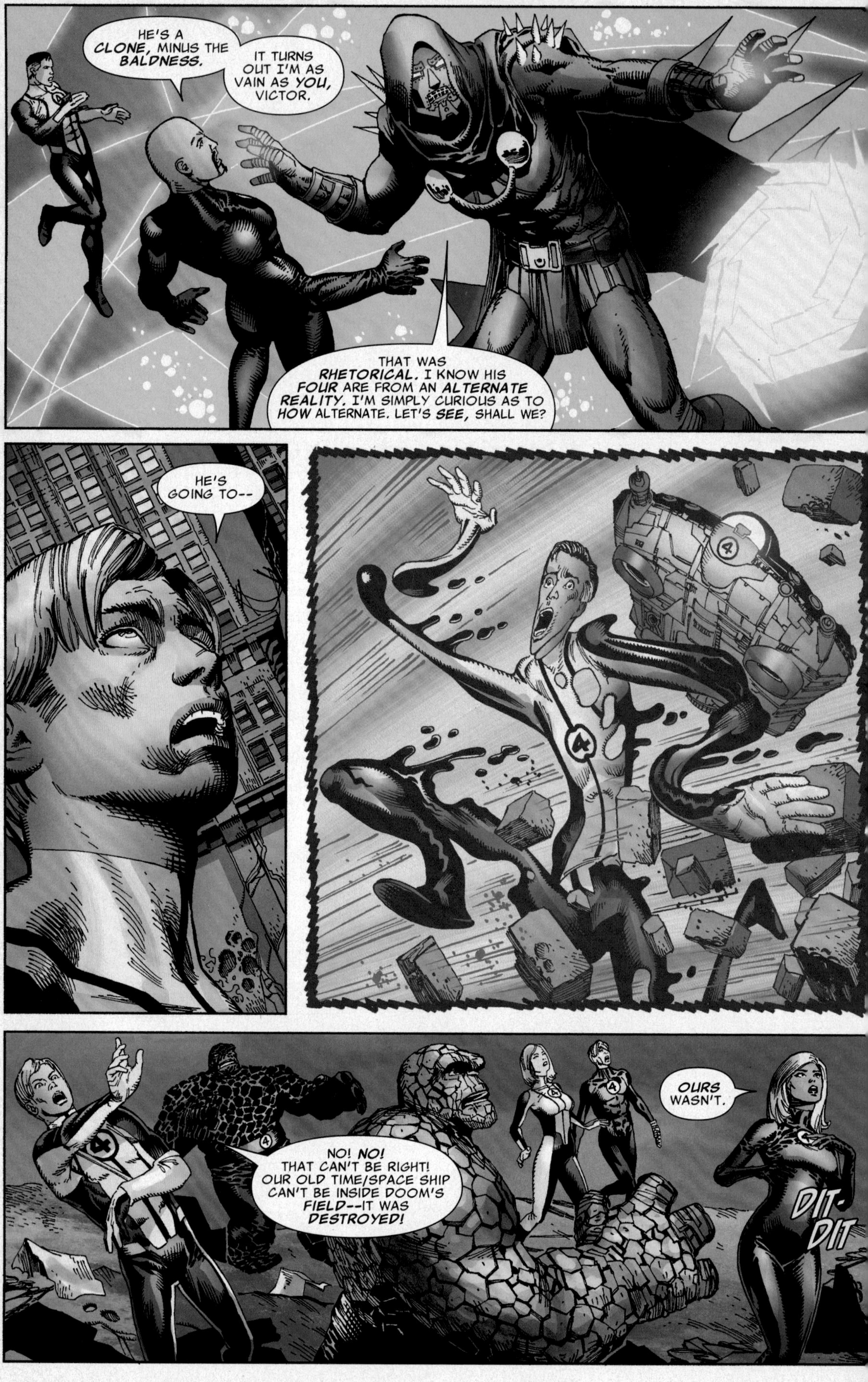
HE'S A CLONE, MINUS THE BALDNESS.
IT TURNS OUT I'M AS VAIN AS YOU, VICTOR.
THAT WAS RHETORICAL. I KNOW HIS FOUR ARE FROM AN ALTERNATE REALITY. I'M SIMPLY CURIOUS AS TO HOW ALTERNATE. LET'S SEE, SHALL WE?
HE'S GOING TO--
NO! NO! THAT CAN'T BE RIGHT! OUR OLD TIME/SPACE SHIP CAN'T BE INSIDE DOOM'S FIELD--IT WAS DESTROYED!
OURS WASN'T.
DIT-DIT

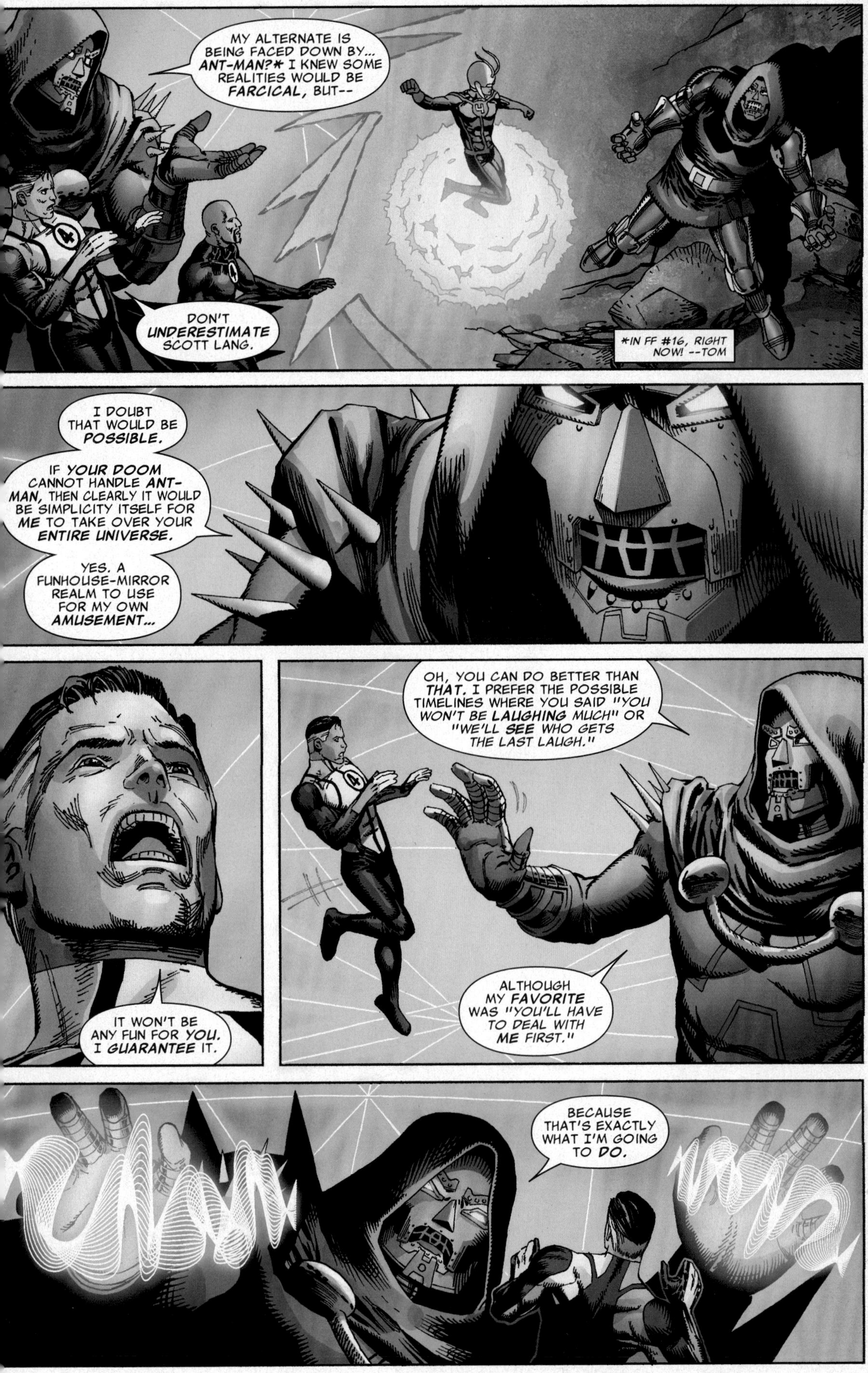
MY ALTERNATE IS BEING FACED DOWN BY... ANT-MAN?* I KNEW SOME REALITIES WOULD BE FARCICAL, BUT--
DON'T UNDERESTIMATE SCOTT LANG.
*IN FF #16, RIGHT NOW! --TOM
I DOUBT THAT WOULD BE POSSIBLE.
IF YOUR DOOM CANNOT HANDLE ANT-MAN, THEN CLEARLY IT WOULD BE SIMPLICITY ITSELF FOR ME TO TAKE OVER YOUR ENTIRE UNIVERSE.
YES. A FUNHOUSE-MIRROR REALM TO USE FOR MY OWN AMUSEMENT...
IT WON'T BE ANY FUN FOR YOU. I GUARANTEE IT.
OH, YOU CAN DO BETTER THAN THAT. I PREFER THE POSSIBLE TIMELINES WHERE YOU SAID "YOU WON'T BE LAUGHING MUCH" OR "WE'LL SEE WHO GETS THE LAST LAUGH."
ALTHOUGH MY FAVORITE WAS "YOU'LL HAVE TO DEAL WITH ME FIRST."
BECAUSE THAT'S EXACTLY WHAT I'M GOING TO DO.

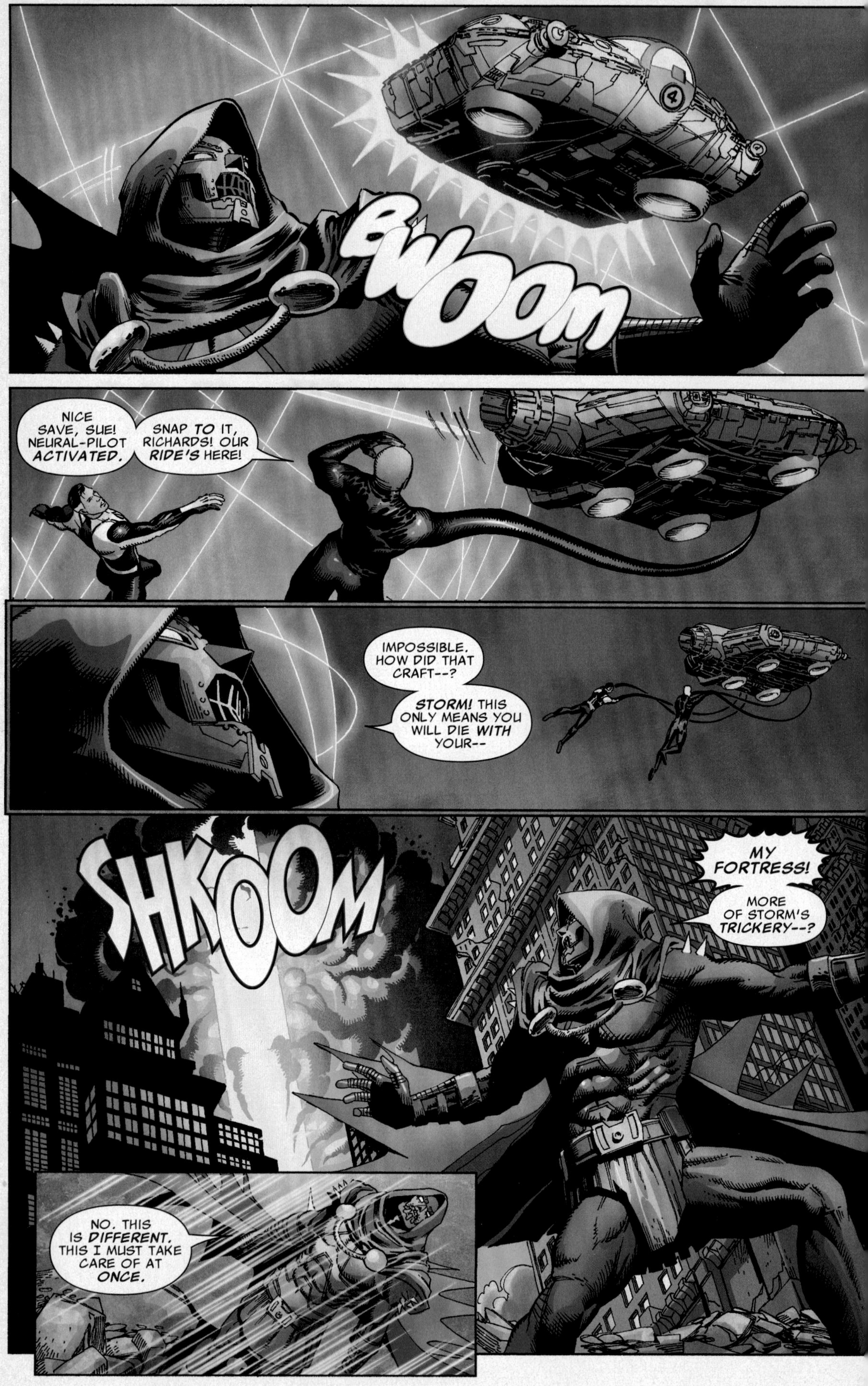

BWOOM
NICE SAVE, SUE! NEURAL-PILOT ACTIVATED.
SNAP TO IT, RICHARDS! OUR RIDE'S HERE!
IMPOSSIBLE. HOW DID THAT CRAFT--?
STORM! THIS ONLY MEANS YOU WILL DIE WITH YOUR--
SHKOOM
MY FORTRESS!
MORE OF STORM'S TRICKERY--?
NO. THIS IS DIFFERENT. THIS I MUST TAKE CARE OF AT ONCE.

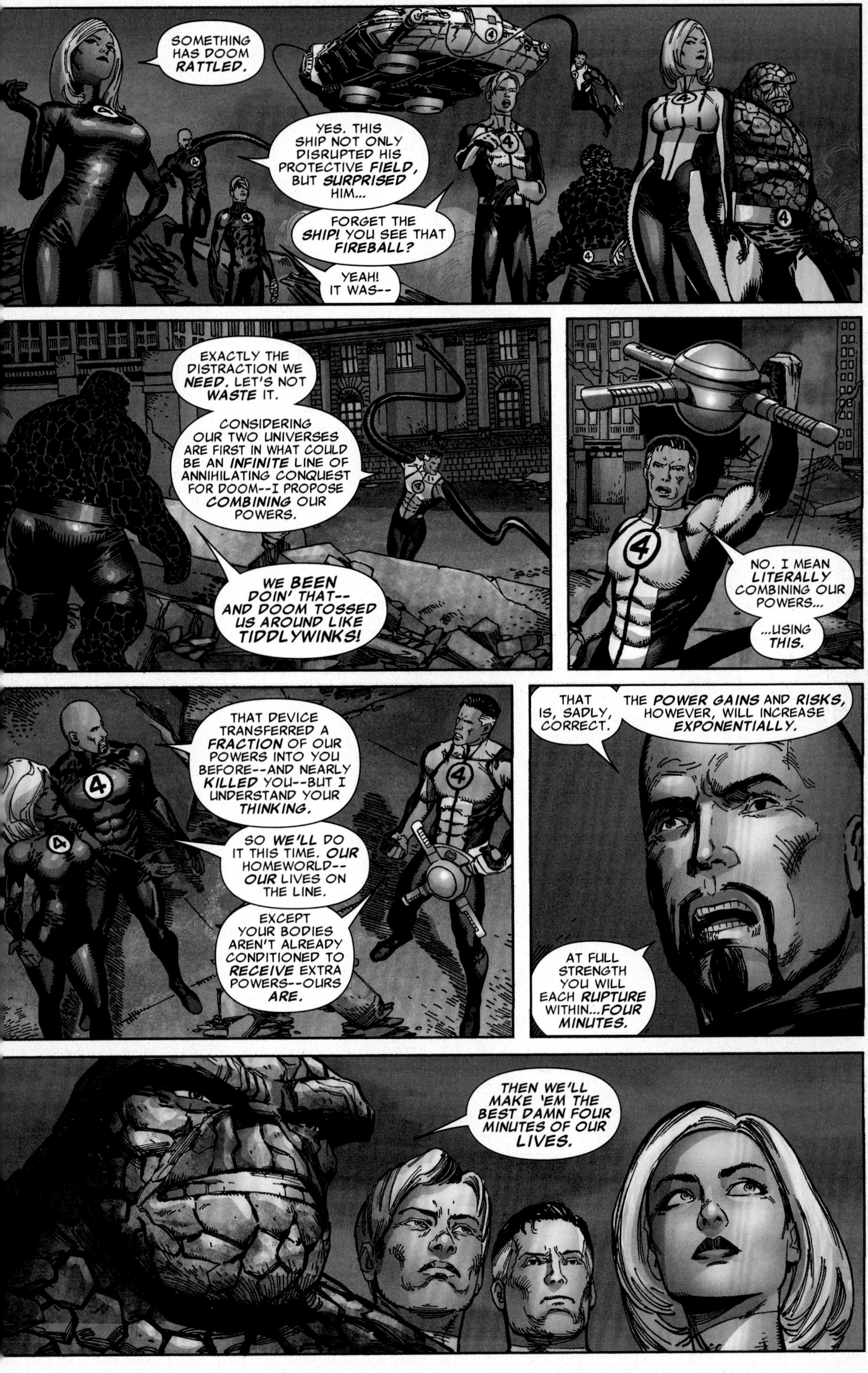

SOMETHING HAS DOOM RATTLED.
YES. THIS SHIP NOT ONLY DISRUPTED HIS PROTECTIVE FIELD, BUT SURPRISED HIM...
FORGET THE SHIP! YOU SEE THAT FIREBALL?
YEAH! IT WAS--
EXACTLY THE DISTRACTION WE NEED. LET'S NOT WASTE IT.
CONSIDERING OUR TWO UNIVERSES ARE FIRST IN WHAT COULD BE AN INFINITE LINE OF ANNIHILATING CONQUEST FOR DOOM--I PROPOSE COMBINING OUR POWERS.
WE BEEN DOIN' THAT-- AND DOOM TOSSED US AROUND LIKE TIDDLYWINKS!
NO. I MEAN LITERALLY COMBINING OUR POWERS...
...USING THIS.
THAT DEVICE TRANSFERRED A FRACTION OF OUR POWERS INTO YOU BEFORE--AND NEARLY KILLED YOU--BUT I UNDERSTAND YOUR THINKING.
SO WE'LL DO IT THIS TIME. OUR HOMEWORLD-- OUR LIVES ON THE LINE.
EXCEPT YOUR BODIES AREN'T ALREADY CONDITIONED TO RECEIVE EXTRA POWERS--OURS ARE.
THAT IS, SADLY, CORRECT.
THE POWER GAINS AND RISKS, HOWEVER, WILL INCREASE EXPONENTIALLY.
AT FULL STRENGTH YOU WILL EACH RUPTURE WITHIN...FOUR MINUTES.
THEN WE'LL MAKE 'EM THE BEST DAMN FOUR MINUTES OF OUR LIVES.

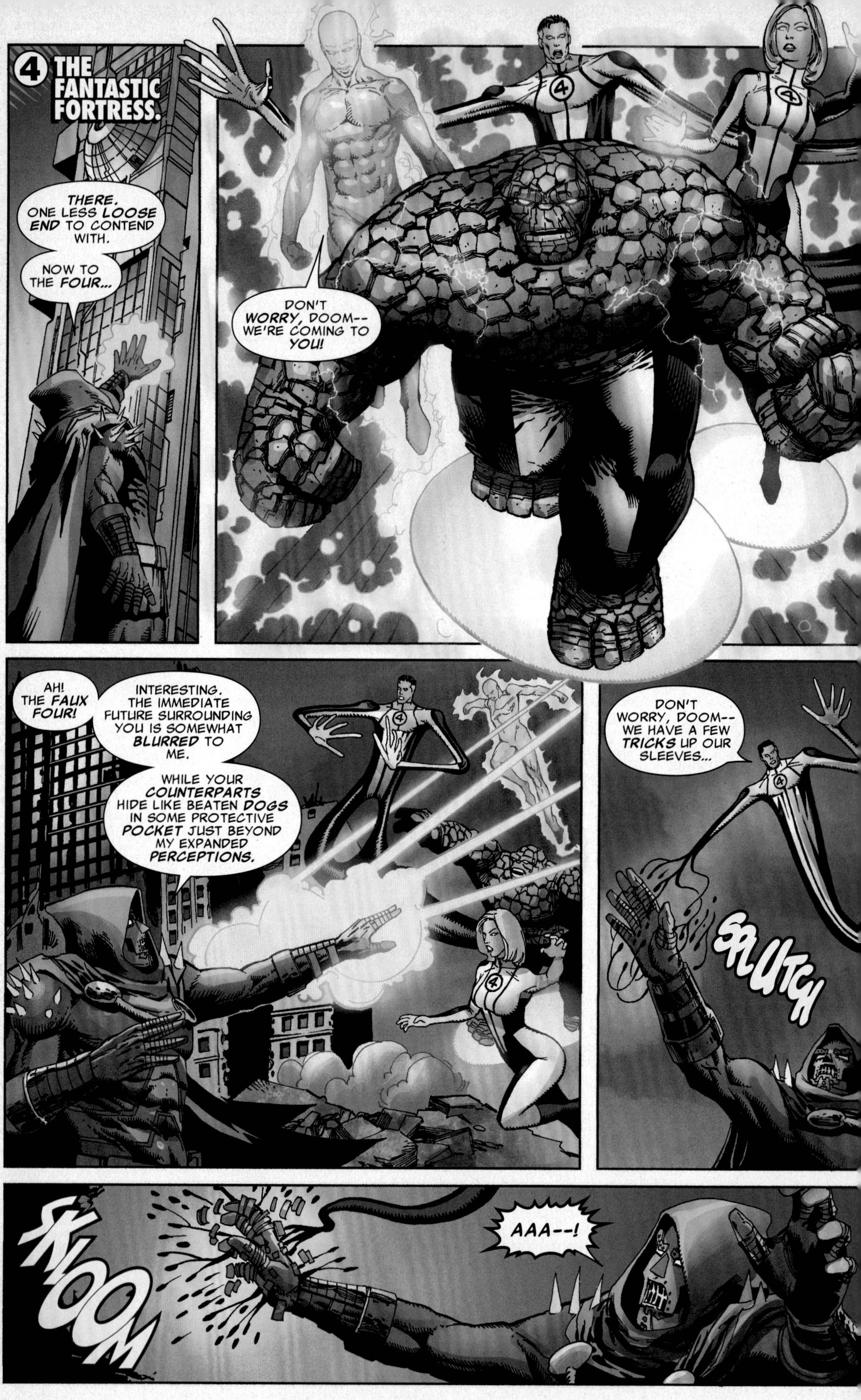
4 THE FANTASTIC FORTRESS.
THERE. ONE LESS LOOSE END TO CONTEND WITH.
NOW TO THE FOUR...
DON'T WORRY, DOOM-- WE'RE COMING TO YOU!
AH! THE FAUX FOUR!
INTERESTING. THE IMMEDIATE FUTURE SURROUNDING YOU IS SOMEWHAT BLURRED TO ME.
WHILE YOUR COUNTERPARTS HIDE LIKE BEATEN DOGS IN SOME PROTECTIVE POCKET JUST BEYOND MY EXPANDED PERCEPTIONS.
DON'T WORRY, DOOM-- WE HAVE A FEW TRICKS UP OUR SLEEVES...
SPLUTCH
SKOOM
AAA--!

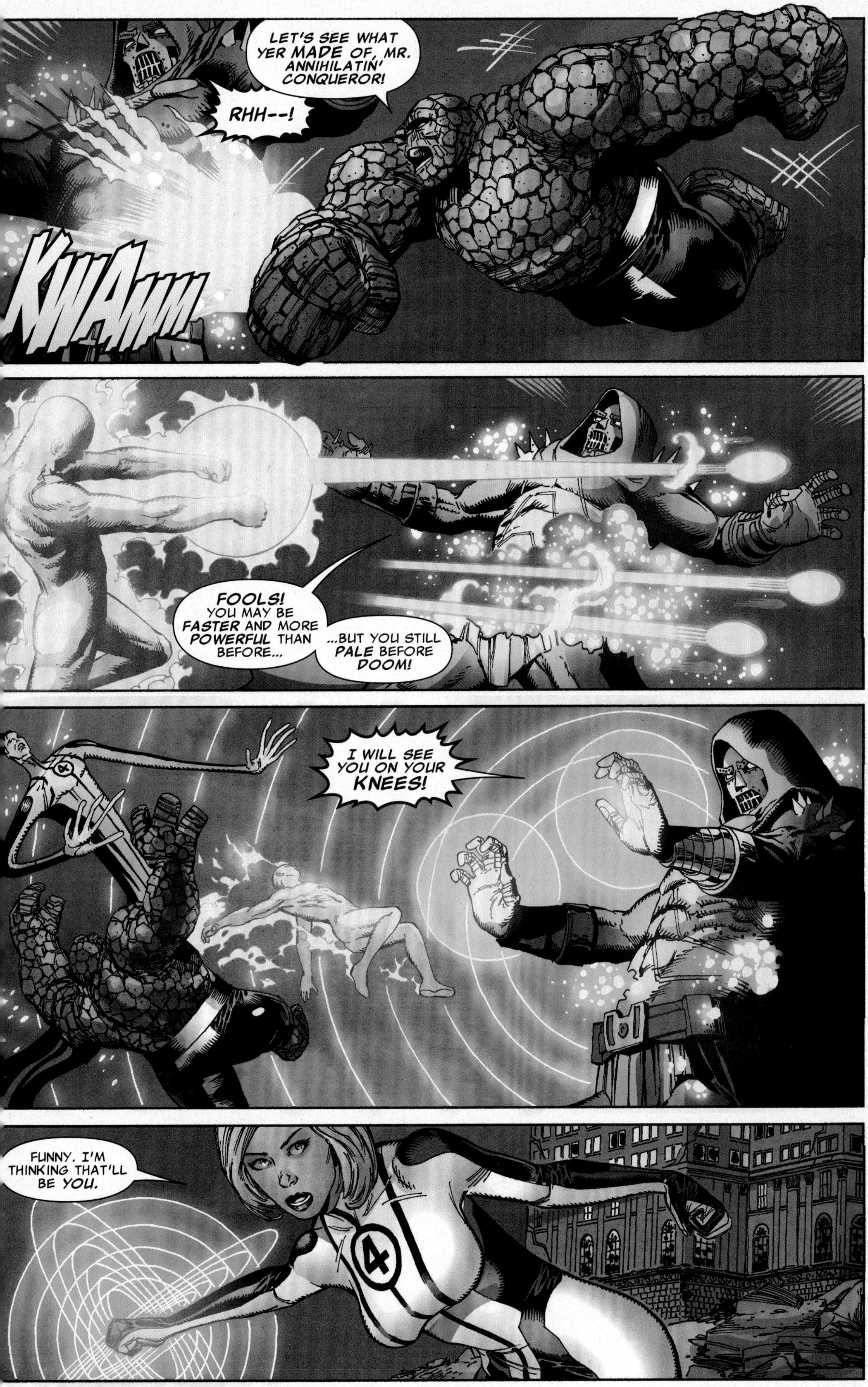

LET'S SEE WHAT YER MADE OF, MR. ANNIHILATIN' CONQUEROR!
RHH--!
KWAMM
FOOLS! YOU MAY BE FASTER AND MORE POWERFUL THAN BEFORE...
...BUT YOU STILL PALE BEFORE DOOM!
I WILL SEE YOU ON YOUR KNEES!
FUNNY. I'M THINKING THAT'LL BE YOU.

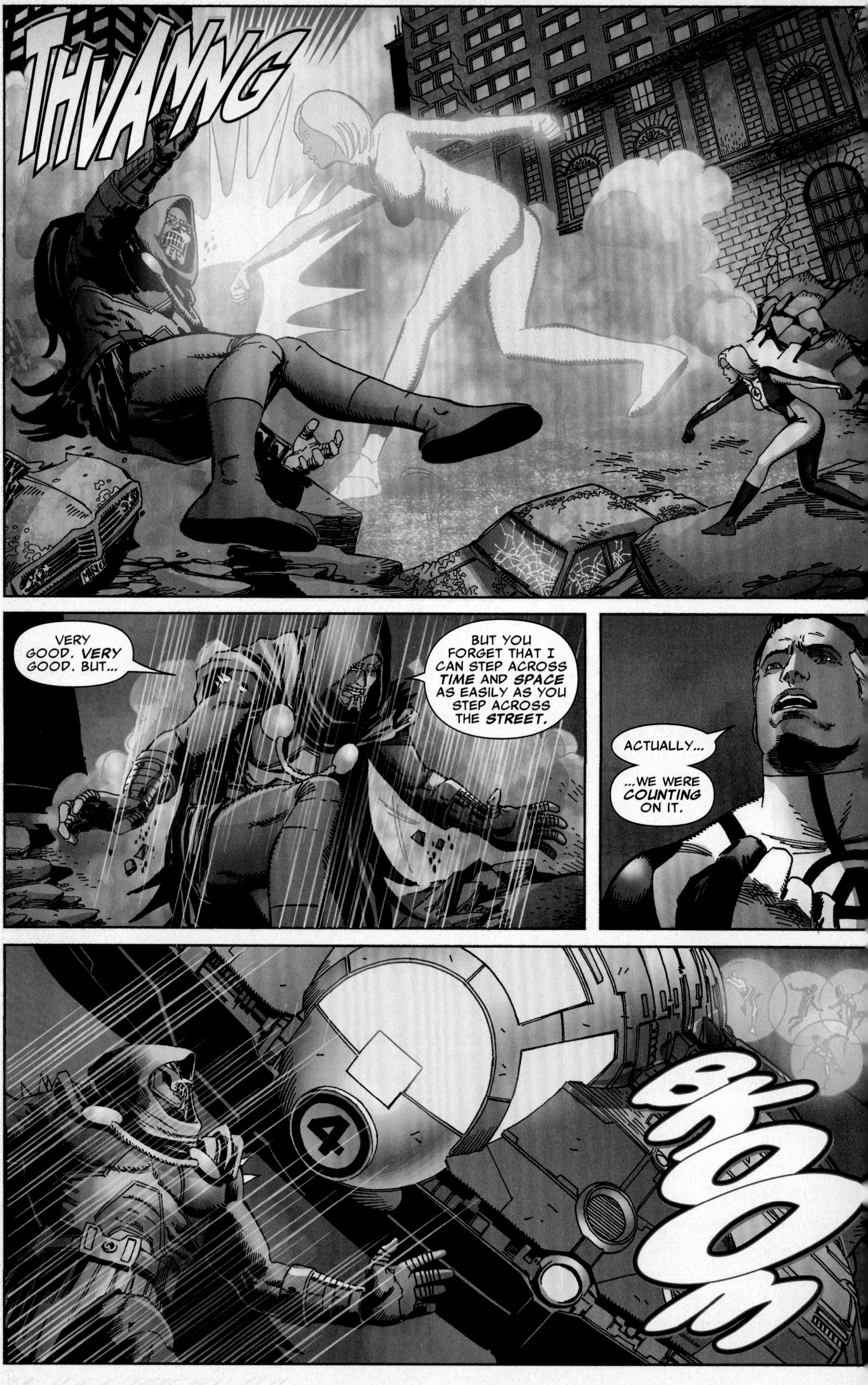
THVANNG
VERY GOOD. VERY GOOD. BUT...
BUT YOU FORGET THAT I CAN STEP ACROSS TIME AND SPACE AS EASILY AS YOU STEP ACROSS THE STREET.
ACTUALLY...
...WE WERE COUNTING ON IT.

KRANOOM

YOU WERE *RIGHT*--THE SHIP WAS A *BLINDSPOT* TO HIM. DOOM NEVER SAW IT COMING.

WHAT'S *IMPORTANT* IS WHAT COMES *NEXT*...

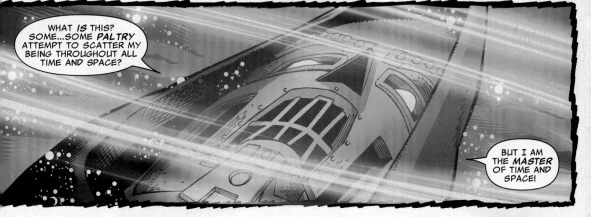

WHAT *IS* THIS? SOME...SOME *PALTRY* ATTEMPT TO SCATTER MY BEING THROUGHOUT ALL TIME AND SPACE?

BUT I AM THE *MASTER* OF TIME AND SPACE!

I AM ITS *MASTER*--!

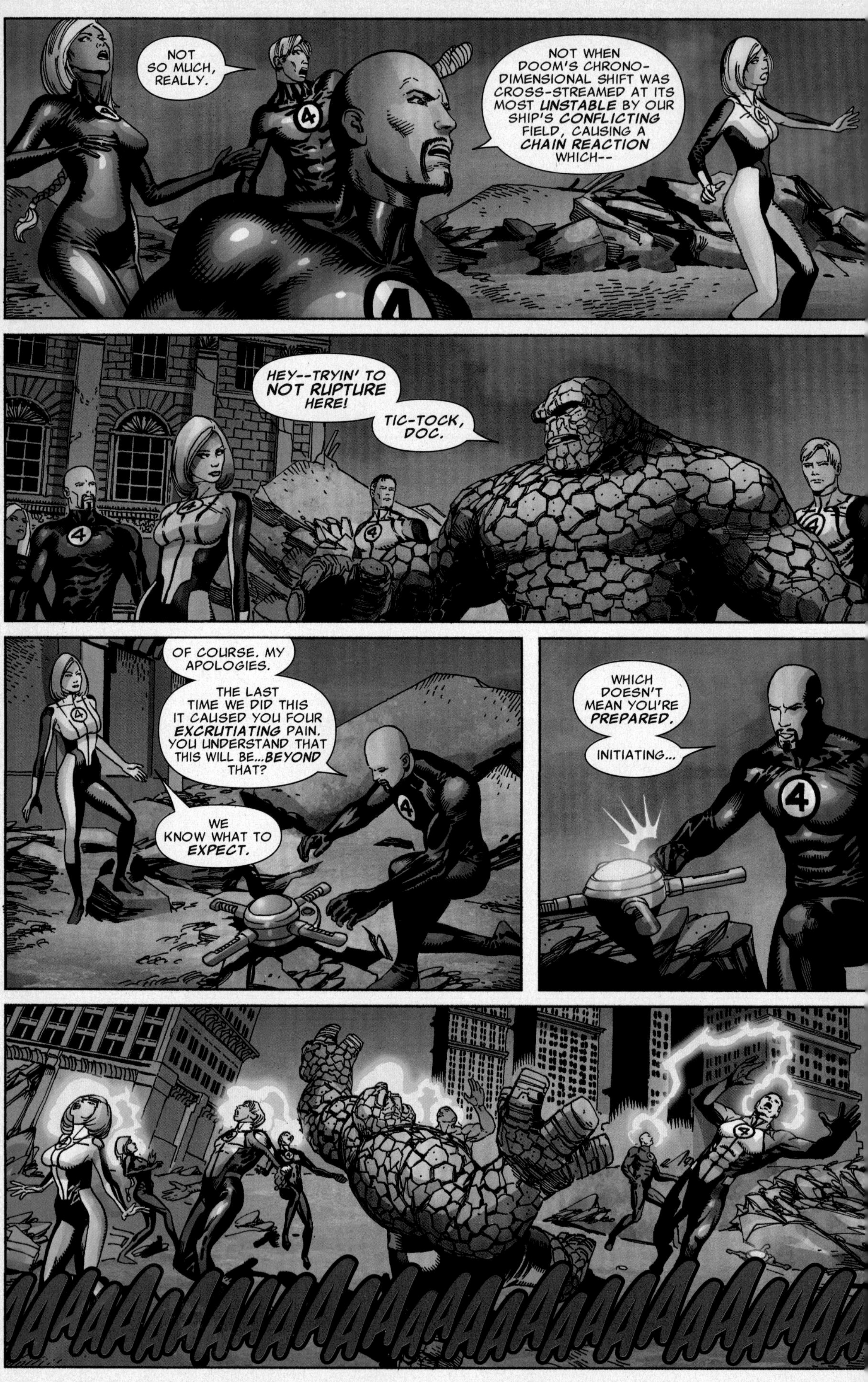
NOT SO MUCH, REALLY.
NOT WHEN DOOM'S CHRONO-DIMENSIONAL SHIFT WAS CROSS-STREAMED AT ITS MOST UNSTABLE BY OUR SHIP'S CONFLICTING FIELD, CAUSING A CHAIN REACTION WHICH--
HEY--TRYIN' TO NOT RUPTURE HERE!
TIC-TOCK, DOC.
OF COURSE. MY APOLOGIES.
THE LAST TIME WE DID THIS IT CAUSED YOU FOUR EXCRUTIATING PAIN. YOU UNDERSTAND THAT THIS WILL BE...BEYOND THAT?
WE KNOW WHAT TO EXPECT.
WHICH DOESN'T MEAN YOU'RE PREPARED.
INITIATING...
AAAAAAAAAAAAAAAAAAAAAAAAAAAAAAAAAAAAAAAAAAAAAAAAAAAAAAAAA

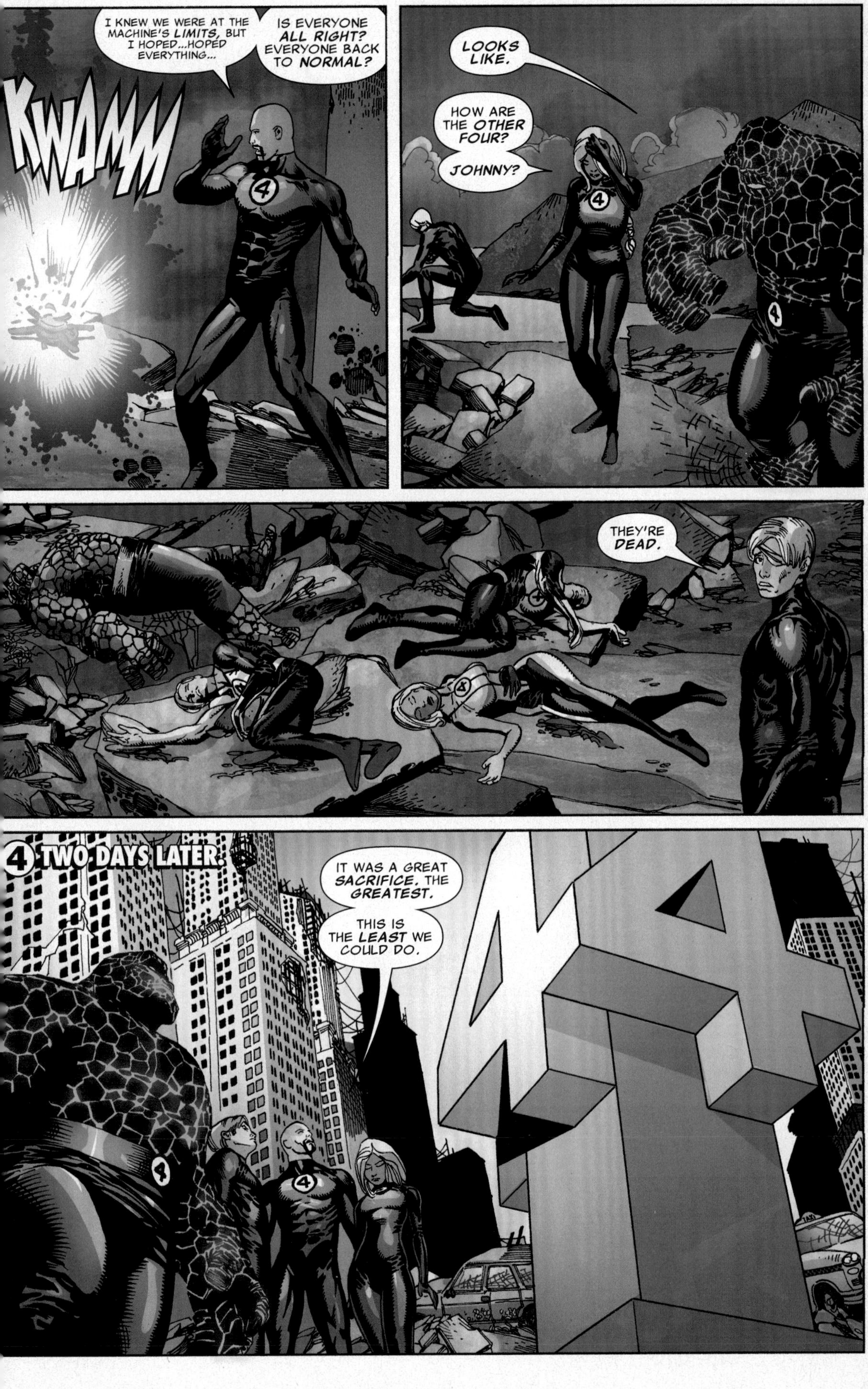
KWAMM
I KNEW WE WERE AT THE MACHINE'S LIMITS, BUT I HOPED...HOPED EVERYTHING...
IS EVERYONE ALL RIGHT? EVERYONE BACK TO NORMAL?
LOOKS LIKE.
HOW ARE THE OTHER FOUR?
JOHNNY?
THEY'RE DEAD.
TWO DAYS LATER.
IT WAS A GREAT SACRIFICE. THE GREATEST.
THIS IS THE LEAST WE COULD DO.

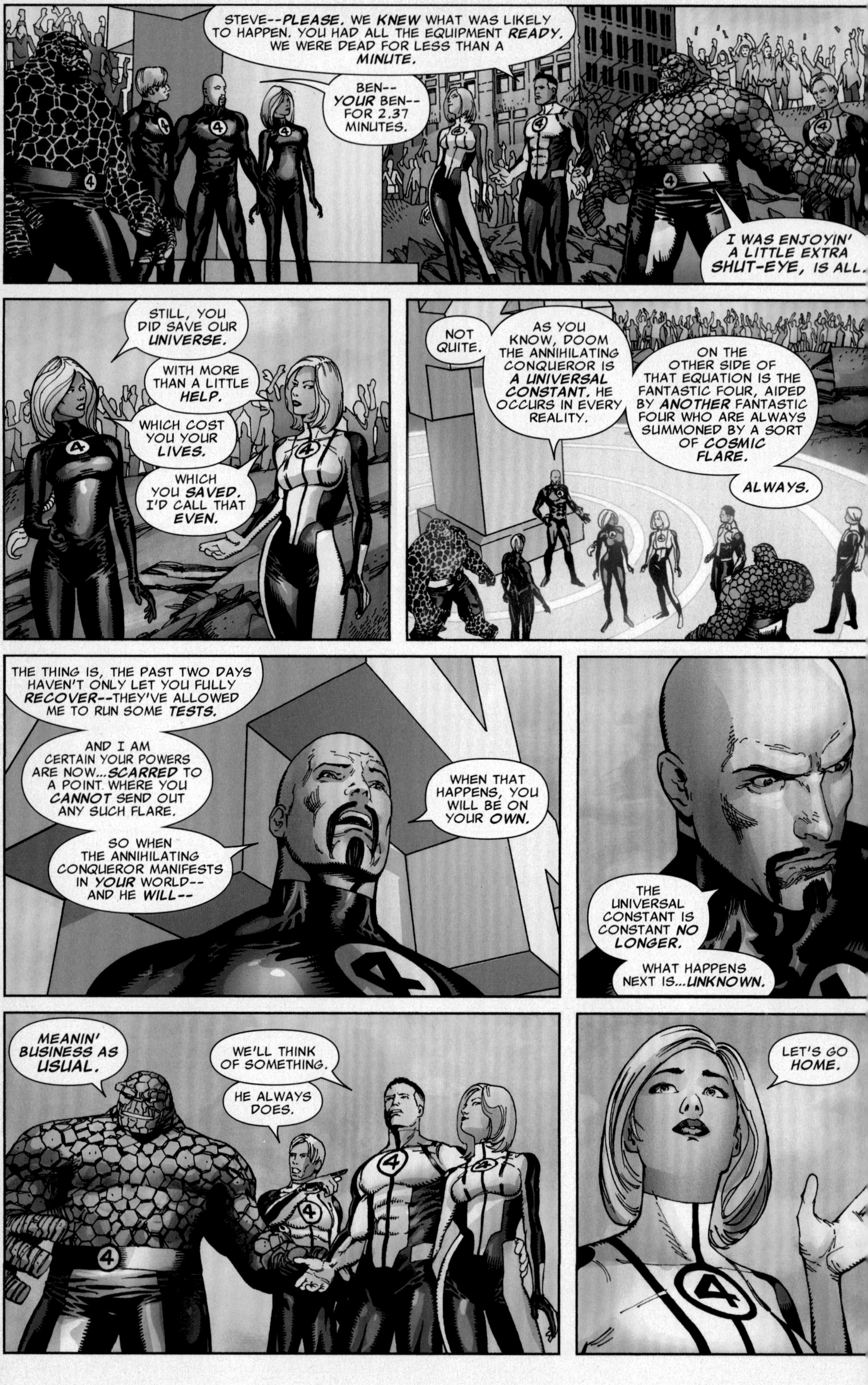
STEVE--PLEASE. WE KNEW WHAT WAS LIKELY TO HAPPEN. YOU HAD ALL THE EQUIPMENT READY. WE WERE DEAD FOR LESS THAN A MINUTE.
BEN-- YOUR BEN-- FOR 2.37 MINUTES.
I WAS ENJOYIN' A LITTLE EXTRA SHUT-EYE, IS ALL.
STILL, YOU DID SAVE OUR UNIVERSE.
WITH MORE THAN A LITTLE HELP.
WHICH COST YOU YOUR LIVES.
WHICH YOU SAVED. I'D CALL THAT EVEN.
NOT QUITE.
AS YOU KNOW, DOOM THE ANNIHILATING CONQUEROR IS A UNIVERSAL CONSTANT. HE OCCURS IN EVERY REALITY.
ON THE OTHER SIDE OF THAT EQUATION IS THE FANTASTIC FOUR, AIDED BY ANOTHER FANTASTIC FOUR WHO ARE ALWAYS SUMMONED BY A SORT OF COSMIC FLARE.
ALWAYS.
THE THING IS, THE PAST TWO DAYS HAVEN'T ONLY LET YOU FULLY RECOVER--THEY'VE ALLOWED ME TO RUN SOME TESTS.
AND I AM CERTAIN YOUR POWERS ARE NOW...SCARRED TO A POINT WHERE YOU CANNOT SEND OUT ANY SUCH FLARE.
SO WHEN THE ANNIHILATING CONQUEROR MANIFESTS IN YOUR WORLD-- AND HE WILL--
WHEN THAT HAPPENS, YOU WILL BE ON YOUR OWN.
THE UNIVERSAL CONSTANT IS CONSTANT NO LONGER.
WHAT HAPPENS NEXT IS...UNKNOWN.
MEANIN' BUSINESS AS USUAL.
WE'LL THINK OF SOMETHING.
HE ALWAYS DOES.
LET'S GO HOME.

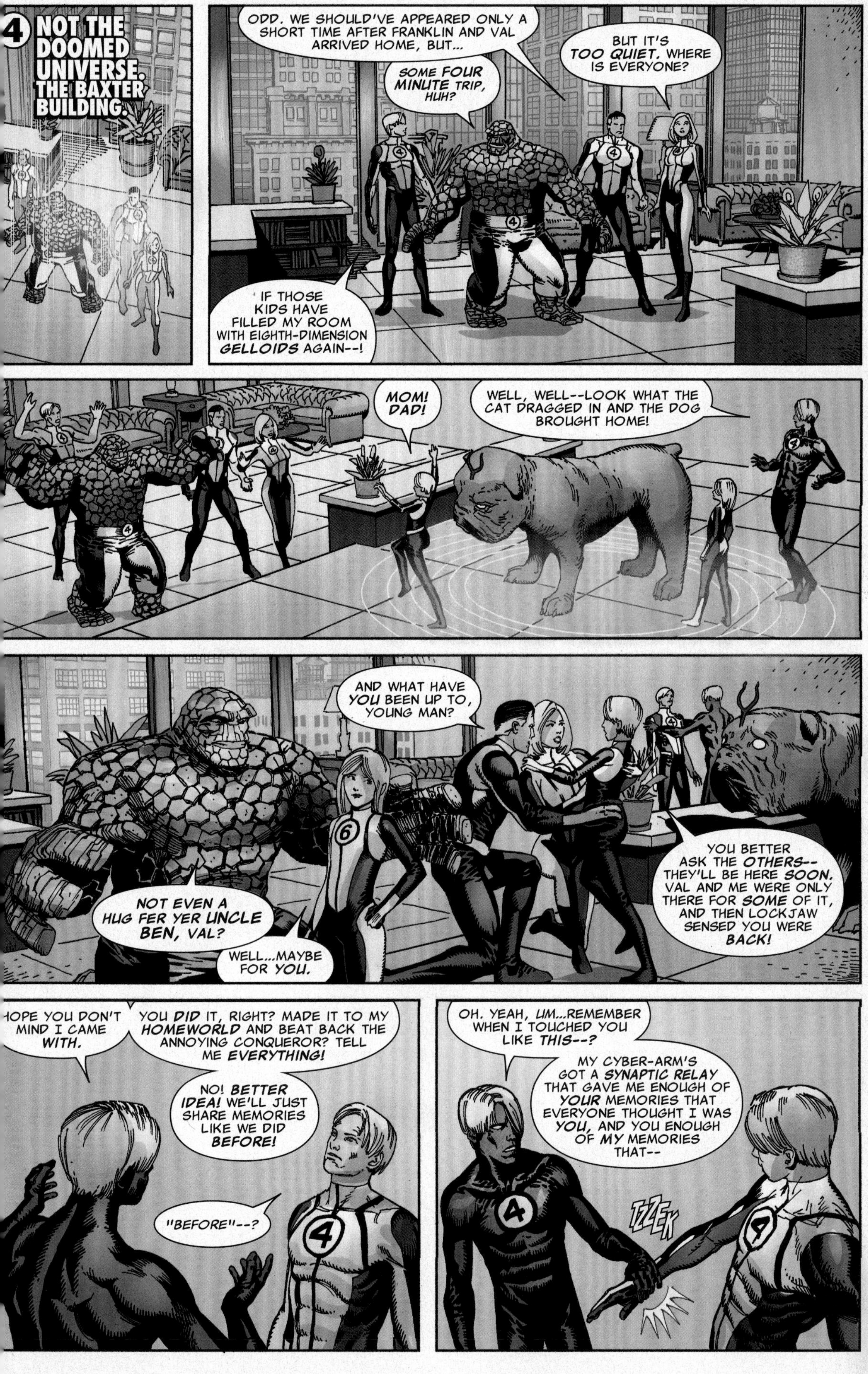

NOT THE DOOMED UNIVERSE. THE BAXTER BUILDING.
ODD. WE SHOULD'VE APPEARED ONLY A SHORT TIME AFTER FRANKLIN AND VAL ARRIVED HOME, BUT...
SOME FOUR MINUTE TRIP, HUH?
BUT IT'S TOO QUIET. WHERE IS EVERYONE?
IF THOSE KIDS HAVE FILLED MY ROOM WITH EIGHTH-DIMENSION GELLOIDS AGAIN--!
MOM! DAD!
WELL, WELL--LOOK WHAT THE CAT DRAGGED IN AND THE DOG BROUGHT HOME!
AND WHAT HAVE YOU BEEN UP TO, YOUNG MAN?
YOU BETTER ASK THE OTHERS--THEY'LL BE HERE SOON. VAL AND ME WERE ONLY THERE FOR SOME OF IT, AND THEN LOCKJAW SENSED YOU WERE BACK!
NOT EVEN A HUG FER YER UNCLE BEN, VAL?
WELL...MAYBE FOR YOU.
HOPE YOU DON'T MIND I CAME WITH.
YOU DID IT, RIGHT? MADE IT TO MY HOMEWORLD AND BEAT BACK THE ANNOYING CONQUEROR? TELL ME EVERYTHING!
NO! BETTER IDEA! WE'LL JUST SHARE MEMORIES LIKE WE DID BEFORE!
"BEFORE"--?
OH. YEAH, UM...REMEMBER WHEN I TOUCHED YOU LIKE THIS--?
MY CYBER-ARM'S GOT A SYNAPTIC RELAY THAT GAVE ME ENOUGH OF YOUR MEMORIES THAT EVERYONE THOUGHT I WAS YOU, AND YOU ENOUGH OF MY MEMORIES THAT--
TZZEK

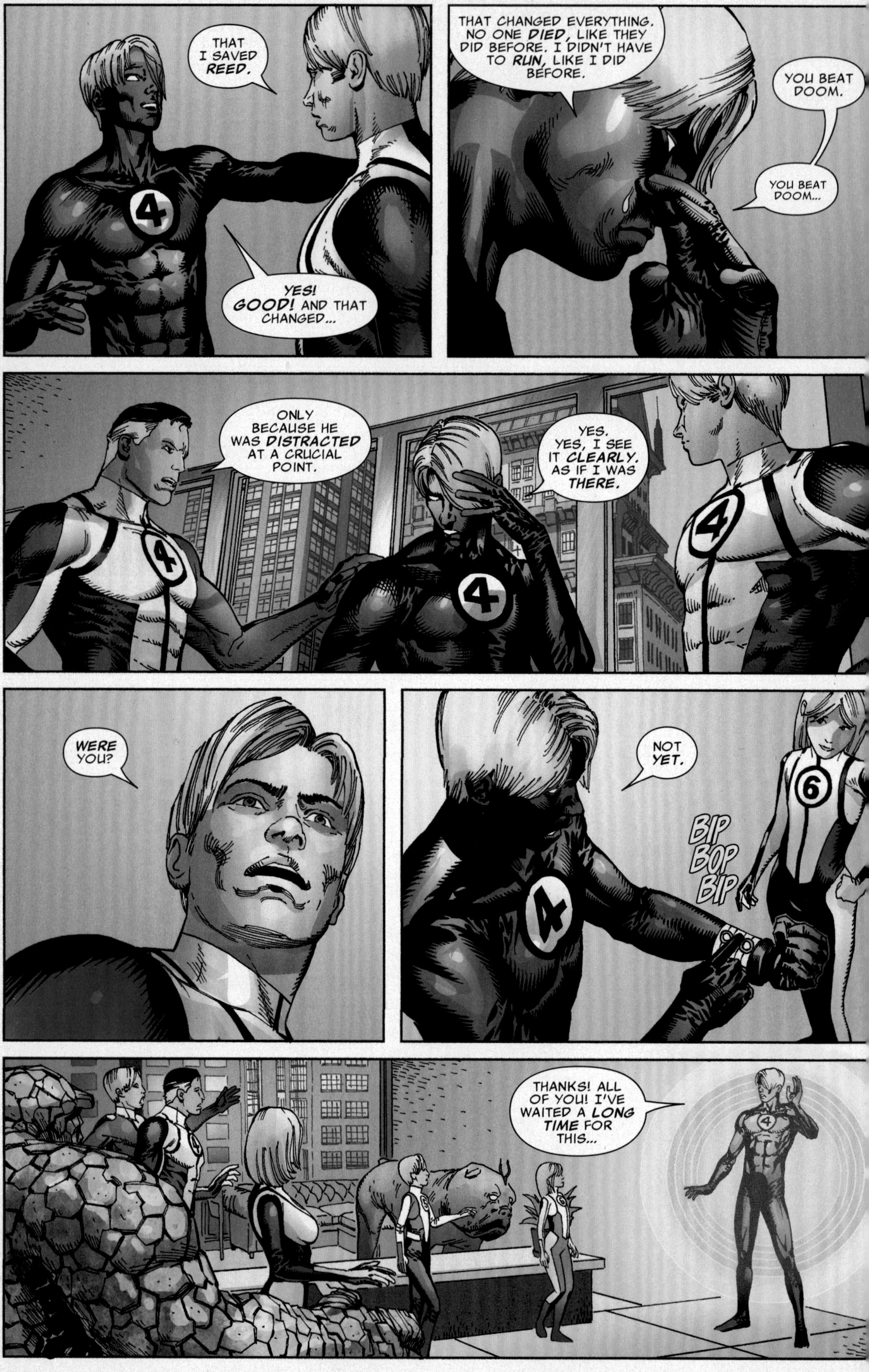
THAT I SAVED REED.
YES! GOOD! AND THAT CHANGED...
THAT CHANGED EVERYTHING. NO ONE DIED, LIKE THEY DID BEFORE. I DIDN'T HAVE TO RUN, LIKE I DID BEFORE.
YOU BEAT DOOM.
YOU BEAT DOOM...
ONLY BECAUSE HE WAS DISTRACTED AT A CRUCIAL POINT.
YES. YES, I SEE IT CLEARLY. AS IF I WAS THERE.
WERE YOU?
NOT YET.
BIP BOP BIP
THANKS! ALL OF YOU! I'VE WAITED A LONG TIME FOR THIS...

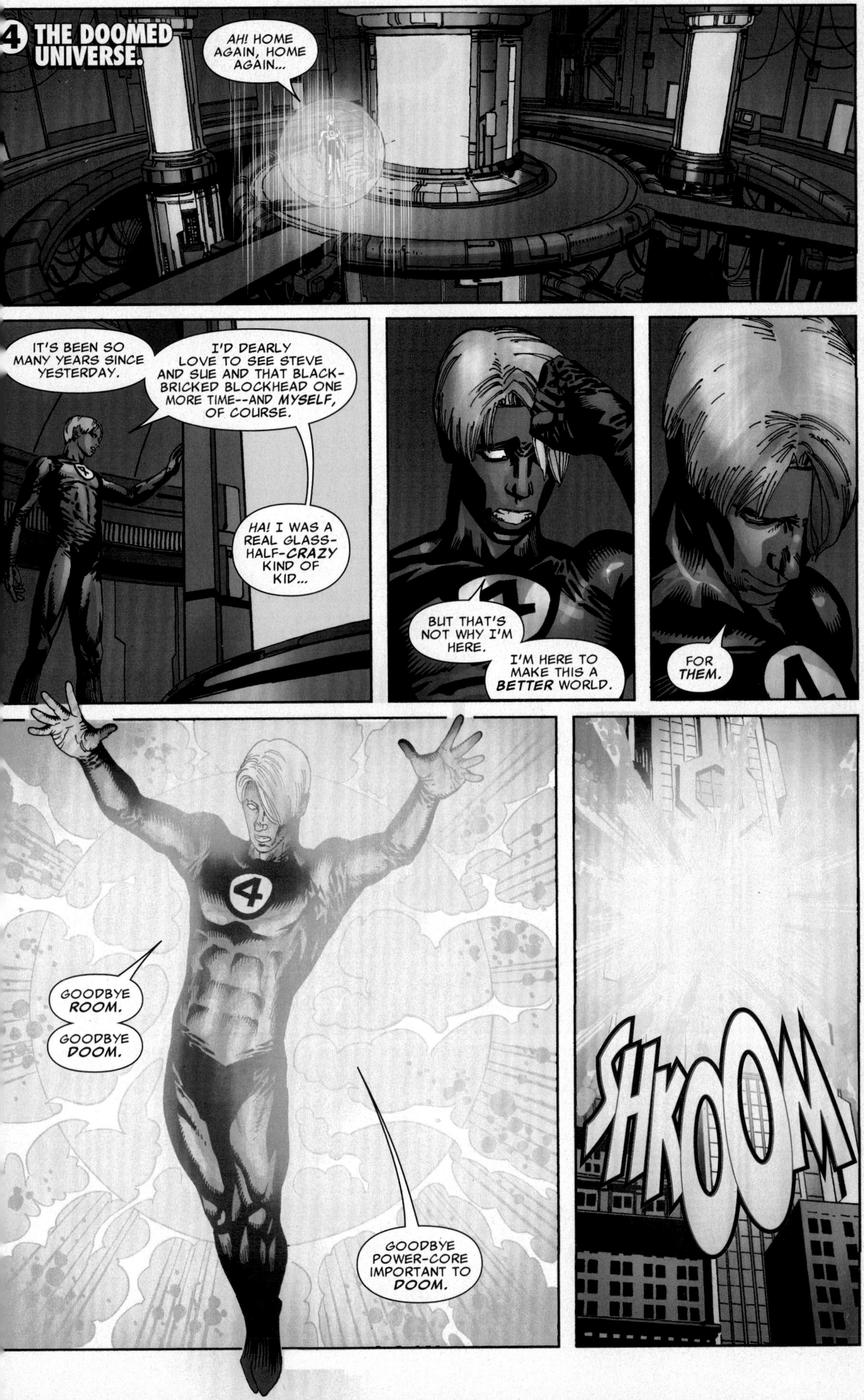

4 THE DOOMED UNIVERSE.
AH! HOME AGAIN, HOME AGAIN...
IT'S BEEN SO MANY YEARS SINCE YESTERDAY.
I'D DEARLY LOVE TO SEE STEVE AND SUE AND THAT BLACK-BRICKED BLOCKHEAD ONE MORE TIME--AND MYSELF, OF COURSE.
HA! I WAS A REAL GLASS-HALF-CRAZY KIND OF KID...
BUT THAT'S NOT WHY I'M HERE.
I'M HERE TO MAKE THIS A BETTER WORLD.
FOR THEM.
GOODBYE ROOM.
GOODBYE DOOM.
GOODBYE POWER-CORE IMPORTANT TO DOOM.
SHKOOM

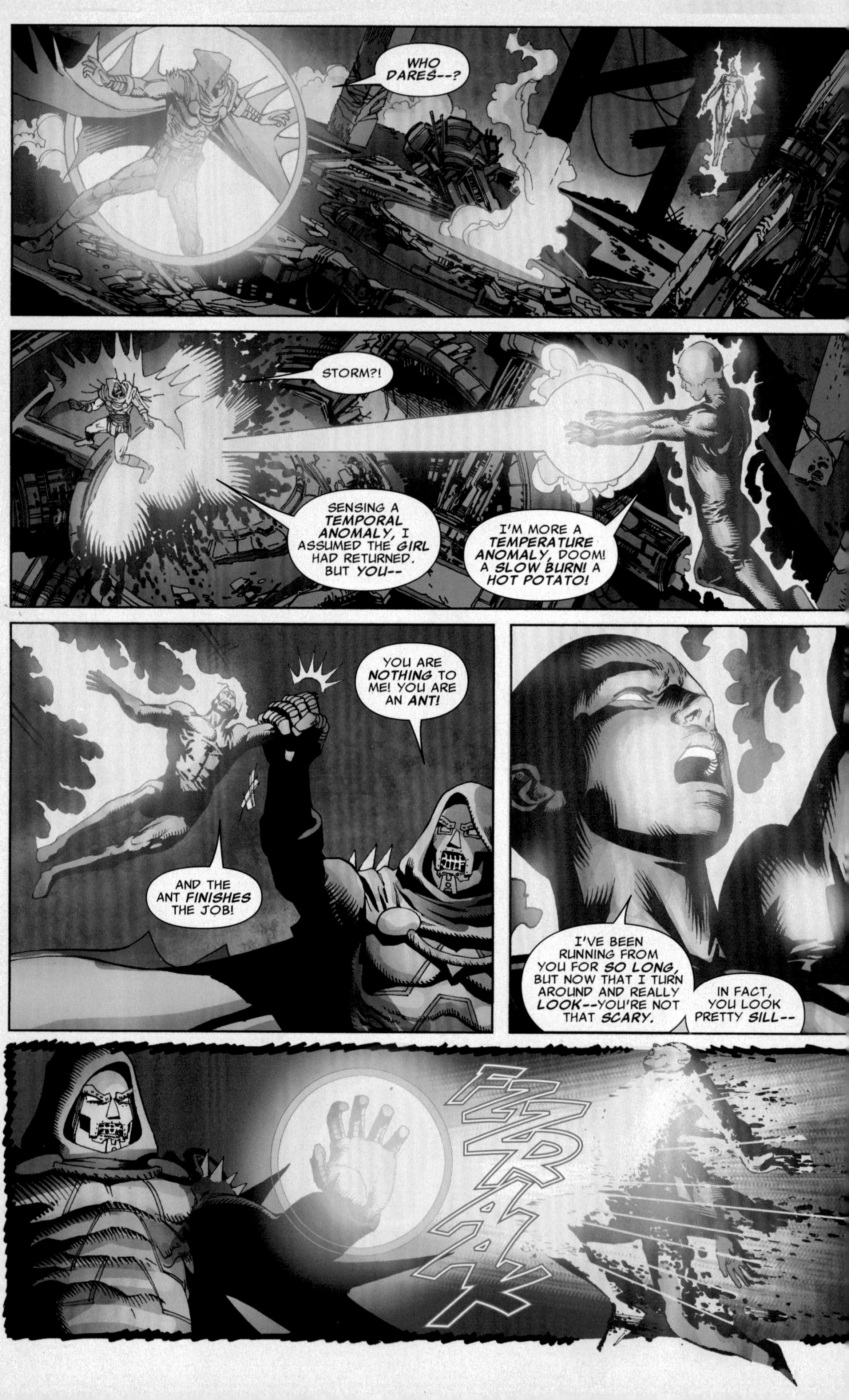
WHO DARES--?
STORM?!
SENSING A TEMPORAL ANOMALY, I ASSUMED THE GIRL HAD RETURNED. BUT YOU--
I'M MORE A TEMPERATURE ANOMALY, DOOM! A SLOW BURN! A HOT POTATO!
YOU ARE NOTHING TO ME! YOU ARE AN ANT!
AND THE ANT FINISHES THE JOB!
I'VE BEEN RUNNING FROM YOU FOR SO LONG, BUT NOW THAT I TURN AROUND AND REALLY LOOK--YOU'RE NOT THAT SCARY.
IN FACT, YOU LOOK PRETTY SILL--
FZZRAKK

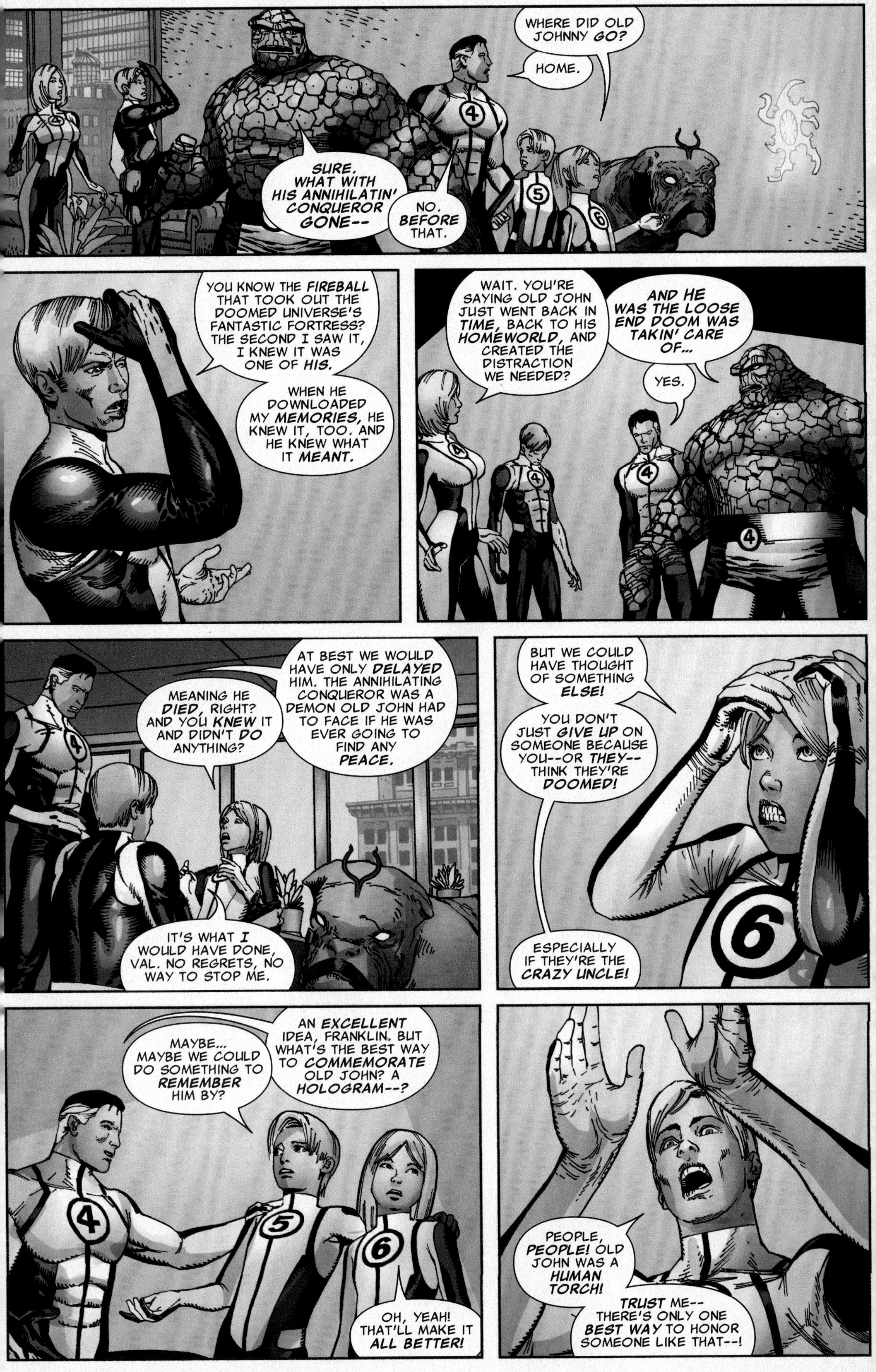
WHERE DID OLD JOHNNY GO?
HOME.
SURE. WHAT WITH HIS ANNIHILATIN' CONQUEROR GONE--
NO. BEFORE THAT.
YOU KNOW THE FIREBALL THAT TOOK OUT THE DOOMED UNIVERSE'S FANTASTIC FORTRESS? THE SECOND I SAW IT, I KNEW IT WAS ONE OF HIS.
WHEN HE DOWNLOADED MY MEMORIES, HE KNEW IT, TOO. AND HE KNEW WHAT IT MEANT.
WAIT. YOU'RE SAYING OLD JOHN JUST WENT BACK IN TIME, BACK TO HIS HOMEWORLD, AND CREATED THE DISTRACTION WE NEEDED?
AND HE WAS THE LOOSE END DOOM WAS TAKIN' CARE OF...
YES.
MEANING HE DIED, RIGHT? AND YOU KNEW IT AND DIDN'T DO ANYTHING?
AT BEST WE WOULD HAVE ONLY DELAYED HIM. THE ANNIHILATING CONQUEROR WAS A DEMON OLD JOHN HAD TO FACE IF HE WAS EVER GOING TO FIND ANY PEACE.
IT'S WHAT I WOULD HAVE DONE, VAL. NO REGRETS, NO WAY TO STOP ME.
BUT WE COULD HAVE THOUGHT OF SOMETHING ELSE!
YOU DON'T JUST GIVE UP ON SOMEONE BECAUSE YOU--OR THEY-- THINK THEY'RE DOOMED!
ESPECIALLY IF THEY'RE THE CRAZY UNCLE!
MAYBE... MAYBE WE COULD DO SOMETHING TO REMEMBER HIM BY?
AN EXCELLENT IDEA, FRANKLIN. BUT WHAT'S THE BEST WAY TO COMMEMORATE OLD JOHN? A HOLOGRAM--?
OH, YEAH! THAT'LL MAKE IT ALL BETTER!
PEOPLE, PEOPLE! OLD JOHN WAS A HUMAN TORCH!
TRUST ME-- THERE'S ONLY ONE BEST WAY TO HONOR SOMEONE LIKE THAT--!

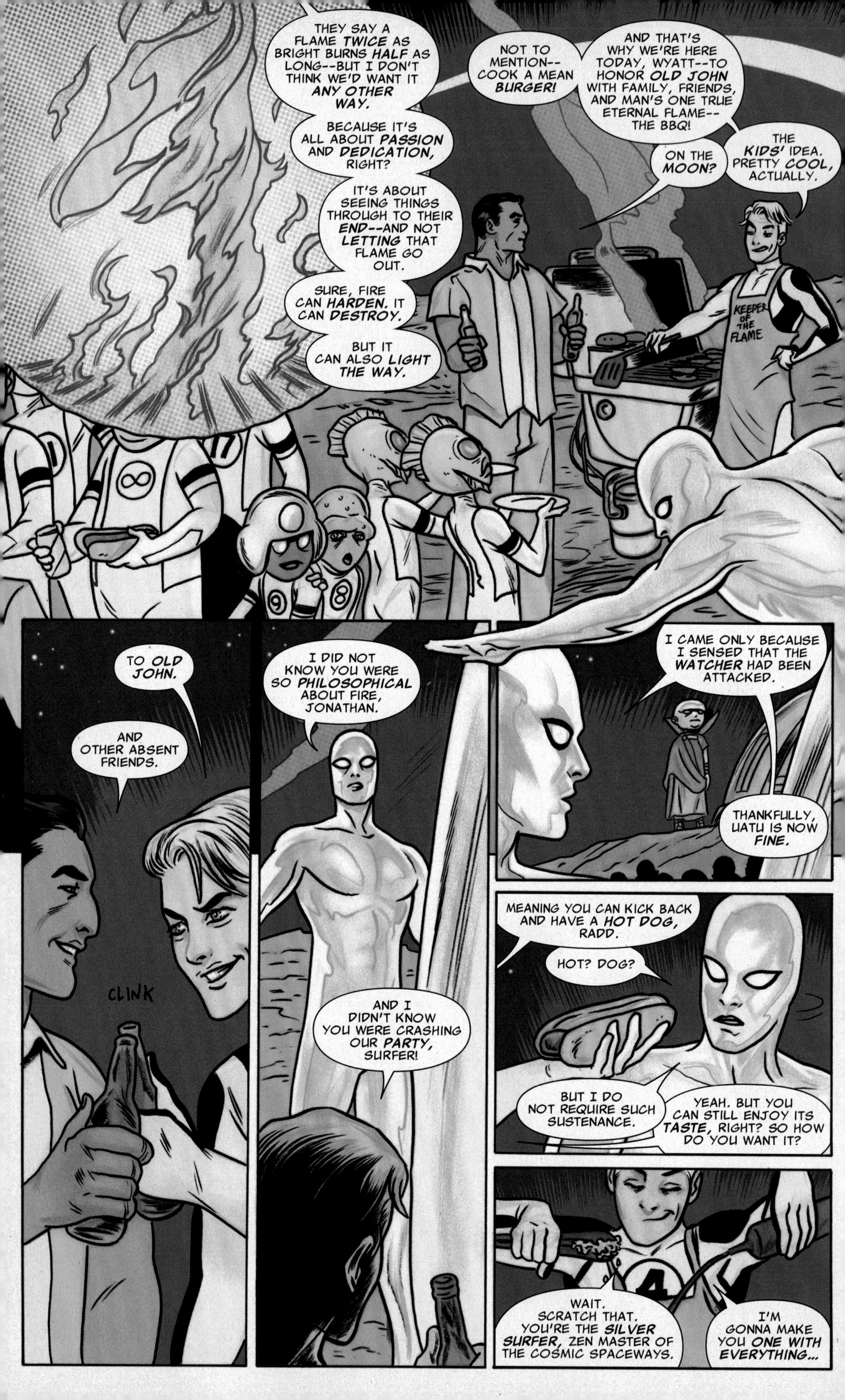
THEY SAY A FLAME TWICE AS BRIGHT BURNS HALF AS LONG--BUT I DON'T THINK WE'D WANT IT ANY OTHER WAY.
BECAUSE IT'S ALL ABOUT PASSION AND DEDICATION, RIGHT?
IT'S ABOUT SEEING THINGS THROUGH TO THEIR END--AND NOT LETTING THAT FLAME GO OUT.
SURE, FIRE CAN HARDEN. IT CAN DESTROY.
BUT IT CAN ALSO LIGHT THE WAY.
NOT TO MENTION--COOK A MEAN BURGER!
AND THAT'S WHY WE'RE HERE TODAY, WYATT--TO HONOR OLD JOHN WITH FAMILY, FRIENDS, AND MAN'S ONE TRUE ETERNAL FLAME--THE BBQ!
ON THE MOON?
THE KIDS' IDEA. PRETTY COOL, ACTUALLY.
KEEPER OF THE FLAME
TO OLD JOHN.
AND OTHER ABSENT FRIENDS.
CLINK
I DID NOT KNOW YOU WERE SO PHILOSOPHICAL ABOUT FIRE, JONATHAN.
AND I DIDN'T KNOW YOU WERE CRASHING OUR PARTY, SURFER!
I CAME ONLY BECAUSE I SENSED THAT THE WATCHER HAD BEEN ATTACKED.
THANKFULLY, UATU IS NOW FINE.
MEANING YOU CAN KICK BACK AND HAVE A HOT DOG, RADD.
HOT? DOG?
BUT I DO NOT REQUIRE SUCH SUSTENANCE.
YEAH. BUT YOU CAN STILL ENJOY ITS TASTE, RIGHT? SO HOW DO YOU WANT IT?
WAIT. SCRATCH THAT. YOU'RE THE SILVER SURFER, ZEN MASTER OF THE COSMIC SPACEWAYS.
I'M GONNA MAKE YOU ONE WITH EVERYTHING...

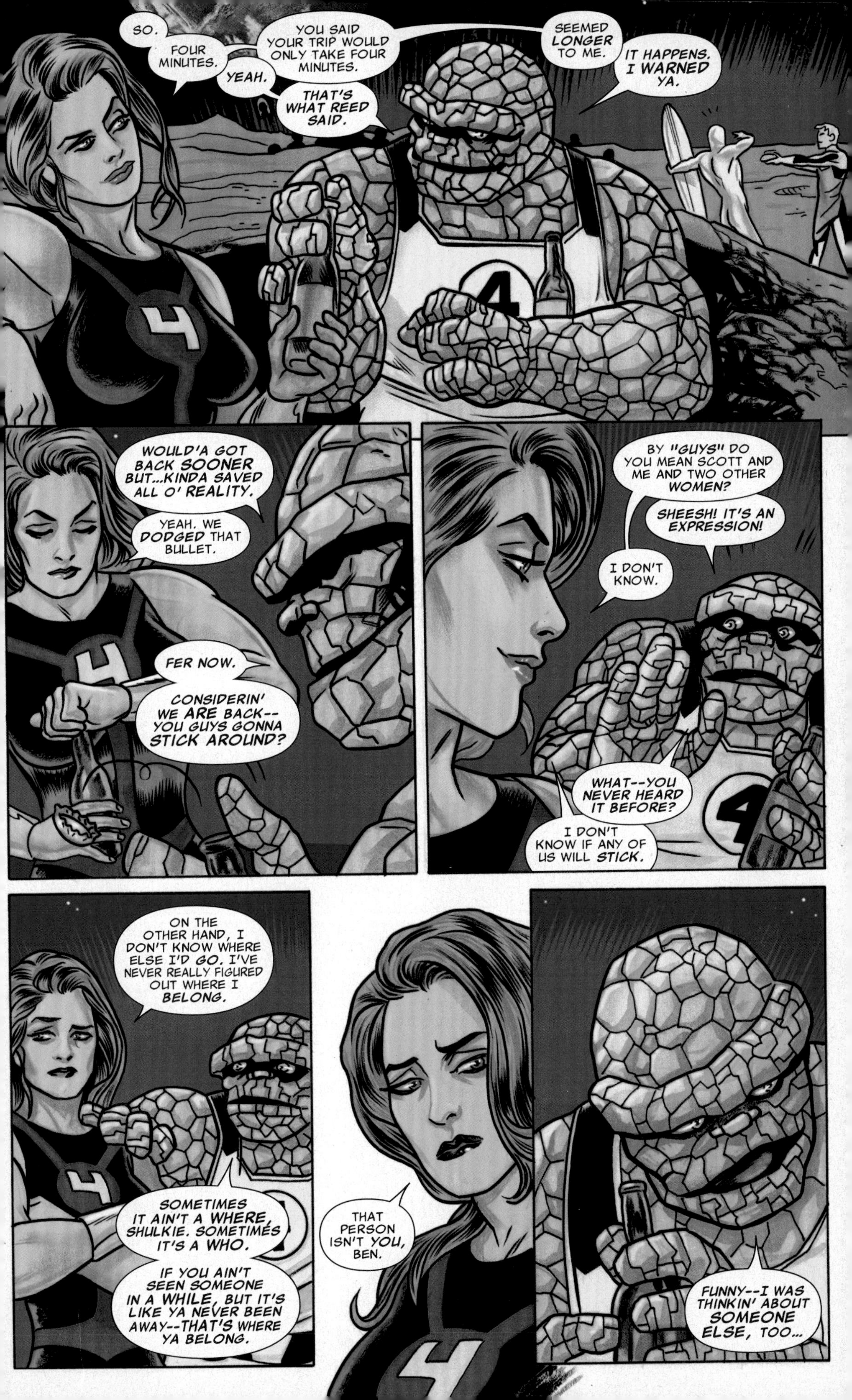
SO.
FOUR MINUTES.
YOU SAID YOUR TRIP WOULD ONLY TAKE FOUR MINUTES.
YEAH.
THAT'S WHAT REED SAID.
SEEMED LONGER TO ME.
IT HAPPENS. I WARNED YA.
WOULD'A GOT BACK SOONER BUT...KINDA SAVED ALL O' REALITY.
YEAH. WE DODGED THAT BULLET.
FER NOW.
CONSIDERIN' WE ARE BACK-- YOU GUYS GONNA STICK AROUND?
BY "GUYS" DO YOU MEAN SCOTT AND ME AND TWO OTHER WOMEN?
SHEESH! IT'S AN EXPRESSION!
I DON'T KNOW.
WHAT--YOU NEVER HEARD IT BEFORE?
I DON'T KNOW IF ANY OF US WILL STICK.
ON THE OTHER HAND, I DON'T KNOW WHERE ELSE I'D GO. I'VE NEVER REALLY FIGURED OUT WHERE I BELONG.
SOMETIMES IT AIN'T A WHERE, SHULKIE. SOMETIMES IT'S A WHO.
IF YOU AIN'T SEEN SOMEONE IN A WHILE, BUT IT'S LIKE YA NEVER BEEN AWAY--THAT'S WHERE YA BELONG.
THAT PERSON ISN'T YOU, BEN.
FUNNY--I WAS THINKIN' ABOUT SOMEONE ELSE, TOO...

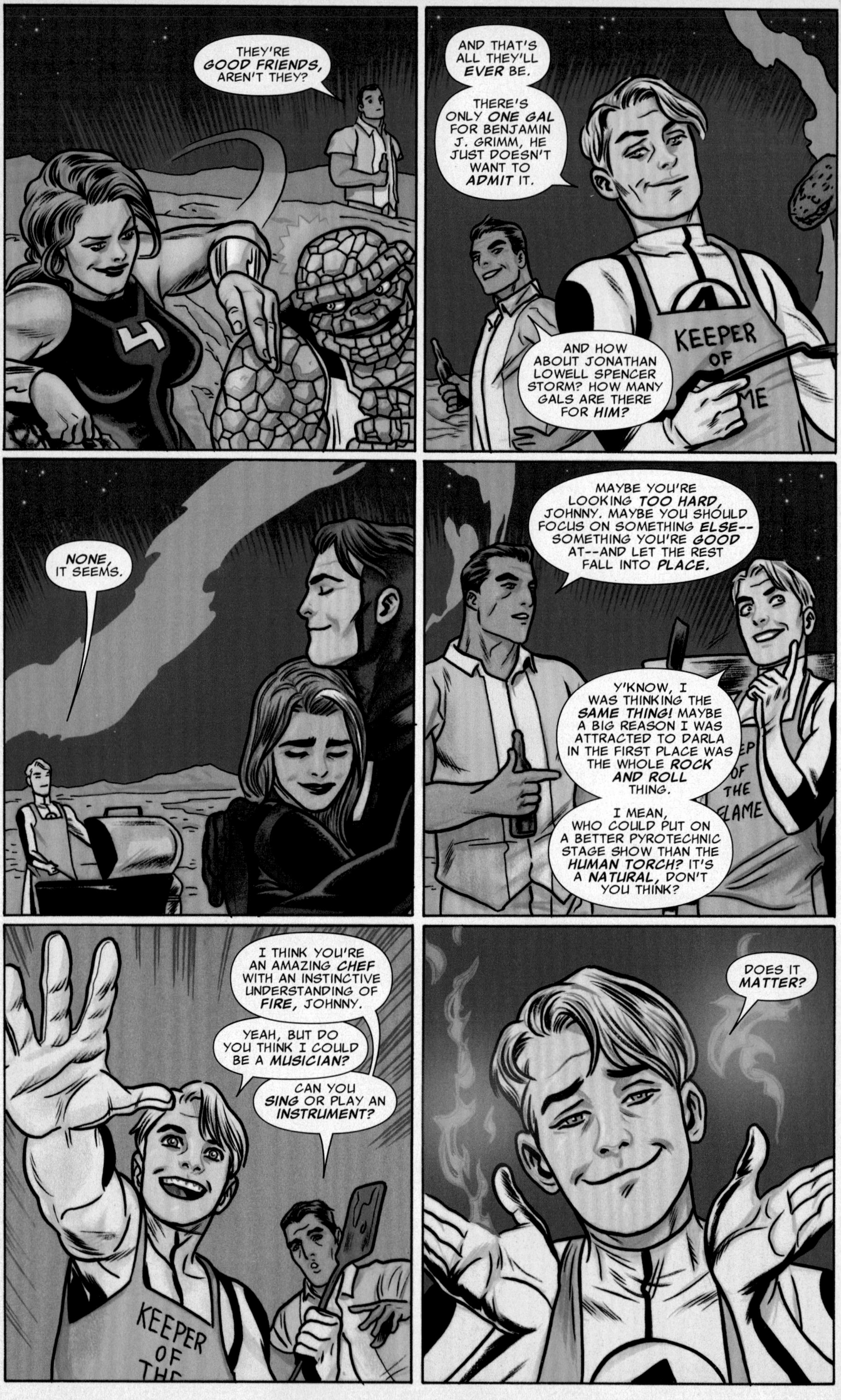
THEY'RE GOOD FRIENDS, AREN'T THEY?
AND THAT'S ALL THEY'LL EVER BE.
THERE'S ONLY ONE GAL FOR BENJAMIN J. GRIMM, HE JUST DOESN'T WANT TO ADMIT IT.
AND HOW ABOUT JONATHAN LOWELL SPENCER STORM? HOW MANY GALS ARE THERE FOR HIM?
KEEPER OF
NONE, IT SEEMS.
MAYBE YOU'RE LOOKING TOO HARD, JOHNNY. MAYBE YOU SHOULD FOCUS ON SOMETHING ELSE--SOMETHING YOU'RE GOOD AT--AND LET THE REST FALL INTO PLACE.
Y'KNOW, I WAS THINKING THE SAME THING! MAYBE A BIG REASON I WAS ATTRACTED TO DARLA IN THE FIRST PLACE WAS THE WHOLE ROCK AND ROLL THING.
I MEAN, WHO COULD PUT ON A BETTER PYROTECHNIC STAGE SHOW THAN THE HUMAN TORCH? IT'S A NATURAL, DON'T YOU THINK?
I THINK YOU'RE AN AMAZING CHEF WITH AN INSTINCTIVE UNDERSTANDING OF FIRE, JOHNNY.
YEAH, BUT DO YOU THINK I COULD BE A MUSICIAN?
CAN YOU SING OR PLAY AN INSTRUMENT?
KEEPER OF
DOES IT MATTER?

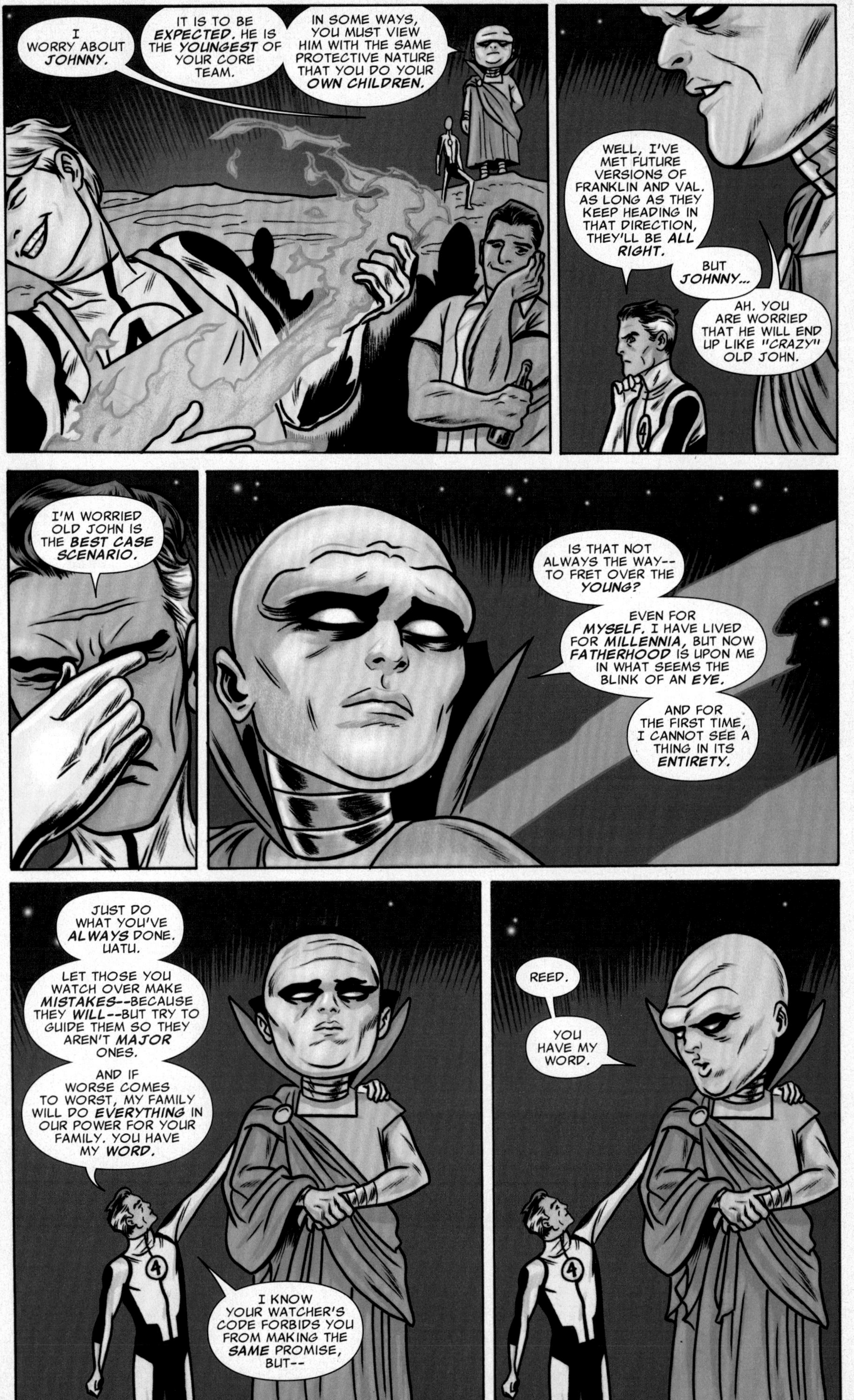
I WORRY ABOUT JOHNNY.
IT IS TO BE EXPECTED. HE IS THE YOUNGEST OF YOUR CORE TEAM.
IN SOME WAYS, YOU MUST VIEW HIM WITH THE SAME PROTECTIVE NATURE THAT YOU DO YOUR OWN CHILDREN.
WELL, I'VE MET FUTURE VERSIONS OF FRANKLIN AND VAL. AS LONG AS THEY KEEP HEADING IN THAT DIRECTION, THEY'LL BE ALL RIGHT.
BUT JOHNNY...
AH. YOU ARE WORRIED THAT HE WILL END UP LIKE "CRAZY" OLD JOHN.
I'M WORRIED OLD JOHN IS THE BEST CASE SCENARIO.
IS THAT NOT ALWAYS THE WAY-- TO FRET OVER THE YOUNG?
EVEN FOR MYSELF. I HAVE LIVED FOR MILLENNIA, BUT NOW FATHERHOOD IS UPON ME IN WHAT SEEMS THE BLINK OF AN EYE.
AND FOR THE FIRST TIME, I CANNOT SEE A THING IN ITS ENTIRETY.
JUST DO WHAT YOU'VE ALWAYS DONE, UATU.
LET THOSE YOU WATCH OVER MAKE MISTAKES--BECAUSE THEY WILL--BUT TRY TO GUIDE THEM SO THEY AREN'T MAJOR ONES.
AND IF WORSE COMES TO WORST, MY FAMILY WILL DO EVERYTHING IN OUR POWER FOR YOUR FAMILY. YOU HAVE MY WORD.
I KNOW YOUR WATCHER'S CODE FORBIDS YOU FROM MAKING THE SAME PROMISE, BUT--
REED.
YOU HAVE MY WORD.

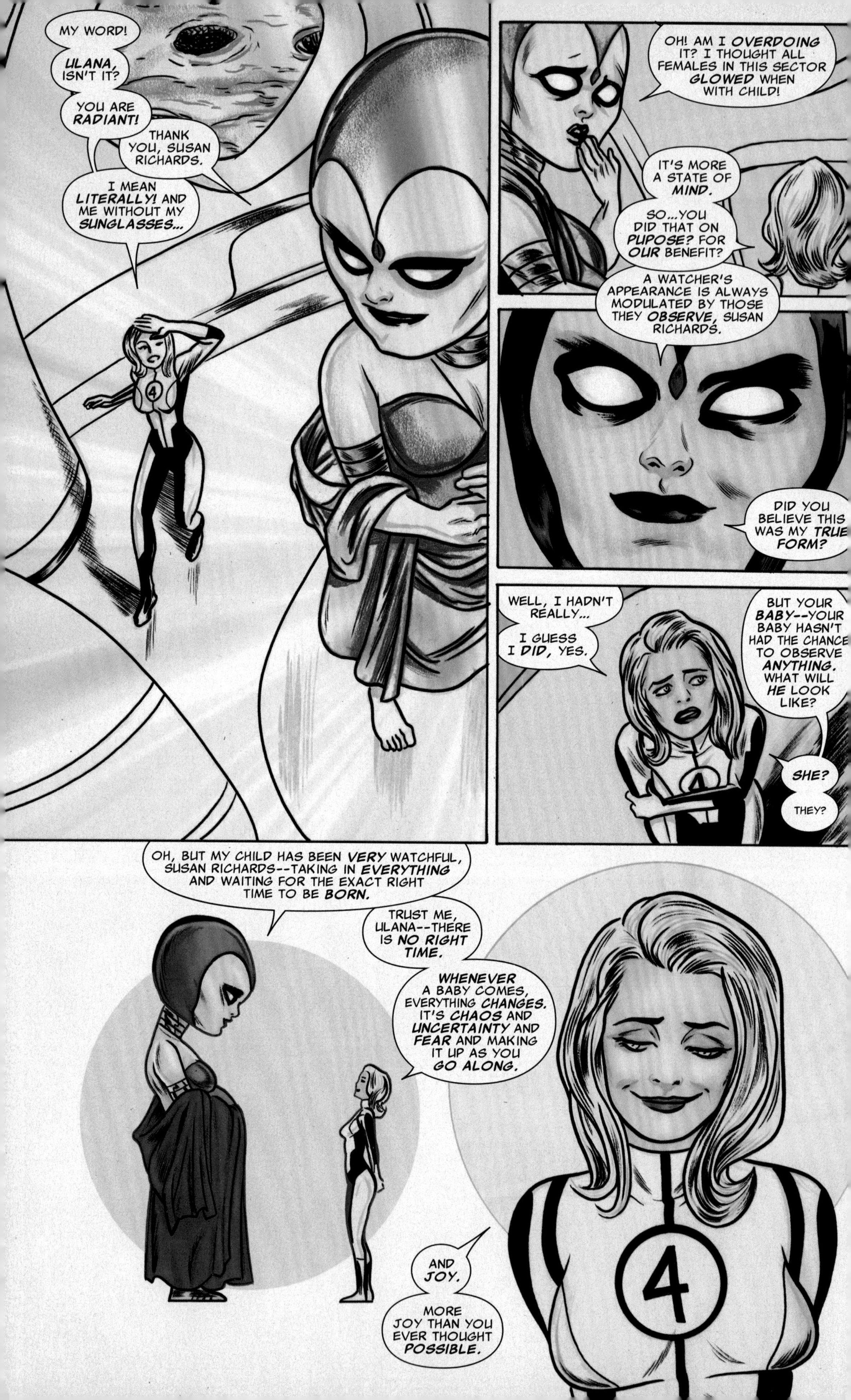
MY WORD!
ULANA, ISN'T IT?
YOU ARE RADIANT!
THANK YOU, SUSAN RICHARDS.
I MEAN LITERALLY! AND ME WITHOUT MY SUNGLASSES...
OH! AM I OVERDOING IT? I THOUGHT ALL FEMALES IN THIS SECTOR GLOWED WHEN WITH CHILD!
IT'S MORE A STATE OF MIND.
SO...YOU DID THAT ON PUPOSE? FOR OUR BENEFIT?
A WATCHER'S APPEARANCE IS ALWAYS MODULATED BY THOSE THEY OBSERVE, SUSAN RICHARDS.
DID YOU BELIEVE THIS WAS MY TRUE FORM?
WELL, I HADN'T REALLY...
I GUESS I DID, YES.
BUT YOUR BABY--YOUR BABY HASN'T HAD THE CHANCE TO OBSERVE ANYTHING. WHAT WILL HE LOOK LIKE?
SHE?
THEY?
OH, BUT MY CHILD HAS BEEN VERY WATCHFUL, SUSAN RICHARDS--TAKING IN EVERYTHING AND WAITING FOR THE EXACT RIGHT TIME TO BE BORN.
TRUST ME, ULANA--THERE IS NO RIGHT TIME.
WHENEVER A BABY COMES, EVERYTHING CHANGES. IT'S CHAOS AND UNCERTAINTY AND FEAR AND MAKING IT UP AS YOU GO ALONG.
AND JOY.
MORE JOY THAN YOU EVER THOUGHT POSSIBLE.

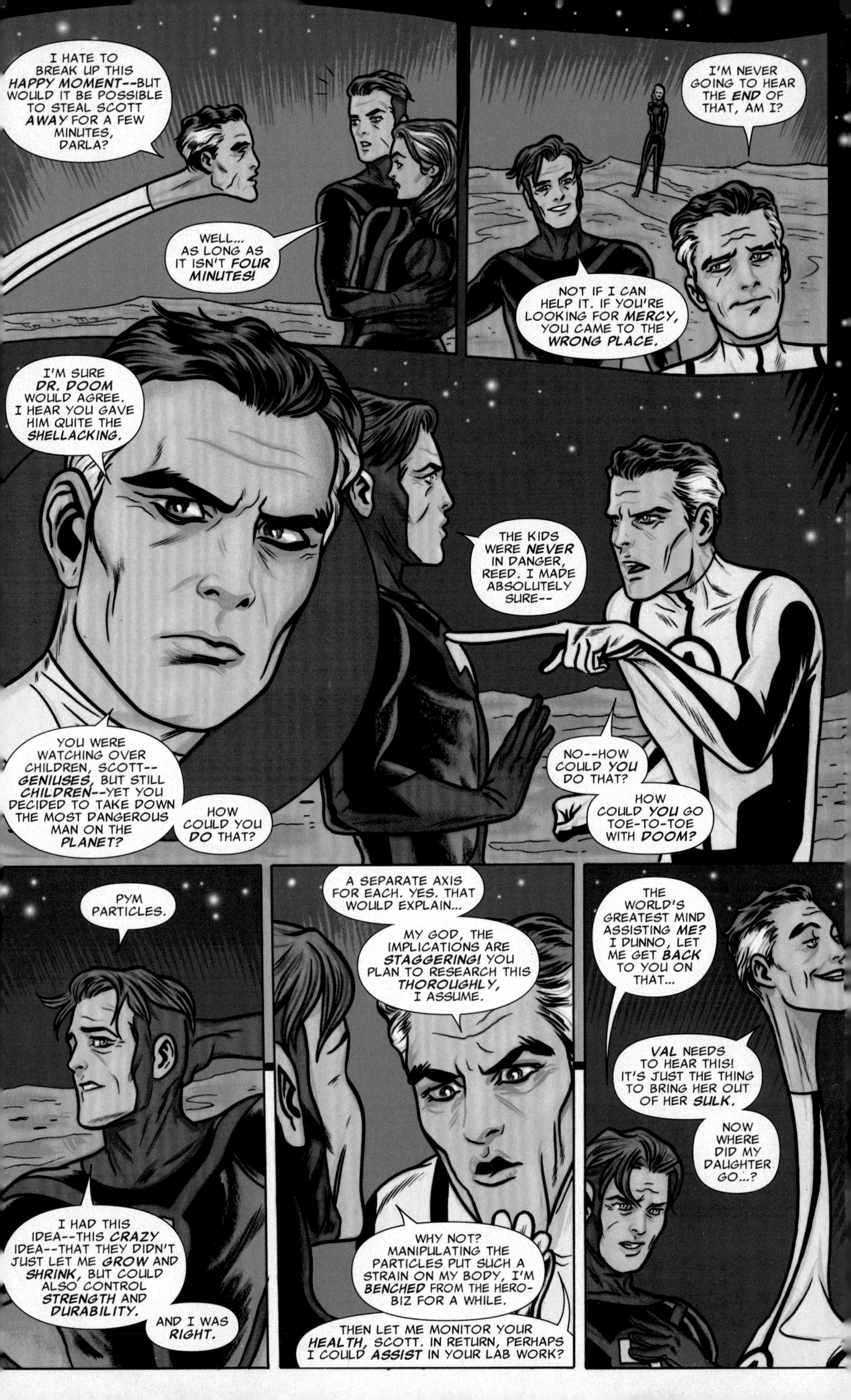

I HATE TO BREAK UP THIS HAPPY MOMENT--BUT WOULD IT BE POSSIBLE TO STEAL SCOTT AWAY FOR A FEW MINUTES, DARLA?
WELL... AS LONG AS IT ISN'T FOUR MINUTES!
I'M NEVER GOING TO HEAR THE END OF THAT, AM I?
NOT IF I CAN HELP IT. IF YOU'RE LOOKING FOR MERCY, YOU CAME TO THE WRONG PLACE.
I'M SURE DR. DOOM WOULD AGREE. I HEAR YOU GAVE HIM QUITE THE SHELLACKING.
THE KIDS WERE NEVER IN DANGER, REED. I MADE ABSOLUTELY SURE--
YOU WERE WATCHING OVER CHILDREN, SCOTT--GENIUSES, BUT STILL CHILDREN--YET YOU DECIDED TO TAKE DOWN THE MOST DANGEROUS MAN ON THE PLANET?
HOW COULD YOU DO THAT?
NO--HOW COULD YOU DO THAT?
HOW COULD YOU GO TOE-TO-TOE WITH DOOM?
PYM PARTICLES.
I HAD THIS IDEA--THIS CRAZY IDEA--THAT THEY DIDN'T JUST LET ME GROW AND SHRINK, BUT COULD ALSO CONTROL STRENGTH AND DURABILITY.
AND I WAS RIGHT.
A SEPARATE AXIS FOR EACH. YES. THAT WOULD EXPLAIN...
MY GOD, THE IMPLICATIONS ARE STAGGERING! YOU PLAN TO RESEARCH THIS THOROUGHLY, I ASSUME.
WHY NOT? MANIPULATING THE PARTICLES PUT SUCH A STRAIN ON MY BODY, I'M BENCHED FROM THE HERO-BIZ FOR A WHILE.
THEN LET ME MONITOR YOUR HEALTH, SCOTT. IN RETURN, PERHAPS I COULD ASSIST IN YOUR LAB WORK?
THE WORLD'S GREATEST MIND ASSISTING ME? I DUNNO, LET ME GET BACK TO YOU ON THAT...
VAL NEEDS TO HEAR THIS! IT'S JUST THE THING TO BRING HER OUT OF HER SULK.
NOW WHERE DID MY DAUGHTER GO...?

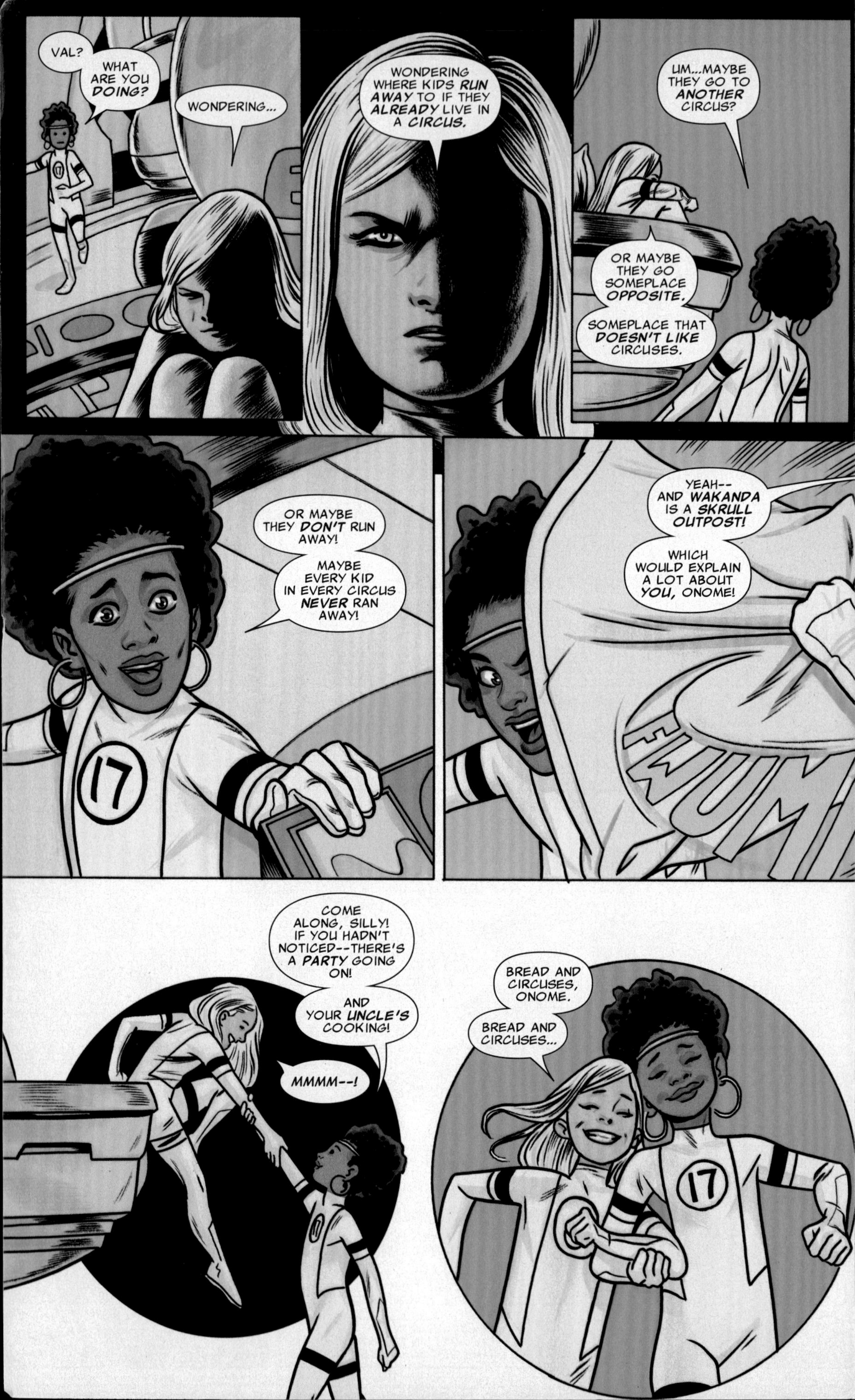
VAL? WHAT ARE YOU DOING?
WONDERING...
WONDERING WHERE KIDS RUN AWAY TO IF THEY ALREADY LIVE IN A CIRCUS.
UM...MAYBE THEY GO TO ANOTHER CIRCUS?
OR MAYBE THEY GO SOMEPLACE OPPOSITE.
SOMEPLACE THAT DOESN'T LIKE CIRCUSES.
OR MAYBE THEY DON'T RUN AWAY!
MAYBE EVERY KID IN EVERY CIRCUS NEVER RAN AWAY!
YEAH-- AND WAKANDA IS A SKRULL OUTPOST!
WHICH WOULD EXPLAIN A LOT ABOUT YOU, ONOME!
COME ALONG, SILLY! IF YOU HADN'T NOTICED--THERE'S A PARTY GOING ON!
AND YOUR UNCLE'S COOKING!
MMMM--!
BREAD AND CIRCUSES, ONOME.
BREAD AND CIRCUSES...

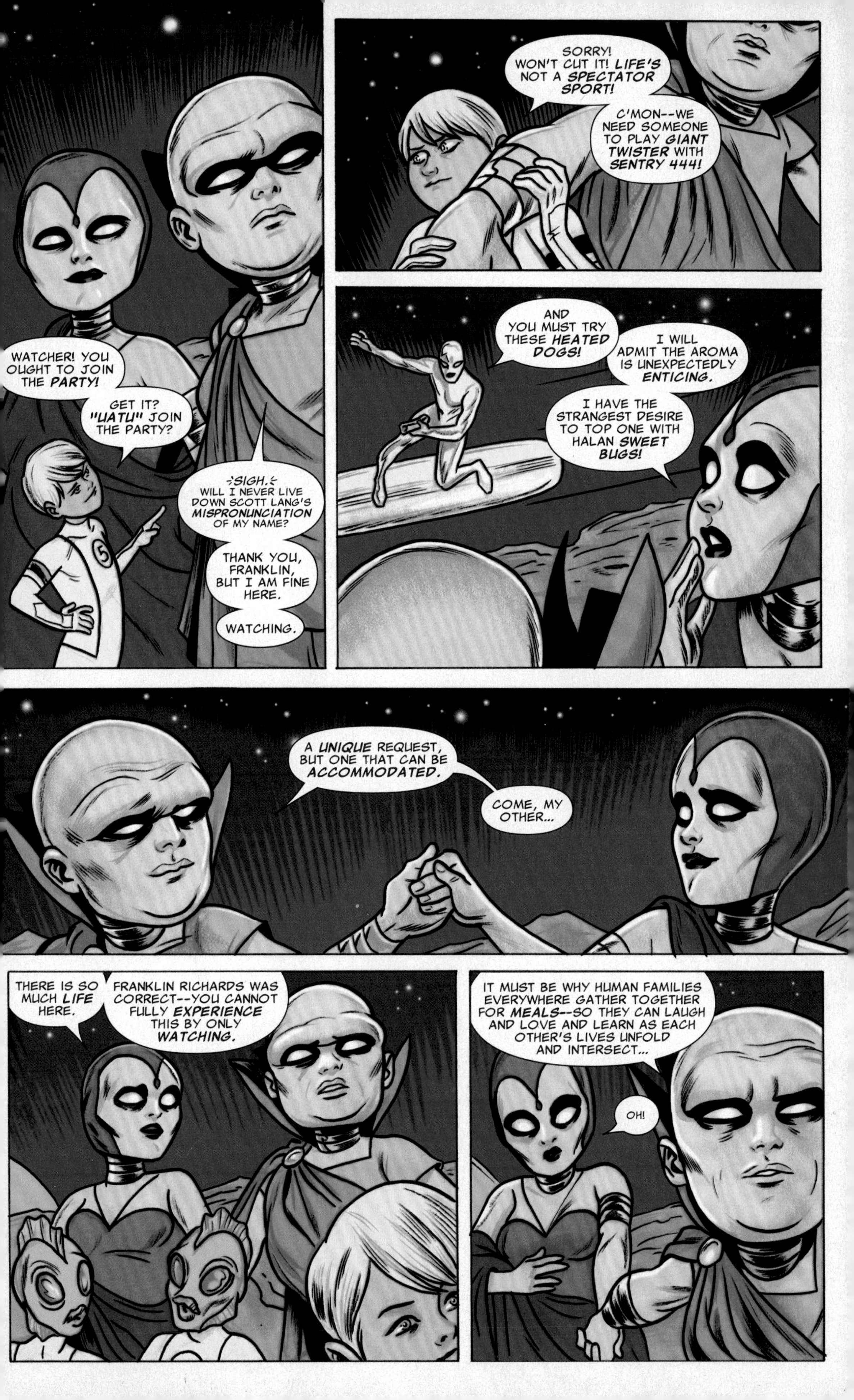
WATCHER! YOU OUGHT TO JOIN THE PARTY!
GET IT? "UATU" JOIN THE PARTY?
SIGH. WILL I NEVER LIVE DOWN SCOTT LANG'S MISPRONUNCIATION OF MY NAME?
THANK YOU, FRANKLIN, BUT I AM FINE HERE.
WATCHING.
SORRY! WON'T CUT IT! LIFE'S NOT A SPECTATOR SPORT!
C'MON--WE NEED SOMEONE TO PLAY GIANT TWISTER WITH SENTRY 444!
AND YOU MUST TRY THESE HEATED DOGS!
I WILL ADMIT THE AROMA IS UNEXPECTEDLY ENTICING.
I HAVE THE STRANGEST DESIRE TO TOP ONE WITH HALAN SWEET BUGS!
A UNIQUE REQUEST, BUT ONE THAT CAN BE ACCOMMODATED.
COME, MY OTHER...
THERE IS SO MUCH LIFE HERE.
FRANKLIN RICHARDS WAS CORRECT--YOU CANNOT FULLY EXPERIENCE THIS BY ONLY WATCHING.
IT MUST BE WHY HUMAN FAMILIES EVERYWHERE GATHER TOGETHER FOR MEALS--SO THEY CAN LAUGH AND LOVE AND LEARN AS EACH OTHER'S LIVES UNFOLD AND INTERSECT...
OH!

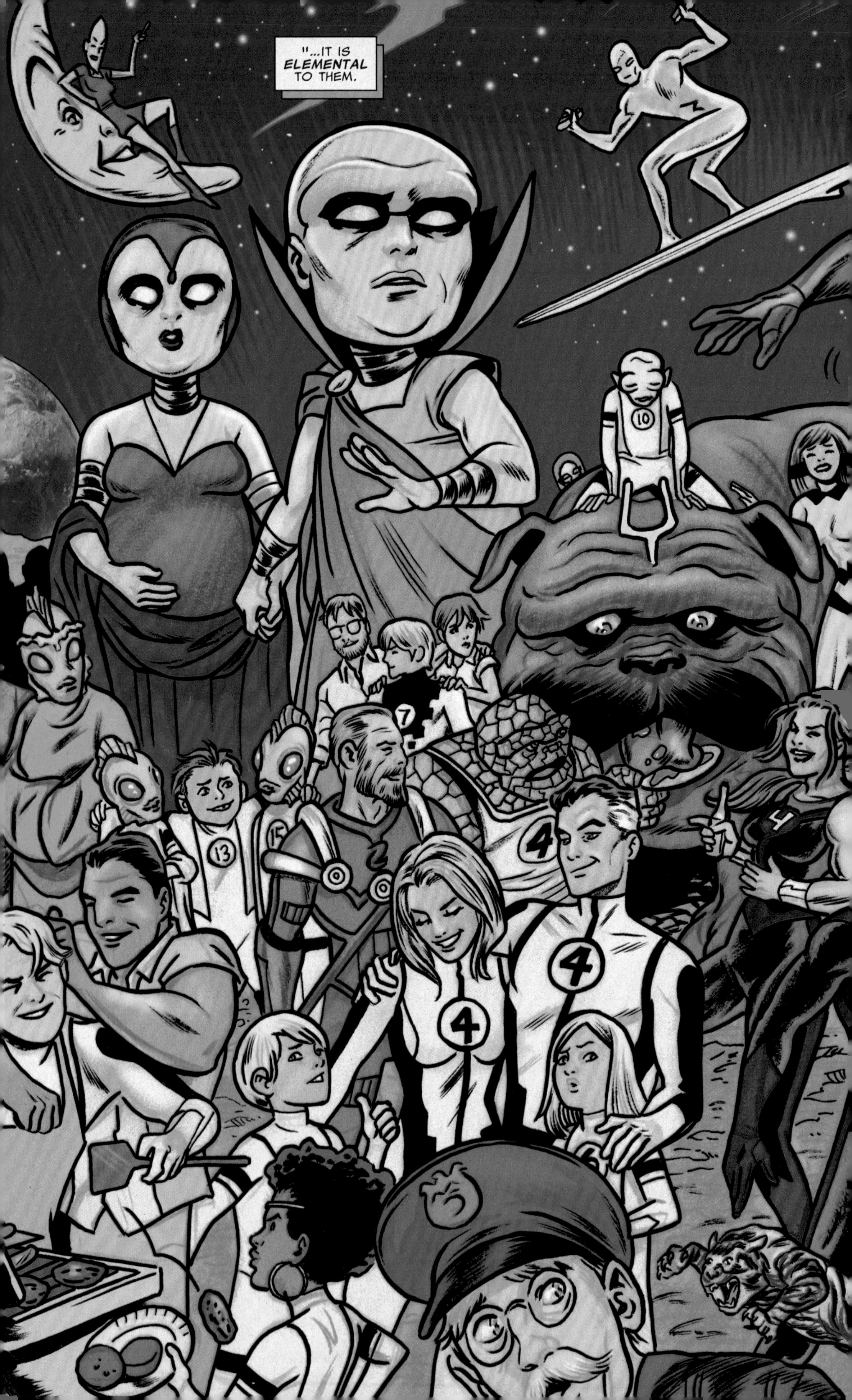
"...IT IS ELEMENTAL TO THEM.

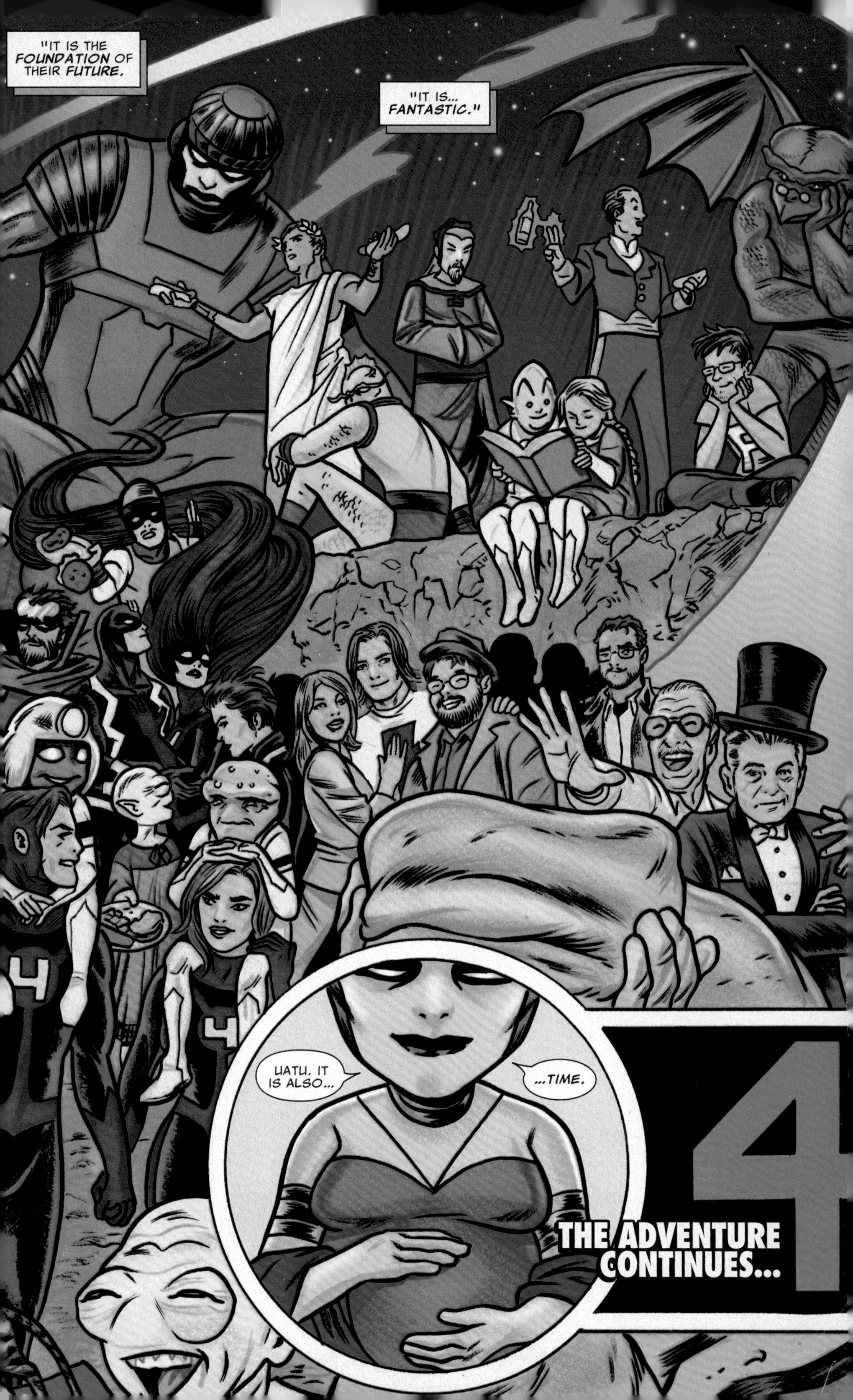
"IT IS THE FOUNDATION OF THEIR FUTURE.
"IT IS... FANTASTIC."
UATU. IT IS ALSO...
...TIME.
THE ADVENTURE CONTINUES...

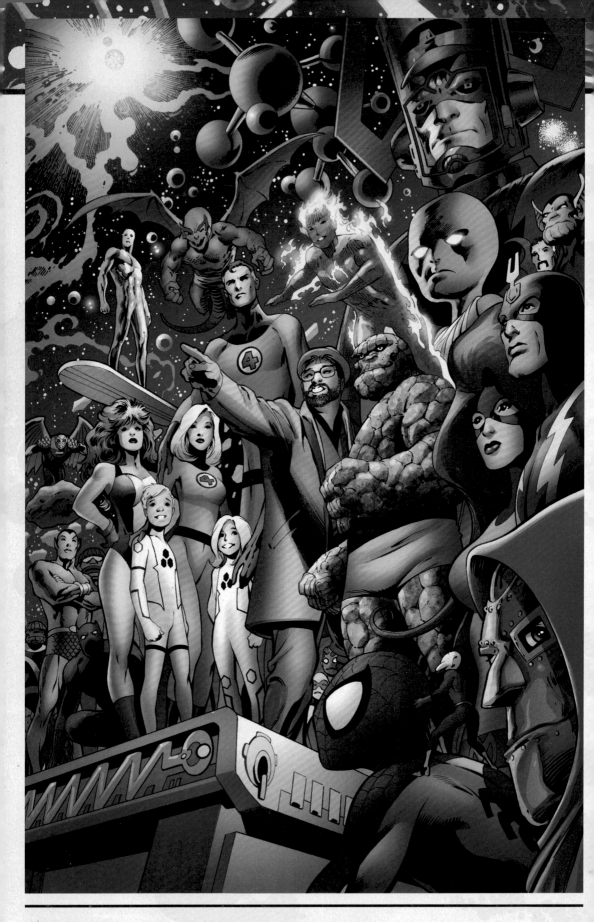

FANTASTIC FOUR #16 VARIANT BY ALAN DAVIS, MARK FARMER & PAUL MOUNTS